FEB 2 7 2003

Getting Right with God

Southern Baptists and Desegregation, 1945–1995

RELIGION AND AMERICAN CULTURE

Series Editors
David Edwin Harrell Jr.
Wayne Flynt
Edith L. Blumhofer

Getting Right with God

*Southern Baptists
and Desegregation, 1945–1995*

Mark Newman

The University of Alabama Press
Tuscaloosa and London

Copyright © 2001
The University of Alabama Press
Tuscaloosa, Alabama 35487-0380
All rights reserved
Manufactured in the United States of America

1 2 3 4 5 6 7 8 9
09 08 07 06 05 04 03 02 01

Typeface is New Baskerville

∞

The paper on which this book is printed meets the minimum requirements of
American National Standard for Information Science–Permanence of Paper for
Printed Library Materials, ANSI Z39.48-1984.

Library of Congress Cataloging-in-Publication Data

Newman, Mark.
   Getting right with God : Southern Baptists and desegregation,
1945–1995 / Mark Newman.
       p.   cm. — (Religion and American culture)
Includes bibliographical references and index.
   ISBN 0-8173-1060-6 (alk. paper)
   1. Southern Baptist Convention—History—20th century.
2. Segregation—Religious aspects—Southern Baptist
Convention—History—20th century.   I. Title. II. Religion and
American culture (Tuscaloosa, Ala.)
   BX6462.3 .N48 2001
   261.8′348′0088261—dc21
                              2001001287

British Library Cataloguing-in-Publication Data available

Contents

Preface

TRADITIONALLY, BAPTISTS have had no creed. They based their faith and practice on New Testament teachings. Doctrinally, Baptists agreed on the authority of the Bible as the word of God, personal salvation by faith, believer's baptism by immersion and the priesthood of the believer. The Bible, they believed, made personal evangelism and missions central concerns for Christians. To further the missionary enterprise, Baptists created the General Missionary Convention of the Baptist Denomination in the United States for Foreign Missions in 1814 and the American Baptist Home Mission Society in 1832. After a sectional divide over the issue of appointing slaveholders as missionaries, Baptists in the South formed the Southern Baptist Convention (SBC) in 1845 with the continued aim of fostering missions. To facilitate their evangelistic goals, Southern Baptists created the Domestic Mission Board (from 1874 the Home Mission Board or HMB) and the Foreign Mission Board (FMB) as agencies of the new convention. In 1888, Baptist women formed the Woman's Missionary Union (WMU), an auxiliary to the convention, to raise funds for missionary work. Three years later, the convention established the Sunday School Board to publish religious literature for use by its churches. Baptist men organized the Laymen's Missionary Movement in 1907, which became the Brotherhood Commission in 1950.

Although all churches attempt to present themselves in the best moral light, the real opinions and feelings of Southern Baptists on racial issues can be discerned with a greater degree of accuracy than those of members of hierarchical denominations. The congregational nature of Southern Baptist polity ensured that opinions expressed about civil rights issues by denominational messengers, presidents and pastors usually fell within the parameters of mainstream Baptist opinion. Taken together, these views provide an indication of social change over time. The SBC and Baptist state conventions are annual meetings of messengers elected by and from affiliated, autonomous churches. The messengers are not called delegates, because they have not been delegated authority by their churches, rather they carry messages from their congregations. Convention messengers have the power to accept or reject recommendations from convention agencies and institutions, and may suggest their own. Cooperation with denominational programs and compliance with convention resolutions and statements is voluntary; each church decides for itself. Churches control the purse strings of the conventions, by choosing whether and how much they wish to contribute to their annual budgets which fund convention agencies and programs. The SBC and Baptist state conventions control their agencies by means of elected boards, commissions and trustees, but they have no authority over individual churches.

The messengers elect the presidents of the SBC and Baptist state conventions to preside over their annual meetings, appoint their resolutions committees, which consider and choose resolutions to be voted on at the convention, and play a role in the nomination of the trustees of Baptist institutions and agencies. Baptist presidents have no authority to speak officially for the denomination; they can only suggest and persuade. Presidents also serve on convention boards and the executive committee. A convention's executive committee runs the day-to-day affairs of the convention between annual meetings. Any decisions it makes are ultimately subject to approval by the messengers at the next meeting of the convention. Individual churches not only elect convention messengers, they also choose their own pastors and can hire and fire them at will.

The democratic nature of Southern Baptist polity requires consensus and cooperation to function. It has an inbuilt, although not absolute, tendency to avoid controversial and divisive issues, in favor of the unifying themes of evangelism and missions, the very essence of the Southern Baptist cooperative venture. When issues, such as civil rights, highlight a powerful discrepancy between Christian ethics and Christian practice that the messengers feel unable to ignore, they express themselves in resolutions, recommendations, statements and programs. These expressions and activities are analyzed in this book because they are useful barometers of change. However, they reveal little about the broad range and diversity of Southern Baptist opinion and even less about how most Southern Baptists interpreted and responded to them. Consequently, this study also examines the denominational press, letters, surveys of desegregation in Southern Baptist life and opinion polls. To illuminate the diversity of their experience, the book focuses on the eleven states of the Old Confederacy.

It is a commonplace in the sociology of religion that established churches or denominations tend not only to accept the prevailing order but also to legitimize that order by offering a religious justification or explanation for its existence. Thus, most Southern Baptists and the major southern white denominations supported slavery, the Confederacy, the Lost Cause and the development of Jim Crow. The region's white clergymen offered religious sanction for each of these features of southern history, either by citing biblical passages in their support or interpreting them as God's will. Yet, when the United States Supreme Court declared public school segregation unconstitutional in *Brown* v. *Board of Education* (1954), the SBC urged compliance with the court's ruling, even though the overwhelming majority of Baptists favored segregation.

Although most Baptists preferred Jim Crow, they differed in their commitment to its preservation. Militant segregationists defended segregation as biblical and in accordance with God's will. Moderate segregationists, unlike militants, did not accord segregation religious justification. Tradition and acceptance of the prevailing social order as natural and just accounted for their endorsement of racial separation. Throughout the civil rights era, a minority of Baptists, including some lay people, some pastors and some denominational officials, labeled here as progressives, persistently criticized racial inequality and discrimination.

Regardless of their views toward Jim Crow, Southern Baptists shared primary commitments to scripture and evangelism, and, since at least the end of the nineteenth century, to law and order and to public education. Conflict between their primary commitments and the maintenance of segregation in the civil rights era made moderate segregationists amenable to change. Baptists argued that the Bible commanded them to obey the law. They regarded education as necessary to understand Scripture and for the preservation of democracy, a system under which they believed religion best thrived. In the 1950s and 1960s, southern white resistance to desegregation defied federal law, imperiled education and undermined Southern Baptist missions in Africa and Asia. Civil rights direct action campaigns in the first half of the 1960s further revealed American racism, and the Civil Rights Act of 1964 outlawed segregated public accommodations. Consequently, their primary commitments encouraged moderate segregationists, albeit gradually and reluctantly, to acquiesce in the demise of *de jure* segregation.

Progressives and some moderate segregationists in positions of leadership as pastors, editors of Baptist state convention newspapers, and denominational officials encouraged Baptists to accept desegregation by appealing to their primary commitments. They made their appeal from the pulpit, in editorials, public comments and in reports and recommendations to their conventions. The SBC's Christian Life Commission published and promoted a non-segregationist viewpoint in annual reports to the convention.

It challenged the views of biblical segregationists by placing progressive articles in Baptist newspapers, distributing a sizeable tract literature to opinion makers and organizing conferences for Baptist leaders. Influenced by the efforts of progressives and by the South's gradual abandonment of legal segregation, many biblical segregationists relinquished their views.

The approach taken in this study assumes that active Southern Baptists sought, however imperfectly, to apply their religious beliefs to their everyday lives and that these beliefs were more than just a mask to justify or rationalize other interests. The SBC's message that their primary commitments required Baptists to accept the end of legal segregation was difficult, threatening and challenging precisely because religious belief played an important part in their lives and worldview. The SBC weaned them away from support for segregation as public policy, which is not to say that the mass of Southern Baptists became active advocates of integration or even favorable to the idea. They simply accepted that enforced segregation and overt racial discrimination were unchristian, and, prompted by this realization, they eventually adjusted to their demise. Subtle rather than seismic, the change was nevertheless an important part of the white South's response to the civil rights movement and federal support in its behalf.

Acknowledgments

T HIS BOOK IS BASED on research originally conducted for my doctoral dissertation at the University of Mississippi. I am very grateful to the members of my dissertation committee, Jack Bass, Winthrop D. Jordan and Ted Ownby, and to my supervisor Charles Reagan Wilson for their advice and support. Financial assistance in the form of a graduate assistantship and fellowship from the University of Mississippi enabled me to survive through hard times. A study grant from the Historical Commission of the Southern Baptist Convention eased research costs in Nashville. I am especially grateful to the Louisville Institute for the Study of Protestantism and American Culture for a generous dissertation fellowship.

I owe a great debt to the staff of the Southern Baptist Historical Library and Archives in Nashville, Tennessee, especially Pat Brown and Bill Sumners, who always responded to my requests promptly and courteously and suggested additional materials for examination. I also thank the Baptist Joint Committee for allowing me to rummage through its office files in Washington, D.C. aided by the Committee's research assistant Rosemary Brevard, Eljee Bentley of the Woman's Missionary Union for her many helpful suggestions and willingness to find materials, and the staff of the Southern Baptist Sunday School Board Archives, particularly Pat Huddleston. The interlibrary loan staff at the University of Mississippi and the University of Derby provided an essential service by obtaining key materials.

Although based on my dissertation research, this book bears virtually no resemblance to the original dissertation, except in the thrust of its interpretation. Richard H. King, Peter Ling, Ted Ownby and Michael Simpson offered helpful comments and advice during the process of revision. I am grateful to Tony Badger and John White for allowing me to try out ideas at conferences.

Earlier versions of some of the material here have appeared elsewhere: "The Alabama Baptist State Convention and Desegregation, 1954–1980,"

Alabama Baptist Historian; "The Arkansas Baptist State Convention and Desegregation, 1954–1968," *Arkansas Historical Quarterly;* "The Baptist General Association of Virginia and Desegregation, 1931–1980," *Virginia Magazine of History and Biography;* "The Baptist State Convention of North Carolina and Desegregation, 1945–1980," *North Carolina Historical Review;* "The Baptist State Convention of South Carolina and Desegregation, 1954–1971," *Baptist History and Heritage;* "The Florida Baptist Convention and Desegregation, 1954–1980" *Florida Historical Quarterly;* "The Georgia Baptist Convention and Desegregation, 1945–1980," *Georgia Historical Quarterly;* "The Mississippi Baptist Convention and Desegregation, 1945–1980," *Journal of Mississippi History;* "Southern Baptists and Desegregation, 1945–1980," in *Southern Landscapes*, Transatlantic Perspectives 7, edited by Tony Badger, Walter Edgar and J. Norby Gretland (Tübingen: Staffenburg Verlag, 1996); and "The Tennessee Baptist State Convention and Desegregation, 1954–1980," *Tennessee Historical Quarterly*. I would like to thank these publishers for their kind support and for their permission to reprint portions of these articles here.

For their generous offers of help and convivial company during research trips, I thank James L. Baggett, Bart and Sharon Bartleson, Frank and Linda Clover, Robert Ginn, and Sheila Moore.

Jonathan Osmond offered wise counsel when I first considered graduate study. Kees Gispen encouraged me in my work and even donated a much needed and much appreciated computer during my time in Mississippi. My entire graduate and professional academic career has been underpinned by the advice, guidance and encouragement of Michael Simpson as both mentor and friend. I have never known a scholar to be so generous of his time and knowledge with his students and former students, despite a great many professional commitments and a thriving research career.

Mark Newman

The Southern Baptist Convention and African Americans, 1845–1944

D<small>ISGRUNTLED WHITE SOUTHERNERS</small> formed the SBC in 1845 after the General Missionary Convention of the Baptist Denomination in the United States for Foreign Missions refused to appoint slaveholders as missionaries. The sectional split among Baptists prefigured the divisions of the Civil War. Southern Baptists endorsed secession and the Confederate cause. After the South's defeat, many celebrated the Lost Cause. Constituting nearly one-third of Southern Baptist membership, African Americans formed their own churches during Reconstruction, when whites refused to grant them equality within biracial churches. Southern Baptists endorsed segregation as God ordained, as they had once done slavery, and defended southern disfranchisement of African Americans. Most Baptists believed in black inferiority and supported white supremacy, although some Baptist bodies denounced lynching. Consistent criticism of enforced racial inequality, but not segregation, emerged in the SBC and many Baptist state conventions only in the late 1930s and 1940s. The demands and successes of the nascent civil rights movement for equality, and the fight against Nazi Germany, engendered a growing sensitivity about racial injustice within America. Yet in 1944, few Baptists saw any inconsistency between segregation and their primary commitments to scripture, evangelism, law and order, and public education.[1]

In the late eighteenth century, slavery had some vigorous critics among white Baptists in the Upper South, but, as the institution expanded across the South during the next century, the region's Baptists increasingly defended it as biblical and a means by which they could evangelize heathen Africans. Baptists enjoyed the greatest success of any denomination in recruiting African Americans. Many slaveholders encouraged conversion in the belief that the emphasis Baptist preachers placed on obedience and morality might render their slaves more subservient. By contrast, slaves found in the Baptist faith, which they fused with African belief systems, a means to combat dehumanization.[2]

Nearly all antebellum Baptist churches in the South were biracial, and, in some congregations, black members spoke in disciplinary procedures against whites. However, white churches normally allocated slaves a separate area during worship services. At white insistence, slaves often convened in separate services presided over by a slaveholder or white minister. African Americans preferred their own worship meetings, held outside white control. Some slaves participated in clandestine services on the plantation away from their masters. Southern white churches also spawned over 150 antebellum African-American churches in which blacks enjoyed autonomy in worship services.[3]

Although white ministers sometimes trained African-American slaves for missionary activity and even emancipated a few of these missionaries, they defended the peculiar institution. Stung by increasing abolitionist sentiment among northern Baptists during the 1830s and 1840s, those in the South became increasingly strident in their support of slavery. The attempt of the General Convention to maintain an uneasy neutrality over the issue came unstuck in 1844 when the Georgia Baptist Convention sponsored slaveholder James E. Reeve as a missionary to the Cherokees in a test case. When the General Convention's Home Mission Society rejected Reeve's nomination and its Foreign Mission Board affirmed later in the year that it would not appoint a slaveholder, southerners concluded that abolitionists had seized control of the convention. In response, they met in Augusta, Georgia, in May 1845 and organized the SBC.[4]

As the issue of slavery and its expansion split the nation in the 1850s and 1860s, white Southern Baptists rallied to the South's defense. The South Carolina Secession Convention first met in Columbia's First Baptist Church. The degree of enthusiasm Baptists held for secession reflected that in their particular states, with those of the Deep South first championing secession. Once the eleven southern states had seceded and the Civil War broke out, white Southern Baptists lauded the Confederacy's cause. In May 1861, the messengers to the SBC adopted a resolution that declared: "We most cordially approve of the formation of the Government of the Confederate States of America, and admire and applaud the noble course of that Government. . . . " Southern Baptists reconciled their belief in law and order with secession by arguing that they were acting in defense of liberty and so enjoyed God's approval. The Confederacy's military victories in the Civil War reflected His blessings and its defeats His chastisement for southerners' failings. In 1863, the SBC described the war as "just and necessary" and detected the "divine hand in the guidance and protection of our beloved country."[5]

Convinced that theirs was a holy cause, Baptist ministers remained confident of ultimate victory. Defeat, then, required a religious explanation, which white southerners found in the Lost Cause. As historian Charles Reagan Wilson has explained, a substantial body of southern clergymen, many of them prominent leaders within their denominations, became prime exponents of this myth. They "interpreted the Civil War as demonstrating the height of Southern virtue, as a moral-religious crusade against the atheistic North." Southern whites, their clergymen told them, were a peculiarly virtuous people chosen by God, and their religion was the most pure form of Christianity. The Confederate defeat did not mean that the Almighty had abandoned the South, rather it was part of God's plan, "a form of discipline," that would prepare southerners for a more glorious future, if they maintained Christian-Confederate values.[6]

Race, Wilson contends, was connected to but not central to the Lost Cause, which focused primarily on the religious virtue of the Confederates. Southern whites had fought the war, their ministers contended, not to preserve slavery but to defend a godly, southern society and the principles of the American Revolution. Throughout the century, southern white clergymen nevertheless continued to defend slavery as part of God's plan to evangelize African Americans. But the Almighty, they maintained, had also decreed emancipation in 1865. Many Baptists argued that God had ended slavery because it had achieved His purpose by converting and civilizing blacks, a prerequisite for their return to Africa to evangelize the continent. Some Baptists claimed, more pessimistically, that emancipation represented God's judgement for their failure to fulfil adequately their evangelistic duties to the slaves.[7]

After the Civil War, most Southern Baptists intended that African Americans should remain within their denomination but in a subordinate, segregated position. Unwilling to accept a continued inferior status within the church, blacks withdrew from biracial congregations to establish their own. White Baptists initially opposed separation. They feared that African Americans, as Baptists in Edgefield County, South Carolina, explained in 1865, might become subject to "the guidance of ignorant, unqualified, and unauthorized persons." However, by the late 1860s, most white Baptists regarded separation as both inescapable and desirable, and, sometimes, they helped in the creation of African-American churches.[8]

The SBC's annual meeting in 1869 revealed that a consensus had emerged in favor of excluding African-American churches from Southern

Baptist associations and conventions. In debate, the messengers firmly rejected biracial organization. Outside Maryland and Florida, few black churches remained in Southern Baptist associations after the early 1870s. Several thousand African Americans maintained their second-class membership in predominantly white congregations, but their numbers gradually declined; by 1902 none officially remained on church membership rolls. Except for a few African Americans who continued to attend its churches, the SBC had become almost entirely white, as it was to stay until the 1950s.[9]

The Southern Baptist rejection of biracialism reflected fears that it would involve racial equality within the church. In 1869, the SBC declared that the Bible recognized "social distinctions." Behind the fear of social equality lay a dread of miscegenation. Jeremiah B. Jeter, senior editor of the *Religious Herald,* a Southern Baptist weekly newspaper published in Virginia, warned in 1869 that black equality within the church would lead to "the *mongrelization* of our noble Anglo-Saxon race. . . . " As African Americans departed from their churches, Southern Baptists exhibited decreasing interest in their welfare. They listened to convention reports that called for black ministerial training but developed few evangelistic or educational programs for African Americans until late in the century.[10]

Northern whites, following in the trail of Union soldiers, took the lead in missionary activity among the former slaves. Southern Baptists feared that the missionaries would instill radical, egalitarian ideas among the freedmen. Their concerns seemed justified when the American Baptist Home Mission Society proposed a joint program of missions with the SBC in 1868 that would "lift up the millions of freedmen to the exercise of all the rights and duties of citizenship and Christian brotherhood." The convention promptly rejected the northern approach, and the society continued its missionary program alone.[11]

The weekly newspapers of Southern Baptist state conventions frequently criticized northern missionaries for bringing, as the Atlanta-based *Christian Index* complained, "influences from abroad estranging the colored population from the white for political ends." Southern Baptists opposed the Reconstruction policies of the federal government, designed to create a biracial democracy in the South by adding the thirteenth, fourteenth and fifteenth amendments to the Constitution, abolishing slavery, granting citizenship to the native-born, and outlawing racial discrimination in the franchise. Inaccurately, they charged that southern state governments were dominated by African Americans, who, hampered by political inexperience, fell victim to the machinations of northern white carpetbaggers and southern-born Republican scalawags. Editors of Baptist newspapers seized upon instances of corruption among Republican-controlled state governments in the South to condemn Reconstruction and black suffrage.[12]

Southern Baptists also denounced the biracial thrust of Reconstruction, just as they had rejected integration within their churches. They maintained that God had intended for the races to be separate. Although Baptists agreed that all humans were descended from Adam and Eve, most argued that God had created differences between the races that made African Americans inferior. Misreading *Genesis* 9:25–27, they claimed that God had cursed Ham and his descendants with black skin and condemned them to perpetual servitude. Southern Baptists believed that whites had a duty to maintain their blood untainted, since miscegenation would create an inferior, hybrid race in defiance of God's plan for racial purity. Accordingly, Baptists lambasted the civil rights bill of 1875, which forbade segregation in public accommodations.[13]

The violence of the Ku Klux Klan represented the most extreme form of white resistance to African-American equality during the Reconstruction era. Although there is little direct evidence that Baptist ministers joined the Klan, Baptist newspapers did not condemn its activities and most ignored them. Occasionally, they asserted their belief in law and order but argued that, in their supposed absence, the extralegal methods of the Klan were understandable.[14]

A series of federal Enforcement Acts and mass prosecutions undermined the Klan in the early 1870s, by which time southern Democrats had already redeemed several states from Republican rule, with the use of intimidation and violence. By 1876, the Republicans had lost control of every southern state but Louisiana, Florida and South Carolina. Reconstruction finally ended when incoming President Rutherford B. Hayes withdrew federal troops from the South and allowed the last Republican governments there to fall in 1877. With the restoration of Democratic rule in the South and the overturning of the Civil Rights Act by the Supreme Court in the *Civil Rights Cases* (1883), Southern Baptists believed that whites had reestablished the divine order in race relations. In the late 1880s and 1890s, they shared and contributed to an emerging southern white consensus that a new generation of African Americans, unschooled by slavery, had become too assertive.[15]

Baptists fully supported southern disfranchisement of African Americans in the wake of the Populist movement that had raised the specter of a biracial coalition of impoverished farmers. Although most Baptist newspapers did not discuss the South's adoption of Jim Crow laws in the 1880s and 1890s, upheld by the Supreme Court in *Plessy* v. *Ferguson* (1896), they frequently defended segregation as God's will. The *Christian Index* declared in 1889 that "The color line remains just where the Almighty put it, and there it will remain." Baptists supported public education, but they insisted that the races should be educated separately. African Americans, in their view, should receive sufficient education to allow them to read the Scriptures and secure employment as laborers. Baptists claimed that both races supported segregation. According to the *Christian Index,* "The line of demarcation is observed as rigidly by Negroes as by whites."[16]

African Americans who did not exhibit the subservience whites expected of them risked being lynched, often for the spurious accusation of raping white women. Lynching reached its peak between 1890 and 1915. At first, some Baptists viewed lynching, as they had once seen Klan violence, as a regrettable but understandable response to an absence of effective law enforcement. However, as lynching became more frequent, most Baptist newspapers and many state conventions condemned the practice, which offended their commitment to law and order.[17] Although they rejected lynching and other forms of white violence, Southern Baptists placed the responsibility for racial harmony on African Americans, who, they believed, should acquiesce in their subjugation. The HMB argued in its 1891 report that evangelism would encourage blacks to accept a "subordinate place" that would "settle this race question forever." Limited, uncoordinated and disparate, Southern Baptist missionary work among African Americans seemed to enter a new phase when, in 1894, Northern and Southern Baptists agreed on a coordinated approach to evangelism with black Baptist state conventions, known as the New Era Plan. However, the plan only operated in six states. By 1900, it stood largely in abeyance, a casualty of the unwillingness of whites to offer black Baptists the egalitarian relationship they desired. In the meantime, African-American Baptists had created their own national organization, the National Baptist Convention.[18]

The WMU worked closely with female leaders from the National Baptist Convention. In the 1890s, it began operating a program of industrial schools and mothers' meetings for African-American women with support from the HMB. The WMU influenced the formation of the Woman's Convention in 1900, an auxiliary to the National Baptist Convention, which parallelled its own function within the SBC. WMU leader Annie Armstrong persuaded the HMB to hire female African Americans as field workers for the Woman's Convention.[19]

Both Southern and National Baptists thrived, and their numbers rapidly expanded. During the 1890s, the SBC became the largest white denomination in the region. By 1900, there were 1,657,996 Southern Baptists. They interpreted their growth as a sign of God's blessing. In common with racists in the North and Britain, Southern Baptists believed that God had entrusted Anglo-Saxons with a mission to spread civilization and Christianity. They maintained that in the South, whites had kept the purity of their Anglo-Saxon blood by practicing racial segregation, and because their region had remained relatively immune to immigration from southern and eastern Europe. The purity of their religion and of their blood, Southern Baptists believed, marked them as God's agents for saving the South, America and then the world. In 1896, the SBC declared that "No portion of this [Anglo-Saxon] race has been dowered with more magnificent advantages than that one which inhabits this Southern land. . . . Who can doubt that he means to give it the post of honor as the light-bearer of the world?"[20]

Concerned primarily with the conversion of southern whites as a prerequisite to world evangelism, Southern Baptists neglected the religious and secular needs of African Americans. In 1905, the HMB's annual report lamented that "Southern Baptists ought to be expending for mission work among the negroes of the South more money annually than they are now contributing to all the objects of the Board. . . . " At ease with the subordination of blacks, the SBC declared at the same meeting that "It is no affair of this Convention to solve the so-called negro problem." The convention confined its criticisms of race relations to lynching. In 1906, it declared that "lynching blunts the public conscience, undermines the foundations on which society stands, and if unchecked will result in anarchy." Even then, the convention assumed those lynched to be guilty of raping white women. It affirmed that "our condemnation is due with equal emphasis, and in many cases with even greater emphasis, against the horrible crimes which cause the lynchings." Not surprisingly, the SBC maintained a modest program of evangelistic work with African Americans. In the decade preceding World War One, it employed missionaries jointly with the National Baptist Convention, who, in some years, numbered thirty or more. However, the work conducted with African Americans by the WMUs of the Southern Baptist state conventions declined.[21]

Although at the turn of the century the SBC became increasingly involved with social issues, such as alcohol, appointing a Committee on Temperance in 1908, it did not address inequalities between the races. The convention created a Social Service Commission in 1913, designed to provide Baptists with guidance on ethical issues. After issuing its first report in 1914, the convention replaced it with a Committee on Temperance and Social Service. Although in 1915 the new committee condemned sweatshops, inadequate tenement housing, political corruption and ruthless corporate profiteering, it remained preoccupied by the alcohol question until ratification of the Eighteenth Amendment, mandating national prohibition, in 1919. During prohibition, the committee, now renamed the Social Service Commission, continued, under chairman A. J. Barton, who wrote the bulk of its reports until his death in 1942, to give more emphasis to temperance than to any other single issue.[22]

The commission's silence about race relations left the HMB as the only Southern Baptist agency that habitually addressed the issue. However, the board's conception of civil rights did not extend beyond freedom from mob violence, and it regularly prefaced calls for the conversion and protection of blacks with the claim that they comprised a "weaker race." The assumption of African-American inferiority informed all aspects of Southern Baptist interest in race relations. A report to the SBC in 1915 concluded that the "greatest . . . need of the Negro is the construction of character."[23]

Many African Americans sought to escape from southern discrimination, segregation and violence. Beginning in 1915, thousands of blacks migrated from the rural South to northern cities, as demand for American goods abroad and the end of mass migration from war-torn Europe created an industrial labor shortage. A race riot broke out in East St. Louis, Illinois, in July 1917, and twenty-five race riots occurred in the North and South during the summer of 1919. Initiated by whites, the riots had diverse causes, among them white fears of interracial liaisons, residential proximity to blacks, and in Phillips County, Arkansas, opposition to a black tenant farmers' union.[24]

Cognizant of "the considerable feeling of unrest on the part of the negro" and "mob violence and other outbreaks of racial prejudice," the Committee on Temperance and Social Service addressed race relations in its 1920 report to the SBC. The committee first assured Baptists that segregation remained immutable, before calling for improvements in the living conditions and employment opportunities afforded blacks. It also acknowledged that African Americans suffered injustices before the law. However, with few race riots after 1919, the committee turned its attention away from economic and social problems faced by blacks, and limited its message on race to condemnations of lynching and calls for the protection of accused criminals from mob violence.[25]

Influenced by wartime developments, the WMU took a renewed interest in race relations. In October 1920, three Baptist women attended a meeting of the Commission on Interracial Cooperation, a southern interracial body, that created a Department of Women's Work. The WMU's Executive Committee agreed to participate in the department, which focused its efforts on promoting racial equality within segregation. Some Baptists objected to the commission's connection with the ecumenical Federal Council of Churches, and many preferred to emphasize evangelism as the answer to racial problems.[26]

Discussions between black and white Baptists, begun before the war, resulted in the establishment of the American Baptist Theological Seminary in Nashville, Tennessee, in 1924. Owned and operated by the National Baptist Convention, U.S.A., Inc., and the SBC, the seminary trained African-American ministers. Southern Baptists contributed $50,000 toward opening the seminary and $10,000 annually for its maintenance. The institution had two boards of trustees, one with a white majority that oversaw property and financial issues, and the other with a black majority that ran everyday operations. Although its rules stipulated that a National Baptist serve as president, whites effectively controlled the seminary. Poorly funded, and with the fluctuating contributions of the National Baptist Convention, U.S.A., Inc., always below those from the SBC, the seminary offered an inferior education. Consequently, the best financed and most able African-American theological students pursued their education in the North.[27]

Less concerned with ministerial training, the SBC's Social Service Commission, as the Committee on Temperance and Social Service became known in 1920, devoted most of its comments on race relations during the 1920s toward condemnations of lynching. With only three exceptions, the commission published lynching statistics between 1925 and 1946, usually accompanied by appeals for self-regulation at a time when the National Association for the Advancement of Colored People (NAACP) lobbied for a federal antilynching law.[28]

The WMU also took a stand against lynching in the 1920s and 1930s. In the annual Week of Prayer for Home Missions in 1927, the WMU included an appeal against lynching. Four Southern Baptists, all prominent WMU officers, were among the twenty-three women who founded the Association of Southern Women for the Prevention of Lynching in 1930. Led by Jesse Daniel Ames, the association, which grew to 40,000 members, mobilized community opinion whenever mob violence threatened to occur. After Ames spoke at its annual meeting in 1932, the WMU adopted a resolution that denounced lynching. Partly under the influence of the association, the number of lynchings fell from eight in 1936 to three in 1939.[29]

With lynching in decline, the SBC began to address other racial problems that had gained prominence. The NAACP's campaigns against disfranchisement and for equality in education, including equal pay for black school teachers, increased the sensitivity of the convention to these issues in the late 1930s. Although the administration of Franklin D. Roosevelt steadfastly refused to endorse federal antilynching bills and New Deal agencies practiced discrimination and segregation in their programs, Roosevelt helped to legitimize black aspirations for equality by appointing African Americans to administrative posts and beginning the desegregation of federal offices. He also appointed Supreme Court justices who rendered decisions that increasingly favored the NAACP.[30]

Influenced by the changing national climate, the HMB's report to the SBC in 1937 catalogued racial inequalities in education, housing, the administration of justice and employment. The board denounced racial supremacy and denied that God had condemned African Americans to perennial subordination. Its work with blacks, which had declined after the convention experienced financial problems in the 1920s and early 1930s, revived with the appointment of Noble Y. Beall in 1937 as director of the Department of Cooperative Work with Negroes. Beall began a program of deploying teacher-missionaries, who worked with African-American colleges in the training of ministers. The convention also created a Committee on Negro Ministerial Education that first met in 1938, and later held joint meetings with similar committees appointed by the Northern Baptist Convention and the National Baptist Convention, U.S.A., Inc. A study and discussion group, the committee examined inadequacies in training available to black Baptist pastors in the South and suggested remedial measures.[31]

The SBC moved beyond discussion in 1939 by adopting three race relations resolutions proposed by the Social Service Commission. The resolutions reflected the messengers' commitments to law and order, and to public education. The convention denounced the "lawlessness" of lynching and reaffirmed its "unalterable opposition to all forms of mob violence." Unwilling to move beyond the requirements of existing law, the resolutions offered no support for efforts in the U.S. Congress, none of them successful, to secure antilynching legislation. Instead, the convention urged "all citizens to contend earnestly for the administration of justice under the orderly processes of law. . . . " The messengers recognized and promised to work for the correction of inequalities facing African Americans in "the disproportionate distribution of public school funds, the lack of equal and impartial administration of justice in the courts, inadequate wages . . . and the lack of adequate industrial and commercial opportunity. . . . "[32]

The convention adopted similar resolutions proposed by the Social Service Commission in 1940, while the commission's report also drew attention to the lower salaries paid to black teachers. However, the commission tempered its commitment to equality by arguing in its report that, although African-American laborers endured lower wages and fewer employment opportunities than whites, "we would not assert that no differential in wages paid could ever be justified because of difference in social position and living requirements." Furthermore, the report suggested limitations to educational equality. "We recognize," the commission stated, "the fact that absolute equality in the distribution of public funds for education would perhaps not be feasible."[33]

In June 1940, the Fourth Circuit Court of Appeals ruled against racial differentials in teachers' salaries in *Alston v. Board of Education of the City of Norfolk,* and in November the Supreme Court refused to hear an appeal by the Virginia city's school board. The Social Service Commission's report to the SBC in 1941 welcomed the advances it claimed had occurred toward equal justice in the courts and in education, particularly "in the fixing of teachers' salaries." The messengers adopted resolutions regarding African Americans that affirmed their concern "for the welfare of the race, both economic and religious[,] and for the defense and protection of all the civil rights of the race." In another resolution, they expressed support "for the creation and maintenance of law and order and for the suppression of all mob violence. . . . "[34]

While Southern Baptists debated, African Americans challenged discrimination using direct action, as well as litigation and lobbying of Congress. By threatening to organize a mass march on Washington, D.C., A. Philip Randolph pressured President Roosevelt into establishing the temporary Fair Employment Practices Committee (FEPC) by executive order in June 1941. The FEPC sought to eliminate racial discrimination in hiring and the workplace, but it lacked the necessary enforcement powers. The Congress of Racial Equality (CORE), organized by a biracial group of northerners in 1942, pioneered sit-ins against segregated facilities in their region. The wartime labor shortage in the North boosted the long-term pattern of southern black migration to northern industrial cities. Enfranchised in key urban areas in the North, African Americans became increasingly important to presidential candidates who, as a consequence, responded to some of the demands made by civil rights organizations.[35]

Blacks who remained in the South also challenged discrimination. In October 1942, prominent African Americans met in North Carolina and issued the Durham Statement that called for voting rights, abolition of the poll tax, a stronger FEPC, and equal educational opportunities. A conference of southern whites, including Kathleen Mallory, a leader in the WMU, met in April 1943 and replied with the Atlanta Statement. Signed by over three hundred people, it conceded the existence of racial discrimination and supported "civil rights and economic opportunities" for blacks.[36]

Race riots broke out in Harlem, Detroit and Beaumont, Texas, in 1943. Racial violence also occurred during the war at military bases in Georgia, Mississippi, Texas and Louisiana. In their appeals to Asian opinion, the Japanese contrasted America's profession of democratic values and equal opportunities with the reality of racial discrimination faced by African Americans. Some Americans also became sensitized to the issue of racism by the fight against Nazi Germany and its anti-Semitic policies.[37]

In response to wartime developments, the Social Service Commission gave increasing attention to race relations, spurred on by J. B. Weatherspoon, who became its chairman in 1943. A member of the commission since 1930, Weatherspoon had taught ethics, including race relations courses, in the Department of Christian Sociology at The Southern Baptist Theological Seminary in Louisville, Kentucky, since 1929. He prepared the commission's report to the SBC in 1943, which asked, in a pointed reference to the racism of Nazi Germany and the recent riots in America, "Have we adopted irretrievably the Germanic principle?" and insisted that "America cannot go with Germany." Weatherspoon also acknowledged the demands of the civil rights movement. He praised the Durham meeting of black leaders and quoted approvingly from the Atlanta Statement. However, Weatherspoon did not challenge segregation, which had to be overturned before any real amelioration of racial inequality could occur. Refusing to recognize any contradiction in his position, he argued "What we seek is a *modus operandi* that will diminish friction, eliminate injustices, and promote friendly co-operation."[38]

Weatherspoon did not address voting rights until 1944, after the Supreme Court's ruling in *Smith* v. *Allwright* had outlawed white primary elections, which effectively elected officials in the South. Rather than offering an outright endorsement of the recent decision, he sought to disentangle the question of desegregation from those of voting rights and economic opportunity. Weatherspoon's report stated that "Indiscriminate social commingling is regarded by the majority of both races as undesirable and impossible. . . . Shall we not then distinguish between the issue of social equality and that of political and economic freedom, and deal with the latter on its own merits and in all good conscience?" The commission's recommendation, which the messengers adopted, merely reaffirmed resolutions approved three years earlier in support of the welfare and civil rights of African Americans.[39]

Although the messengers habitually adopted the reports and recommendations of the Social Service Commission, which appealed to their primary commitments, their influence on the mass of Southern Baptists can easily be overestimated. The commission's reports reflected what most messengers considered best practice. They could endorse them at the convention, aware that they were not binding. The commission had no staff and very limited finances; it did not distribute any literature on race relations. It spent $1,272 in 1940, $1,150 in 1941, $73 in 1942, nothing in 1943 and only $38 in 1944. Most Southern Baptists paid little attention to the commission; since their churches were independent, they did not need to. Several state conventions created social service committees on the lines of the SBC's commission, but lack of funds, staff and influence also hampered them. Reports from many state social service commissions nevertheless suggest that, to some extent, Baptist messengers to the state conventions shared and were influenced by ideas from the regional commission.[40]

At the request of E. C. Dargan, president of the SBC, Baptist conventions in Georgia and Virginia established the first social service committees at the state level in 1911. They preceded the SBC's own commission, which Dargan appointed. Within a few years, Baptist state conventions in North Carolina, South Carolina, Texas and Alabama also established social service commissions. Until World War Two, the state committees, for the most part, avoided discussion of specific racial problems, other than, sometimes, to condemn lynching and report black poverty. Instead, they issued general admonitions that Baptists should apply the golden rule in dealing with those of other races. The committees did not question segregation or wage differentials between the races. Baptist conventions in Virginia, North Carolina, and Texas also created race relations committees.[41]

According to historian John Lee Eighmy, the Committee on Inter-Racial Relationships established by the Baptist General Association of Virginia in 1931, was not only the most active of the three in promoting meetings with African-American Baptists, but was also the most critical of Southern Baptists for reneging on Christian principles in race relations. In both 1941 and 1942, the Virginia committee called for adherence to the *Alston* ruling and opposed racial discrimination in the national defense program. It contrasted the American fight for democracy abroad in 1943 with the denial of rights to blacks and other minorities at home. The committee also recognized "an increasing tension between the races in some areas, heightened by war conditions," and appealed for "a progressive and Christian solution . . . to assure the best of relationships between the two groups." In 1944, the committee urged pastors and church leaders to study the reports of the Durham and Atlanta conferences, and called on them to support the Southern Regional Council, an Atlanta-based biracial organization founded that year to promote racial equality within segregation. Each year the General Association adopted the committee's reports and recommendations, but except for teachers' salaries, they shied away from mentioning specific African-American grievances.[42]

The race relations committee of the Baptist State Convention of North Carolina focused on evangelism, but its Committee on Social Service and

Civic Righteousness addressed some specific black complaints. In 1942, the committee called upon North Carolinians "to see that fair treatment and justice are extended Negroes in employment, in militay [*sic*] service, and in the courts of our land." It "greatly deplored" the race riots of 1943. The committee declared that "The unwillingness on the part of many white people to accord Negroes full opportunity for growth in a genuine democracy, and the bitterness shown by some of the colored leaders in seeking to obtain rights denied them, are not in accord with Christian ideals for living together." A year later, it called "upon our government, both federal and local, to see that our Negro brothers are accorded justice in the courts, and that he has a fair chance in the business world in matters of employment and wage."[43]

Generally less outspoken about particular facets of discrimination than the convention in North Carolina, the Baptist General Convention of Texas placed greater emphasis on improving race relations at the local level. Until it appointed a Committee on Inter-Racial Relations that first reported in 1943, the convention had considered African Americans almost solely in terms of evangelism. The committee's report, that year, gave favorable coverage to the Durham and Atlanta conferences on civil rights. At its prompting, the convention voted to establish a Department of Interracial Cooperation, partly as a culmination of its earlier missions efforts, but also in response to the civil rights movement and to the dangers of racism exemplified by Nazi Germany. The vote was probably also influenced by a race riot in Beaumont that had occurred in June and highlighted the state's racial problems.[44]

Under its director A. C. Miller, the Department of Interracial Cooperation emphasized the necessity of African-American ministerial education and cooperative missions with minority groups. It decided to prepare "A wholesome and informative literature . . . dealing with various phases of racial misunderstanding." The department also promoted the establishment of standing committees on interracial cooperation in the state's Baptist associations.[45]

The remaining Baptist state conventions either mostly ignored racial problems, or were as fully concerned and, in some cases, as advanced on race issues as the SBC. Conventions in Tennessee, Arkansas and Mississippi disregarded civil rights altogether, while the Alabama Baptist State Convention occasionally broke its silence on the issue. In its report to the Alabama convention in 1941, the Social Service Commission deplored "race conflicts and persecutions" and "those who fan the fires of race hatreds." It also declared that "All minority racial groups should be given the same rights and privileges that the majority groups claim for themselves." Having advanced too far in front of Baptist opinion in Alabama, the commission avoided racial issues in subsequent years.[46]

By contrast, the Louisiana Baptist Convention became more willing to offer support for African-American rights as the war continued. Reporting to the convention in 1941, the Committee on State Missions noted the development of "a rising consciousness among Negroes of their own inherent abilities to look out for themselves." Rather than addressing the substance of black demands, the committee asked the convention's Executive Board to increase its efforts to train African-American ministers. It assured Baptists that there were "still many wide open doors for us in this field. . . . " The convention's Social Service Committee ignored racial problems until 1944, when, in a delayed response to America's race riots of the previous year, it condemned "busy bodies and adjectators [*sic*] who have stirred up much confusion within our nation among the Negroes in particular." However, the report, which the messengers approved, also endorsed resolutions in support of civil rights adopted by the SBC in 1941 and reaffirmed in 1944.[47]

The Georgia Baptist Convention took a stronger position than its Louisiana counterpart. The convention adopted a Social Service Commission report in 1941 that deplored "excitement of racial feeling and hatreds," and supported "civil, economic, and educational justice" for African Americans. Three years later, the commission acknowledged that the war had worsened race relations, reassured Baptists that blacks did not seek "social equality" and argued that Christians should support equality of opportunity for all.[48]

The Baptist state conventions in Florida and South Carolina took particularly outspoken approaches to racial problems. In 1941, the Baptist State Convention of South Carolina adopted a report from its Commission on Social Service that expressed "horror at the ruthless way Germany has dealt with her minorities" and warned Baptists that "We must be careful to be above reproach in handling our own minority problem." The report criticized "politicians, organizations, and interested forces" that used "race prejudice to further their selfish ends." It welcomed the recent decline in southern lynching, and progress toward equalizing educational opportunities. The committee called for equal justice in the courts for African Americans, and it recognized that "recent Supreme Court decisions have brought us face to face with racial discriminations."[49]

In 1942, the Florida Baptist Convention's Temperance and Social Service Committee praised steps made toward fair trials for black defendants, greater public expenditure on black education and improved salaries for black teachers. The committee made a strong appeal to the primary commitments of Southern Baptists in its repudiation of racial discrimination. It declared that "In the interest of our educational, industrial, civic and religious health, we must remove the differential, the injustices and inequalities suffered by the Negro race. . . . " The committee also made an impassioned plea against lynching and called for "law and order."[50]

Race riots imperiled law and order, and highlighted the saliency of racial problems. In 1943, the Florida Baptist Convention adopted a Social Service and Temperance Committee report that announced "We deplore the race riots that have occurred in our country during the past year." The Baptist State Convention of South Carolina adopted recommendations from its Commission on Social Service that "We should do all we can to keep relations between white and colored people good. There are great problems here. Hoodlums cannot solve them."[51]

The social service bodies in both conventions decried race prejudice as unchristian. In 1944, the Florida Baptist Convention adopted a Social Service and Temperance Committee report that declared: "We deplore the presence of race prejudice among our people and we reaffirm the great principle of respect for the personality of every man taught by Jesus." In South Carolina, the Committee on Social Service also noted that "Jesus put supreme valuation on personality. . . . " It cautioned Baptists that "Race hatred undermines respect which is due to every person made in the image of God." Both conventions linked the fight against totalitarianism abroad with the need to cultivate democracy at home. The Florida committee contended that "It is inconsistent for us to boast that we are fighting for democracy throughout the world, when we are denying fundamental rights to the negro within our borders." The South Carolina commission deplored political racial demagoguery, and the convention adopted its recommendation that "We must seek to demobilize hatred, seeking to prevent it from being directed against minority groups and leading to Fascism here in America."[52]

For a Deep South state, the Baptist State Convention of South Carolina was very outspoken in defense of African Americans. Proportionately, the Deep South had the greatest black population in the South. Largely in consequence, whites in the region were more fearful of and therefore more repressive toward African Americans. Yet to judge by their convention reports, Baptists in South Carolina were almost as advanced in their advocacy of black rights as those in North Carolina, and Georgia's Baptists were, in some ways, as concerned with racial problems as those in Texas. In part, the paradox reflects the fact that social service committees throughout the South attracted as members those Baptists who were most aware of and concerned to alleviate social problems. Even so, as the example of Alabama illustrates, they could not move too far ahead of Baptist opinion in their states. Equally important, the committees became most outspoken whenever racial problems threatened disorder, most notably in 1941 and 1943, and when they feared that whites might defy Supreme Court decisions favoring African-American plaintiffs. The committees were often as concerned with law and order as they were with black rights.[53]

The weekly newspapers published by the state conventions provide another means of gauging Southern Baptist opinion. In his 1949 dissertation, Foy Valentine, who served as executive secretary of the SBC's Christian Life Commission between 1960 and 1987, examined editorials, articles and letters in the Southern Baptist denominational press in Texas, Mississippi, Kentucky and North Carolina to ascertain changing Southern Baptist attitudes toward African Americans between 1917 and 1947. He identified the most important reactionary attitudes as a belief in the Curse of Ham, "support of the Ku Klux Klan, an explanation bordering on a justification of lynching, the fear that the Negroes would lower the level of civilization which the whites had established, and the expression of white superiority and Negro inferiority." Progressive trends included a growing awareness of and desire to overcome racial problems, opposition to lynching and the Ku Klux Klan, and "a genuine interest in aiding the Negro in the securement of all his rights. . . . "[54]

Valentine concluded that although neither progressive nor reactionary attitudes dominated throughout or even at any particular time between 1917 and 1947, overall "the reactionary element persisted but its intensity abated," while "the progressive element . . . was gradually intensified, becoming more genuinely progressive all the time." The few favorable references made to the Ku Klux Klan found in the 1920s did not recur thereafter, while reactionary expressions declined most sharply in the 1940s. Valentine's analysis indicates that racial attitudes expressed in the Baptist press tended to be less progressive than those of the SBC's Social Service Commission and the more advanced social service commissions among the state conventions.[55]

Whatever the disposition of Southern Baptists toward civil rights, the SBC gave greater financial support in the 1940s to the evangelism of African Americans and black ministerial education. In 1940, the WMU began an annual series of interracial institutes in southern cities "to train black women as leaders of missionary societies in their own churches." The SBC increased its support for the HMB's work with blacks from $33,000 in 1944 to $109,000 in 1945. Many state conventions also increased their rhetorical and, sometimes, their financial commitment to missions. The Report on State Missions of the Louisiana Baptist Convention noted in 1941 that "Our

Negro Mission work has been all a matter of well-wishing until recently a few hundred dollars was given." The convention requested the Executive Board to increase funding for the work. A year later, the Baptist State Convention of South Carolina voted to appoint a committee "to study the problem of Negro Baptist Ministerial Education. . . . " The Mississippi Baptist Convention adopted a recommendation from its Convention Board to "enlarge our work with the races" and accordingly increased its missions budget for "Negro Work" from $2,400 in 1944 to $4,000 in 1945.[56]

As African-American militancy grew, Southern Baptists increasingly viewed evangelism not only as desirable in itself but also as a way to improve race relations without disturbing Jim Crow. Some Baptists supported greater missionary work among blacks with the implied, but unstated, hope that it might deflect African-American attention away from the desegregation demands of the civil rights movement. The HMB hired its first black staff member, Roland Smith, in 1942 as a liaison between Southern and National Baptists. Committed to segregation, the board denied Smith an office, and he had to work from home. *Home Missions,* the monthly publication of the HMB, editorialized in 1943 that the board's activities "makes it possible for Southern Baptists to cross all racial lines in preaching the Gospel without raising the question of racial or social relationships." The HMB's Department of Cooperative Missions with Negroes declared in 1944 that its work sought "to train the Negro leadership for Christian service and to help create better race relations between white and Negro people."[57]

Many state conventions presented a similar message. In 1943, the Florida Baptist Convention's Social Service and Temperance Committee argued that interracial missions could create "a more wholesome and Christian relationship between the . . . races." It also reassured Baptists that "a happy relation between the races does not mean an amalgamation." In 1944, A. Hamilton Reid, president of the Alabama Baptist State Convention, called on Southern Baptists to "show more spiritual concern for and lend more spiritual assistance to the negro Baptists in an effort to maintain a harmonious and Christian understanding between the two great races. . . . " In an article promoting the work of the Department of Interracial Cooperation, A. C. Miller assured Texas Baptists that it was "better to develop our people within our own races." At the end of World War Two, missionary endeavor seemed entirely compatible with segregation and for some Baptists even a means to secure its preservation.[58]

The vast majority of Southern Baptists, like other southern whites, favored Jim Crow. Their support derived from a range of sources, among them a conviction that God had created segregation, a presumption that African Americans were inferior in intelligence and morals, a fear of miscegenation, an acceptance of prevailing social norms and obedience to the law. A poll of white southerners conducted in 1942 found school desegregation supported by 2 percent, public transportation desegregation by 4 percent and residential desegregation by 12 percent. Only 21 percent believed that blacks had equal intelligence.[59]

Although Baptists endorsed segregated education, during the war their conventions increasingly called for greater public expenditure on black education. Like other southern whites, many Baptists saw the equalization of the public schools as a way to stave off challenges to segregated education by the NAACP, but it also reflected their commitment to public education. Some Baptist conventions supported the equalization of teachers' salaries, which reflected not only their commitment to education, but also their belief in the rule of law as the courts decided in favor of parity. When the judiciary outlawed the white primary and chipped away at injustices within Jim Crow education, Baptist conventions tended to support constitutional rights without discussing specific court rulings. The same commitment to law and order also led them to deplore lynching and race riots.

By the end of World War Two, the first signs of incompatibility between the primary commitments of Southern Baptists and the maintenance of segregation had begun to emerge. However, few Baptists were aware of a conflict, and the vast majority of them supported Jim Crow. Prompted by lynching, the emerging civil rights movement, federal court rulings, race riots and the virulent racism of Nazi Germany, many Baptist conventions had begun to develop an awareness of and a growing discomfort with the worst aspects of racial discrimination and inequality. However, it was only in the quarter century after the war, with the emergence of a larger and more successful civil rights movement, a federal government and Supreme Court more supportive of civil rights, and the expansion of the Baptist missions into the newly independent countries of Asia and Africa, that most Baptists found themselves unable to reconcile their commitments with the existence of Jim Crow.

2

An Overview: Southern Baptists and Desegregation, 1945–1971

IN THE CIVIL RIGHTS ERA, the SBC was the largest white denomination in the South and the largest Protestant denomination in the United States. Its membership, concentrated overwhelmingly in the South, numbered 5.9 million in 1945, 9.9 million in 1961 and 11.8 million in 1971, and included nearly half of the southern white population. For decades prior to the civil rights movement, the vast majority of Southern Baptists had supported racial segregation. Subsidiary to their devotion to God and scripture, Baptists held primary commitments to evangelism, law and order, and public education. Until the 1950s and the 1960s, Baptist commitments seemed compatible with the maintenance of Jim Crow. However, on May 17, 1954 the Supreme Court declared public school segregation unconstitutional in *Brown* v. *Board of Education*. The *Brown* ruling and subsequent federal civil rights legislation, together with the white South's massive resistance to desegregation, created a conflict between segregation and the primary commitments of Southern Baptists. Most editors of Southern Baptist newspapers, some agency heads, many of the Social Service and Christian Life commissions of the SBC and state conventions, and a few scattered pastors encouraged Baptists to accept the demise of legal segregation. By 1971, many Baptists rejected segregation in principle, but few desired or actively sought genuine integration.[1]

Until the mid-1960s, the majority of white southerners and Southern Baptists favored segregation. Opinion polls taken in the 1950s and early 1960s consistently found that approximately 64 to 70 percent of southern whites favored "strict segregation." However, Southern Baptists, like other whites, differed in the depth of their devotion to racial separation. While hard-line segregationists supported Jim Crow unyieldingly, many Baptists were moderates who preferred segregation but not at the expense of social peace and lawful order.[2]

Hard-line segregationists justified racial segregation as biblical and cited selected verses, mostly drawn from the Old Testament, in their support. Moderate segregationists, unlike hard-liners, did not accord segregation racial justification. Their support for the separation of the races derived from custom and an acceptance of the existing social order. Believing that the Bible neither advocated nor condemned segregation, moderates could eventually acquiesce in desegregation because it posed no threat to their religious beliefs.[3]

A progressive minority of Baptists persistently criticized racial discrimination. Between 1945 and 1954, most progressives argued that blacks should be accorded equal treatment within segregation, although a few also criticized racial separation in principle. In the years after the *Brown* decision, progressives contended that biblical teachings stressed the unity of mankind and did not legitimate segregation. Progressives included some denominational officials, some heads of SBC agencies, the SBC and some state convention Christian Life commissions, some Baptist student unions (BSUs), a few editors of Baptist newspapers and a few pastors and lay people. They argued, in meetings of the SBC and state conventions, the denominational press and pamphlet literature, and also in a few churches, that biblical teachings stressed the unity of mankind and did not legitimate segregation.[4]

Whatever their views toward segregation, Baptists held primary commitments to evangelism, law and order, and public education. Religion infused their commitments. Baptists argued that *Matthew* 28:19–20, the Great Commission, required them to convert the unsaved at home and abroad. Citing *Romans* 13:1–2 and *Titus* 3:1, they insisted that the Bible taught Christians to obey the law. Baptists heralded Jesus as the prince of peace. They considered the public school system essential for producing an educated citizenry that could read and understand biblical teachings and so "constitute a rich field for the gospel." Baptists also viewed public education as vital for the maintenance of a democratic and free society, conditions under which, they believed, Christianity prospered.[5]

Dedicated progressives sought to persuade Baptists that segregation and its maintenance militated against their primary commitments. Conflict between their commitments and Jim Crow made moderate segregationists amenable to change. Massive resistance by some southern states to school desegregation in the second half of the 1950s and early 1960s defied federal law, threatened education and, by publicizing American racism to the world, undermined Southern Baptist evangelism in non-white countries. In the 1960s, civil rights direct action campaigns also exposed American racism. The Civil Rights Act of 1964 made segregation of public facilities unlawful. During the 1950s and 1960s, therefore, the core values held by moderate segregationists pushed them gradually toward acceptance of the end of legal segregation.

Influenced by social change and the progressives' rebuttal of the biblical defense of Jim Crow, even some hard-line segregationists undertook a painful review of their belief in a biblical justification for segregation. Although some hard-liners maintained their views throughout the 1970s, many concluded that the Bible did not endorse segregation as they had once believed. Like the vast majority of Baptists, they came to reject enforced segregation in principle as discriminatory and unchristian.[6]

Southern Baptists passed through three stages in their response to the issue of desegregation. In the first stage, between 1945 and 1954, Baptists continued to support segregation but argued that African Americans should be given equal opportunities within it. In their second stage, after the *Brown* decision, their primary commitments began to push Baptists, however reluctantly and incrementally, towards an acceptance of change. In their third stage, after the passage of the Civil Rights Act of 1964, more and more Baptists abandoned their commitment to segregation and repudiated racism as unchristian. Although they did not seek integration, most rejected overt discrimination.

During their first stage, most Baptists favored racial segregation. SBC presidents, elected by the messengers at the convention's annual meetings, defended segregation and insisted that it benefitted both races. In 1948, M. E. Dodd, a former SBC president, declared that "The Negro in the South has developed faster than anywhere in the world, through the efforts of Southerners themselves. . . . The Jim Crow law is for the protection of the Negroes themselves." In many southern states, editors of Southern Baptist state convention newspapers endorsed segregation as biblical and part of God's plan for mankind. Garbling *Acts* 17:26 and ignoring its implicit rejection of racial differences, E. D. Solomon, editor of the *Florida Baptist Witness,* wrote: "Segregation yes, forever. God has so ordained. 'He made of one nation (race) of man to dwell on all the face of the earth'—He made them that way—That way they must stay."[7]

In the 1940s and early 1950s, Southern Baptist progressives in the social service commissions, like most contemporary southern white liberals, urged that African Americans be accorded equal opportunities, facilities and justice within the system of segregation. In line with their primary commitments, the SBC and most state conventions adopted the commissions' reports and recommendations. They also condemned lynching and mob violence. Some conventions denounced the Ku Klux Klan. The Baptist State Convention of North Carolina called the "Ku Klux Klan's propaganda of white supremacy . . . a denial of the Scripture." Editors of state conven-

tion newspapers, including many in the Deep South, adopted similar positions.[8] By the early 1950s, the social service commissions of the Texas, Virginia and North Carolina conventions had each criticized segregation in
their reports. The SBC's Social Service Commission and the WMU also
attacked segregation in some of their publications. Fearful of advancing
too far ahead of their constituency, they did not sponsor resolutions condemning Jim Crow.[9]

Commitment to evangelism led most Southern Baptist seminaries to rescind their whites-only policies in the early 1950s. Although the SBC continued to cooperate with African-American Baptists in helping to finance
the American Baptist Theological Seminary, the school remained poorly
funded and inferior. In 1950, Edward A. McDowell, chairman of the SBC's
Committee on Negro Ministerial Education, told the convention: "The
need for better trained ministers among our Negro Baptist brethren grows
ever more acute. This need cannot be supplied alone by the American Baptist Seminary at Nashville. . . . The time has arrived for our Convention to
co-operate with Negro Baptists in providing ministerial training on the
higher academic levels." Trustees of Southern, Southwestern and New Orleans Baptist Theological Seminaries agreed to implement nondiscriminatory admissions policies beginning in 1951 and 1952. The trustees of the
seminaries presented the move as a practical means of offering black ministers adequate training rather than as an attack on segregation. A news
release from The Southern Baptist Theological Seminary, explained that
"The action of Southern Seminary trustees has in it no radical implications
concerning the race issue. A Baptist need has been met on the practical
Christian level." The SBC commended the seminaries' action at its annual
meeting in 1952.[10]

During their second stage, beginning in 1954, SBC and some Baptist
state convention leaders and editors urged Baptists to accept the *Brown*
ruling. Baker James Cauthen, executive secretary of the SBC's Foreign Mission Board, argued that "The decision will strengthen American influence in many countries and will reduce some obstacles to missionary work
among the races." SBC president J. W. Storer insisted that Christians had
to obey the Supreme Court's decision on the basis that it was the law, and
"We 'Render to Caesar the things that are Caesar's, and to God the things
that are God's.'" L. S. Sedberry, executive secretary of the American Baptist
Theological Seminary, warned that "We must not permit prejudices, racial
antagonism, and petty politics to lead us into confusion, violence, and possible bloodshed." The WMU also supported the *Brown* decision.[11]

Southern Baptist leaders did not endorse the *Brown* decision as being in
itself Christian. Only A. C. Miller, executive secretary of the SBC's Christian

Life (formerly Social Service) Commission, took that position. Miller told the *Baptist Press* that "The decision was the inevitable result of social progress based on the Christian teaching that all men are included in the love of God and have dignity and worth in the sight of God."[12]

In its report to the convention, the Christian Life Commission urged Baptists to support the *Brown* ruling because it was legal, "vital to our Christian missionary enterprises," and based on "the scriptural teaching that every man is embraced in the love of God." The commission also argued that the public school system was "one of the greatest factors in American history for the maintenance of democracy and our common culture. . . . " The convention adopted the commission's recommendation endorsing *Brown,* by a vote of approximately nine thousand to fifty.[13]

Only the Virginia and North Carolina conventions specifically approved the *Brown* decision, but no convention went on record against it. Most Baptist state conventions appealed for Southern Baptists to be calm and respond peacefully. Some conventions also insisted on the need to be law-abiding and to preserve the public school system. Diehard segregationists in Arkansas, Tennessee, Louisiana and Mississippi succeeded in silencing their conventions.[14]

Regardless of their personal views about segregation, most Southern Baptist editors urged compliance with *Brown*. David M. Gardner, the biblical segregationist editor of the *Baptist Standard* of Texas, declared that "Whether we like the decision or not, it is now the law of the land, a fact which we must face and adjust ourselves to as good citizens and loyal Americans. . . . It is now imperative and incumbent upon Negroes and whites alike to cooperate in calm, clear thinking and courageous action in the interest of saving our free public school system." Only the editors of the *Baptist Record* in Mississippi and the *Baptist Message* in Louisiana expressed disapproval of the ruling and the SBC's resolution in its support.[15]

Immediately after the *Brown* ruling, all the Deep South states, except Alabama, approved laws forbidding public school desegregation. Alabama, Florida, Louisiana, Mississippi and North Carolina passed pupil assignment laws designed to evade or at least limit desegregation. Hard-line segregationists formed Citizens' Councils designed to silence white critics of Jim Crow and to intimidate blacks from petitioning for its removal. In May 1955, the Supreme Court ruled on the implementation of *Brown*. Public schools, the Court decided in a supplementary decision known as *Brown II,* had to begin desegregation with "all deliberate speed." By giving federal district courts discretion as to the pace of desegregation, the Court unwittingly encouraged the white South to obstruct the process.[16]

White resistance hardened in the wake of *Brown II* and in response to a growing number of school desegregation petitions filed by African Americans. The Citizens' Councils spread to most southern states. In March 1956, 101 of the South's 128 congressmen signed the Southern Manifesto, which declared the Supreme Court's ruling unconstitutional and supported all "lawful means" to "resist forced integration." By mid-1957, eight states had passed interposition laws to block implementation of *Brown*. In 1958, the governors of Virginia and Arkansas closed public schools subject to desegregation.[17]

In the second half of the 1950s, the SBC faced mounting opposition to its pro-desegregation position. Ardent Baptist segregationists wanted their conventions to endorse Jim Crow, but most white southerners simply wanted the churches to refrain from supporting desegregation or discussing racial problems. Many Southern Baptist pastors ignored the subject of race, either because they supported segregation, or because they rejected involvement in social and political issues. Other ministers bowed to segregationist community pressure. Some congregations fired clergymen who refused to endorse segregation or spoke out in favor of integration.[18]

With the exception of the Christian Life Commission, the SBC largely fell victim to its constituency's wish for silence regarding racial problems. The Southern Baptist commitment to peace and stability inhibited SBC executives from speaking out. Their primary commitments placed denominational officials in a dilemma. To urge obedience to the law by condemning massive resistance would create division and disorder within the convention, and risk the withdrawal of segregationist financial contributions. Yet to say nothing implied tacit support of law-breaking.[19]

The SBC and Baptist state conventions responded by refusing to endorse massive resistance and by continuing to call for peace and order. Accordingly, in 1956 the Georgia Baptist Convention adopted a Social Service Commission report that declared: "Certainly Christ would not have His followers become a party to any group that would incite mob violence or would break down respect for constituted authority and the law of the land." Although some conventions fell silent under segregationist pressure, most refused to countenance the abolition of the public school system, or any other measure designed to evade desegregation. Only the Alabama and Louisiana conventions openly declared themselves in favor of segregated education.[20]

SBC denominational leaders set the pattern followed by most state conventions. In April 1956, twenty leading Southern Baptists, including SBC president C. C. Warren, the heads of SBC agencies and prominent pastors, signed a widely-publicized "Appeal For a Christian Spirit in Race Relations." Although the Appeal did not constitute official convention policy and simply urged Baptists to apply Christian principles to race relations and remain calm, it did, in effect, disassociate the convention from supporters of massive resistance. However, the Appeal was also designed, according to signatory Porter Routh, executive secretary of the SBC's Executive Committee, to "forestall any debate or division over the matter" of race relations and segregation at the forthcoming convention meeting in Kansas City.[21]

In his presidential address to the 1956 convention meeting in Missouri, C. C. Warren declared that he concurred "in the feeling that it will be unwise for us to reopen any discussion of it [the Supreme court decision] here." Warren warned that "extremists and agitators" were doing "incalculable harm," because they overlooked "the fact that economic and social relationships . . . simply cannot be changed overnight." He also cautioned against "open defiance" of *Brown* because that would "endanger our foreign mission work throughout thirty-five areas of the earth and play right into the hands of the Communist[s]. . . ."[22]

Segregationist messengers applied pressure that kept the Christian Life Commission on a tight budget, but they failed to prevent it from carrying out its educative role. Instead of trying to force through divisive resolutions at the SBC's annual meetings, progressives in the commission sought to cultivate racial understanding and reconciliation by publishing an extensive tract literature. The tracts attacked the biblical defense of segregation, called for tolerance of other races, and pointed out that domestic racism hampered the work of Southern Baptist missionaries. The commission mailed its literature to the denomination's pastors, and to state and local leaders. Many pastors and lay church leaders, especially in the Deep South, indicated that the commission's race relations material helped both them and their congregations to understand racial problems better. Maxwell Baker, pastor of Sparkman, Alabama's First Baptist Church wrote to A. C. Miller: "Race relations is really a hot bed here and I have waited a long time for some sane material on the subject." However, some SBC agencies responded to segregationist pressure by downplaying race relations. The HMB withdrew a study book on the subject, *The Long Bridge,* because of the issue's sensitivity, even though the book's mild tone did not challenge Jim Crow.[23]

Southern Baptist state conventions did not, for the most part, simply follow popular segregationist sentiment. Even in states that experienced bitter desegregation clashes, Baptist conventions refused to endorse resistance. After the failed attempt of Autherine Lucy to desegregate the University of Alabama in 1956 and during the ongoing Montgomery Bus Boycott against discriminatory seating, the Alabama Baptist State Convention endorsed public school segregation. However, it did not support massive resistance and condemned an amendment to the Alabama Constitution that authorized the abolition of public education should the federal courts order its desegregation. In 1957, President Eisenhower sent troops to enforce school desegregation in Little Rock, Arkansas, against the opposition of Governor Orval Faubus. One year later, Virginia Governor J. Lindsay Almond Jr. closed schools facing desegregation. The Arkansas Baptist State Convention declined to take sides on the Little Rock issue. The Baptist General Association of Virginia "overwhelmingly" rejected a resolution backing the state's governor, and it opposed the use of churches to establish private, all-white schools.[24]

Many Southern Baptist editors vigorously condemned the mechanisms of massive resistance and none supported them. They denounced nullification, interposition, tuition grants to allow pupils to attend private schools and local option schemes designed to evade desegregation. Richard N. Owen, editor of the *Baptist and Reflector* of Tennessee, declared that "Any proposal for nullification of the Supreme Court's school [de]segregation decision is only reckless bravado. . . . We owe it to all our children and we owe it to the future to preserve our public schools." Editors reproved white mobs that tried to prevent the implementation of school desegregation and some warned that racial incidents hindered Baptist missions abroad. After printing a letter from a missionary in Argentina on the front page, Erwin L. McDonald, editor of the *Arkansas Baptist,* announced that "The cause of missions and of democracy have suffered inestimably from the 'Little Rock' incident."[25]

School desegregation suits by the NAACP localized the issue and forced Southern Baptist pastors to take a stand. As members of Baptist or interdenominational organizations, Baptist pastors appealed for peaceful acceptance of court-ordered school desegregation in cities such as Dallas, Little Rock and Atlanta. They declared that the law had to be obeyed and the education system maintained. Some pastors personally acted in support of integration. Tennessee pastor Paul Turner suffered a beating from segregationists in 1956 for escorting black children to recently-integrated Clinton High School.[26]

In 1959, Arkansas and Virginia abandoned massive resistance. School desegregation orders brought token integration into every state by 1964, as even the Deep South abandoned overt resistance. At the same time, the civil rights movement adopted direct action, in the form of sit-ins, boycotts and demonstrations, designed to overturn segregation and achieve voting rights. Both white mobs and southern law officers frequently attacked civil rights protestors.[27]

The combination of violence and increased court-ordered school desegregation forced moderate segregationists to respond, as their primary commitments came under unprecedented, sustained pressure. In 1961, whites in Alabama beat the biracial Freedom Riders for testing the Supreme Court's *Boynton* v. *Virginia* decision outlawing segregation in terminal facilities used by interstate buses. The SBC adopted a resolution that condemned mob violence. In a concession to the Deep South that also reflected Baptist commitment to stability and order, the convention criticized "unwarranted provocation" as well. The resolution reminded Baptists that "We cannot afford to let pride or prejudice undermine . . . either our Christian witness at home or the years of consecrated, sacrificial missionary service among all the peoples of the world." Missionaries and Home and Foreign Mission Board leaders spoke more forcefully against racial discrimination in America during the early 1960s than they had ever done before. As civil rights protests and marches reached their peak in 1963, Baker James Cauthen declared: "I have never known missionaries to be more concerned than they are now becoming about this serious matter. We could find it necessary to bring missionaries out of some countries and some mission work may have to close as a direct result of these tensions."[28]

Confronted with imminent school desegregation, some of the Deep South conventions and their leaders urged Baptists to obey the law and preserve public education. In 1960, the Georgia Baptist Convention appealed to the state government to abandon its massive resistance stance. In the Deep South, site of most of the direct action and voter registration campaigns of the civil rights movement between 1961 and 1965, Baptist state conventions condemned civil rights protests and segregationist violence as threats to public order. Some conventions in the peripheral South adopted a more progressive line. The Texas and North Carolina conventions called for Baptist churches and educational institutions to be open to all races. A small number of churches and several Baptist colleges in the two states complied.[29]

Baptist editors mirrored the response of their respective conventions. Token school desegregation in Alabama and Georgia, and the desegregation of the universities of Georgia (1961) and Mississippi (1962) and South Carolina's Clemson College (1963) forced even Deep South editors to urge obedience to federal law. As a few Alabama schools prepared to desegregate in 1963, Leon Macon, the biblical segregationist editor of the *Alabama Baptist,* urged his readers to accept the inevitable. Macon declared: "The Federal Courts' decisions are tantamount to law, and although many do not agree with these decisions, it becomes a Christian to obey the law. We believe God's Word instructs Christians to obey the authorities of the state."[30]

Their primary commitments induced some editors, with varying degrees of enthusiasm, to support the goals, although not the tactics, of the civil rights movement. In 1963, city police commissioner "Bull" Connor set dogs on civil rights demonstrators in Birmingham, Alabama. Richard N. Owen wrote in the *Baptist and Reflector* that "Baiting the police and inciting violence through mass demonstrations won't solve these problems, nor will police dogs stop people who are determined to be free from the stigma of second class citizenship because of their color." In the early 1960s, editors in Texas, Arkansas and North Carolina called on Baptists to open their churches to African Americans and embrace integration, while John Jeter Hurt Jr. also cautiously conceded the justice of black demands in Georgia's *Christian Index*. Explaining his change of views, former segregationist E. S. James, editor of the *Baptist Standard,* wrote: "[W]e lived in a culture where segregation was practiced, and we thought little about it until circumstances forced it upon our attention. The extension of missionary work in Africa and the emergence of new nations there, together with the [*Brown*] court decision and the persistent efforts of some of our own church people who had a conscience about it, have caused many of us to examine our own hearts."[31]

Segregationist letters to the denominational press remained common in the early 1960s, but a growing number of pastors and lay people declared their opposition to Jim Crow. The danger racism posed to missions prompted many Baptists to speak out for the first time. Grace Bryan Holmes wrote in 1960: "This is my answer to missionary Virginia Cobb's letter published in . . . *The Christian Index*. I would like for her to know there is one Christian on the homefront who does not 'think that way.' But like so many others who are sadly in the minority, I have kept silent on the subject of race prejudice. I cannot keep silent any longer on this 'crucial issue' which has caused conflict in my soul ever since I can remember. I was born and bred in the South and I was brought up a Baptist. But I could never reconcile the philosophy of segregation and what politicians refer to as 'our sacred way of life' with the doctrine of Christianity." Nevertheless, most Southern Baptists wanted their society's racial customs to remain unchanged. According to a *Newsweek* poll conducted in 1963, only 29 percent of southern whites favored desegregation of public accommodations.[32]

Although most Southern Baptists wanted to maintain segregation, progressives in the SBC's Christian Life Commission urged them to support and embrace change. In May 1964, the commission recommended to the convention's annual meeting that it approve church desegregation and "pledge to support the laws designed to guarantee the legal rights of Negroes in our democracy and to go beyond these laws by practicing Christian love and reconciliation in all human relationships. . . . " In its recommendation and literature, the commission tried to prepare Baptists to accept the pending civil rights bill. Convention messengers rejected the commission's recommendation and instead adopted a pallid substitute, hastily prepared by ministers from Louisiana, Mississippi and Alabama. Adopted, amid charges of ballot-rigging, by a margin of only 335 votes out of 8,000 cast, the substitute recommendation ignored civil rights legislation. It asserted that "the final solution to these [race relations] problems must come on the local level, with Christians and churches acting under the direction of the Holy Spirit and in the spirit of Jesus Christ."[33]

During their third stage, beginning with the passage of the Civil Rights Act in July 1964, continued racial violence and the demands of law led a growing number of Southern Baptists to accept the end of legal discrimination. At the same time, more and more Baptists rejected biblical segregation as they responded to the ongoing educational campaign by progressives and to the call of missionaries abroad. Days after the Civil Rights Act passed, SBC president Wayne Dehoney declared that "as Christian citizens, we are charged by the word of God to give voluntary, peaceful obedience to every letter of this law." Dehoney supported his words with action. At President Lyndon B. Johnson's request, he joined the National Citizens' Committee for Community Relations, designed to foster compliance with the act.[34]

As the civil rights bill was now the law of the land, the SBC passed a resolution in its support in 1965, modeled on that offered by the Christian Life Commission a year earlier. The messengers promised to promote "peaceful compliance with laws assuring equal rights for all" and "to go beyond these laws in the practice of Christian love." Concern for missions and peace and order, as much as a commitment to the rule of law, explained the passage of the resolution. Its opening paragraph drew attention to "the major responsibility" Southern Baptists had "for the Christian witness both in the homeland and around the world." The resolution also criticized disruptive civil rights protestors and their violent opponents: "We deplore the open and premeditated violation of civil laws, the destruction of property, the shedding of human blood, or the taking of life as a means of influencing legislation or changing the social and cultural patterns."[35]

The Virginia and North Carolina conventions endorsed the Civil Rights Act and the Baptist General Convention of Texas praised desegregation. No convention condemned the act. Although ignored by a few editors, many of them called upon Baptists to accept the new law. Richard N. Owen urged Baptists to give the act "voluntary, peaceful obedience" as "a test of our citizenship and of our Christianity." Seeking to reconcile the demands of law with what he claimed were the demands of God, Leon Macon argued that Southern Baptists could obey the Civil Rights Act and still serve the intended purpose of segregation laws, the avoidance of miscegenation, by refusing to marry African Americans. Despite their frequently-stated opposition to the civil rights movement, both Reuben E. Alley of the *Religious Herald* and W. G. Stracener of the *Florida Baptist Witness* now conceded that blacks faced discrimination and needed some form of redress. Stracener claimed that "it may be that the force of new law is essential for insuring the liberties of those who are being discriminated against."[36]

The cumulative effect of the editors' endeavors was to encourage Baptists to adjust to desegregation. Editors in Arkansas, North Carolina and Texas joined progressives in SBC agencies, such as the Christian Life Commission, the HMB and the WMU, in urging Baptists to advance integration. Progressives published integrationist articles in Southern Baptist magazines and journals. Their combined efforts, together with secular change mandated by the federal government, led increasing numbers of segregationists to reject Jim Crow. Some former biblical segregationists confessed their change of heart in denominational publications. Mrs. S. A. Williams of Arkansas explained in December 1964: "The new Civil Rights Bill only forces us to do that which the Constitution has always guaranteed should be done to all its citizens. . . . Once I was very bitter and very prejudiced where our colored people are concerned. . . . After much Bible searching and much prayer on the subject, I no longer believe in race superiority as I once did." Whereas 61 percent of white southerners opposed token school integration in 1963, only 24 percent did so by 1966.[37]

Incidents in which civil rights workers tried to enter Southern Baptist churches suggest that a significant proportion of regular churchgoers throughout the South sympathized with open admissions policies. More churches adopted open than closed policies. Even when churches barred African Americans, most members either could not bring themselves to vote for exclusion, or were intimidated into abstaining by segregationists. Exclusion votes usually represented a small minority of the congregation and came largely from the ranks of older and irregular church attendees. In a typical example, an anonymous Georgia pastor recalled that when his church voted 150 to 95 not to seat blacks: "At least 60 non-resident and inactive members voted. At least 12 people voted who have not been in church since I have been here—four and a half years. Many others voted who did not attend church more than once or twice per year. . . . [A]t least 80 percent of the work of the church and the financial support of the church is represented by the 95 people who voted 'yes.'" Most of the 625 resident church members did not even vote.[38]

Whatever their disposition, continued secular pressure and upheaval forced more and more Baptists to confront the issue of segregation. Threatened with the loss of federal grants and loans to students and themselves by the Civil Rights Act of 1964 and the Higher Education Act of 1965, Southern Baptist universities and colleges adopted open admissions policies. Baptist colleges in the Deep South held out longest in refusing to sign the required civil rights compliance pledge, but all did so by 1970.[39]

The assassination of Martin Luther King Jr. in 1968 and the riots that followed shocked Southern Baptist leaders. Many of them realized that Southern Baptists and the nation as a whole needed to make real and substantial efforts to deal with white racism, and the underlying social and economic causes of riots that had plagued America annually since 1964. In the aftermath of King's assassination, seventy-one SBC and state convention leaders and editors signed "A Statement of Christian Concern." The statement acknowledged Southern Baptists' "share of responsibility for the injustice, disorder and wickedness of our land" and asked the SBC's Executive Committee to create a task force from relevant SBC agencies "to deal with these problems in the most effective manner possible. . . . "[40]

At its annual meeting, the SBC voted 5,687 to 2,119 in favor of a modified version of the statement that weakened the Baptist confession of responsibility for the racial crisis, affirmed the Baptist role in preaching God's love and urged minorities to respect "the person and property of others." The messengers declared that "we are shocked by the potential for anarchy," and urged Baptists to act because "we have had riots and have tolerated conditions that breed riots, spread violence, foster disrespect for the law, and undermine the democratic process." Equally important, America's race relations, the statement claimed, threatened Baptist evangelism. "We believe," the messengers affirmed, "that a vigorous Christian response to this national crisis is imperative for an effective witness on our part at home and abroad." The statement committed Baptists to securing open churches, equal rights, and equal opportunities in education and employment. Opposition to the statement came mainly from the Deep South.[41]

Denominational interest and commitment to the resolution of racial problems peaked between 1968 and 1971, but Southern Baptists faced a formidable task to achieve the aspirations of their convention. A survey conducted in 1968 revealed that in the eleven southern states only 127 of their churches had at least one African-American member, while 686 churches were willing to receive black members. A year after King's assassination, the Supreme Court ruled in *Alexander v. Holmes County Board of Education* that school desegregation had to be completed in 1970. Some Southern Baptist churches and their congregations, particularly but not exclusively in the Deep South, responded to the Supreme Court's ruling by setting up private schools and, more generally, by relocating to the suburbs to escape desegregation. In both 1970 and 1971, the SBC adopted resolutions that expressed its support of the public school system and condemned the establishment of private church schools for the purposes of avoiding racial integration. Across much of the South but especially in the Deep South, the region most affected by the *Alexander* decision, their primary commitments led some conventions and many denominational leaders to urge Baptists to support the public education system as it desegregated. Most Baptist editors made similar appeals. Hudson Baggett, editor of the *Alabama Baptist,* warned that "private schools cannot take the place of our public school system and state institutions of higher learning."[42]

Resolutions adopted by the SBC in 1969, 1970 and 1971 commended open churches and condemned racial prejudice. They indicate the continued decline, but not extinction, of racism within the convention. Even in the Deep South, some change occurred. Messengers from Mississippi and Alabama sponsored the 1970 and 1971 resolutions. Southern Baptist opposition to segregation was also indicated, albeit negatively, by the *Becoming* incident. In 1971, the Sunday School Board authorized the cancellation and revision of 140,000 copies of *Becoming,* a church training quarterly for teenagers, because it contained a photograph of a male, African-American teenager talking with two white female teenagers and a text that supported open churches. Over twenty state Baptist conventions and groups across the nation adopted resolutions concerning the withdrawal of *Becoming,* and over four hundred people wrote to the board about its action. Every resolution, except that adopted by the Mississippi Baptist Convention, and 314 of the letters opposed the board's decision.[43]

In effect, many Southern Baptists joined an increasingly conservative, white American mainstream in the late 1960s and early 1970s, opposed to legal racial discrimination and segregation but unwilling to make sacrifices to achieve integration. With the civil rights acts firmly in place, most Southern Baptists and most white Americans felt that government action in behalf of African Americans had gone far enough, and they opposed measures to offset the effects of past racism.[44]

Reflecting national white opinion, the SBC rejected "in total" the "outrageous" demands made by the National Black Economic Development Conference's Black Manifesto in 1969 for white denominations to pay African Americans $500 million in reparations for their complicity in racism. At the same time, the messengers called on everyone "to work for racial justice, economic improvement, political emancipation, educational advancement, and Christian understanding among all peoples of the nation and the world."[45] Florida pastor Glenn Lawhon successfully moved the deletion of a passage from the resolution that would have urged Southern Baptists to "support all governmental and social service agencies" that sought to help the needy. Lawhon's objection that Baptists should not support simply any "hairbrained idea" that the government might employ in its anti-poverty program reflected a nationwide distrust of government action that had helped to elect Republican Richard Nixon to the White House in 1968. The inefficiency and mismanagement that accompanied some of the economic and social programs of President Johnson's Great Society had produced widespread public disillusionment with the ability of government to deal effectively with social problems.[46]

A year later, in 1970, the SBC adopted resolutions that supported law and order, and commended the Nixon administration's "vigilant and peaceful efforts to contain radical extremists. . . . " Ostensibly not connected with racial issues, the resolutions reflected hostility towards radical black groups, such as the Black Panthers, that had been targeted by the Nixon government, as well as radical white student and fringe groups. Attentive to public opinion, Democrats coopted the law-and-order theme to effect in the 1970 congressional elections, another sign that the convention shared the national mood on social and racial issues.[47]

By 1971, Southern Baptists increasingly resembled other white Americans in their approach to race relations. Baptist leaders had helped to persuade many of their coreligionists away from a commitment to Jim Crow. Denominational officials and editors were mostly divided between progressives and moderate segregationists, while hard-line, biblical segregationists formed a substantial minority of SBC membership. While progressives urged the Baptist masses to embrace the inclusive and color-blind nature of Christianity and appealed to their fidelity to scriptural teachings, moderate segregationists took a more pragmatic approach. Baptists, moderates argued, had to relinquish forced segregation and obey federal law to save Baptist missions, public education and the South from violence and chaos. In combination the progressive and moderate approach, disseminated through the Baptist media and churches, provided a secondary pressure, behind that exerted by the civil rights movement and federal government, on religious white southerners to accept a new order in race relations. Some Baptists accepted the collapse of *de jure* segregation only as a *fait accompli* and actively sought to escape it by joining white flight to the suburbs and private schools. Even the majority of Baptists did not seek residential or school integration. Nevertheless, Southern Baptists increasingly viewed segregation in principle as incompatible with Christian belief, even as many struggled with the idea of opening their churches to all regardless of race.

3

The Sociology of Religion
and Social Change

Sociologists identify beliefs and practices, the polity of a religious organization and the social location of religion as key elements in understanding religion and social change. These factors inhibited the SBC and Baptist state conventions from responding in prophetic tones to the civil rights movement and its demands, and determined that their responses would be channeled toward caution and, sometimes, evasion. Nevertheless, Baptist conventions usually assumed more progressive positions regarding race relations than the mass of their membership. Sociologists have also examined the role of the local minister in dealing with social change. Their studies provide an understanding of the muted response of the majority of Southern Baptist clergymen to an era of marked racial change.

In the South, evangelical Protestantism, which places supreme emphasis on personal redemption through the medium of the conversion experience, has enjoyed religious hegemony since the 1830s and especially since the Civil War. Southern Baptists have not formed *the* church in the South in the sense of being an established church and have been but one of three major competing denominations, alongside the Methodists and the Presbyterians. However, their superior numbers, the regional hegemony of evangelical Protestantism as a whole, and the fact that many lay Southern Baptists have held important positions of social and political power in the region have given Southern Baptists and the SBC many characteristics associated with an established, albeit regional, church.[1]

"The Church," wrote sociologist Ernst Troeltsch, "is that type of organization which is overwhelmingly conservative, which to a certain extent accepts the secular order, and dominates the masses. . . . " Using this definition, the SBC can be considered the church in the South. The history of the development and spread of Southern Baptists from a sect among the poor, opposed to the lifestyles and values of the southern elite, in the eighteenth century, to a church largely in harmony with the elite during the course of the nineteenth, also fits closely with Troeltsch's conception of the development of a church. According to Troeltsch: "The fully developed Church . . . utilizes the State and the ruling classes, and weaves these elements into her own life; she then becomes an integral part of the existing social order; from this standpoint, then, the Church both stabilizes and determines the social order; in so doing, however, she becomes dependent upon the upper classes, and upon their development." Thus Southern Baptists supported slavery and the Civil War was fought, in large part, to defend it, even though many of them had no material stake in slavery.[2]

Less concerned with the development of sects into churches than Troeltsch, sociologist Emile Durkheim also recognized the role of religion in promoting and maintaining social and moral order. The church, according to Durkheim, uses ritual both to remind adherents of and to call them to uphold their shared values and beliefs. It supports the order and cohesion of society. Southern Baptists promoted social stability by inveighing against drunkenness, gambling and dancing. They contributed to the social integration of southern white society by idealizing the South as a region with a religion purer than any to be found elsewhere and, most obviously, by supporting the Confederacy.[3]

Working in the Durkheimian tradition, American sociologists Charles Y. Glock and Rodney Stark agree that religion supports social integration and harmony. They also regard the church as "an adaptive institution in society, an institution which is prone to compromise with the dominant secular point of view." Glock and Stark concur with F. Ernest Johnson's observation that "As the church becomes broadly inclusive and representative, it inevitably takes on the character of the community as a whole." When they conflict, religious norms tend to lose out to secular norms. Nevertheless, Glock and Stark contend that "The church does not merely support the *status quo,* nor merely follow the lead of its parishioners in the formulation of its social and economic policy. . . . [T]he church is in fact ahead of (more liberal than) its laity on most issues. It is more receptive to social change than its parishioners." The SBC and especially its Christian Life Commission, and some Baptist state conventions and their commissions, were clearly ahead of the mass of Southern Baptists in assuming a non-segregationist and, later, an integrationist posture during the 1950s and 1960s.[4]

The SBC and Baptist state conventions, with rare exceptions, did not follow southern white segregationist sentiment during the civil rights struggle. But they could not afford to get too far in front of their coreligionists. Of necessity, they tended to hedge on segregation, even as they sought to persuade Baptists to accept the inevitability of its demise. Rather than adopting a strong condemnation of segregation, the SBC endorsed the *Brown* decision in 1954 as both lawful and Christian. It also recommended that Baptists apply Christian principles to the expected crisis: "[W]e urge our people and all Christians to conduct themselves in this period of adjustment in the spirit of Christ; . . . we pray that God may guide us in our thinking and our attitudes to the end that we may help and not hinder the progress of justice and brotherly love. . . . " SBC president J. W. Storer responded to *Brown* in as nonpartisan a fashion as he could, even as he urged compliance based on Christian values. Storer declared that "Since the Supreme Court has made its ruling it is the duty of all Christians to respect that ruling and pray that God shall guide its implementing within the framework of mutual understanding and consideration."[5]

Many Baptist state conventions equivocated in their response to the *Brown* decision. In its discussion of the ruling, the Georgia Baptist Convention's Social Service Commission relied on the normative principles of Christianity: "These issues should be met by Christian men and women on the basis of spiritual teaching that every man is embraced in the love of God, every man has value in the sight of God, and every man is included in the plan of God." In a final act of equivocation, which avoided the issue of whether equal rights could exist under a system of segregated education, the commission urged "all Christians [to engage] in positive thinking and planning so that all people, of all races, would have equal rights as God would have it."[6]

Conventions took a much stronger stand on the need for Southern Baptists to be Christian in their relationships with African Americans than they did on the issue of segregation. Baptists could generally accept statements calling for courtesy in their relationships with those of other races, if they were not coupled with either an endorsement of or a call for desegregation. In the early 1960s, the Christian Life Commission published pamphlets that dealt with general, moral approaches to racial problems, such as *Christian Principles Applied to Race Relations.*[7]

The relationship between religion and culture is a dialectical one: each shapes and influences the other. This is not to claim that they do so equally, only that the relationship between them is not inherently biased in favor of one side. Religion can be a force for social continuity or for social change. Although a long-entrenched denomination will tend to support existing societal arrangements, endogenous and exogenous factors determine the relationship between a particular church or denomination and society. The ethical standards of a religion influence not just the degree of social involvement advocated by its adherents but also the nature of the involvement they espouse.[8]

Although some Southern Baptists participated in social Christianity, particularly in the first two decades of the twentieth century, it was also true that most Baptists emphasized individual morality, rather than attacking corporate sin. They criticized alcohol, dancing and gambling, rather than calling for social justice. In the civil rights era, Southern Baptists tended to emphasize the private morality of treating African Americans well in individual dealings, rather than the public morality issue of the collective injustice meted out to blacks under segregation. The Reverend Paul Jones, head of the Christian Action Commission of the Mississippi Baptist Convention, recalled in 1984, that "Integration was touted as a matter of corporate morality. It was the institutions that initially desegregated. Baptists just don't think in terms of corporate morality; we begin with the individual. We can see the drunk, the effect of the abuse of drugs in a family. Race was part of a societal experience, and when morality gets beyond the personal we sometimes tend not to see it."[9]

Voluntaristic belief systems, such as those of Southern Baptists, often argue that social problems are the product of individual sins multiplied on a large scale. Therefore many Southern Baptists tended to recognize racism only as the sum of individual prejudices, and they could not conceive of institutional and impersonal racism. Furthermore, as historian Edward L. Queen II has argued, most Southern Baptists did not hate African Americans. Devoid of personal hostility to blacks, they were either oblivious to the racism of southern white society or believed that blacks were currently occupying an inferior position because of educational and cultural disadvantages that they would, somehow, surmount over time. James F. Burks, the segregationist pastor of Norfolk, Virginia's Bayview Baptist Church, asserted in 1956 that "There is absolutely neither a feeling of animosity in my heart nor an attitude of inferiority as regards the colored race." Convinced that they were not themselves racist and that they had no part in discrimination, many Southern Baptists could not understand the issues raised by the civil rights movement. H. M. Stroup, a retired North Carolina minister, claimed in the mid-1950s that "The negro in the South has had every advantage given him. He is not mistreated in our state. He has been advanced as he has been able to take it."[10]

Most Southern Baptists considered that race relations in the South were good. They prided themselves on their cordial relations with African Americans, without reflecting upon the subordination they demanded from blacks in their interaction with them. M. A. Webb, a layman from Cleveland, Mississippi, explained in 1955: "I am a Southerner, born and reared in the Mississippi Delta where the Negro predominates in number. I have lived with them all my life, and have no feelings against them, other then complete segregation. I have many friends among the negores [*sic*], and I feel sure that many count me as a friend. If any one of them wants or needs anything, he comes to me and I work out the problem with him—whether it be for a small loan 'until Saturday,' an order to the Doctor, or, for help in buying something over a period of payments." A substantial majority of Southern Baptists in the civil rights era had what theologian H. Richard Niebuhr described as a Christ of culture approach to their society. Niebuhr wrote about such Christians: "They feel no great tension between church and world. . . . On the one hand they interpret culture through Christ; . . . on the other hand they understand Christ through culture, selecting from his teaching and action as well as from the Christian doctrine about him such points as seem to agree with what is best in civilization."[11]

As they equated racism with personal hatred of other races, Southern Baptists were inclined to advocate the conversion of the sinner away from individual prejudice under the guiding spirit of Christ, instead of expressing support for measures to protest and remedy collective injustice, such as civil rights demonstrations and legislation. Writing in 1964, W. Levon Moore, pastor of Pontotoc, Mississippi's First Baptist Church, explained that "the southern minister understands that prejudice, hate, injustice, and discrimination cannot be alleviated by external laws and violent pressure tactics, but are banished only by love; love that comes as the result of an inward experience of regeneration through the redemptive work of Christ."[12]

Although there were and are Southern Baptists who have accorded importance to both evangelism and social Christianity, many others have stressed the primacy of personal redemption. Baptists believe that the saved will go to heaven and the unsaved, the lost, will go to hell. Given this perspective, evangelism is far more important for many Baptists than attempts to cure the ills of this world. The Reverend Moore noted that a "serious study of the scriptures has convinced many southern ministers that their call is not a call to re-make an imperfect society, but rather to serve as ambassadors of Christ in re-making a lost humanity, preparing it for habitation of the 'new heaven and the new earth' which God Himself shall create." Furthermore, some Southern Baptists adhere to a premillennialist view. They believe that the end of the world will be preceded by an ever-increasing spiral of worldly problems. Hence, social reform seems to them not only misdirected but futile.[13]

The primacy of the individual in Southern Baptist thinking is reflected not only in an emphasis on the individual's personal redemption and regeneration but also in the doctrine of the priesthood of the believer. The democratic implications of Baptist individualism are reflected in Baptist polity. Consequently, progressive Baptist leaders in the postwar era could not order Southern Baptist churches to integrate. They had to tread softly in their approach to racial problems lest they alienate their coreligionists, who through their individual churches could refuse to provide the financial support essential to the survival of the agencies, commissions and institutions of the SBC and the Baptist state conventions. After Martin Luther King Jr. spoke at The Southern Baptist Theological Seminary in April 1961, thirty-one churches in Alabama designated that no portion of their gifts to the SBC's Cooperative Program (budget) go to the seminary, and some churches ceased all contributions to the program. Concerned with denominational growth, denominational leaders at both the SBC and Baptist state convention levels tended to be consensus builders, who shied away from controversy and preferred to avoid divisive issues whenever possible.[14]

Besides the endogenous factors outlined above, the social location of religion or even a particular denomination is important in determining its relationship with social change. Traditionally, Southern Baptists have, to a large extent, emphasized private morality. Their religion has been privatized. They are not alone. Indeed all mainstream religions in America have been subject to privatization. Sociologist Meredith McGuire offers a definition of the phenomenon: "Privatization is the process by which certain differentiated institutional spheres (e.g., religion, family, leisure, the arts) are segregated from the dominant institutions of the public sphere . . . and relegated to the private sphere. This segregation means that the norms and values of the private sphere are irrelevant to the operations of public sphere institutions." Religions subject to privatization, McGuire explains, "do not have to legitimate society directly—they support it indirectly by motivating retreat into the private sphere." The privatization of religion means that even denominations or ministers who openly support civil rights legislation and affirmative action may have little or no influence on their parishioners.[15]

According to sociologist Peter L. Berger, privatization explains "why the churches have had relatively little influence on the economic and political views of even their own members, while continuing to be cherished by the latter in their existence as private individuals." Even if many Southern Baptist ministers had spoken out for civil rights laws, conceivably they might not have affected their congregations, whose members would have dismissed their views as irrelevant to secular concerns and instead urged pastors to stick to the Bible. By rejecting the biblical defense of segregation, however, Baptist progressives concentrated on the one area, biblical interpretation, which their coreligionists, as people of the book, could not simply dismiss as irrelevant to the secular world.[16]

However, only a minority of Southern Baptist ministers assumed a forthright progressive position during the civil rights era. It is unclear how many southern ministers supported school desegregation. According to a survey conducted in 1958 by *Pulpit Digest,* 78 percent of Protestant ministers in the South and border states favored compliance with *Brown*. Denominational differences of opinion were small—75 percent of Baptists endorsed desegregation and 82 percent of Methodists and Presbyterians. Support for desegregation in the Deep South ran 18–28 percent lower than the 78 percent regional average. With justice, historian Howard Dorgan questions the validity of the *Pulpit Digest* poll. He argues that "a majority of 1958 white Protestant clergymen in at least South Carolina, Alabama, Arkansas, and Mississippi were not in favor of compliance." Dorgan contends that the poll was "skewed toward a liberal bias," because it was voluntary and attracted replies from ministers of prestigious urban churches, who formed the majority of the magazine's subscribers. He also notes that 6 percent of the respondents were black and can reasonably be expected to have supported *Brown*. The survey included the border south states "where integration plans typically were instituted with greater ease than in the Deep South." Furthermore, some Southern Baptist pastors publicly defended segregation.[17]

Even if many Southern Baptist ministers had wanted to speak out for equal rights or for integration, there were powerful incentives for them not to. Southern Baptist congregations hired and fired their own pastors; given the segregationist convictions of many lay Baptists the risk of dismissal was high. The Reverend Will D. Campbell, a Southern Baptist chaplain at the University of Mississippi in the 1950s, explained that "Because of Baptist church polity you work for the congregation, and no one wants to pay someone who opposes them." It was a brave minister who decided to stand against the opinion of the majority of his congregation and in so doing risk his job and his ability to provide for his family. Theology professor John R. Bodo argued in 1964 that "economic pressure on the pastor is probably the greatest deterrent to his exercising prophetic leadership. . . . "[18]

Yet throughout the civil rights era, there were some Southern Baptist pastors who advocated desegregation in defiance of their congregations. Some of these pastors kept their pulpits and even won over members of their congregations, but many were either fired by their churches or felt compelled to resign after encountering hostility from their parishioners. The congregation of Macon, Georgia's Tattnall Square Baptist Church voted for the resignation of its pastor Thomas J. Holmes in September 1966, after he had opposed the policy of excluding blacks recently adopted by its membership.[19]

Aside from dismissal, ministers risked violence and intimidation from segregationist communities against both themselves and their families. William P. Davis served as director of the Mississippi Baptist Convention's Department of Negro Work between 1957 and 1972. Although Davis had not called for integration, his evangelistic work with African-American ministers provoked the wrath of militant segregationists in the state. Driving along a dirt road in south Mississippi during the summer of 1961, Davis found his path blocked by flaming timbers placed by men whose car headlights shone in the distance. They pulled Davis from his car and called him a "nigger lover" and "do gooder" before they assaulted him. Davis's assailants urinated on him as he lay pegged to the ground. He escaped with his life and continued to work with blacks, despite constant threats and intimidation. Occasionally, violence against Baptist ministers took a more extreme form. In July 1958, segregationists bombed the home of Warren Carr, pastor of Watts Street Baptist Church and chairman of the interracial human relations committee in Durham, North Carolina. Both Carr and his wife escaped injury.[20]

Generally, segregationist violence did not exceed attacks on property. Insults and troublesome telephone calls constituted the most common form of harassment against integrationist ministers and their families. E. J. Kearney, pastor of Bonham, Texas's Seventh and Main Baptist Church, who pleaded for improved race relations, explained to his fellow pastors in the Fannin County Association in September 1957 that "To preach this message on race relations may well cost some of us our pulpits. It may mean a cross burned in our yards. It may mean the stoning of our churches, the insulting of our families, the physical harm to our children." It would be uncharitable to castigate Southern Baptist ministers, who labored in such conditions, for remaining silent.[21]

If an overtly integrationist minister did not lose his job, he still ran the risk of splitting his church or alienating enough of the congregation to have a damaging effect upon membership and financial donations. In 1964, Louis Wilhite became pastor of West End Baptist Church, which lay in an area of Birmingham, Alabama that soon underwent rapid transition from a white to a black neighborhood. Wilhite encouraged African Americans to participate in church programs, while many white members joined the exodus to the suburbs. The pastor and his family suffered harassment and threats. His church eventually split in 1972. Wilhite and over a hundred members left to form the Arlington Baptist Church. Both churches closed a few years later.[22]

According to Benjamin B. Ringer and Charles Y. Glock, those who were the most active in the church and often its largest contributors were also its most conservative members. They were likely to be the congregants who were most committed to segregation. To risk alienating them could also mean to endanger the "success" of a ministry. G. Jackson Stafford resigned the pastorate of Batesburg, South Carolina's First Baptist Church in October 1955 after a sustained campaign by United States Federal Judge George Bell Timmerman Sr., chairman of the deacons and the father of South Carolina's governor, to oust him. As a messenger to the convention, Stafford had voted for the SBC's resolution on *Brown* in 1954. Timmerman believed in biblical segregation. The judge's campaign against Stafford divided the church's deacons, but Timmerman enjoyed majority support from them. Stafford, who had hitherto presided over a marked expansion in the church's membership and budget, left rather than subject the church to controversy. Only twenty to twenty-five of the three hundred members present voted to accept his resignation, while none voted against. Yet, Timmerman, despite the reluctance of the congregation to see Stafford depart, enjoyed such dominance that he could force the pastor out.[23]

T. B. Maston, professor of Christian Ethics at the Southwestern Baptist Theological Seminary in Fort Worth, Texas, observed how crucial the idea of success was to Southern Baptist denominational figures, ministers and lay people alike. Maston explained that "Unfortunately, success is measured almost exclusively in material terms—numbers, buildings, income. . . . Some seem to want peace and quiet at any price, fearful of the effect of any difference of opinion or disturbance on the growth in numbers or the increase in financial support of the church or agency." Under these circumstances, there was little incentive for a minister to defend integration before a hostile congregation. Sociologists Ernest Q. Campbell and Thomas F. Pettigrew argue that "the minister [tends] to base his self-image, hence his sense of worth or unworth, on his success in managing a corporate enterprise." To achieve such success, they explain, "The minister is required to be a cohesive force, to 'maintain a fellowship in peace, harmony, and Christian love,' rather than to encourage action that divides the members." Many lay people and pastors saw the premier tasks for Southern Baptist ministers as evangelism and the expansion of church membership and buildings. Clergymen who wanted to preach racial justice but did not could justify their silence to both themselves and the church hierarchy by arguing that segregationist feelings were so strong among their congregations that they dared not speak out.[24]

"[T]he higher the socioeconomic and educational level of the congregation," Campbell and Pettigrew argue, "the greater the freedom of the minister to defend and support integration values." In 1954, an SBC survey of nearly 2,200 Southern Baptist ministers found that 73 percent had rural origins, including 63 percent of the convention's urban clergymen. Of the

SBC's 30,000 churches that year, 14,700 stood in open country, almost 9,000 in villages and towns, and less than 6,300 in cities. Poverty limited the per capita donations of rural congregants to $29 per year. An earlier SBC survey in 1949 discovered that one-third of Baptist pastors had achieved a high-school diploma or even less. Insufficient income from their pastoral duties forced some rural and small-town clergymen to operate a bivocational ministry as they took secular employment to support themselves and their families. Proportionately, Southern Baptists tended to have more members and pastors with lower income and educational levels than the other major Protestant denominations. Maston explained that "These are the very people who, because of the economic threat of the Negro and their own insecurity, are generally the most prejudiced against the Negro." Consequently, Southern Baptist ministers who were so inclined faced a difficult task in trying to change the segregationist beliefs of their congregations.[25]

Some pastors contended, therefore, that segregationist views among their congregations could only be undermined by a long and patient program of Christian education, which also had the welcome consequence of relieving the minister of the need to take a clear and immediate stand against Jim Crow. Clergymen maintained that they could not take too strong a position for fear that they would alienate the very people they were trying to reach. Ernest White, pastor of St. Joseph, Missouri's Wyatt Park Baptist Church, explained that "If a pastor is asked to leave a church over such a cause as the equality of rights for all races, it will be more difficult than ever for those people to be persuaded as to the moral rightness of the cause." In putting forward such an argument, clergymen were not necessarily simply offering a rationalization for their silence on racial issues. Colbert S. Cartwright observed in 1956 that some southern ministers who spoke out against segregation had lost their pastorates, only "to be replaced by less qualified ministers of limited social conscience." An outspoken biblical segregationist, Byron M. Wilkinson, replaced Thomas J. Holmes, after his forced resignation as pastor by Tattnall Square Baptist Church. The removal of integrationist pastors by their congregations and apparent lack of accomplishment deterred other like-minded ministers from speaking out.[26]

Owen Cooper, a segregationist layman who later championed integration and then served as president of the SBC, argued in 1984 that many Southern Baptist ministers never received the credit they deserved for their quiet, but effective, race relations work. Cooper recalled that "Some of them [pastors] were accused of not positioning themselves," but he insisted that had they supported integration they would have faced dismissal. He declared: "What would have been accomplished? True leadership is to accept people where they are and bring them along."[27]

Some clergymen were emboldened to speak out on racial problems when the SBC and its agencies, and Baptist state conventions did so. An unnamed minister told a race relations conference, organized by the SBC's Christian Life Commission in 1964, that "What you say makes it easier for us to speak to the issue." Pastors could argue that they were only reflecting the views that Baptists had themselves endorsed in convention meetings. When the Reverend G. Avery Lee preached a sermon in support of integration to Rustin, Louisiana's First Baptist Church in April 1956, he read out the full text of the resolution passed by the SBC in support of *Brown,* two years before. Lee then asked his parishioners "What more Christian attitude can we find as a pattern to follow?"[28]

Reference to convention sentiment, though, could be a double-edged sword since conventions could backtrack from a previous stance for racial justice or simply retreat into silence on the issue, leaving an outspoken progressive minister isolated. Historian Andrew Manis observes in his study of the Deep South that "the Baptist state conventions that in 1954 had been relatively compliant with the Supreme Court decision had become more vocally critical of it by 1956." In regard to social issues, Glock and Stark maintain that "Where the church has made up its mind, so have the ministers; where the church is equivocal, so are the ministers."[29]

Apart from relaying denominational resolutions, integrationist pastors, Campbell and Pettigrew note, employed seven techniques to communicate their views without alienating their parishioners. The law and order approach enabled ministers to appeal for compliance with court-ordered school desegregation, without revealing their own views, by arguing that it was the law of the land and obedience to the law was essential to the maintenance of social order. In November 1957, nine Baptist pastors joined an interdenominational group of Atlanta clergymen in signing a statement that disavowed support for "amalgamation of the races," but declared, concerning the *Brown* ruling, "As Americans and as Christians we have an obligation to obey the law." In the "messenger of the Lord technique," ministers maintained that integration was God's will and consequently they had no choice but to proclaim this truth. Johnny Jackson preached to the First Baptist Church of Walnut Hills, Dallas, Texas, in September 1957 that "I do not believe any close student of the Bible, especially the New Testament, can justify any kind of racial segregation or discrimination on the basis of God's will."[30]

Pastors who employed the "exaggerated southerner technique" stressed their credentials as southerners, in an effort to deflate the notion that they were outside agitators and so ensure a hearing for their views, before going on to assert their support for integration. In his integrationist sermon, the Reverend G. Avery Lee reminded his congregation that "As an Oklahoman, I grew up in the general traditions of the South. My folks shared about the same prejudices as others." In the "every-man-a-priest technique," the minister stated "his own opinion while expressing tolerance for contradictory ones and reminding his listeners that their access to God's truth is equal with his."[31] The "deeper issues technique" did not involve discussion of racial problems but instead stressed the Christian values of brotherhood and equality in the hope that the listener would connect these with the integration issue. In "the segregationists are stupid technique," the pastor dismissed rabid segregationists as ignorant haters and attacked their argument that desegregation would lead to interracial marriage and the destruction of the white race. More equivocal than the others, the "God is watching technique" simply required an assertion from clergymen that "the matter of race does have religious significance" and so his listeners "should 'act like Christians' in matters pertaining thereunto."[32]

Most of the techniques described by Campbell and Pettigrew did not require the minister to identify himself as an integrationist and only two of them directly asserted that segregation was not God's will. In most cases, the listener was left to make the connections for himself with the degree of inference provided by the pastor varying from one technique to another. Apart from reducing the likelihood of friction with the congregation, these techniques also gave clergymen the psychological comfort that they had addressed civil rights issues, although their congregations might not always have made the connections required even to be aware of the fact.[33]

In February 1957, Harold E. Fey of the *Christian Century* visited Koinonia Farm, an interracial community in southwest Georgia led by Clarence Jordan, a graduate of The Southern Baptist Theological Seminary. During the previous week and over the past few months the farm had been fired upon, and in other incidents a house had been burned and Koinonia's farm market destroyed by dynamite because it members did not conform to segregation. On his drive down to Koinonia, Fey visited an affluent "Baptist church in a county seat town south of Atlanta." A visiting pastor delivered the sermon to a packed congregation. Fey reported that "The atmosphere suddenly got tense when in the middle of the sermon he referred to the way in which Hitler exploited tensions between 'groups.' He said that some people in our society try to make scapegoats of minority 'groups.' But the crisis passed without the forbidden word 'race' having been spoken, and the sermon wandered off into safer speculations. The congregation was never told why the minister chose as his text Jeremiah 7:9–10. . . . But perhaps the people knew that the text applied to the story of Koinonia Farm. . . ."[34]

Progressive Southern Baptists, whether denominational officials or local pastors, faced formidable obstacles, cultural, religious, and strategic, in trying to prepare Southern Baptists to adjust to changes in race relations. Maston summed up their problem: "They have the responsibility to move the people to whom they minister toward the Christian ideal, but they must do this in such a way as to maintain an effective working rapport with the people." One of the first tasks progressives faced in trying to prepare Baptists to accept racial change was to wean a substantial group of them away from their belief that racial segregation was not just a preferable social arrangement but one that God had originated.[35]

4

Southern Baptists and the
Biblical Defense of Segregation

Scholars have often failed to appreciate the significance of religion in the segregationist world view. Indeed, historian Edward L. Queen II writes that among Southern Baptists "opposition to integration, with perhaps one exception, was never formulated on the basis of religion." In fact, for many Southern Baptists, the Bible was the linchpin of their defense of segregation. If the civil rights movement was a religious movement, opposition to it was, at least in part, a kind of religious movement as well. Many preachers and lay persons of both sexes insisted not only that segregation was in the best interests of African Americans, as well as whites, but, more importantly, that it had been ordained by God. Baptists who centered their support for Jim Crow on the Bible could be found throughout the South in the 1940s, 1950s and 1960s. They predominated in regions in which African Americans formed a substantial part of the local population, which included, aside from the Deep South, the black belt and plantation areas of the other southern states. Biblical segregationists also formed part of the Southern Baptist population in urban areas to which they and many African Americans had migrated from the countryside during the century.[1]

The importance of the religious defense of segregation cannot be fully understood without an appreciation of the role played by religion in legitimizing southern white society. "By legitimation," sociologist Peter L. Berger explains, "is meant socially objectivated 'knowledge' that serves to explain and justify the social order." Historically, religious legitimations of social arrangements, known as theodicies, have been more potent and effective than any other. Theodicies are so efficacious because they give the social order the sanction of a higher power, God. To uphold and to participate in the institutions of society is to "participate in the divine cosmos." To question social arrangements is to question God Himself. Supported by a theodicy, the social order appears "as the manifestation of something that has been existent from the beginning of time, or at least from the beginning of this group." In sum, a theodicy makes a social structure seem "divinely sanctioned, sacred, and inviolable." Individuals who support and participate in the institutions of society not only have no cause to doubt their role, they feel "an ultimate sense of rightness."[2]

Religion, of course, does not necessarily or always defend existing social conditions. Indeed, according to Berger, "religious perspectives may *withdraw* the status of sanctity from institutions that were previously assigned this status by means of religious legitimation." New perspectives may develop among those who have previously propagated the theodicy, or more likely they will come from outside that group. Religious perspectives can alter because of changes in society that cause people to consider and apply religion or religious ideas in new ways. By the same token, religious ideas can influence and shape the way in which people perceive and pursue, as sociologist Max Weber put it, the "material and ideal interests, [that] directly govern men's conduct."[3]

In order for ideas about the world or about the social order to remain plausible to members of a society, they require constant affirmation and reaffirmation from others. A rival religious view of the world to that advanced by the prevailing theodicy weakens its plausibility structure. Social arrangements lose their mystic sacredness and so can become subject to challenge. Berger observes that "The less firm the plausibility structure becomes, the more acute will be the need for world-maintaining legitimations. Typically, therefore, the development of complex legitimations takes place in situations in which plausibility structures are threatened in one way or another." He argues that all religious world-views are insecure and subject to change. Individuals inhabit a religious world that also exists in a "particular social context within which that world can retain its plausibility." Berger explains that "Since every religious world is 'based' on a plausibility structure that is itself the product of human activity, every religious world is inherently precarious in its reality. . . . '[C]onversion' (that is, individual 'transference' into another world) is always possible in principle."[4]

Many Southern Baptists employed a theodicy to defend segregation during the civil rights movement against those who questioned or sought to challenge racial subordination in the South. They articulated the theodicy most strongly when segregation came under attack, not just from secular sources but from progressive Baptists who challenged their segregationist beliefs. It would be mistaken to assume that most Southern Baptists simply fell into line with the demands of the white South's massive resistance to desegregation and tailored their religious beliefs to its needs. Racial segregation had a long lineage in Southern Baptist thought and action. Many antebellum Southern Baptist churches had practiced it. After Emancipation, white Southern Baptists refused to treat the former slaves equally within their congregations. Rejecting continued subordination to whites, the Freedmen preferred to form their own Baptist churches. Separation came by mutual consent and with white encouragement. Southern Baptists endorsed segregationist legislation in the late nineteenth and early twentieth centuries in the belief that racial separation was biblical. Thus, they contributed to the development of segregation in the South.[5]

Most Southern Baptists, outside the Deep South and the black belt, were moderate, rather than biblical, segregationists in the civil rights era. Biblical segregationists tended to be conservative or fundamentalist in theology, but some, at least in the Deep South, were theological liberals or moderates, and there were progressives and moderate segregationists in each theological camp. In combination with the much larger number of moderate segregationists, who simply wanted to avoid controversy and division, progressives generally succeeded in preventing either consideration or approval of segregationist resolutions at SBC and Baptist state convention meetings. In any case, most Baptist segregationists did not seek to put their conventions on record in favor of Jim Crow, they sought only to prevent them from endorsing integration.[6]

Although they left few traces of their beliefs in the official records of Baptist conventions, many Southern Baptists nevertheless believed that segregation was scriptural and part of God's plan for mankind. In letters (and some editorials) published in official Baptist newspapers and in correspondence with the SBC and its agencies, they asserted biblical support for Jim Crow. Militant Southern Baptist segregationists argued that God's plan required them to maintain His creation of different races. Leon Macon of the *Alabama Baptist* editorialized: "We think it is deplorable in the sight of God that there should be any change in the difference and variety in his creation and he certainly would desire to keep our races pure." Hard-liners maintained that to spurn segregation was to reject the word of God as recorded in the Bible, the sole source of divine authority, and His plan for mankind. O. W. Taylor, editor of the *Baptist and Reflector*, explained that "the plan of God is for diversity of races to continue through earthly time and into eternity. Hence, those who try to break down or obliterate racial distinctions and bring in a mongrel race or mongrel races go contrary to this plan of God." David M. Gardner of the *Baptist Standard* concurred. The editor wrote: "God created and established the color line in the races, and evidently meant for it to remain. Therefore, we have no right to try and eradicate it."[7]

Gardner's view was shared by much of the laity and expressed in some church resolutions. A resolution from the Cameron Baptist Church of

South Carolina declared: "In integrating the races in schools, we foster miscegenation, thereby changing God's plan and destroying His handiwork." Militant segregationist Baptists also expressed their views in the Southern Baptist press. Mrs. Sam Fowler Stowers wrote to the *Baptist Standard:* "This I believe: there is nothing more obvious than the fact that God created the races and set barriers of color, physical characteristics, and innate integrity between them for a purpose; and an intermingling and intermarriage (which is the definition for the word, integration) of the races God separated himself, is unthinkable, disgusting, and contrary to His divine plan!"[8]

Segregationist Baptists asserted that God had created the races for a purpose, although they were unable to identify His intention in doing so. By resolution, Mississippi's Mendenhall Baptist Church called "upon our religious leaders and statesmen to strive to keep the races pure that they may serve out the purpose for which God created them." A. Mims Wilkinson Jr. could not explain God's design in creating different races but had no doubt that a purpose existed. He wrote to the *Christian Index:* "What God intended when he created separate races, I cannot say. However, the many races were created. They are different and we can safely assume there was a reason. . . . "[9]

Making analogies from the Bible, some Baptist segregationists feared that if whites violated God's plan by integrating with blacks, divine retribution would follow. In 1958, E. D. Estes of Jackson, Mississippi, warned Brooks Hays, the president of the SBC, that "God does not want the races integrated. Study the Old Testament! It shows every time the people disobeyed God and integrated with other TRIBES, trouble was upon them and God whipped them one way or another. Where are most of the wars of this world? Wars are where the people are integrated!" The Reverend James F. Burks of Norfolk, Virginia's Bayview Baptist Church, claimed that God had destroyed Sodom and Gomorrah in His anger at racial integration which, Burks alleged, had occurred in these towns. Based on the (unfounded) belief that Semitic people were descended from Shem and blacks from Ham, Burks argued that "Sodom and Gomorrah were within the border of the Canaanites, who were descendants from Ham. Lot, a descendant of Shem, took his belongings and attempted to settle among them. His residence in Sodom got him into serious trouble, God's judgment was finally visited upon Sodom."[10]

For hard-line segregationists it followed that if segregation was biblical, then those who supported integration were guilty of sinful pride by believing that they could improve on the work of God. H. T. Sullivan claimed in the *Baptist Message* that "It was never His will that the races should become so mixed and confused as they are today. Where we have 'fumbled the ball' is [in] trying to improve on God's plan." Some Southern Baptists went further by asserting that integrationists were actually doing the work of the devil. Mrs. Roy McCaa wrote to the *Baptist Message:* "I cannot conceive of any real born again person advocating mixing of the races. . . . The Supreme Court's ruling on race-mixing [*Brown*] is satanic to the core, and may God in his infinite mercy pity them, is my prayer." In the *Arkansas Baptist Newsmagazine* E. R. McCorthy urged Baptists to resist what he saw as the evil of integration. "Let's not follow," implored McCorthy, "the leadership of this Devilish doctrine of destroying the handiwork of God in the creating of the races."[11]

Some Baptist segregationists saw the flourishing commitment of southerners to Christianity, and especially Baptist Christianity, as proof that God favored their devotion to both scriptural teachings and Jim Crow. They detected the Almighty's blessing in the fact that they were members of America's largest Protestant denomination and one that was expanding at a time when other major American Protestant denominations, ostensibly liberal on race, were losing members. Specifically connecting Baptist success and segregation, a resolution of Farmerville, Louisiana's First Baptist Church asked: "For, if segregation became wrong in 1954 why was it not wrong before that year? And, if it is wrong, why has the God of both races so wonderfully blessed the area of the Southern Baptist Convention and made it the Bible belt of the world, yet it is the only area where segregation has been practiced[?]"[12]

Militant segregationists did more than assert that segregation formed part of God's plan for the world or rest their case on the vibrancy of Christianity in their region. As people devoted to the authority of scripture they based their views on biblical passages or "proof texts," which they claimed offered divine sanction for segregation.

Ministers put forward the most detailed form of the biblical defense of segregation. They began with *Genesis*, focusing their arguments on chapters 9–11. According to segregationists, after the flood, God had divided the world among the three sons of Noah: Shem, Ham and Japheth. The descendants of Shem lived in Southern Asia and became yellow-skinned (or lived in the Middle East as the Semitic peoples). God gave Japheth's descendants, the white race, Europe and allotted Africa to the descendants of Ham, who were black. In addition, the supposed Curse of Ham condemned Ham's descendants to perpetual racial segregation and servitude. Despite God's supposed plan for racial segregation, the races had refused to separate and attempted to build a tower that would have reached heaven —the Tower of Babel. In response, God confounded their languages and scattered the three races "abroad upon the face of all the earth [*Genesis*

11:9]." Summing up the segregationist interpretation of *Genesis,* the Reverend T. J. Preston explained to the *Christian Index:* "The Lord at Babel gave them their languages and the bounds of their habitation. The White race in Europe, the copper colored races in Asia and the Black or Negro race in Africa. If the Lord had wanted us to all live together in a social way, why did he separate us in the beginning[?]." Segregationists also used the biblical history of the Jews to justify their position, by contending that God, beginning with Abraham, had segregated the Israelites to be the Chosen People and had forbidden them to marry members of other races.[13]

In dealing with the New Testament, hard-line segregationists argued that since it did not condemn racial segregation, God had not withdrawn His approval of the practice. In answer to the question had Jesus been a segregationist, Carey Daniel, pastor of West Dallas, Texas's First Baptist Church and executive vice-president of the Dallas Citizens' Council, wrote: "The burden of proof, my dear friend, rests with you to prove that He was NOT a segregationist. . . . Jesus was the same identical God who spoke through the lips of Moses, and He never once repudiated a single statement He ever made. If ever He did then our God is divided against Himself and His kingdom cannot stand." Segregationist ministers found the strongest New Testament support for their position in the words of Paul. According to *Acts* 17:26, Paul told the Athenians, "[God] hath made of one blood all nations of all men for to dwell on all the face of the earth, and hath determined the times before appointed, and the bounds of their habitation." In the minds of biblical segregationists, who incorrectly equated "nations" with races, Paul's words offered conclusive proof that God intended for the races to be separate, since He had purposefully given each race its own distinct living space. Where the races inhabited the same geographical area due to the accident of history, segregationists reasoned, they had to be segregated according to God's original wishes.[14]

The biblical defense of segregation was not confined to a few specialists. It was often put forward in church resolutions. In October 1957, Summerton Baptist Church in South Carolina adopted a resolution that opposed integration because "(1). God made men of different races and ordained the basic differences between races; (2). Race has a purpose in the Divine plan, each race having a unique purpose and a distinctive mission in God's plan; (3). God meant for people of different races to maintain their race purity and racial identity and seek the highest development of their racial group. God has determined 'the bounds of their habitation.'" Camden, South Carolina's Hermitage Baptist Church rested its defense of segregation on the story of the Tower of Babel. Its resolution stated: "We believe that God Himself instituted the segregation of all races. We also believe

God had a purpose in confounding the language of mankind, and scattering them abroad upon the face of all the earth." Another South Carolina church, Manning Baptist Church, passed a resolution which claimed that "Segregation of races was instituted by God Himself with the Jewish people."[15]

Baptist segregationists expressed their views not only in church resolutions but also in letters to the denominational press and to the SBC and its agencies. Mrs. Dave Miles wrote to the *Baptist Standard* in 1958: "I believe that if the peoples of America would study God's Word more[,] they would see that God intended for each nation to multiply and have its own social standards. Read Genesis 9:21–27 and 10:6–9." Mississippian A. A. Kitchings wrote to H. Franklin Paschall, president of the SBC, in defense of the Curse of Ham. He claimed that "The Canaanites had been cursed by Noah. Read Genesis 9:19–27. The offspring of Canaan are listed in Genesis 10:15–18. Did God respect the curse of Noah? Read Genesis 15:18–21. Did it last through the centuries? Read Deuteronomy 7:1–4. Read Ezra 9th and 10th chapters." Baptists seldom included every major segregationist "proof text," but they quoted many of them directly.[16]

Segregationists cited *Acts* 17:26, with its reference to God having determined the bounds of habitation of "all nations of men," in their support more frequently than any other biblical text. They frequently expressed exasperation that integrationists omitted the second half of the verse, which, segregationists believed, confirmed God's segregation plan. Don Keleg reproached the *Baptist Standard:* "In a recent anti-segregation article in the Standard the author as usual quoted only the first half of Acts 17:26 and left out the last half. Would you please be so good as to print the whole verse in your good paper?" Many lay Baptists simply expressed the belief that the Bible supported segregation, without resorting to particular verses to buttress their view. Writing to the *Baptist Record,* Bob Weems asserted that "We are told in scores of scriptures that everything should reproduce 'after its own kind.'" A North Carolina layman wrote to A. C. Miller, executive secretary of the SBC's Christian Life Commission, "The Bible I use (King James Version) is just literally full of incidents where God segregated his people," but he gave no examples. Lay Baptists often expressed the simple view that "God made one race white, one black and meant for them to stay that way."[17]

Baptist segregationists argued, correctly if spuriously, that Christ did not condemn racial segregation and also that the Bible did not advocate racial integration. "I know of nothing in the Bible", wrote Baptist deacon and Federal District Judge George Bell Timmerman Sr. of South Carolina, "that records Christ as having condemned segregation, although segregation was practiced while He was on earth, even in the synagogues." Segregationists argued that "Jesus was not a member of any group for the advancement of social, economic, or racial groups while he was on this earth" and that He "did not say go and preach integration, but the gospel of salvation." Writing to A. C. Miller, layman J. D. Butler employed a favorite segregationist device. "Would you please show to me," asked Butler, "any place in the Bible where racial segregation is condemned?"[18]

Those segregationists who were fundamentalist in theology, often coupled the biblical defense of segregation with attacks on integration as a manifestation of the Social Gospel and Modernism. In their view, God's plan required only that Baptists evangelize the world by urging mankind to accept God's forgiveness for their sins through the medium of the conversion experience. Although the Social Gospel called on the church to minister to the whole person by tending to both his spiritual and physical needs, fundamentalists believed that it substituted social action for evangelism and thereby prevented people from being saved. Leon Macon claimed that "There is no Scripture whatsoever instructing us to join [social] reformers but we have plenty of instructions to seek to win the world, through the individual, for eternity."[19]

Fundamentalists insisted that only God could save sinful man and only saved men could improve society. Macon stated that "God knows the only permanent way to solve inequities in society is by permeating society with regenerated individuals." Segregationists warned that man should not succumb to the fallacy of the Social Gospel by expecting continual social progress and interpreting that progress as steps towards the eventual return of Christ. The Reverend Hugh Cantrell of First Baptist Church, Stephens, declared, in the annual sermon to the Arkansas Baptist State Convention in 1957, that "God has never indicated that this world will go on forever with an endless, upward spiral of living conditions and prosperity." It followed that Baptists should not devote their energies to social reform but to evangelism, and that reform would not advance the coming of the kingdom. The primacy of evangelism similarly informed the attitudes of some fundamentalists towards African Americans and their acceptance of segregation. Samuel S. Hill Jr. explained in the mid-1960s that "The white Christian's duty toward the Negro, as seen by the southern church, is to convert him and befriend him (in a paternal framework), not to consider altering the social traditions and arrangements which govern his (and everyone else's) life to so significant a degree."[20]

Just as many Southern Baptists denounced the Social Gospel and its implications for race relations, so too did they reject Modernism. Modernists discarded the Genesis account of man's origins in favor of the theory of evolution. They also argued that biblical stories reflected the influence of their many human authors and cast doubt on the literal occurrence of miracles. By discrediting the notion of the Fall and removing the supernatural from religion, Modernism, fundamentalists contended, banished God from the world, eliminated the hope of eternal life and, in expunging the concept of sin, encouraged man to run wild. Furthermore, Modernism suggested that the different races of the world had been created not by God, as segregationists believed, but by the process of adaption to environment. Segregationists argued that integrationists wanted to mix the races biologically. Consequently, in segregationist minds, integration represented a form of Modernism since it implied that the races should not be regarded as immutable. Indeed integrationists, segregationists believed, went beyond the theory of evolution by advocating that man, rather than natural selection, work actively to change the (allegedly) distinct characteristics of the races. The Reverend James F. Burks wrote in the *Religious Herald* that "the amalgamation of races is part of the spirit of anti-christ. The Word of God is the surest and only infallible source of our facts of ethnology, and when man sets aside the plain teachings of this blessed book and disregards the boundary lines God Himself has drawn, man assumes a prerogative that belongs to God alone."[21]

Rejecting Modernism, fundamentalists insisted on what they considered to be God's timeless truths revealed in scripture. To them it followed that if segregation was biblical, then those who supported integration were falling prey to the Social Gospel and Modernism. In 1967, Virginia Barker reacted angrily to the mildly integrationist editorials of *Home Missions*. She complained: "I am sick unto death, figuratively speaking, about race relations. . . . Where are you going with the magazine? Sounds like you are getting off on a social gospel. I am afraid the Southern Baptists are getting into modernism." Louisianan O. P. Bazer sought to discredit integration by linking it to the Social Gospel. He wrote to *Home Missions:* "I do not believe that belief in "integration" is the test of a Christian and that it happens to be the unshakable will of God, as the proponents of the social gospel loudly proclaim. God segregated us by making us different." Mr. and Mrs. Scarborough of Alabama were equally forthright in asserting their biblical segregationist beliefs and condemning integration as an example of the Social Gospel. They wrote: "Unless our Boards: Home, Foreign, Sunday School, etc., wake up and realize that we are in the business of saving souls rather than trying to solve social ills, I fear that it will be necessary for those Southern Baptists with firm convictions toward segregation to take drastic action to preserve what we feel is God's will."[22]

Whatever their theological orientation, biblical segregationists often employed secular "evidence" that they claimed demonstrated God's prudence in making racial segregation a part of His plan for the world, and proved that an ungodly inspiration lay behind the drive for integration. As evidence of God's wisdom in segregating the races, Baptists argued, on the one hand, that both African Americans and whites favored segregation, and, on the other, that both black behavior and the practical results of integration in American cities provided ample evidence of God's wisdom in ordaining segregation. In support of the latter point, some Baptist segregationists took a white supremacist stance. These Baptists alleged that blacks were inferior and prone to criminality and immorality and so whites should be protected from them by segregation. Furthermore, integration would mean the destruction of the white race and the superior civilization it had created under God's guidance.

Segregationists frequently charged that integration was either Communist-inspired or in the Communist interest. Integration served Communism, they believed, by undermining American resistance to its supposedly aggressive aims. Conflict over integration, segregationists argued, weakened American unity. White supremacist Baptists insisted that Communists championed integration in order to "weaken" the white race through intermarriage and so make America less able to resist a Communist takeover. The atheistic nature of Communism, segregationists believed, provided additional confirmation that segregation was godly. Segregationists contrasted the repression of the Soviet Union with the freedoms Americans enjoyed. They claimed that since God had "chosen America," He had also "sanctioned its constitutional arrangements." Segregationists argued that desegregation violated the Constitution and therefore God's wishes, because it undermined the freedom of the individual to choose his associates.[23]

Southern Baptists frequently noted and took pride in the fact that southern blacks, like southern whites, were a religious people. As religious folk, Southern Baptist segregationists assumed that blacks, like themselves, recognized the biblical nature of segregation and, as God intended, preferred it. As late as 1963, only 35 percent of southern whites believed that African Americans strongly favored school desegregation. Writing in the *Religious Herald*, John J. Wicker Jr. noted, in support of his claim that blacks preferred segregation, that "the big majority of Negro church members are much happier with their own churches, and certainly would not give them up for a mixture." In 1957, the Louisiana Baptist Convention insisted "that in the main the Negroes of Louisiana prefer to have schools and churches of their own." Baptist segregationists frequently mentioned that African Americans had chosen to withdraw from white churches after the Civil War to form their own, but failed to note that discrimination by white-run churches had precipitated the black exodus. "As for our churches," wrote Leon Macon, "the present segregated conditions were brought about by the expressed desire and wish of our colored brethren." If blacks favored segregation, it followed that civil rights groups, such as the NAACP, that campaigned for integration had to be under the influence of an alien, that is to say unAmerican and ungodly, group or ideology.[24]

In the Cold War era, most Americans felt threatened by the Soviet Union and believed that it headed an international conspiracy to spread Communism throughout the world. Consequently, many Southern Baptists found it easy to believe that the civil rights movement was a tool, consciously or otherwise, of the Communists as southern demagogues claimed. The Arkansas Baptist State Convention adopted a report on State Missions in 1954 that asserted: "The Communists make their approach through the underprivileged group. And they have interfered with the work among the Negroes in some areas." Segregationist pastors and lay people often shared such views. According to W. H. Prescott, a Texas layman: "For years the Negro of the South was perfectly satisfied with his lot. I am fearful it is a communist-agitated move that has stirred up our problem." A South Carolina pastor was more blunt. "Certainly," he claimed, "it is an established fact that the Communist [*sic*] are using the NAACP." Writing in the *Baptist Message,* H. T. Sullivan called the NAACP "an agency of Communism." Sullivan noted that the NAACP and the Communist Party of the United States of America voiced the same demands for racial justice and, on this basis, argued that integration was "one of the steps toward the Communist ideal and the sinister aim of world-socialism."[25]

The Reverend William T. Bodenhamer, a member of the executive committee of the Georgia Baptist Convention, a state representative, and the executive secretary of the segregationist States' Rights Council of Georgia, Inc. made a direct link between black demands for integration, and Communism and the Cold War. In a letter sent to Atlanta ministers who had signed a statement in 1957 calling for peaceful race relations and the preservation of the public school system, Bodenhamer wrote: "The Communists planned over thirty years ago to inflame 'the Negro minority against the whites' and 'to instill in the whites a guilt complex for their exploitation of the Negroes.' How they have succeeded! In addition they have infiltrated our governmental agencies and stolen scientific secrets which have placed them ahead in the world today." Southern Baptists were not significantly out of step with mainstream America in the McCarthy era when they labeled liberals, in their case racial liberals, as Communists or Communist dupes.[26]

Baptists were naturally antagonistic to Communism because of the avowed atheism of that creed. They also denounced Communism because it rejected the idea of a personal God, exalted material improvement over spirituality and insisted that man could create a beneficent society through his own efforts. In essence, Southern Baptists contended that Communism deified man. Segregationist Southern Baptists argued that Communists pursued racial integration in defiance of biblical teachings. The Reverend J. M. Drummond claimed in the *Alabama Baptist* that "integration is nothing but Communism, and it is strictly against God's Holy Word." Communists, segregationists charged, sought to blend the races into one in defiance of God's plan for mankind. A resolution by Jacksonville, Florida's Ridge Boulevard Baptist Church declared that "since God made the races, and appointed the bounds of their habitations . . . attempts to force racial union in social life would lead to the communist hope of producing a 'one world hybridized human,' against the Word and will of God. . . ."[27]

Southern Baptists' hostility to Communism and Socialism, which they regarded as a form of Communism or a step towards its adoption, also reflected their commitment to what they believed to be God-given, individual rights. In protecting the individual, Baptists argued, the American political system followed biblical injunctions. "The recognition of the individual's right to 'life, liberty, and the pursuit of happiness,'" argued layman W. I. Pittman, "stems from the teachings of Christ." Accordingly, Baptists vigorously opposed Communism, which to them epitomized centralized, bureaucratic government control and interference in the affairs of the individual.[28]

For white southerners, the American Constitution's primary function was to protect the freedom of the individual from the encroachments of government. Any such encroachments *ipso facto* marked a step on the road to Socialism and ultimately Communism. Virginian S. J. Thompson claimed that "the ultimate goal of those who are now agitating for segregation [integration?], is complete amalgamation of all races into one, and a completely socialistic state. I personally believe these things are contrary to the best interest of the American people, and contrary to the principles upon which this country was founded." To Southern Baptists, any person or group, such as Martin Luther King Jr. or the NAACP, which advocated an expanded role for government (civil rights laws) or a diminution of the rights of the individual ("forced integration") had to be Communist or at least Socialist.[29]

White southerners regarded the civil rights movement, the *Brown* ruling and civil rights legislation as attempts to undermine the freedom of the individual to choose his own associates and to run his life or business without interference from the federal government or civil rights protestors.

John G. Swafford, a Tennessee layman, complained in 1964 that "The passage and enforcement of the civil rights bill would mean the end of the freedom of private business and the end of the rights of the individual in the American way of life." In the minds of many Southern Baptists, segregation laws, rather than depriving the individual of his rights to free association, actually protected them. In 1956, W. A. Criswell, pastor of Dallas, Texas's First Baptist Church, the largest Baptist church in the world, and one of the most widely-read Southern Baptist preachers of the twentieth century, addressed a joint session of the South Carolina state legislature. Criswell pleaded: "Don't force me by law, by statute, by Supreme Court decision, . . . to cross over in those intimate things where I don't want to go. Let me build my life. Let me have my church. Let me have my school. Let me have my friends. Let me have my home. Let me have my family."[30]

Southern Baptist segregationists often claimed that the NAACP sought to remove segregation laws merely as a first step towards its real aim of fostering the intermarriage of blacks and whites. In making the argument, some Southern Baptists took an overtly white supremacist position. Supremacists sometimes argued that Communists, who were supposedly influencing the NAACP, favored intermarriage as a means to destroy the (allegedly) superior white race so that America and the world might more easily fall victim to the international Communist movement. According to Alabamian G. C. Moore Jr.: "[T]he Communists . . . have divided this nation's peoples —white against black—purposely to reduce the viability of the white race and make preparations for a Communist takeover."[31]

Most supremacists simply argued that blacks were physically and mentally inferior. Therefore, racial intermarriage would produce inferior offspring. Assuming black inferiority, T. C. Hardman wrote to the *Christian Index:* "To enforce social equality, as would result from mixed schools, would mean miscegenation and this brings about amalgamation, degeneration and approach to the level of the lower of the race." Supremacists frequently offered fallacious historical examples designed to prove that societies which mixed the races inevitably declined. In 1956, an Alabama layman cited the following fallacies in his defense of segregation: "The historical factors of civilization development (the negro being the only race to never develop a written language, a sail boat, or a form of government) the weakness of countries like Spain, France and Italy who have already destroyed their race by miscegenation as compared to countries like England, Germany and the Netherlands, the fall of the Roman Empire. . . ."[32]

Supremacists claimed that white civilization was superior to any other and that this superiority was proof that God had chosen the white race to carry out His purpose. The Reverend Montague Cook contended in a sermon to his congregation at Moultrie, Georgia's Trinity Baptist Church that "Our present day western civilization is the concrete evidence of God's purpose for the white European. This is the case for racial segregation. It has been necessary to produce people through whom God could work out his purposes in the world, through whom he could bless all the rest of mankind. As at one time the Jew was God's man, in other times the white European was God's man. To meet the requirements of being God's chosen for a purpose, racial purity is essential."[33]

Aside from alleging that African Americans were intellectually and culturally inferior, supremacists claimed that blacks were also prone to criminality and immorality. Hence, segregation was necessary to protect whites. In 1963, Leon Macon argued that as a result of African-American migration to Washington, D.C.: "It is now declared that it is unsafe to be out in the streets of Washington at night, churches are barring their windows and entrances, women are carrying protective weapons, and crimes are flourishing in our Capital." Integration, supremacists claimed, increased the supposed criminal tendencies of black people. In August 1961, Alabama banker W. D. Malone wrote to Duke McCall, president of The Southern Baptist Theological Seminary: "I am thankful to note that participation in the integration movement is gradually being recognized as unchristian. The racial crime rate has increased enormously since this agitation started." Some supremacists implied that God had sanctioned segregation to insulate whites from the vices that they associated with African Americans. The Reverend Billy G. Pierce wrote to the *Arkansas Baptist Newsmagazine* in August 1963: "Since the church was organized by Christ it has always stood for segregation. A drop of poison in a glass of water makes the entire glass of water bad. It is a known fact that the Negro illegitimate birth rate, venereal disease, robbery, and unlawful acts are far out of porportion [*sic*] to that of the White race."[34]

In the second half of the 1960s, some Southern Baptists seized on black riots and looting in American inner cities to support their argument that integration bred crime and dissension. Riots, supremacists implied, demonstrated God's wisdom in segregating the races. A Mississippi layman wrote in 1966, one year after the Watts riot in Los Angeles: "It was God who created the white man white and the black man black. He put them on separate continents. Why—I do not know except that He wanted us this way. Now man has made some changes. Let's look at some of them. Let's think of integrated Washington, D.C., and Los Angeles, California. They have about the highest crime rates in the country and race riots are beginning in each place. Now consider segregated Mississippi. Here we have the lowest crime rate in the United States until agitators come in (FBI). We have no racial hatreds here."[35]

Despite the continued salience of the biblical defense of segregation, by the mid-1960s the white Baptist South appeared less firmly committed to it. Biblical segregationist letters and church resolutions to the denominational press and to the SBC and its agencies from Southern Baptists living in the peripheral South gradually declined after 1964. Opinion polls found that opposition to token school desegregation among southern white parents declined from 61 percent in 1963 to 16 percent in 1970. However, public avowals of biblical segregation from Southern Baptists living in the Deep South continued into the early 1970s.[36]

Token school desegregation came earlier to the peripheral South. As the 1960s wore on, it seemed increasingly futile to Southern Baptists in that region, faced with a *fait accompli,* to voice the biblical segregationist argument. Furthermore, because the peripheral South had proportionately fewer African Americans than the Deep South, the impact of desegregation was less intrusive. Evasion, tokenism and white flight to the suburbs and to private, often Southern Baptist, whites-only schools also limited racial integration. Conceivably, some Southern Baptists retained their belief in biblical segregation but, with integration restricted in its practical application, the anxiety that had motivated them to proclaim their views publicly had receded.[37]

Southern Baptists living in the Deep South had always had the greatest trepidation about integration, because the population in their states had the highest proportion of blacks to whites in the South. Furthermore, the brunt of black activism occurred in Alabama, Georgia and Mississippi and so whites in these states felt the greatest urgency in reiterating a biblical case for segregation. White schools in the region began to desegregate fully under court order in 1970. As anxiety about *Brown* and the civil rights movement had earlier motivated Baptists to express publicly their biblical segregationist views, so anxiety over school desegregation continued to provoke the same response in the late 1960s and early 1970s. However, after 1972, biblical segregationist protests diminished sharply in the Deep South. The reasons for the decline mirrored those which had earlier accounted for the demise of public affirmations of the biblical defense in the peripheral South. In the Deep South, as elsewhere in the region, tokenism, evasion, and white flight muted the impact of school desegregation. In addition, some whites sent their children to hastily opened private secular and Southern Baptist schools.[38]

To some extent biblical segregationists across the entire South retreated into racially exclusive churches, educational, and social institutions as *de jure* segregation came to an end. They and the region's predominantly white officialdom found ways to circumvent integration. Many Southern Baptists, also, found that school desegregation and the outlawing of segregation in public facilities did not bring the explosion of racial intermarriage that they had feared. Thus, public segregation laws no longer seemed necessary to protect "racial integrity."

However, many former biblical segregationists gradually abandoned their views, after a great deal of contemplation and searching of the scriptures. Collectively, the civil rights movement, federal intervention on behalf of desegregation, and the educational efforts of influential Southern Baptists who rejected the biblical segregationist defense led biblical segregationists to reexamine and reconsider their beliefs. The African-American freedom movement destroyed the myth that blacks were content with segregation, inferior in their abilities and unable to organize their own lives. It also convinced some segregationists of the inequality of the southern system of racial segregation. Federal government legislation and judicial rulings also rested on the premise that segregation was unjust. Under the impact of these developments, segregationists attempted to reconcile what they perceived as biblical segregationist teachings with secular evidence that segregation undermined black personhood and worth. The long-term, educational efforts of progressive Baptists helped to convince segregationists that the Bible did not support segregation and, in part, facilitated their adjustment to the demise of *de jure* segregation in the South.

Influenced by the progressives, the SBC endorsed the *Brown* decision and the Civil Rights Act of 1964, and in 1968 it urged Baptists to work to achieve desegregation and equal opportunities in both the churches and the secular world. Testimonies from former biblical segregationists demonstrate that progressives influenced individual Baptists, as well as Baptist institutions. Twelve years after making his Jim Crow address to the South Carolina legislature, W. A. Criswell declared that biblical segregationists "do not read the Bible right." Explicitly disavowing his past, Criswell declared that "I don't think that segregation could have been or was at any time intelligently, seriously supported by the Bible." Owen Cooper also recanted his earlier biblical segregationist views. Cooper, then president of the SBC, explained in 1974: "The reasoning I had undertaken to build or to maintain my position began to melt away in the light of an open-minded search of the scripture and the growing Christian conviction that all men are equal in the sight of God, that we are all children of God, and if children, then brothers in Christ. [Actions of the Southern Baptist Convention] which was ahead of me at this time, also gave me cause to think."[39]

By the mid-1970s, expression of segregationist views had ceased to be publicly acceptable, even amongst most Southern Baptists in the Deep South. In 1974, defiant segregationist Morris H. Gardner wrote to the *Alabama Baptist:* "I firmly believe in each race having its own schools, social organizations, and churches. Of course, what I am suggesting will be considered ridiculous and absurd by today's liberal and brainwashed public and I will be labeled a dirty old racist and bigot. Regardless of how I may be ridiculed for my viewpoints, I am going to state my convictions, come what may." Once commonplace among southern whites, biblical segregationist views had became the preserve of a tiny minority.[40]

Most Southern Baptists opposed the desegregation demands of the civil rights movement. Many did so in the belief that they were upholding the will of God expressed in the scriptures. Zealous in their adherence to biblical teachings, such Baptists found numerous verses in the Bible that, they were convinced, proved that God had commanded the separation of the races as part of His plan for mankind. Religious belief informed the intense opposition of many Baptists to desegregation, just as it inspired many supporters of integration. Although their religion helped bring white Baptists around, finally, to an understanding of the need for civil rights, for many years it was also religion that informed their support of segregation. Progressive Baptists played an important part in facilitating the transformation of their views.

5

Progressive Southern Baptists and Civil Rights

ALTHOUGH SOME HISTORIANS note that a progressive minority of Southern Baptists sought to persuade their coreligionists to accept desegregation, they have not appreciated the magnitude or impact of their efforts. "Protestant churches," writes historian Numan V. Bartley, "had little or no positive influence on the racial attitudes of even their most devoted laymen." In fact, a small number of Southern Baptist leaders, labeled the "progressive elite" by Andrew Manis, exerted a real and partially effective influence on Baptists to confront and discard their support for racial discrimination in the civil rights era. Progressives rejected the dominant racial mores of the southern white community, and, by the 1950s, they challenged the biblical defense of segregation. With rare exceptions they did not participate in the civil rights movement, and they usually trailed behind the federal courts, the federal government and, of course, the movement in their advocacy of racial justice. Nevertheless, progressives played a significant, but secondary role in undermining Southern Baptist support for overt discrimination and segregation.[1]

The progressive elite comprised some faculty members of Southern Baptist seminaries, the Social Service and Christian Life commissions of the SBC and some of its member state conventions and a few denominational leaders at the regional and state levels. Segregationists, who comprised the majority of Southern Baptists in the postwar decades, could not dismiss Baptist progressives as meddling outside agitators who knew nothing about the South and its race relations, since progressives, like themselves, were products of the South and its largest denomination. Most Baptists respected progressive leaders, even when they disagreed with them about race, because they were the best educated Southern Baptists, the "experts" on biblical interpretation and understanding. By condemning racial discrimination and denying that the Bible endorsed segregation, the progressive elite created a crisis in the plausibility structure of the segregationist Southern

Baptist majority. Progressives successfully challenged the mystic, sacred and seemingly immutable character of segregation, and in this way helped Southern Baptists eventually to adjust to the desegregation demands of the civil rights movement and to the civil rights acts of the 1960s.

Southern Baptist congregational polity deprived members of the progressive elite of the power to impose their views and standards on their churches and coreligionists. Nevertheless, the influence of the progressive elite extended well beyond their numbers as they used convention meetings, Social Service and Christian Life commission reports, resolutions, conferences, seminars, pamphlets, seminary classes, and Baptist newspapers and newsletters to disseminate their views. Progressives concentrated their efforts on Baptist leaders, whether they were denominational leaders, convention messengers, editors of Baptist publications, seminary students or local pastors. They affected the opinion makers in Baptist life and through them the larger Baptist constituency.

Progressives came from all regions of the South, including the Deep South. William P. Davis, who headed the Mississippi Baptist Convention's Department of Negro Work, was a native Mississippian. Nevertheless, progressives were far more numerous and outspoken in the peripheral than in the Deep South. Texas provided some outstanding progressive leaders, including A. C. Miller, Foy Valentine, Jimmy Allen and James Dunn, who successively led the state convention's Christian Life Commission. Both Miller and Valentine later directed the SBC's Christian Life Commission. Some progressives, such as Blake Smith, pastor of Austin, Texas's University Baptist Church, were liberal in theology, but many, including Valentine and T. B. Maston, professor of Christian Ethics at Southwestern Baptist Theological Seminary in Fort Worth, Texas, between 1922 and 1963, remained committed to a conservative theology. Conservatives placed supreme emphasis on the saving of souls, but they also believed that saved people had a duty to apply Christian teachings in their approach to social issues.[2]

Whatever their theological disposition, progressive Baptists derived principles from the Bible, particularly the New Testament, that fostered their belief in the equal treatment of all, regardless of race, and their rejection of segregation. They argued that since God had created all men in His own image (*Genesis* 1:27) and Jesus had died for all men no matter their race (*Hebrews* 2:9), then every man should be treated with equal respect and without racial prejudice. Progressives cited the first half of *Acts* 17:26 "[God] hath made of one blood all nations of men for to dwell on all the face of the earth . . . ," and Peter's perception, after he had at first refused to associate with Gentiles, "that God is no respecter of persons" (*Acts* 10:34) as incompatible with the maintenance of Jim Crow. Christians had to reject segregation and racial prejudice since "There is neither Jew nor Greek, there is neither bond nor free, there is neither male nor female: for ye are all one in Christ Jesus." (*Galatians* 3:28).[3] Progressives contended that "Jesus never practiced racial discrimination," and that he had crossed the racial divides of his time by healing and helping "people of all races." Consequently, Christians could not support racial segregation. T. B. Maston summarized the progressive view in *Segregation and Desegregation,* published in 1959. He explained: "The Christian ideal would demand the elimination of all segregation, by law or custom, based on class or color. This is true because segregation, which inevitably means discrimination, is contrary to the spirit and teachings of Christ."[4]

Besides the scriptures, progressives attributed their views to the influence of parents and their childhood environments, revulsion at racial violence perpetrated by whites, exposure to African Americans who rejected the subservient role southern whites expected of them, and the effects of seminary or college education in ethics and race relations. Clarence Jordan also influenced some progressives in the 1940s, and Billy Graham affected a larger number of Southern Baptists in the 1950s and 1960s.

The circumstances of their upbringing were often crucial in creating progressives. Some of them spent all or part of their childhoods in areas where few African Americans lived and overt racism was less marked. Born in 1916, Carlyle Marney, an influential religious writer and pastor in both Austin, Texas and Charlotte, North Carolina, grew up in the east Tennessee town of Harriman, which had stayed loyal to the Union during the Civil War and had a tradition of independent thinking. Maston, born in 1897, also came from East Tennessee, which had a small black population, and spent much of his childhood in Ohio. W. R. Grigg, secretary of the Department of Interracial Cooperation of the Baptist State Convention of North Carolina between 1957 and 1966, originated from Illinois where he was born in 1910. He moved to North Carolina at age eighteen with his widowed North Carolinian mother. Many Texas progressives, such as A. C. Miller who was born near San Angelo in 1891 and grew up in Colorado City, came from the less racially repressive central and western parts of the state.[5]

A large number of progressives, including Grigg, Marney, Maston and William P. Davis, recalled the crucial influence of unprejudiced parents upon them. Foy Valentine, born near Edgewood, Texas, in 1923, recollected: "It was my father who taught me by example and precept that everybody is somebody, that blacks must be related to as full fellow human beings, and that neighbors who succumbed to . . . be involved with the Ku Klux Klan . . . were doing . . . an un-American and un-Christian thing." As a boy in North Carolina, Victor Glass, who headed the HMB's Department of Work with National Baptists between 1965 and 1974, observed his plumber father threaten his inspector after the man had shoved a black youth out of the way.[6]

Some progressives emerged from militant segregationist areas, where they were outraged by random violence against African Americans. W. W. Finlator, who played a prominent role on the Baptist State Convention of North Carolina's Committee on Social Service and Civic Righteousness and served as chairman of the North Carolina Advisory Committee to the U.S. Commission on Civil Rights between 1971 and 1980, grew up in eastern North Carolina, where he had been born in 1913. Personal observation of racial discrimination made him into a progressive. During his wartime pastorate at Weldon Baptist Church, Finlator witnessed police brutality against an African American, who had done no more than been adjudged to have been too near whites at the entrance to a movie theater. Outraged by the incident, he vowed to challenge racial discrimination. Revulsion at Nazi Germany's racial policies, the publication of Gunnar Myrdal's 1944 critique of American racism, *An American Dilemma,* and the report of President Harry S. Truman's Committee on Civil Rights, *To Secure These Rights,* in 1947 also heavily influenced Finlator.[7]

William P. Davis, born in 1903, remembered his shock as a young pastor, when he encountered a white friend in Mississippi who had shot and killed a fleeing black man for answering him back. Davis saw the body lying in a stream. An inquest returned a verdict of justifiable homicide. Davis recalled: "As I looked at that man [the deceased], and later when I went to visit his wife and children and talked to them, heard their screaming, I resolved then I was going to try and do something to help the race situation in Mississippi."[8]

Personal experience of a different kind reinforced W. R. Grigg's progressive approach to race relations. Grigg made friends with African Americans, while working alongside them on a North Carolina farm during his youth, and he learned to respect their individuality. Victor Glass shared food and conversation with blacks when he worked with them on a construction site in Virginia as a young man. He recalled that "This was really my first contact with black people. It was here I met black people who did things other than just yard work or servant work. . . . "[9]

Several prominent progressives who regarded African Americans as worthy of respect and equality did so influenced in part by Clarence Jordan. Born to a comfortable Georgia family in rural, impoverished Talbotton in 1912, Jordan, as a child, readily saw a discrepancy between biblical teachings about brotherhood and the racial and economic inequalities that the members of his Baptist church did nothing to change. Determined to alleviate the poverty that afflicted both black and white, he decided to become a scientific farmer and earned a degree in the subject from the University of Georgia. To undergird his vision of relieving rural poverty with religious understanding, Jordan enrolled in graduate studies at The Southern Baptist Theological Seminary. While still a doctoral student, Jordan directed the missions work with African Americans of the Long Run Association at Louisville, Kentucky. Appointed full-time director of missions after his graduation, Jordan recruited Victor Glass, a student at the seminary, to lead the Fellowship Center. His work brought Glass into regular contact with blacks, and he joined an African-American Baptist church.[10]

With Martin England, an alumnus of The Southern Baptist Theological Seminary, Jordan cofounded Koinonia Farm in southwest Georgia during 1942 as an experiment in Christian brotherhood and interracial living. His work attracted the interest of Baptist college and seminary students. After graduating from Baylor University, Foy Valentine spent the summer of 1944 working at Koinonia. Jordan condemned segregation in addresses to state BSU conventions and Baptist colleges. His words influenced Jimmy Allen who had been reared in a segregationist family and frequently engaged in fistfights with African Americans in Dallas, Texas, during the 1940s. Allen heard Jordan speak at a Young Men's Conference in Ridgecrest, North Carolina, in 1944 and the experience left him unable to reconcile his racism with Christianity. Jordan supported a vote by Baptist students on retreat at Ridgecrest in 1946 to overturn a ban on African-American students. However, the Sunday School Board, which operated Ridgecrest, refused to desegregate the assembly grounds. Jordan's support for the students led to his effective exclusion from most official Southern Baptist gatherings until the 1960s. Despite a local economic boycott and violent attacks upon it in the second half of the 1950s, Koinonia Farm survived.[11]

Although he supported acquisitive capitalism that Jordan rejected, Billy Graham, born in Charlotte, North Carolina, in 1918, also exerted a progressive influence on Southern Baptists in race relations. A member of Dallas, Texas's First Baptist Church pastored by W. A. Criswell, Graham was nevertheless ecumenical in his approach. He held no official position within the SBC and did not work with its progressive members. Graham influenced Baptists by example. Beginning in 1953, the popular evangelist held his southern crusades on a desegregated basis, and he publicly stated that the Bible did not sanction segregation. Graham addressed the SBC in 1956 and praised its 1954 resolution in support of *Brown*. He told the messengers that they would have to face the situation "realistically" and urged the convention not to "lag behind." Two years later, Graham moved the location of an integrated crusade from the statehouse grounds in Columbia, South

Carolina, to the federal military base at nearby Fort Jackson, after Governor George Bell Timmerman Jr. denied permission for it to be held on state property. According to W. T. Moore, a HMB worker, Graham's preaching and example "had a deep influence on Southern Baptists."[12]

Graham, like Jordan, mainly operated outside of Southern Baptist institutions. Within the convention, seminary professors, specializing in Christian ethics and sociology, exercised the most progressive influence on Baptists. Professors joined pastors and laymen in serving on the Social Service and Christian Life commissions of the SBC and Baptist state conventions. They also frequently wrote articles on race relations for the commissions, other Southern Baptist agencies, and denominational newspapers.[13]

J. B. Weatherspoon, born in Nelson, North Carolina, in 1886 and T. B. Maston were outstanding among progressive seminary professors. Weatherspoon taught sociology and preaching at The Southern Baptist Theological Seminary between 1929 and 1958. He served as chairman of the Social Service Commission of the SBC (renamed the Christian Life Commission in 1953) between 1943 and 1955. Weatherspoon wrote many of the commission's reports and recommendations, and also some of its pamphlet literature. T. B. Maston was active in both the Christian Life commissions of the Baptist General Convention of Texas and the SBC. Maston also joined the NAACP, the National Urban League and the Southern Regional Council. He published a host of articles, pamphlets and books on race relations, used by the Christian Life commissions of the SBC and his home convention, the WMU, the HMB, and state convention newspapers. Besides Weatherspoon and Maston, other professors, such as Olin T. Binkley and Edward A. McDowell both at The Southern Baptist Theological Seminary and C. W. Scudder at Southwestern Baptist Theological Seminary, also exercised a progressive influence.[14]

Seminary professors inculcated greater awareness and sensitivity about civil rights among many of the thousands of students they taught. Mississippian Clayton Sullivan accepted segregation without question during his youth, but his racial views changed during his studies at The Southern Baptist Theological Seminary in the 1950s. Sullivan remembered that "All of my professors at the Louisville seminary were vocal in criticizing the South's traditional racial views. Louisville seminary was the place where I first heard Jim Crow openly challenged. I became an admirer of Dr. Martin Luther King and a believer in integration." Students at both The Southern Baptist Theological Seminary and Southwestern Baptist Theological Seminary not only took classes in race relations, they often worked in African-American churches and institutions. Encouraged by professors and students, the trustees of Southwestern, Southern and New Orleans seminaries agreed to drop racial barriers to admission in 1951 and 1952.[15]

Students often took their progressive influence with them as they became editors of Baptist newspapers, pastors and denominational leaders and officials. Weatherspoon taught Clarence Jordan. Hugh A. Brimm, another Weatherspoon student, served as executive secretary of the SBC's Social Service Commission between 1947 and 1952. A. C. Miller, Brimm's successor, was influenced by Dr. Charles Gardner, who introduced him to the Social Gospel in his Christian sociology classes at The Southern Baptist Theological Seminary, from which Miller graduated in 1921. Foy Valentine became a Maston student at the Southwestern Baptist Theological Seminary after his summer at Koinonia. Jimmy Allen and James Dunn also studied ethics under Maston.[16]

In the postwar era, Southern Baptist progressives passed through three stages. During their first stage between 1945 and 1953, most progressives advocated making the "separate but equal" policy of segregation truly equal for both races. A minority questioned and even condemned segregation but most did not do so until the *Brown* decision in 1954 forced the issue. In their second stage between 1954 and 1959, the majority of progressives articulated and promoted a non-segregationist viewpoint as southern white resistance to school desegregation mounted. They refuted the biblical defense of segregation in an attempt to ease the path for desegregation. In their third stage, beginning in 1960, progressives advocated integration of the races in the churches and in society.

During their first stage, progressives appealed for African Americans to be accorded courtesy and respect, and given equal facilities and justice. Wartime conditions prevented the SBC from holding its annual meeting in 1945. Nevertheless, Weatherspoon wrote a Social Service Commission report for the convention in which he appealed for adjustments in race relations within segregation. Specifically he urged equal opportunities in education, employment, government and the armed forces. Weatherspoon insisted that the constitutional rights of blacks be respected and called for equal justice in the courts. He also called for the inclusion of African-American residences in housing improvement programs.[17]

A minority of progressive Baptists publicly criticized segregation. Frustrated by the convention's conservatism, a group of North Carolina–based pastors and lay people began publishing an independent monthly journal, *Christian Frontiers,* in January 1946 as an outlet for progressive ideas. Edited initially by Das Kelly Barnett, pastor of the Baptist Church of Chapel Hill, and later by W. W. Finlator, the journal never achieved a circulation greater than one thousand copies. During its brief existence, *Christian Frontiers* condemned racism, the Ku Klux Klan, and biblical "proof texts" employed by segregationists. It also called for the abolition of the poll tax and the passage of a federal anti-lynching law. Dependent on donations and subscriptions, *Christian Frontiers* ceased publication in January 1949 under financial pressure.[18]

The journal's editors Das Kelley Barnett and W. W. Finlator played an active role in the Baptist State Convention of North Carolina's Committee on Social Service and Civic Righteousness. Barnett helped write the committee's report to the convention in November 1946. It advocated the immediate passage of a federal anti-lynching law, together with state and national legislation to ensure equal employment opportunities, equal treatment in the workplace, and equal pay for equal work. The report condemned the Ku Klux Klan and accused churches that excluded African Americans of denying biblical teachings. Adopted unanimously, it made the state convention the first "official Baptist body in the South" to condemn segregation.[19]

Although it was not binding on the churches, the press, according to committee chairman Louis S. Gaines, misled the public and then convention messengers "into the idea . . . that our Baptist churches had been ordered to throw open their doors to a polyglot membership henceforth." As a result, and despite the fact that some committee members and two-thirds of the 1,360 convention messengers had returned home, malcontents prevailed. The depleted convention reviewed the report and deleted the section calling church segregation unchristian by a vote of 253 to 158. It also withdrew support for equal employment legislation. Influenced by the lynching of African-American veterans in eastern North Carolina and other parts of the South after World War II, the convention remained on record in support of an immediate federal anti-lynching law.[20]

Race violence and African-American demands for equality made Southern Baptists anxious about the future of their region's race relations. Accordingly, the SBC agreed to Weatherspoon's recommendation in 1946 that it create a special committee to study "the whole race situation." A year later, the convention adopted the report and recommendations of the Committee on Race Relations, chaired by Weatherspoon. The report outlined a Charter of Principles in Race Relations that the *Christian Century,* a nondenominational weekly, believed "would be a credit to any denomination." The charter urged Baptists to "protest against injustice and indignities against Negroes" and called on them to endorse the constitutional rights of blacks to vote, serve on juries, receive justice in the courts and secure a "just share" of educational funds.[21]

The committee's recommendations committed Baptist boards, agencies, newspapers and state Social Service committees to promote Christian solutions to racial problems in their reports and literature. It assigned the SBC's Social Service Commission with responsibility to oversee and encourage the educative program. The SBC agreed, at Weatherspoon's prompting, to provide the commission with a $10,000 budget and an executive secretary. Fearful of arousing opposition, the Social Service Commission did not support civil rights legislation in its reports. In 1948, it commended the "major objectives" of the report of President Truman's Committee on Civil Rights as "in keeping with the American way of life as guaranteed by the Bill of Rights" but sidestepped its specific and wide-ranging legislative recommendations for overturning segregation and discrimination.[22]

Its budget was inadequate for the tasks assigned the Social Service Commission and some key Southern Baptist agencies, such as the Sunday School Board, did not respond to the entreaties of the convention on race relations. Nevertheless, under its newly appointed executive secretary, Hugh A. Brimm, the commission developed a vigorous program in race relations. It regularly issued press releases and statements that condemned the resurgent Ku Klux Klan, called for equal rights and publicized the recommendations of the conferences on race it sponsored. The commission's monthly newsletter, *Light*, took a much bolder stand than its annual reports to the SBC. Articles in *Light* refuted the "proof texts" used by biblical segregationists and criticized Jim Crow. Reaching a maximum circulation of 13,000, *Light* addressed the converted. However, occasionally, the commission distributed it to all of the SBC's pastors. In 1949, the commission held an interracial workshop for sixty lay people, professors of Baptist colleges, and ministers at Ridgecrest, North Carolina, on "Next Steps in Race Relations." The meeting called on Baptists to join the National Urban League, the NAACP and the Southern Regional Council.[23]

Sympathetic editors of Baptist state convention newspapers, such as L. L. Carpenter of North Carolina's *Biblical Recorder*, used the commission's statements in editorials and ran its articles. Even hostile editors published its material. The reports of the Social Service and race relations committees of the Baptist state conventions frequently reflected the influence of the SBC commission, and they sometimes copied sections from its reports. Members of the SBC's Social Service Commission also addressed the state conventions' annual meetings. Prompted by their Social Service and race relations committees, the North Carolina, South Carolina, Tennessee, Florida and Virginia conventions adopted the Charter of Principles in Race Relations. Progressives exerted some influence even in the Deep South. The Alabama Baptist State Convention urged Baptists to study the SBC's charter, and in the 1940s the South Carolina, Georgia and Alabama conventions called on them to support equal opportunities and facilities for African Americans within segregation. State convention newspapers frequently carried the reports of the SBC and state Social Service committees, ensuring that they received a wider audience.[24]

In the years immediately preceding the *Brown* decision, Southern Baptist progressives became increasingly critical of Jim Crow but only a few called for its abandonment. In 1949, J. B. Weatherspoon wrote in a Social Service Commission pamphlet: "Jim Crow laws cannot solve the race problem. In a particular place segregation may be the demand of stubborn social circumstances—proclaiming conflict, but it does not create a racial harmony that reaches to any depth; it is the symptom of an ill and not a remedy for it." Progressives in the Virginia and Texas conventions also questioned segregation. In 1950, the report of the Ministry With Minorities in Texas claimed: "It is neither voluntary nor social segregation to which minority peoples object. It is legal segregation they oppose. They oppose it because it assumes the superiority of one race and the inferiority of another. Such an assumption is an affront to every person of another race who cares enough for his personal worth and dignity to challenge it." The Baptist General Association of Virginia's Inter-Racial Committee argued in 1952 that "It would be most difficult to justify" segregation "either by Scripture or by the Christian conscience."[25]

Many progressives evolved into critics of segregation because the African-American struggle against Jim Crow forced them to examine biblical teachings about human relations. G. Avery Lee, pastor of Ruston, Louisiana's First Baptist Church and a member of the SBC's Christian Life Commission, explained: "My thinking has been the gradual process of growing up which has led me to believe that all forms of prejudice because of race, and all restrictions because of race . . . are morally wrong because they are denials of the sacredness of human personality and thus do not represent the real expression of the Christian faith." Yet, it was only after the *Brown* decision that most progressive Southern Baptists publicly rejected segregation. They did not want to oppose the law and, before the Supreme Court's ruling, opposition to public school segregation meant opposition to state law in the South. Progressives were also reluctant to attack segregation, because it was an established racial custom that the majority of Southern Baptists supported. Such attacks would have been divisive and might have resulted in segregationists withdrawing financial support from denominational programs.[26]

In their second stage between 1954 and 1959, most progressive Southern

Baptists adopted a non-segregationist, rather than an integrationist, view-point. Proponents of non-segregation did not set forth integration as a positive goal. They simply held that legal segregation was wrong and should be abandoned because it was discriminatory, unchristian and indefensible on biblical grounds. Progressives also contended that segregation and resistance to court-ordered desegregation hindered Southern Baptist missions abroad.

A. C. Miller, who had succeeded Hugh A. Brimm as head of the SBC's Christian Life Commission, sought to prepare Southern Baptists for the inevitability of desegregation. In a press release issued four months before the *Brown* ruling, Miller told Baptists that the Supreme Court had out-lawed racial discrimination in almost every case it had accepted during the previous forty years, and he intimated that they should expect it to rule against school segregation. When the Supreme Court handed down its anti-segregation ruling in May 1954, SBC leaders and agency heads called for its acceptance. Most Baptist editors across the South, including some in the Deep South, urged Baptists to accept *Brown* calmly. In addition, many editors either reprinted or quoted from Miller's article. "American Christianity," wrote the *Christian Century,* "has reason to be grateful that it has in the Southern Baptist Convention[,] leadership which speaks responsibly and courageously at this critical time and on this important matter."[27]

The Christian Life Commission presented the SBC with a recommendation in June 1954 that urged acceptance of *Brown.* It read in part: "We recognize the fact that this Supreme Court decision is in harmony with the constitutional guarantee of equal freedom to all citizens, and with the Christian principles of equal justice and love for all men." The commission's report made clear the progressives' commitment to non-segregation, rather than integration. It claimed that "It will be easier for us to understand the issues involved in this whole question of segregation when we look at it in terms of voluntary separation instead of legal segregation. It is not that the Negro objects to being separated from white people. The facts are, it is not interracial commingling which he desires so much as it is the freedom from the legal system of segregation which denies him that free-dom." Despite its mild tone, the convention adopted the Christian Life Commission's recommendation only after a dramatic intervention by J. B. Weatherspoon, which testified to his influence. After two biblical segregationists, with strong vocal support from the majority of the messengers, had proposed that the recommendation be rejected, Weatherspoon gave a stirring speech in its support and called on Baptists to do "the Christian thing." The convention gave him "long and loud applause" and adopted the resolution overwhelmingly. The *Christian Century* argued that by its action the SBC "did more than any other group in the country could to secure cooperation with the court's verdict."[28]

Most Baptist editors received the SBC's recommendation with equanimity. L. L. Carpenter praised it warmly, while moderate editors used it to reinforce their pleas for calm acceptance of *Brown*. The SBC's action also encouraged some pastors to speak out. Endorsing the recommendation in the *Baptist Record* as "the painfully right action," Chester Molpus, pastor of Mississippi's Belzoni Baptist Church, quoted Weatherspoon's speech to the SBC. Prompted by progressives, the North Carolina and Virginia conventions endorsed the *Brown* ruling. The Alabama Baptist State Convention adopted a Social Service Committee report that quoted the SBC's recommendation in full, while the Baptist State Convention of South Carolina adopted a Social Service Commission recommendation that called on Baptists to "strengthen our public schools." The Georgia Baptist Convention unanimously adopted a Social Service Commission report urging "all Christians in positive thinking and planning so that all people, of all races, would have equal rights as God would have it." In Texas, the Christian Life Commission recommended that Baptists ignore "demagogues or radicals," and its report implied that segregation was unchristian. The commission also produced *The Bible Speaks on Race*, which refuted the arguments of biblical segregationists. "Hundreds" of pastors, James Dunn remembered, used the pamphlet as "sermon outlines." The convention's newspaper, the *Baptist Standard*, published a series of articles by W. R. Grigg that attacked segregation and racial prejudice.[29]

Southern whites became more defiant in their opposition to school desegregation after May 1955, when the Supreme Court ordered its completion with "all deliberate speed." In 1956, over one hundred southern congressmen signed the Southern Manifesto by which they swore to oppose *Brown* by all legal means. President Dwight D. Eisenhower sent troops to overcome Governor Orval Faubus's defiance of a federal court order to desegregate Little Rock's Central High School in September 1957.[30]

The new mood of defiance put Southern Baptist progressives on the defensive. The SBC's Christian Life Commission offered no race relations recommendations in the second half of the 1950s. However, its reports continued to call for peaceful adjustment to change and obedience to the law, and to remind Baptists that any other course hampered their worldwide program of evangelism. Segregationist opposition forced the commission to present its reports to the convention as information rather than for adoption. Although embattled, progressives fought off repeated efforts by Deep South segregationists to cut the commission's funding and weaken its reports. The *Christian Century* credited A. C. Miller and the Christian Life Commission with persuading the convention not to retract its 1954 resolution on *Brown*. Progressives operating at the state level also faced a holding operation. Segregationists managed to defeat proposed endorsements of the *Brown* decision by the Social Service committees of the Tennessee and Georgia conventions in 1956.[31]

Frustrated by opposition from segregationists, progressives sought to outflank them. Unable to persuade the SBC's hostile Finance Committee to recommend a significantly greater allocation for its activities, the Christian Life Commission obtained a grant of $30,000 in 1956 from The Fund for the Republic, an agency of the Ford Foundation. Armed with these funds, the commission produced an extensive literature, which it mailed to every Southern Baptist pastor and to the leadership of SBC and state convention agencies and boards. The commission advertised its literature in Baptist state convention newspapers and mailed pamphlets on request. It printed some 400,000 copies of ten pamphlets in 1957 alone. The commission also tackled race relations in the *Christian Life Bulletin,* a monthly publication introduced in 1955 to replace the by-now defunct *Light,* which it sent to the SBC's 25,000 pastors and to an additional 5,000 people who requested it "for distribution in their churches and church organizations."[32]

Collectively the commission's literature rebutted the biblical defense of segregation, declared that segregation undermined evangelism at home and abroad, attacked white supremacy and dismissed fears that integration would produce miscegenation. The *Information Service* of the ecumenical National Council of Churches claimed in 1956 that the Christian Life Commission had "prepared and sent out some of the most effective materials, aimed at correcting appeals to Scripture in support of segregation."[33]

Progressives began their attack on the segregationist defense by addressing the biblical verses used by segregationists to support their case. The Curse of Ham justification for the second class status of blacks, they claimed, was no more than a myth. Noah and not God had placed the curse and, anyway, the curse was placed not on Ham but on Canaan whose "descendants lived in Palestine and not in Africa." Progressives also dismissed the Tower of Babel incident as irrelevant to race relations. It dealt with idolatry and differences in languages, they asserted, not racial segregation. According to progressives, the biblical injunction to the Jews not to marry those belonging to other nations, referred not to racial intermarriage but to marriage across religious lines.[34]

Segregation's critics had only one "proof text" to tackle in the New Testament, *Acts* 17:26, which claimed that God had created "all nations of men" and determined "the bounds of their habitation." R. Lofton Hudson, pastor of Kansas City, Missouri's Wornall Road Baptist Church, argued in *Is Segregation Christian?* that Paul's words were designed to demonstrate to his proud Greek audience at Athens that its members were no better than any other people, since all were descended from the same blood or parentage. According to Hudson, "There is nothing in this passage that remotely suggests the idea of segregation." In the pamphlet *The Bible Speaks on Race,* the Christian Life Commission argued that *Acts* 17:26 referred to nations, rather than races. It added: "Those who use this verse to defend prejudice in America do not suggest that modern Americans move out of the United States and give this land back to the Indians to whom the Lord originally appointed it." Progressives countered the segregationist argument that Jesus was not opposed to segregation by demonstrating that He had crossed the racial divides of His time. He did so, for example, when He talked to the Samaritan woman at the well (*John* 4). Progressives pointed out that Jews despised the Samaritans as half-breeds of mixed blood and refused to have any dealings with them, yet Jesus did, and in *Luke* 10:25–37 he made a Samaritan the hero of a parable.[35]

If Baptists were to spread Jesus' message across the planet, they had to remember that, as the title of a Christian Life Commission pamphlet emphasized, race relations was a factor in world missions. G. Avery Lee declared in another of the commission's pamphlets: "Our foreign missionaries, and our mission boards tell us that they are embarrassed in their activities with the non-whites of the world because our treatment of racial minorities is not in keeping with the spirit of Christ." Aside from emphasizing the needs of the Great Commission and attacking the biblical defense of segregation, progressives challenged the secular arguments used by segregationists that African Americans were inherently inferior. "The psychologists have told us, and produced evidence as proof," countered Maston, "that races are not innately superior or inferior." Dale Cowling, pastor of Little Rock, Arkansas's Second Baptist Church, insisted, in a sermon during the city's school desegregation crisis, that science proved that if some blacks appeared to be inferior to whites in intelligence, hygiene, and rates of disease, especially sexually transmitted disease, these conditions reflected a poor and deprived environment rather than genetic inheritance.[36]

Progressives rejected the segregationist argument that the civil rights drive to overturn the "separate but equal" doctrine was Communist-inspired or served the interests of Communism by dividing Americans against each other. Maston turned the segregationist charge on its head by maintaining that denial of equal citizenship rights to African Americans advanced the Communist cause. G. Avery Lee declared: "The accusation that these men of the [Supreme] Court are influenced by Communists is ridiculous. Those who make such statements infer that Democracy is weaker at this point than Communism. That is an inference I will not accept. Those who make such charges infer that Christianity, and the Christian heritage in America, is weaker at this point than Communism. I will not accept that reasoning."[37]

Cautious in their non-segregationist approach, progressive Baptists also sought to calm popular fears about the consequences of desegregation, which, they insisted, need not and did not mean immediate full-scale integration. "It is possible," wrote Maston, "to have separation without segregation and desegregation without much integration." Maston even conceded that "one might justify voluntary racial separation and even conceivably defend legal segregation as a necessary social policy in some areas for the present. . . . " Nevertheless, Baptists should not forget that "the segregation pattern is out of harmony with the spirit and the teachings of the Bible, particularly as revealed in the life and ministry of Jesus." Progressives tried to defuse the segregationist fear that school integration would result in interracial marriage. Dale Cowling stated that "Our fears of these new social relationships are so great until they keep us from looking calmly at other communities where they have already been met. Surely, the same culture, training, and background that operates presently in the choice of our friends will continue to operate." In *Race Relations—A Christian View*, J. B. Weatherspoon dismissed fears of miscegenation. He wrote that "the far-off specter of 'race amalgamation' or 'social equality' must not keep Christian people from what is presently just."[38]

In letters to A. C. Miller and the SBC's Christian Life Commission, pastors and officials across the South applauded the commission's efforts and testified to their impact. Most of the correspondents lived in the Deep South, suggesting that the commission succeeded in bypassing the hardline segregationists, who dominated the region's public life. Francis E. Stewart, moderator of the Central Baptist Association of Georgia, asked for two hundred copies of the commission's pamphlet *The Unity of Humanity* in March 1957. Stewart commented: "I think that it is one of the most constructive bits of writing I have yet seen. It comes at a most opportune time." Some state denominational leaders extolled the commission's work. Charles F. Sims, general secretary-treasurer of the Baptist State Convention of South Carolina, wrote to Miller in July 1957 that "I think I could very well use here in the office 50 copies of the Christian Life Commissions' [*sic*] report to the Southern Baptist Convention. I appreciate your sending this to all of our pastors. . . . "[39]

The commission's literature encouraged clergymen to address race relations. James H. Fox Jr., pastor of Front Royal, Virginia's Marlow Heights

Baptist Church, wrote to Miller that "You have given many of us pastors encouragement and strength as we have taken a stand for Christ on many issues." Progressives also influenced the laity. Florence, South Carolina, pastor W. E. Maring told the SBC's Christian Life Commission in November 1957 that its reports on race relations "are helping to condition the minds and hearts of at least many." Ministers sometimes used the commission's pamphlets in church. Richard A. Harris Jr., pastor of Richmond, Virginia's Westhampton Baptist Church, wrote to Miller that "Last Sunday, as we in our church tried to face up to some of the issues of our racial relationships (about which, to masterfully understate, there is some divided opinion!), it was so helpful to have many of your C.L.C. publications as resource material." In the late 1950s, at the apex of massive resistance, favorable letters to the Christian Life Commission about its work exceeded unfavorable letters by a margin of thirty-five to one.[40]

In addition to its literature, the commission sponsored conferences on race relations for pastors and lay people in Louisiana, Mississippi, South Carolina, Tennessee, and Kentucky. It set a practical example by helping to establish the Nashville Conference on Human Relations in 1957, designed to promote peaceful compliance with school desegregation. The commission also targeted SBC and state convention leaders. Over 250 Baptist leaders attended a Christian Life Commission conference in North Carolina during August on "Racial Understanding and the Bible." In addition, the commission worked with seminary classes and student pastors.[41]

Progressives made direct appeals to Baptists. As president of the SBC between 1957 and 1959, Brooks Hays, a former chairman of the Christian Life Commission, spread the progressives' message in speeches to the SBC and Baptist state conventions. Hays declared in his presidential address to the SBC in 1959: "Our research in Biblical teaching on race has disproved the claim that existing patterns are divinely prescribed. . . . [S]criptural support for state segregation laws cannot be claimed." Hays's words had special poignancy, because in 1957 he had tried, as a U.S. congressman from Arkansas, to mediate a settlement in the Little Rock school desegregation crisis. His intervention on the side of compliance with federal law cost Hays reelection to congress. Despite segregationist opposition, the SBC approved a resolution, at the conclusion of his presidency, that commended Hays's "courageous stand on the great issues of our day."[42]

Like Hays, the SBC's Christian Life Commission sought a middle path between those who advocated immediate desegregation and diehard segregationists. In 1959, the commission reported that "The issue has been complicated by the radical demands for immediate and complete removal of all forms of segregation on the one hand, and by an equally radical insistence on the maintenance of the traditional system of segregation on the other." In answer to segregationist letters, A. C. Miller insisted that "We are not trying to promote integration of the races in the public schools." He did not advocate integration, but neither did he support segregation by law. Miller wrote to one pastor that "This Commission does not believe that rabid integration can take place in some areas of our Southland, and we are certainly not working to bring this about. In some areas it is no doubt advisable for the separation of the races to continue. But we believe that this can be achieved by good will and understanding, without having to force legal segregation down the throats of those who cannot help themselves."[43]

Miller claimed that African Americans did not "have any quarrel with the idea of the separation of the races," but he insisted that "the system of legal segregation should not be maintained." Miller, as Eldie F. Hicks, pastor of Magee, Mississippi's First Baptist Church, protested, refused to face the logical conclusion of his and the commission's non-segregationist message. Hicks complained that "If segregation is morally wrong, if it is a violation of Christ's ethic, then, to be consistent, it must be argued [*sic*] that *all* segregation ought to be abolished; in our churches, in our colleges, in our homes, and in our marriages."[44]

Progressives entered their third stage of development in 1960, by calling for integration in church and society. The collapse of massive resistance in Virginia and Arkansas in 1959, and the beginnings in February 1960 of successful African-American student sit-ins at lunch counters that denied blacks service made integration seem not only possible but increasingly likely. The sit-ins also revealed the dissatisfaction and determination of young blacks to overturn segregation.[45]

The SBC's Christian Life Commission's 1960 report acknowledged the influence of African-American protests. Accepted by the convention as information and not for adoption, it read: "In the light of recent efforts on the part of Negro citizens in many areas in securing equal rights . . . the Commission urges our Southern Baptist people to make use of every opportunity to help Negro citizens to secure these rights through peaceful and legal means and to thoughtfully oppose any customs which may tend to humiliate them in any way." Foy Valentine, who succeeded Miller as the commission's executive secretary in 1960, frequently condemned segregation when introducing its reports. In 1961, he told the SBC's annual meeting: "We can be the light of the world in a social order hamstrung by segregation. . . . " Afraid of moving too far ahead of its constituency, the commission made no recommendations on race relations in the early 1960s.[46]

Some progressives operating at the state and local level urged Southern Baptists to support integration. The Baptist State Convention of North Carolina called for church desegregation, while its sister convention in Texas commended churches which had open policies. The Baptist General Association of Virginia claimed that "Any system which is designed to make a group feel inferior and unworthy should not be a part of our Christian practice." Progressive Baptist editors in North Carolina, Texas, Arkansas and the HMB called for equal rights and desegregation.[47]

Across the South progressive Baptists responded to but trailed behind secular trends. The SBC's Christian Life Commission did not propose nor endorse legislative solutions to racial problems in advance of action by government. Not until a civil rights bill outlawing segregation in public accommodations seemed likely to pass in 1964 did the commission offer its support. Only then did it recommend open admissions policies in Southern Baptist churches. The commission channeled articles supporting desegregation and racial equality to Baptist publications. It also targeted denominational leaders and editors. The commission brought one hundred and fifty prominent Baptists to a Christian Life Seminar in Washington, D.C. in March 1964, where President Lyndon Johnson urged them to support the civil rights bill. In June, a month before the bill's enactment, the Christian Life Commission's report condemned segregation and the "thunderous silence" of Southern Baptists in failing to speak out against it. Adopted by the SBC, the report also recognized that civil rights protests sought "redress of legitimate grievances." The commission recommended that the messengers endorse open churches and pledge themselves to "go beyond" civil rights laws. However, they narrowly rejected the recommendation.[48]

The Christian Life Commission held conferences on "Christianity and Race Relations" at Glorieta, New Mexico, and Ridgecrest, North Carolina, in August 1964 for 3,290 denominational leaders and officials. The *Christian Century* enthusiastically praised the meetings: "Characterized by hardhitting, forthright explorations of Southern Baptist default in the area of racial crisis, the well attended conferences not only made Southern Baptist history but also summoned the whole convention to a new day in its approach to the racial crisis." Influenced by the commission and the disastrous effect that racism was having on Baptist foreign missions, the WMU and the HMB featured race relations and condemned segregation in their magazines. Victor Glass told state convention executive and missions directors that "To stand in the way of the Negro achieving all that he is capable of achieving, is to oppose God in his plan for every life."[49]

Encouraged by progressives, the Upper South and Texas state conventions called for obedience to the Civil Rights Act. The Baptist General Association of Virginia adopted recommendations in support of the act in 1964 and praised the work of the SBC's Christian Life Commission in race relations. The Baptist General Convention of Texas adopted recommendations from its Christian Life Commission that welcomed "the increasing number of schools, churches, and hospitals which minister to all persons in the name of Christ without regard to race." The Baptist State Convention of North Carolina adopted a Christian Life Commission report that commended and encouraged open churches, and desegregation of public accommodations. Other state conventions kept silent, for fear of alienating segregationists. However, William P. Davis took a courageous personal stand in testimony before the U.S. Commission on Civil Rights in Jackson, Mississippi. Davis told the commission's public hearing in February 1965: "Any citizen worthy of the name is entitled to his civil rights. Intimidation or discrimination used to deny a citizen his civil rights should not be tolerated in Mississippi or anywhere in the United States of America. Human beings matter more than empty tradition."[50]

The SBC passed a resolution supporting the Civil Rights Act in 1965, based on the recommendation made by its Christian Life Commission a year before. The convention also adopted a commission report that condemned segregation as "an offense to the gospel" and "a sin against God." Ralph McGill, publisher of the *Atlanta Constitution,* called the SBC's actions "historic" and "a great breakthrough for moral and Christian truth in the South." The *Christian Century* wondered if the meeting marked the beginning of "A New Climate Down South?" Editors of Baptist newspapers in Arkansas, Florida, North Carolina, Tennessee and Texas commended the SBC's resolution and the Christian Life Commission's report.[51]

The SBC's action encouraged conventions that had previously been reticent to address segregation. The Florida Baptist Convention condemned segregation and the Alabama Baptist State Convention welcomed "encouraging strides forward" in key civil rights concerns, which it listed as "employment practices, public accommodations, schools, and voting rights." The Baptist State Convention of South Carolina praised progress made toward school desegregation and equal job opportunities in the state. It also criticized continued inequalities between the races in housing and in "representation on public boards and agencies."[52]

The most prominent civil rights leader, Martin Luther King Jr., was assassinated in April 1968. His murder led to a wave of riots and disturbances. SBC leaders asked Foy Valentine and Clifton J. Allen, editorial secretary of the Sunday School Board, to draft a statement in response. At the SBC's annual meeting in June, 72 percent of the messengers voted for the "Statement Concerning The Crisis In Our Nation," which committed them to work for an end to segregation in churches and housing, and for equal opportunities in public services, education and employment. The crisis statement was endorsed by the Virginia and Texas conventions, the Christian Life agencies of the North and South Carolina conventions, and the Executive Board of the Tennessee Baptist Convention. It also received the support of most state convention officials and editors, except for many from the Deep South.[53]

Only a "small number" of Southern Baptists wrote to the SBC in Nashville criticizing the statement and many praised it. Mississippian Kathleen Hilton wrote to SBC president H. Franklin Paschall that "southern churches have remained silent far too long." Pastors also used the statement. Donald Atkinson, pastor of Birmingham's Hillview Baptist Church, told the *Alabama Baptist:* "In a recent business conference, our church discussed the statement adopted by the Southern Baptist Convention on the racial and crime crisis in our country. I am delighted to share with you that we had an open and free discussion; and I feel we reached a higher level of understanding concerning our Christian responsibility."[54]

The crisis statement marked an important stage in the SBC's and Southern Baptists' gradual and still uncompleted abandonment of racism. Progressives had succeeded in making their views on race those of the convention. Although the SBC elected leading fundamentalist W. A. Criswell, a frequent critic of social Christianity and one-time defender of segregation, as president in 1968, he commended the "spirit" of the crisis statement and publicly repudiated the biblical defense of segregation. A survey of messengers to the SBC in 1969 found that 6 percent thought race should be a factor in determining church membership, while 52 percent disagreed and 40 percent believed each church should decide for itself. Erwin L. McDonald, editor of the *Arkansas Baptist Newsmagazine,* concluded that "The voices of those who would try to use the Bible to argue that God meant for Negroes—or any other racial group—to be kept in an inferior state has been muted by that of a more intelligent and more humane Baptist majority."[55]

In the many resolutions it adopted between 1969 and 1971, the SBC supported most of the positions on race relations promoted by the Christian Life Commission. The convention adopted a resolution in 1969 that reaffirmed its crisis statement of the year before and urged everyone "to work for racial justice, economic improvement, political emancipation, educational advancement, and Christian understanding" for all. Significantly, the SBC's resolutions on race-related issues were not sponsored by its Christian Life Commission. The commission did not need to do so because a consensus had emerged in the SBC in support of justice and against discrimination. In another important development, messengers from the Deep South sponsored progressive resolutions on race relations for the first time. In 1970, former biblical segregationist and Christian Life Commission opponent Owen Cooper of Mississippi successfully moved the adoption of a resolution that commended those Southern Baptist churches that had opened themselves to persons of all races and urged greater interracial cooperation between Christians. The following year the convention adopted a resolution against racial prejudice presented by Lamar Jackson of Alabama.[56]

Through their patient and persistent efforts progressives influenced many Baptist leaders and opinion makers. John H. Buchanan Jr., pastor of Birmingham, Alabama's Southside Baptist Church, and later a U.S. congressman, told Brooks Hays that "You've influenced me. I altered my views about national policy on integration as a result of studying your addresses and articles and what you have had to say." Members of the Christian Life Commission in Texas helped to change the views of E. S. James, editor of the *Baptist Standard,* who had supported segregation in the 1950s. Through their reports and literature, progressives also undermined segregationist thought and belief among many pastors and lay people, even in conventions dominated by vocal segregationists. Dillard Wilbanks, a minister of education and music at Manchester, Georgia's Northside Baptist Church, wrote to Jack U. Harwell, the integrationist editor of the *Christian Index,* that "Those who enraged me by suggesting that I would have to accept integration endured my scorn for a time but have now come to see that . . . their efforts were not in vain. With patience you will reap a rich harvest. May God richly bless you as you stand firm upon the leadership of the Holy Spirit in your very special calling to Christian journalism."[57]

During the course of the 1970s, Baptist colleges and universities that had not already done so adopted non-discriminatory admissions policies, as did many Southern Baptist churches. Integration of Baptist institutions seldom extended beyond tokenism but segregation in principle had become largely unacceptable.[58]

Southern Baptist progressives played a supporting role, behind the civil rights movement and the federal government, in the transfiguration of the South's race relations. Although they did not initiate change, progressives did help many Southern Baptists to adjust to and eventually accept it. They did so by criticizing the inequities of segregation in the 1940s and early 1950s, and, after the *Brown* decision, by attacking the main components of the segregationist ethos, especially the biblical defense of segregation. Progressives gradually destroyed the sacred nature of segregation, making Baptist acceptance, however reluctantly, of its legal demise possible. From non-segregationists in the second half of the 1950s, progressives became champions of integration in the first half of the 1960s. They helped influence the vast majority of Baptist institutions to adopt nondiscriminatory policies in the late 1960s and 1970s. Progressives achieved minimal integration within the SBC, but they nonetheless helped to make flagrant segregation and discrimination unacceptable among most Southern Baptists.

6

Public School Desegregation

By THE LATE nineteenth century most Southern Baptists had developed a strong commitment to public education. They contended that it provided people with the skills to read and interpret the Bible, and strengthened the nation's democracy. However, the demands of the civil rights movement for equal educational opportunities and facilities in the 1930s and 1940s and for school desegregation after that placed a great strain on Baptist support for the public school system. Progressive Southern Baptists and Baptist leaders frequently urged their coreligionists to accept school desegregation, rather than withdraw their children into private education or allow public schools to be closed to prevent integration. Most Baptists preferred to see Jim Crow education maintained and, unlike their leaders, they consistently supported measures designed to prevent or severely limit desegregation. When school desegregation reached their state or locality, a minority of Baptists withdrew their children into private schools, sometimes operated by their churches, despite the opposition of many SBC and Baptist state convention leaders. However, most Baptists, motivated by a combination of principle and the high cost of private schooling, retained their commitment to public education and reluctantly accepted desegregation as the price of preserving it.

In the 1940s, progressive Baptists, particularly in the SBC and the North Carolina, Texas and Virginia conventions, were occasionally able to obtain support from their conventions for improving educational opportunities for African Americans. The SBC's Social Service Commission suggested in 1945 "That in educational opportunities provided for out of public funds Negro children and white children shall share equally in proportion to their numbers." The commission also commended school equalization programs and welcomed desegregation of graduate education at the University of Arkansas and some border state universities. It reasoned that equalization of higher education facilities was prohibitively expensive.[1]

Even some hard-line segregationists supported the principle of equal opportunity within Jim Crow education. David M. Gardner, editor of the

Baptist Standard, expressed support in 1945 for "equal opportunities in the realm of economics and education" but warned that "we must seek such improvements within the racial groups" and avoid "an amalgamation of the races." Baptist state conventions in Alabama, Georgia and South Carolina also supported improved, but segregated, education for African Americans in the late 1940s. The Commission on Social Service of the Baptist State Convention of South Carolina reported in 1949, after it had met "a representative group" of African Americans, that "They are not insisting on being enrolled in our schools or universities along with white students, but they are insisting upon equal opportunities of education being provided for our Negro population, comparable to that provided for our white population."[2]

Many Southern Baptist segregationists, like southern state governments that embarked on programs of upgrading African-American schools in the late 1940s and early 1950s, supported school equalization in the hope that it would satisfy blacks and deter the courts from outlawing segregation. The Georgia Baptist Convention adopted a Social Service Commission report in 1949 that placed its faith "in improved educational facilities for the Negro" as a solution to "racial tensions." A year later, the convention adopted a commission report that praised efforts to equalize education in the state. It declared: "We rejoice in the sustained efforts of many of our cities and counties, even at great cost, to improve the school facilities for negroes. The answer to the appeal for further advance lies not in law suits to end segregation. If such a suit prevailed it would accentuate rather than lessen the problem." As NAACP litigation, challenging segregated education, worked its way through the court system in the early 1950s, most of the conventions and editors who had once called for equalization ignored education altogether. The Georgia and South Carolina conventions voted in 1953 against taking a position on the forthcoming Supreme Court decision on school segregation.[3]

However, when the Supreme Court handed down the *Brown* ruling in May 1954, the SBC and a large majority of the Baptist state conventions and their newspaper editors reminded Baptists of the necessity of preserving public education, whatever their feelings about integration. The SBC adopted a recommendation from its Christian Life Commission in support of *Brown* that reminded Baptists that public education was essential to the nation's democracy. It noted that desegregation would not be immediate and commended the Court for deferring implementation of its decision "until the nation shall have had time to work out methods by which transition from the present practice may be effected." The North Carolina and Virginia conventions also endorsed the ruling. The Baptist General Association of Virginia adopted a Christian Life Committee report that announced: "We feel that basic to the democratic freedom in our republic is our system of free public schools."[4]

Although it avoided commenting on the substance of *Brown,* the Social Service Commission of the Baptist State Convention of South Carolina presented a vigorous defense of public education. The commission reported to the messengers: "Every person should . . . be able to read the Scriptures for himself, and thus the ability to read the Bible becomes basic to the individual's learning about God for himself. . . . Baptists in South Carolina have the greatest stake in the Public Schools, and the most to be lost if our present means of universal education is destroyed." The convention adopted the commission's recommendation that exhorted the state's leaders to bolster public education.[5]

The editors of Baptist newspapers often took a more forthright position than their conventions in support of *Brown* and the SBC's resolution, with only the editors of the *Baptist Message* and the *Baptist Record* expressing criticism of them. Reuben E. Alley, editor of the *Religious Herald,* warned parents against sending their children to private schools. If they tried to circumvent the Supreme Court's decision in that way, he contended, they would endanger the public school system and even perhaps "the operation of democracy in the United States." David Gardner urged Texas Baptists to accept *Brown.* He wrote that "The idea of abolishing our public school system is unthinkable. Such a course would be an indictment against the character of American manhood, doom many of the youths of today and the future to live in ignorance, and imperil the nation."[6]

Some pastors and lay people wrote to the denominational press in opposition to the court's ruling and the SBC's resolution. Malcontents contended that segregation was biblical and that both the decision and resolution were political and therefore wrong. Significantly, they did not argue that the public school system should be abandoned to preserve segregation. Many Baptists reserved judgement about desegregation as they waited for the Supreme Court to decide when and how its ruling would be enforced. Some believed, as Leon Macon editorialized in the *Alabama Baptist,* that "segregation will continue on the whole, even as it is in the north where non-segregation has been practiced."[7]

The editors of Baptist state convention newspapers frequently spoke out in support of public education, when their states proposed legislative measures to preserve segregation that endangered the operation of public schools. However, against the counsel of their leaders, many Baptists joined other whites in voting in state referenda for legislative devices designed to impede desegregation. Only when a stark choice emerged between some desegregation and the closure of the public school system did most southern states abandon resistance and accede to token integration. The majority of Baptists, like other whites, acquiesced in limited desegregation as the price of maintaining public education.

Governor Herman Talmadge tested the commitment of white Georgians to segregation in 1954 by proposing a state constitutional amendment that would allow the legislature to change the public education system into a private one and provide tuition grants for those attending private schools. John Jeter Hurt Jr., editor of the *Christian Index,* urged Baptists to use their votes to defeat the measure in a forthcoming referendum. He declared that "The public school system must not be lost. Lose it and we lose one of the strongholds of democracy. . . . The proposed constitutional amendment must be defeated." The electorate approved the amendment by the narrow margin of 29,340 votes in November, and chose hard-line segregationist Marvin Griffin as their next governor. Although Griffin's election demonstrated that the voters preferred Jim Crow, the close vote on the amendment indicated that many Georgians remained committed to the continuance of public education.[8]

In May 1955, the Supreme Court issued a second *Brown* ruling in which it decided that school desegregation should be implemented at a pace to be decided by federal district courts. The courts issued their first desegregation orders in the peripheral South, in the belief that whites there might be less resistant to them as African Americans formed a smaller percentage of the population than in the Deep South. In states which sought to evade or limit desegregation, such as Texas, North Carolina and Florida, and to a lesser extent Tennessee, Baptist conventions and leaders tended to speak out in defense of public education. However, in Arkansas and Virginia, which openly defied court-ordered integration, the state conventions retreated into silence until the crisis passed and the states accepted token desegregation.[9]

By the end of 1955, eighty-four school districts in Texas had desegregated. However, Governor Allan Shivers sought to maintain his control over the state's Democratic Party by defending school segregation. Shivers lost control of his party to Price Daniel who succeeded him as governor, but the Advisory Committee on Segregation in the Public Schools, which he had earlier appointed, maintained the segregationist momentum by proposing twenty-one measures to the legislature.[10]

Foy Valentine, head of the Baptist General Convention of Texas's Christian Life Commission, denounced the segregationist bills under consideration by the assembly in 1957 as "unnecessary, inflammatory, discriminatory and . . . unconstitutional."[11] Joseph Martin Dawson, former executive director of the Baptist Joint Committee on Public Affairs, and Blake Smith, pastor of Austin's University Baptist Church, strongly condemned the bills in testimony before the legislature. Dawson claimed that they were based on the "unchristian theme of White supremacy, ill-conceived, basically wrong, an effort to subvert the laws of the nation." Smith told legislators that a proposed pupil assignment bill constituted "basic dishonesty."[12] Carlyle Marney, pastor of Austin's First Baptist Church, also lobbied hard against the legislation. In speaking out against segregation, Valentine, Dawson, Smith and Marney joined the leaders of their state's major denominations. Reporter Ronnie Dugger commented: "But for these unrelenting pressures from the most unassailable of the community's moral leaders, the legislature would have passed . . . all the twelve bills introduced, instead of only two." The two bills enacted comprised a pupil placement bill and a referendum measure that provided for a cessation of state funds and accreditation for any district that desegregated its schools without a petition in favor signed by 20 percent of its voters and a majority vote to the same effect in a special election.[13]

In response, the Baptist General Convention of Texas unanimously adopted a recommendation in 1958 from its Christian Life Commission, drafted by Valentine, that praised "the public schools, one of the cherished strengths of our country." It discerned "a grievous threat" to their "integrity" and warned that they should not be endangered "either through attempts to avoid integration or through indifference and neglect." The public schools remained intact, but the new state laws prevented any further school desegregation in Texas during the remainder of the 1950s.[14]

North Carolina also succeeded in limiting school desegregation to token proportions after flirting with the idea of defying the courts. The state legislature passed a pupil assignment bill in April 1955, and Governor Luther H. Hodges appointed the Pearsall Committee, packed with segregationists, to make further recommendations. L. L. Carpenter, editor of the *Biblical Recorder*, responded by appealing for "calmness, courage, and self-control." He reminded Baptists that the Supreme Court had unanimously called for the end of public school segregation "as soon as practicable." North Carolinians, he wrote, should "follow the course which is dictated by democracy and basic Christian principles of brotherhood and human welfare."[15]

In late July, Carpenter's fears for public education seemed well founded when Governor Hodges raised the possibility of closing schools to avoid desegregation. On August 8, Hodges made a statewide radio and television address designed to rouse whites from the apathy and resignation, he believed, they displayed at the prospect of gradual school desegregation. The governor accused the NAACP of stirring up trouble by sponsoring school desegregation suits, and he implied that it sought miscegenation. Hodges concluded by calling for voluntary segregation in the state's public schools.[16]

Spurred on by Governor Hodges, several North Carolina congressmen and the state legislature, white opposition to desegregation mounted in late 1955 and early 1956. All but three of North Carolina's congressional delegation signed the Southern Manifesto in March 1956, in which over 100 southern congressmen denounced the *Brown* ruling. In May, popular hostility to desegregation ensured the defeats of two of the recalcitrant congressmen in primary elections. The casualties included Charles B. Deane, Recording Secretary of the Baptist State Convention, who was seeking a sixth term in the House of Representatives.[17]

The North Carolina General Assembly met in special session in July 1956 and approved a resolution, supported by Governor Hodges, that condemned the Supreme Court's ruling as a "tyrannical usurpation of power." The special session also considered recommendations by the Pearsall Committee for a state constitutional amendment confirming the authority of local school boards on pupil assignment issues and granting those boards the power to close their schools if racial conditions became unacceptable to local residents. In addition, the amendment guaranteed state-funded tuition grants to assist parents who wanted to send their children to private, segregated schools. L. L. Carpenter opposed the committee's recommendations in the belief that they "could easily destroy public education in North Carolina." Despite Carpenter's plea, the special legislative session overwhelmingly approved the Pearsall Committee's recommendations and a special election was scheduled for September 8 to allow North Carolinians to vote on the proposed constitutional amendment.[18]

Although most North Carolina newspapers and politicians supported the Pearsall Plan, the vast majority of letters to the *Biblical Recorder,* in the summer of 1956, opposed it. They indicated that many Baptists preferred segregated education but not at the cost of undermining the public schools. Bruce E. Whitaker of Raleigh declared that "I for one am not willing to cast my vote to change the Constitution of North Carolina in such a way as to destroy or even weaken the time honored and hard earned public school system in our great state." Whitaker indicated that he preferred to rely on the state's pupil placement law to maintain segregation. Wendell G. Davis, pastor of Statesville's Western Avenue Baptist Church, wrote that "We must remember that there is something worse than having our children go to school with Negroes. Surely an education with Negroes is better than none at all."[19]

A week before the September 8 constitutional amendment referendum

went before the voters, L. L. Carpenter made a final plea for North Carolinians to reject the Pearsall recommendations lest they "pull down the pil-
lars of the temple of education for the children of this state." Despite his
appeal, the electorate approved the plan by a vote of 471,657 to 101,767.
Governor Hodges had succeeded in persuading whites that the plan offered
the surest way of preserving segregated education in most of the state's
public schools. A year later, public schools in North Carolina's three largest
cities—Greensboro, Charlotte, and Winston-Salem—admitted eleven black
pupils, sufficient to satisfy the courts that the state was in compliance with
Brown. North Carolina thereby succeeded in giving most Southern Baptists
what they wanted, maintenance of public school education with minimal
integration.[20]

In Florida, the prospects of outright defiance of the courts and a conse-
quent threat to the public school system seemed more likely, and consequently the Florida Baptist Convention made a strenuous appeal for
preserving public education. Militant segregationists, who enjoyed disproportionate influence in the malapportioned Florida legislature, successfully
sponsored a pupil assignment law in 1955 that gave local school boards authority over student placement. The Florida Baptist Convention responded
by passing a resolution that implored Baptists to support public schools.
The messengers declared their "faith" in public education and urged "our
people to support it in spirit, and . . . through its Parent Teacher's Associations and kindred organizations. . . . "[21]

Most Southern Baptists, like other white Floridians, remained committed
to maintaining segregation. Facing a strong challenge in the Democratic
gubernatorial primary of 1956 from Sumter L. Lowry, a hard-line segregationist, Governor LeRoy Collins affirmed his commitment to preserving
segregation, peacefully and lawfully. Collins also appointed a Special Advisory Committee, chaired by L. L. Fabisinski, to recommend ways of preventing desegregation. W. G. Stracener, editor of the *Florida Baptist Witness*,
called on Floridians to disavow "the extremists on either end of the controversy" and "to be Christian in attitude and action." Unable to propose
"the final answer," Stracener warned that "Whether we like it or not, we are
going to be increasingly faced with the need for a solution to the problem
of segregation."[22]

Collins's overwhelming primary victory confirmed that most whites supported his moderate segregationist policies. In July 1956, Collins endorsed
and the legislature enacted the Fabisinski Committee's proposals by approving a stronger pupil placement law, giving the governor greater power
to regulate public facilities and clarifying the chief executive's powers to
declare an emergency. Collins adjourned the assembly when hard-line seg-

regationists proposed to close schools faced with court-ordered desegregation and called for an interposition resolution nullifying *Brown,* by interposing the authority of the state between Florida's citizens and the federal government.[23]

In his inaugural address in January 1957, Collins warned against defiance of the Supreme Court, pledged his commitment to maintain segregation and conceded the justice of African-American demands for equal opportunities. As Collins became more moderate, militant segregationists in the state assembly became increasingly strident in their defense of Jim Crow. Meeting in November, the Florida Baptist Convention opposed proposals made by hard-line legislators for state tuition grants to fund students who wanted to attend private schools. The messengers adopted a resolution that declared "public funds should not be expended to support or maintain private or religious schools or educational institutions."[24]

Florida did not adopt tuition grants for private, nonsectarian schools and the threat to the public school system subsided. In September 1959, Miami's Orchard Villa Elementary School became the first school in Florida to desegregate, which it did peacefully and voluntarily. However, Orchard Villa served an area that was changing from white to black and the school soon became predominantly African American. Nevertheless, by 1964 a quarter of Florida's school districts had begun desegregation.[25]

Although Tennessee, like Florida, did not adopt massive resistance, school desegregation encountered opposition in some localities. Segregationists in the state assembly sponsored a pupil assignment bill in January 1955. Governor Frank G. Clement, who preferred to wait for the Supreme Court to rule on *Brown*'s implementation, used his supporters in the legislature to table the bill. After the Supreme Court issued the second *Brown* ruling in May, Clement contended that desegregation was a local problem and sought to distance the state government from the issue. In September, the public schools of federally-controlled Oak Ridge, the site of an atomic project, quietly desegregated by order of the federal government. Clement made no attempt to intervene and state-controlled public schools remained segregated.[26]

Richard N. Owen, editor of the *Baptist and Reflector,* argued that the problems generated by segregation "will not be gotten rid of by ignoring them." Owen maintained that "We owe it to all our children and we owe it to the future to preserve our public schools." He claimed that both "forced segregation" and "forced integration" were wrong and pleaded for limited gradual desegregation "in keeping with what can be sustained by public opinion rather than attempting what can only be done at once by force." Owen expressed the hope that both races preferred Jim Crow. "If forced segregation be followed by voluntary segregation," he reasoned, "the crux of the controversy is gone."[27]

Federal court-ordered school desegregation occurred in Clinton (1956) and Nashville (1957), despite some resistance organized by John Kasper, a northern white supremacist outsider, in both locations. Governor Clement ordered the National Guard to disperse a segregationist mob in Clinton, and when some parents boycotted the integrated Nashville schools police intervened against them. Owen condemned resistance to desegregation in both cases. He noted with alarm that in Nashville the "crowds were bent on breaking up our public schools." As the state achieved token desegregation without risking the integrity of the public school system, the Tennessee Baptist Convention did not feel impelled to defend public education.[28]

In Arkansas and Virginia, both Baptist state conventions retreated into silence when their states closed schools subject to desegregation. The conventions proved unwilling to confront determined segregationist resistance. Erwin L. McDonald, editor of the *Arkansas Baptist,* and Reuben Alley provide contrasting reactions to the desegregation crises. McDonald began a campaign to preserve public education, while Alley attacked the *Brown* decision which he had initially called on Virginians to obey.

Token school desegregation proceeded in Arkansas without significant opposition in 1954 and 1955. Running for reelection in 1956, Governor Orval Faubus, who had eschewed racist appeals and supported college desegregation in his term of office, faced hard-line segregationist Jim Johnson. To fend off Johnson's claim that he was weak on segregation, Faubus called for initiative petitions to secure a pupil assignment law and an interposition resolution, asserting the right of the state to interpose its authority to block federally-ordered school desegregation pending an amendment to the United States Constitution to allow dual school systems. Faubus won reelection. Arkansas voters approved two interposition measures in November; a resolution and a nullification amendment to the state constitution. The amendment allowed the state to nullify federal law. Unwilling to challenge segregationist sentiment, the Arkansas Baptist State Convention adopted a lame Social Service Committee recommendation that "in all problems of human relations, the principles of Jesus be applied with faithful convictions and without apology." A year later, when Governor Faubus defied federal court-ordered school desegregation in Little Rock, the convention fell silent about race relations and its Social Service Committee stopped issuing reports.[29]

Little Rock seemed an unlikely site for resistance to desegregation. In 1954, the city's school board had announced its intention of complying with *Brown*. One year later, it developed a court-approved plan for gradual desegregation, beginning with Central High School in September 1957. On September 2 of that year, Governor Faubus called out the National Guard to prevent desegregation of the school. President Dwight D. Eisenhower responded by federalizing the National Guard and dispatching federal troops to ensure desegregation.[30]

When the Supreme Court refused to halt the continued implementation of gradual school desegregation in Little Rock, Faubus closed the city's four high schools in September 1958. The governor assured Little Rock's voters that their children would be able to attend new private, segregated schools. Influenced by his words, over 70 percent of them voted against reopening the city's public schools on an integrated basis. Concerned that children should continue to receive an education, the Pulaski County Baptist Association, which included the capital's Southern Baptists, asked Ouachita Baptist College in Arkadelphia to establish a high school in Little Rock. In October 1958, the association's five hundred messengers overwhelmingly approved the school proposal drawn up by college president Ralph A. Phelps Jr. Avoiding the issue of desegregation, they also adopted a vague resolution calling "for God's will to be done in the public school crisis."[31]

Phelps announced that the new Baptist school would accept children regardless of religious affiliation, provided that they were white. He justified the whites-only policy by claiming that "it seems highly improbable if not totally impossible that a school could be conducted in Little Rock now on any other lines." Phelps argued that the issue was not segregation or integration but the maintenance of education. He said that the school would close once children had access to another school. The Arkansas Baptist State Convention did not fund Baptist High School, which relied on tuition fees and voluntary contributions. Over four hundred children registered for the school, which held classes in three Southern Baptist churches. Erwin McDonald, who had consistently urged Baptists to obey federal law throughout the crisis, acknowledged that Southern Baptists were divided about the establishment of the school. He concluded that "Regardless of individual feelings about the wisdom of the move, now that Ouachita has entered the field she should have our prayers and our hearty support toward maximum success."[32]

At its annual meeting in November, the Arkansas Baptist State Convention received a report from Ouachita Baptist College detailing the establishment of Baptist High School, but it made no official pronouncements about the desegregation crisis. Erwin McDonald argued in February 1959 that Little Rock's public schools had to be reopened. He wrote that "It becomes more and more apparent that we must accept the limited integration as ordered by the Supreme Court of the United States or do away with our public school system altogether. . . . Our public school system is the very bulwark of our democracy. Let us not willingly sacrifice the lives and careers of many of our fine children and further cripple Arkansas and the South. There simply is no way for a system of private schools to replace the public system." The *Arkansas Gazette* reprinted the editorial, and Little Rock's business and community leaders discussed it at the Chamber of Commerce. In March, the Chamber called for the reopening of the schools on a desegregated basis.[33]

McDonald protested when the Little Rock School Board, now dominated by segregationists, fired forty-four teachers and administrators in May for allegedly supporting integration. McDonald, W. O. Vaught, pastor of Immanuel Baptist Church, Dale Cowling, pastor of Second Baptist Church, and John A. Gilbreath, administrator of the Arkansas Baptist Hospital, along with ministers drawn from the other major denominations, joined the 240-member Committee to Stop This Outrageous Purge (STOP), initiated by the Little Rock Parent-Teacher Association. McDonald was quick to point out that the committee took no stand on the issue of integration. Its aims were to have those who had been fired reinstated as well as to force new elections to the school board.[34]

Many teachers, ministers, parents and businessmen rallied behind the STOP campaign in the belief that the public school closures had undermined education, law and order, and the city's economic growth as investors looked to other states in search of a stable business environment. STOP secured sufficient signatures to force a recall election to the school board. Held in May 1959, the election produced a new board pledged to comply with school desegregation. The following month, a federal district court declared the state's school closing law unconstitutional. In July, Baptist High School announced that, in anticipation of the public schools resuming operations, it would not reopen in the fall, as parents had registered only twenty-two students. Little Rock's formerly white public schools peacefully reopened on a desegregated basis in August, and the crisis ended.[35]

The Arkansas elections of 1960 confirmed that the new mood of moderation was not confined to Little Rock. Although Governor Faubus won reelection by a large majority, the voters overwhelmingly defeated a Faubus-supported constitutional amendment permitting local communities to close their public schools to avoid desegregation. Faubus adjusted to the new situation by appealing for unity, industrial growth and even African-American support. Token school desegregation continued in the new decade.[36]

Virginia, like Arkansas, also played a leading part in massive resistance to *Brown*. Governor Thomas B. Stanley appointed a Commission on Public Education in August 1954, popularly known as the Gray Commission, to study the implications of the *Brown* decision. Chaired by state senator Garland Gray, a committed segregationist, and dominated by militant segregationists from the Southside, Virginia's black belt, the commission soon hinted that it would recommend a policy of local option on school desegregation. Only days before the commission reported in November 1955, the Baptist General Association of Virginia held its annual meeting. The Christian Life Committee defended free public schools and warned against any plan that might eliminate them "directly or indirectly." The committee's expectations were disappointed when the Gray Commission recommended a pupil placement law, abolition of compulsory school attendance, and tuition grants for children whose parents wanted them to attend private, segregated schools. Staunchly protecting public education, Reuben Alley opposed tuition grants on the grounds that they would undermine the public schools.[37]

Since Virginia's constitution did not allow state payments to private schools, the commonwealth held a referendum on whether to call a convention to revise the constitution. In January 1956, Virginians voted two to one in favor of holding a convention. The majority of the Old Dominion's whites supported the Gray Commission's plan of token compliance with *Brown* as the best means of preserving public education with minimal desegregation. But committed to the maintenance of segregation everywhere, U.S. Senator Harry F. Byrd, a fervent segregationist and head of a powerful state political organization, and Southside legislators jettisoned the recommendations of the Gray Commission and pushed a package of massive resistance laws through the state assembly. These measures passed in close votes.[38]

By the time the General Association met in November 1956, Virginia had adopted an interposition resolution, which declared that the state would resist the Supreme Court's "illegal encroachment upon our sovereign powers," mandated the closing of any school that desegregated under court order, and denied state funds to those that desegregated voluntarily. In the face of massive resistance and fearful of deepening Baptist divisions, the General Association retreated into near silence. It adopted a Christian Life Committee report that offered nothing more than a plea for Baptists to reject racial discrimination.[39]

In a gesture of defiance against federal interference in Little Rock, Virginians in 1957 overwhelmingly elected as their governor J. Lindsay Almond, the massive resistance candidate. Fearing the backlash, the Christian Life Committee withdrew its report to the General Association's meeting that year. More concerned with unity and institutional survival than justice, the General Association adopted an innocuous motion, proposed from the floor, that merely acknowledged "the sincere differences of opinions among Christians on the matter of race relationships" and petitioned for "divine leadership." Reversing himself, Reuben Alley rescinded his support of the SBC's resolution on *Brown*. In justification, Alley argued that the majority of Baptists were segregationists, the convention's racial pronouncements "caused distress," and segregation was a political question, outside the bounds of the SBC's authority. He declared that "We see little merit in proclaiming from the platform statements of Christian convictions which disagree with facts. The Southern Baptist Convention is not a proper platform for pronouncements on political issues."[40]

Resistance reached its apogee in September 1958, when Governor Almond closed nine schools in Warren County, Charlottesville, and Norfolk rather than desegregate them under federal court order. The example of Warren County, northern Virginia, demonstrates how, during the height of massive resistance, an active unyielding segregationist minority silenced the accommodationist majority. Warren had a small African-American population. Most of the county's Southern Baptists preferred segregation but not at the cost of public education. As members of the Front Royal Ministerial Association, Southern Baptist pastors signed a statement that declared: "The overriding issue before us is not whether we agree with a court order requiring the end of segregation. The overriding issue is the urgency of keeping our public schools open. The education of our children is at stake. . . . " The clergymen urged their parishioners to accept token desegregation and warned them against any attempt to use church buildings for private, segregated schools.[41]

A minority of hard-line segregationist lay people forced public votes in which they succeeded, over the objections of their pastors, in intimidating Baptist, Methodist and Episcopalian churches into voting to allow their facilities to be used for private education. At Front Royal's First Baptist Church only 153 of the 800 resident members voted on the issue, 110 in favor and forty-three against. Some members walked out when they realized that the vote would not be secret. According to Paul L. Stagg, the church's pastor, "Others who were opposed to the motion voted for it when the vote was by standing."[42]

The Christian Life Committee reported to the General Association in 1958 that "many churches and pastors" had been silent about segregation during the past four years. Only the issue of using church buildings for private schools, the committee admitted, had forced churches to take sides on the issue of massive resistance. The committee urged churches not to become "allied with groups or organizations having purely secular purposes" and advised them to stand by the Baptist principle of the separation of church and state. The report was adopted. The General Association also indicated its support for public education in a negative fashion by overwhelmingly defeating a segregationist proposal that it go on record in support of Governor Almond. In January 1959, both the state and federal courts of appeal ruled unconstitutional Almond's closure of public schools and withdrawal of state funds from them. Consequently, Virginia abandoned massive resistance as state policy, peacefully reopened the affected schools, and accepted token desegregation under a local option policy.[43]

The closure of schools in Virginia and Arkansas by state governors marked the zenith of massive resistance to school desegregation. In the Deep South, where African Americans comprised over one third of the population and 90 percent of whites opposed desegregation according to a poll in 1956, the courts expected sustained opposition. Yet, when court-ordered educational desegregation came to the region in the early 1960s, every Baptist state convention there, except Mississippi, spoke out in favor of maintaining the public school system.[44]

The desegregation of schools in New Orleans in 1960 illustrated starkly the conflict between Southern Baptist support for segregation and commitment to public education. Fourteen African Americans were admitted to two formerly all-white schools in the city in November only to be met by a mob that congregated for days. Most white students also boycotted the schools. The Louisiana legislature passed one school segregation law after another, but the federal courts overturned each new law. The Louisiana Baptist Convention met in the midst of the crisis. The convention's Committee on Public Affairs refused to abandon its commitment to the public school system. The committee's adopted report read: "We pause here . . . to reaffirm our belief in the American public schools. We commend your efforts on behalf of our children and our way of life. We pray in these troubled times that you are cherished and protected, encouraged and strengthened, and rewarded for all your efforts." Despite the initial difficulties, the desegregation of New Orleans schools went ahead.[45]

Georgia's battery of massive resistance legislation also posed a threat to public education. The state's malapportioned legislature allowed hard-line, rural segregationists to dominate politics. Consequently, the assembly overwhelmingly approved legislation in January 1956 that barred state funding of desegregated school districts, and required the governor to close any school system that contained a desegregated school. The legislature also adopted an interposition resolution in February that declared the *Brown* ruling "null, void and of no effect." In response, Methodist Bishop

Arthur J. Moore of Atlanta and Atlanta pastor Louie D. Newton, a former president of the SBC, issued a joint statement advising against "hasty or unwise action." Its text stressed their commitment to public education. The two leaders declared that "Almost from the beginning of our national history, our public schools have been honored as a great and indispensable support of our democratic way of life. If America is to have long life and fulfill its God-given destiny, our public schools are essential."[46]

Nevertheless, segregationist resistance intensified. In 1957, the Georgia assembly approved further legislation designed to protect segregation by allowing the governor to suspend the compulsory school attendance law. Eighty Atlanta Protestant ministers, including nine Southern Baptists, signed a public statement in November that supported public education. The clergymen declared: "The public school system must not be destroyed. It is an institution essential to the preservation and development of our democracy. To sacrifice that system in order to avoid obedience to the decree of the Supreme Court would be to inflict tremendous loss upon multitudes of children, whose whole lives would be impoverished as a result of such action."[47]

However, white Georgians remained overwhelmingly opposed to any school desegregation. In 1958, they elected S. Ernest Vandiver, who had promised to maintain segregated education, as their governor in a landslide. Less than two weeks after Vandiver's victory, a federal court agreed to set a trial date for a school desegregation suit filed by African-American Atlantans with the support of the NAACP. Under Georgia's massive resistance laws, the state would automatically close all of the city's schools if just one desegregated. John Jeter Hurt Jr. appealed to Christians to speak out for maintenance of public education. Hurt warned Baptists that "There is not a greater blow to our way of life than will come with the closing of the public schools." Faced with the prospect of school desegregation, Atlanta ministers issued a second statement in November 1958. It reiterated their call for preservation of the public schools. The 312 signatories included sixty-two of the 146 Baptist ministers in the Atlanta area. Hurt called on Baptists to support the appeal.[48]

Although most Atlanta politicians were prepared to concede token desegregation as the price of maintaining public education, the state assembly passed additional segregation legislation in January 1959. It authorized the governor to close any single school that desegregated, rather than all of the district's schools, allowed him to close any part of the university system subject to court-ordered desegregation and, in an attempt to deter Atlanta schools from desegregating, abolished the tax-levying power for schools of municipalities subject to desegregation orders. Six months later,

U.S. District Court Judge Frank A. Hooper ordered the Atlanta school board to present a desegregation plan. Confronted with the inevitability of a clash between the federal courts and the state government, the Georgia Baptist Convention called for preservation of the public schools. The convention adopted a Social Service Commission report in November 1959 that reaffirmed "our faith in the public school system" and called "upon our people to maintain it. . . . "[49]

In January 1960, Judge Hooper approved Atlanta's plan for gradual school desegregation, beginning in September. The predominantly white Atlanta Baptist Pastors Conference unanimously adopted a resolution supporting the preservation of public schools "as indispensable to our way of life" and local option on school desegregation. It sent the resolution to Governor Vandiver, state legislators and Atlanta Mayor William B. Hartsfield. The legislature responded to Hooper's decision by appointing a commission, chaired by Atlanta banker and lawyer John A. Sibley, to study desegregation. By a majority of eleven to nine, the Sibley Commission's report recommended local option tuition grants for students who withdrew to private schools and a pupil placement law to minimize desegregation. Judge Hooper responded by scheduling school desegregation for 1961, to allow the state time to rescind its segregation laws.[50]

The Social Service Commission prepared its annual report in July 1960. Only eight of the commission's members were present at the final drafting. The report reflected the segregationist views of commission chairman Montague Cook. It argued that "our religious practice and sense of practical right would be violated by any forced integration of the races in public schools." John Jeter Hurt Jr. protested in the *Christian Index* that the report "lacked any strong expression in behalf of the public schools," the loss of which would be Georgia's "greatest disaster since Sherman's armies burned their way to the sea." The report and Hurt's editorial generated an extensive correspondence in the *Christian Index*. A minority of writers, confined largely to the black belt, attacked Hurt's editorial and accused him of advocating integration. A. T. Fleming of Blakely, Early County, told Hurt: "[T]here are many parents who place maintaining the purity of the white race above reading, writing and arithmetic." The vast majority of readers supported Hurt, attacked the commission's report and called for preservation of the public schools. Layman Charles G. Johnson wrote to Hurt: "I definitely could not vote to adopt this report . . . for two outstanding reasons. First, I am a Christian and I do not think the Social Service Commission report gives a genuine Christian view. Secondly, I have two boys whom I hope to educate in the public schools of Georgia. . . . "[51]

As the convention's meeting drew near, Hurt urged Baptists to reject the

Social Service Commission's report and take a positive stand for public education. The convention discarded the report and voted, almost unanimously, in favor of a substitute that petitioned Georgia's Governor and General Assembly to take "such steps" as were necessary to maintain the public school system. Georgia abandoned massive resistance as the convention had hoped. The crisis came when a federal court ordered the University of Georgia to enrol two African-American students. Their admission in January 1961 led to a campus riot. As an integrated institution, the university faced the withdrawal of state funding under Georgia law. At Governor Vandiver's request the state assembly repealed its segregation laws and adopted the recommendations of the Sibley Commission. Unhindered by the state, Atlanta officials prepared for school desegregation, which occurred peacefully in August.[52]

Unlike Georgia, when school desegregation came to Alabama in 1963, it did so despite last-stand resistance by the state's governor, George C. Wallace. Alabama had reacted calmly at first to the *Brown* decision, but by 1956 it had adopted massive resistance. The state assembly overwhelmingly approved a "freedom of choice" constitutional amendment in January that allowed parents to choose a segregated school for their children, authorized the legislature and local school districts to finance private schools with public funds, and removed the requirement for the state to provide public education. It also approved a resolution that declared the *Brown* ruling "null, void, and of no effect" in Alabama.[53]

In the *Alabama Baptist,* editor Leon Macon opposed the constitutional amendment for fear that it might lead to the funding of religious schools and violate the separation of church and state. Demonstrating their commitment to resistance, Alabamians ratified the amendment by 104,379 to 68,231 votes in August 1956. At its annual meeting in November 1956, the Alabama Baptist State Convention adopted a recommendation from its Christian Life Commission that exhorted "the Christian people of both races to resolve to develop that great Christian middle course which, if yet largely undefined, is capable of finding itself, for the present at least, within the framework of public school segregation as an immediate necessity in order to maintain the social progress attained by both great races. . . . " The recommendation also expressed concern that the constitutional amendment might endanger the separation of church and state. A year later the commission's report declared: "Public school segregation . . . is in the best interest of a peaceful, progressive Christian society at this time."[54]

However, as school desegregation by court order appeared increasingly likely the convention called for adjustment. Its Christian Life Commission noted in 1961 that "There has been much talk about the closing of our public schools rather than have them integrated racially." Consequently, the commission presented a robust defense of public education. Its report argued that "Our public schools for the masses have been an undergirding element in the strength of democracy. . . . If our public schools collapse, the simple truth is funds just aren't available to finance and maintain the quality of education now being enjoyed. . . . We frown most heavily upon any prospect of closing our public schools as part of a politico-legal battle. Our children should not be asked to pay this price." The convention adopted the report.[55]

Governor Wallace tried to block school desegregation after the federal courts had ordered white schools in Macon County, Birmingham, Huntsville, Tuscaloosa and Mobile to admit twenty-four African-American children in September 1963. Wallace demanded that local authorities close the schools affected. Federal court orders and the federalization of the Alabama National Guard by President John F. Kennedy forced him to retreat. Within a week, all of the schools had reopened.[56]

In contrast to Alabama, token school desegregation occurred with little drama under federal court order in South Carolina during 1963. As desegregation loomed, the Baptist State Convention of South Carolina's Christian Life and Public Affairs Committee released a statement in January. The commission declared that "We earnestly and respectfully urge that the public schools be kept open and that every effort be made to prevent the interruption of normal educational processes. Education is essential to the highest interests of both religion and democracy." In November, the convention's messengers adopted a similar statement from the commission in its annual report.[57]

The federal courts ordered the Deep South to move from token to full school desegregation in 1970. With partial success, Southern Baptist leaders urged their members not to abandon the public school system by withdrawing their children into the hastily-created private schools that sprang up in the region, often in Baptist church buildings. The SBC adopted a resolution in 1970 that noted that "Some private church-related schools are being formed simply as a strategy to avoid racial integration," cautioned churches against allowing their buildings to be used for private schools and opposed support for church schools from public taxes. A year later, it adopted a resolution that affirmed its support for equal opportunity in public education, regardless of race, and reiterated "its commitment to our system of public school education as a means of raising the knowledge level of all children in the nation. . . ."[58]

Baptist leaders in the Deep South appealed to whites to support the public schools in the face of desegregation, and some explicitly warned against resorting to private schools. Aware of substantial hostility toward desegregation, none of the region's Baptist state conventions proposed or adopted a resolution concerning the subject, and no convention agency, except the Alabama Baptist State Convention's Christian Life and Public Affairs Commission, made a recommendation regarding education. The onset of full integration fractured the commitment of a significant minority of Baptists to the public schools, and induced caution in the public statements of their conventions.

As desegregation approached, in January 1970 the Christian Life and Public Affairs Committee of the Baptist State Convention of South Carolina issued a statement that pleaded with its members to support public education. The committee reminded them that "our support of public education and our acceptance of every individual as a person to be treated with dignity are crucial steps toward . . . [the] objective of world evangelism." It also urged Baptists to "express Christian attitudes in personal relationships and to show responsible citizenship in the support of those seeking to strengthen public education." The Mississippi Baptist Convention's Christian Action Commission issued a similar statement that called on Christians to eschew racial division, support "school administrators and teachers who seek to carry out [desegregation] mandates or abide by regulations," and respect "human personality regardless of race." William P. Davis, director of the convention's Department of Work with National Baptists, and Owen Cooper, a past president of the convention, joined the state's other major religious leaders in signing a public statement in support of public education and racial harmony in the schools.[59]

George E. Bagley, executive secretary-treasurer of the Alabama Baptist State Convention, also signed a statement in February 1970, alongside leaders of the other major denominations in his state, that gave strong support to the public schools. Its signatories declared: "We affirm our belief that public education is essential and that good public education is still possible. . . . We urge our political leaders at all levels to use their power and influence for the strengthening of the public school system." The leaders also called on African Americans and whites "to work for racial harmony" by supporting "the necessary adjustments in our present school system." Hudson Baggett, editor of the *Alabama Baptist,* insisted that the public education system was vital for the future of the state's children. He affirmed that "Private schools have a place in our society, but they cannot substitute for the public school system. At this time, our public schools need the help and understanding of parents and church officials. The school situation provides a good opportunity to teach children Christian attitudes in our homes, churches and schools."[60]

The Executive Board of the Northwest Louisiana Baptist Association adopted a resolution in support of public education in January 1970. A month later, the Louisiana Baptist Convention's Committee on Public Affairs issued a statement that urged Southern Baptists not to seek tax funds for private schools designed to avoid integration or preserve segregation. The committee also warned that public tax money for parochial or private schools would weaken the public school system and undermine the separation of church and state. James F. Cole, editor of the *Baptist Message,* published the committee's statement and commended Louisiana's secular newspapers for taking "a firm editorial position in defense of the public school system. . . . " Cole argued that public schools were essential to the nation's survival. He wrote: "I cannot recall a country that has gone over to communism that had a strong public school system. The public school system in America has been a bulwark of democracy. . . . "[61]

Support for private education from a minority of Baptists induced caution in the public statements of some Baptist leaders and occasionally emerged in convention debates. In January 1970, the Mississippi Baptist Convention's Christian Action Commission defended the right of parents to send their children to a private school, even as it urged Baptists to support the public system. The Executive Board of the Alabama Baptist State Convention tabled a report from its Christian Life and Public Affairs Commission in 1970 that warned churches not to establish private schools.[62]

By contrast, the Georgia Baptist Convention's Executive Committee urged Baptists in March to reject those who would destroy the public school system "in order to resist integration of our public schools." It warned Southern Baptist churches of the practical problems involved in operating private schools and noted that those engaged in racial discrimination would forfeit tax exempt status from the Internal Revenue Service (IRS). The cost of issuing such an explicit statement was the disunity that the other conventions had not been prepared to risk. Thirteen members of the committee voted against the statement and requested that their opposition be recorded. Jack U. Harwell, editor of the *Christian Index,* later commented in regard to IRS regulations that "It is sad that churches of Jesus Christ have to be so prodded by secular agencies to do what ought to be patently right to any student of the New Testament."[63]

A minority of Baptists abandoned their historic commitment to public education, sent their children to private schools and pressured their churches to allow their buildings to be used for private education. Immediately after the courts ordered desegregation, sixteen of the seventeen Southern Baptist churches in Adams County, Mississippi, cooperated to establish the Adams County Christian Private School in 1970. Jackson Baptist pastor Charles E. Myers recalled that "There was a violent reaction felt in every area of our community when the courts ordered our Jackson, Mississippi[,] public school system to integrate. . . . Many leaders in our community advocated that the churches start parochial schools for the white children and leave the public schools for the blacks." Alarmed by the rapid creation of church schools, the Alabama Baptist State Convention spoke out against them. The messengers approved a recommendation in 1971 which read: "We do not believe the solution of our social problems lies in multiplying private schools if they become both a financial hardship on our people and a peril to our system of public education. *WE* do, however, recognize as tenable the current movement in our state to create a scholarship program for the direct assistance of students choosing to attend private and church related colleges and universities."[64]

Despite the burgeoning private school system, most Baptists kept their children in the public system, either from conviction or because they considered private education prohibitively expensive. Ninety-two percent (534,000) of those enrolled in Mississippi's public schools in 1969 returned in 1970. In South Carolina, only 4 percent of schoolchildren attended private schools in 1972. Only 40,000 schoolchildren, representing 7 percent of the total, attended segregationist academies, religious and secular, across Mississippi in 1973.[65]

However, the migration of whites, including many Baptists, to the suburbs across the entire South in the late 1960s and early 1970s enabled many to avoid school desegregation and keep their children in the public system. Consequently, the Supreme Court in *Swann* v. *Charlotte-Mecklenburg Board of Education* gave authority in 1971 to federal district courts to accomplish the desegregation of school systems by ordering the busing of school children when necessary. A minority of Baptists, throughout the South, reacted to busing by sending their children to private schools, some of them Baptist, while many others moved to areas beyond its reach. Busing was unpopular among whites nationwide. An opinion poll conducted in 1971 revealed that 80 percent of white Americans opposed it. Aware of widespread white disapproval of busing, the SBC and most Baptist leaders ignored the subject.[66]

Opposition to busing derived from a combination of reasons. Some Southern Baptists simply rejected integration, but, at a time when overt racism was becoming unacceptable, they could disguise their racism as a principled objection to busing because it was, they affirmed, disruptive of the education process, community schools and the lives of the children involved. Many Baptists, however, genuinely feared the unsettling implications of busing. Occasionally, their hostility to it surfaced at convention meetings.

At the annual meeting of the Baptist General Association of Virginia in 1971, James Crocker, pastor of Norfolk's integrated First View Church, proposed a resolution that attacked busing as detrimental to the public education system and a violation of the United States Constitution. After a long debate, the messengers passed the resolution with an amendment that endorsed "open housing for all people in all neighborhoods to make our support of neighborhood schools rest on Christian foundations." Julian H. Pentecost, editor of the *Religious Herald,* supported the resolution on busing. Pentecost explained that "There are valid constitutional, educational and economic reasons to oppose forced busing in order to achieve racial balance in the shcools [*sic*], but the more basis [*sic*] issue is the right of every person to have the freedom to select the area in which he will live."[67]

In its report to the Baptist General Convention of Texas in 1971, the Christian Life Commission appealed on behalf of the public schools, but it nonetheless acknowledged the antipathy many Baptists felt toward busing. The commission recognized that "Probably no other current social issue has disrupted family and community life as has school desegregation, particularly where busing is utilized to accomplish desegregation. We are now being asked to pay a difficult price because our earthly fathers achieved less than what was desired by our Heavenly Father." The messengers adopted the report.[68]

Despite their concerns about busing, by the early 1970s most Baptists, like other white Americans, opposed racial segregation in principle. Opposition to token school desegregation among southern white parents fell from 72 percent in 1958 to 16 percent by 1970, and from 13 percent to 6 percent among non-southern white parents. Although they accepted the end of legal racial discrimination, Southern Baptists, like most white southerners, did not seek integration. Baptists, like other whites, tended to move their children to other schools, public or private, when public school desegregation moved substantially beyond tokenism. In 1970, 57 percent of southern white parents and 52 percent of non-southern white parents objected to school integration when African Americans formed at least half or more of a school's enrollment. Aside from simple racism, the phenomenon also reflected a fear by white parents that their children, exposed to a substantial number of African Americans in the public school system, would copy a black culture that, they considered, held values inimical to their own. They also believed, however erroneously, that busing undermined educational performance and created long-term disciplinary problems.[69]

Nevertheless, by 1971 most Southern Baptists accepted school desegregation in principle and rejected overt racism. Despite the calls of Baptist leaders for adjustment to change whenever it became imminent and un-avoidable, the majority of Baptists consistently supported attempts by their political leaders to evade, delay and limit school desegregation. Baptists acceded to token integration as the only means to preserve public education in the face of federal court orders and increasing federal government pressure. That some Baptists joined white flight to the suburbs and sent their children to private schools, while many also opposed busing, suggests that while they accepted the demise of legal discrimination as irrevocable, many did not become truly reconciled to integration. Without the coercion of federal law, it is unlikely even token desegregation would have occurred.

7

Law and Order

WHATEVER THEIR VIEWS about segregation, most Southern Baptists believed that Christians had a religious duty to obey the law and civil authorities, except if they conflicted with God's will. Baptists also desired order,
peace and stability, which inclined them toward social conservatism. Until
the federal government outlawed school segregation in the *Brown* decision
and segregated public facilities in the Civil Rights Act of 1964, there was
no conflict between Southern Baptist support for the law and segregation.
In the late 1940s and early 1950s, the SBC and many Baptist state conventions condemned racist demagoguery and white supremacist organizations,
and called for equal justice under the law within segregation. Most conventions and their newspaper editors called for adherence to the *Brown* ruling
in 1954. Even hard-line segregationists, who criticized the Supreme Court's
ruling, denounced segregationist violence and outright defiance of court-
ordered desegregation. Moderate segregationists and many progressive
Baptists, like militant segregationists, objected to civil rights demonstrations as disruptive and even unnecessary. However, the riots of the 1960s
and Martin Luther King Jr.'s murder in 1968 led some Baptists to appreciate the constructive role played by the nonviolent movement associated
with King. A large majority of Baptists accepted desegregation, but they
did so reluctantly and only when they became convinced that the sole alternative lay in defying the law and risking civil disorder.

Race riots occurred during World War Two in several northern and
southern towns and cities as African Americans migrated to fill the labor
shortage created by the war and whites clashed with northern black soldiers
in southern defense bases. Southern whites lynched some returning African American veterans, who, they feared, would challenge racial subordination, inspired by their wartime fight for freedom and democracy abroad.
At the same time, the NAACP and local civil rights groups raised black
voter registration levels in the South and won Supreme Court rulings
against discrimination in the franchise and on interstate transportation.[1]

After the war ended, many Baptists feared that America's wartime racial conflicts would continue in peacetime. In 1945, the Baptist State Convention of North Carolina's Committee on Social Service and Civic Righteousness warned that "the postwar period brings the threat of racial strife just as after the last war. The chief hope that we have of preventing such misunderstanding is an aggressive leadership on the part of the Christian church at this moment. Such aggressive leadership should have its initiative among the ministers of both races who ought . . . to come together to canvass local problems and to humbly in the spirit of God seek the solution which would prevent the deplorable violence which occurred after the last war." The Baptist General Convention of Texas also displayed considerable fear and anxiety about racial disorder, especially since the state had experienced a race riot in Beaumont during 1943. According to W. W. Melton, the convention's executive-secretary, A. C. Miller had been appointed director of its Department of Interracial Cooperation in 1944 as "a contact man between the several races in the state" to promote interracial understanding in the hope that "We may thereby prevent racial uprisings and racial conflicts."[2]

In reports adopted by their conventions, Social Service committees in Alabama and Georgia condemned mob violence and those in Florida, North Carolina and South Carolina specifically denounced the Ku Klux Klan during the 1940s and early 1950s. Some Baptist state conventions also decried racist demagoguery by southern politicians, while the SBC's Committee on Race Relations lamented the "revival of lawless organizations that fan racial hatred."[3]

Although the editors of Baptist newspapers condemned racial violence, their comments were sometimes tinged with regional defensiveness. A mob of twenty men lynched two African-American men and their wives near Monroe, Walton County, Georgia, in 1946. The lynchings were widely reported and condemned in the North. Segregationist O. P. Gilbert, editor of the *Christian Index*, deplored the lynchings, but he also maintained that if the crime had occurred in a northern city "it would not have thrown the Nation into such a violent agitation." He insisted that the "situation in the North is more to be deplored than any particular crime or violation of the law perpetrated in the South." Reuben E. Alley, editor of the *Religious Herald*, also believed that the nation unfairly singled the South out for criticism. "There are too many moral wrongs in all the nation," he wrote, "for any section or sections to assume a 'holier than thou' attitude toward the South."[4]

While they deplored violence, some Baptists denied that widespread discrimination against African Americans existed. David M. Gardner, editor of the *Baptist Standard*, claimed that southern blacks were content under segregation. He blamed evidence to the contrary on the machinations of "racial rabble rousers" who operated "under the domination of alien influences" and were "paid fabulous sums to promote strife and trouble. . . . " Finley W. Tinnin, editor of the *Baptist Message,* charged northern interference in what he claimed were otherwise harmonious southern race relations. "Criticism of segregation, so far as churches is [*sic*] concerned," wrote Tinnin, "comes not from the Negro Baptists of the South, but from meddlesome Northerners."[5]

Nevertheless, racial violence and fear of racial conflict sensitized the SBC and many Baptist state conventions to some aspects of racial discrimination. They frequently declared their support for African-American constitutional rights, access to the ballot, and "equal justice with others in the courts of the land." The SBC's Charter of Principles in Race Relations, supported by the conventions in Florida, the Carolinas, Tennessee and Virginia, affirmed these goals in 1947. The Georgia Baptist Convention also supported "political self-determination" for African Americans, while the Alabama Baptist State Convention made its support of black citizenship rights contingent on them being extended as fast as blacks could "qualify for them."[6]

Both the SBC and Baptist state conventions expressed reservations concerning legislative solutions to racial inequality. The SBC's Committee on Race Relations argued that "[T]he problem of race relations is primarily a moral and religious problem." It conceded that "Laws create a measure of restraint against injustice" but affirmed that "even the Constitution of our Nation, cannot relax tensions and resentments, nor banish the prejudices and injustices that spring from fallacious thinking and racial feeling." Baptist state conventions often contended that, as the Tennessee Baptist Convention's Committee on Temperance and Social Service reported, "The different races can live together happily, peaceably and profitably, if only both races will manifest the spirit of Christ in all of their dealings with each other."[7]

Heightened racial conflict in a state could, on occasion, lead its Baptist convention to advocate legislative action. Such was the level of racial violence in the South, the Baptist State Convention of North Carolina went on record in favor of a federal antilynching law in 1946, and its sister convention in South Carolina adopted a resolution in 1949 that called for new laws to curb the Ku Klux Klan.[8]

Usually, Baptists contended that the South could solve its racial problems, if only it was left alone. Many Baptists reacted with hostility when in February 1948 President Harry S. Truman urged Congress to create a permanent Fair Employment Practices Committee, and pass legislation to outlaw lynching, the poll tax and segregation in interstate transportation terminals. M. E. Dodd, a former president of the SBC, contended that "You can't legislate good will among races. The South is working out the solution for racial questions and will continue to do so if not interfered with by others." The SBC's Social Service Commission claimed that the South was "of its own volition . . . moving in the direction of the objectives" of Truman's civil rights policies, without commenting on his legislative proposals.[9]

When they expressed an opinion, the Baptist state conventions and their editors were almost uniformly hostile to the president's civil rights message. The Alabama Baptist State Convention adopted the report of its Social Service Commission that declared: "We believe there are grave dangers that threaten peaceful adjustments because of radical demands for the rapid and complete removal of age-long discriminations by legislation. Law cannot relax tensions and resentments nor banish prejudices."[10] John Jeter Hurt Jr., Gilbert's successor as editor of the *Christian Index,* summed up the main features of Baptist objections to civil rights legislation. Hurt maintained that Truman's proposals were unnecessary because "the chief objectives are being reached through the preaching and practice of Christian rights." He claimed, inaccurately, that "lynching has been wiped out," educational equality nearly achieved and "the negro has won his right to vote." Hurt insisted that, if enacted, Truman's proposals would "fan the flames of race hatred," and he warned that the South was not ready to relinquish segregation. L. L. Gwaltney, editor of the *Alabama Baptist,* warned that legislation would "bring about a revival of the Ku Klux Klan or some other similar organization of that kind" and destroy "all the gains which have been made in the amicable relations of the races in the South."[11]

The editors reflected mainstream white opinion in the region. An opinion poll revealed that southern voters opposed the civil rights program by a margin of nine-to-one. Confronted by hostile southern polls and opposition from Southern Democrats in Congress, Truman initially retreated into silence about his proposals, and he did not work hard for their enactment after his election victory in November 1948.[12]

Most Southern Baptists remained wedded to Jim Crow. When the Supreme Court declared segregated public school education unconstitutional in the *Brown* decision, it brought Baptist support for segregation into direct conflict with federal law. Denominational leaders, and most Baptist state conventions and editors responded to the Court's ruling by appealing for calm, order and respect for the law. Searcy S. Garrison, president of the Georgia Baptist Convention, declared that "Our people . . . are facing the problems arising from the decision as loyal Americans. With time and patience our statesmen and people of both races will establish an order in harmony with wisdom and democratic ideals." The Executive Committee of the Baptist General Association of Virginia's Board of Missions and Education met a day after the Court's decision. It unanimously passed a resolution that urged "all men of good will, who believe in law and order, to refrain from excessive statements and actions and to seek a peaceful, orderly, and Christian solution to every problem raised. . . . " Leon Macon, editor of the *Alabama Baptist,* appealed for acceptance of *Brown.* He wrote: "Southern Baptist[s] are not willing to become rebels again, but to work along quietly and sympathetically to carry out the Supreme Court decision in a manner that will result in happiness and peace among the people." John Jeter Hurt Jr. called on Georgians to "listen to wise and deliberate leaders instead of the demagogues and rabble rousers. . . . "[13]

At its annual meeting in May 1954, the SBC adopted a recommendation that endorsed the *Brown* ruling as "in harmony with the constitutional guarantee of equal freedom to all citizens. . . . " Most Baptist state conventions called for obedience to the law, and none opposed the Court's decision. The Baptist General Convention of Texas recommended "That Texas Baptists assume the initiative at once in working out a Christian solution of our race problem, not allowing either demagogues or radicals to rob us as Christians of that moral leadership which God wants us to exert in the solution of this problem which is primarily moral and spiritual." The Baptist State Convention of North Carolina recognized "the validity" of *Brown* and urged Baptists to follow "a policy of *restrained emotions,*" while the Baptist General Association of Virginia stated that *Brown* was the "supreme law of the land which does not violate any cardinal principle of our religion, and as Christian citizens we should abide by this law."[14]

The three Deep South conventions that addressed school desegregation also appealed for law and order. The Baptist State Convention of South Carolina's Social Service Commission affirmed that "as Christian citizens we will always be law-abiding citizens," while the Georgia Baptist Convention unanimously adopted the report of its Social Service Commission that urged Baptists "to handle this issue as good citizens, calm and dispassionate." In neighboring Alabama, the Social Service Commission reprinted the SBC's resolution on *Brown* and expressed the hope that the state would face the expected crisis "calmly and judiciously, working it out in the spirit of Christ to the best interests of both races."[15]

Despite public statements by most conventions for lawful obedience to *Brown,* some ministers criticized the ruling and questioned its constitutionality, but they, like their conventions, still urged calm. John H. Buchanan, pastor of Birmingham, Alabama's Southside Baptist Church, declared that

"It [*Brown*] complicates and damages relations between races in the South. The present court from its cloistered chambers has overlooked the reality of the situation. Our people must exercise sober and sound judgment in facing this crisis."[16]

Some pastors called for obedience to *Brown* as the law. Paul Caudill, pastor of Memphis's First Baptist Church, cautioned that "As followers of Jesus Christ, we have no alternative but to abide by the laws of our land and to co-operate faithfully in every undertaking in behalf of the welfare of all the peoples of our land irrespective of race or station." More boldly, some ministers praised the Court's ruling and as a consequence, they risked losing their pulpits. Segregationists in Chatham, Virginia's Shockoe Baptist Church forced Henry V. Langford to resign his pastorate after he defended the justice and constitutionality of *Brown* in a letter to the local newspaper. Understandably, given the insecurity of their posts, most clergymen did not address the ruling in their sermons.[17]

Aware of popular southern white hostility to *Brown,* only a few lay Baptists praised it publicly. Lacy Williams of Raleigh wrote to the *Biblical Recorder:* "It should fill Southern Baptists, as well as all citizens, with a sense of pride that our Supreme Court has fearlessly and unanimously declared that under our Constitution all children, of whatever race, stand alike, humbly but unawed before the majesty of the law." Many lay Baptists who wrote to the denominational press on the issue attacked *Brown* as unconstitutional. H. L. Baptist of Newport News wrote to the *Religious Herald* that "the decision of the Court is an invasion of states' rights and is a political decision more than an attempt to interpret the Constitution."[18]

On May 31, 1955, the Supreme Court issued a second *Brown* ruling that called for "a prompt and reasonable start toward full compliance" with desegregation. John Jeter Hurt Jr. called for "calm and deliberate thinking" and warned against defiance. He wrote that "This is no time for the political demagogues and the hate organizations to monopolize the headlines with their defiance of the Supreme Court's order. . . . The Supreme Court is the law of the land. Knock it down and this nation which gave birth to democracy becomes the haven for a dictator." Southern white resistance to school desegregation mounted as African Americans petitioned local school boards to register their children at white schools. The Citizens' Councils, organized to maintain white solidarity against desegregation and intimidate African Americans from exercising their rights, proliferated across much of the South, particularly in black-belt areas. Segregationist resistance drove Baptist state conventions in Arkansas and Virginia into silence about race relations, induced more cautious statements from others, and led the Alabama Baptist State Convention to express hostility toward the Supreme Court. Nevertheless, no convention endorsed defiance of court-ordered desegregation and many counseled Baptists to remain calm and orderly.[19]

Reflecting the hardening of segregationist resistance, the Georgia Baptist Convention adopted a Social Service Commission report in 1955 that warned against "hurried and enforced adjustments" away from "the widely accepted principle of segregation." Nevertheless, it appealed for adherence to the law. The report concluded: "We appeal to all responsible leaders . . . to speak in a calm and deliberate manner, based on the inner conviction that the upholding of law and order is every citizen['s] duty." The Alabama Baptist State Convention adopted a Christian Life (formerly Social Service) Commission recommendation that urged Alabamians "to be sober and cautious" in race relations. It also implored them to bypass "various extreme partisan organizations," which the body of the commission's report indicated referred to the Citizens' Councils.[20]

Petitions by African Americans for school desegregation in seven Alabama counties, the beginning of the year-long Montgomery Bus Boycott in December 1955, and the attempt of Autherine Lucy to desegregate the University of Alabama at Tuscaloosa in February 1956, led many white Alabamians to rally behind resistance. Citizens' Council membership swelled substantially in the wake of the university crisis. Six Citizens' Council members attacked African-American singer Nat King Cole in April 1956 during a performance in Birmingham.[21]

Reflecting the new mood of defiance, Alabama's Southern Baptists became openly hostile to desegregation. A month after a white mob had prevented Lucy from entering the University of Alabama, Leon Macon warned that "Traditions and customs cannot be thrown in reverse overnight." He argued that the South had been solving its racial problems until the NAACP interfered, and he claimed that "the Communists are aggravating the problem. . . . " Meeting in Montgomery, as the bus boycott continued, the Alabama Baptist State Convention defended segregation as a practical necessity in the report of its Christian Life Commission, and it condemned Autherine Lucy as "the seeming tool for" the NAACP. However, it also denounced the Citizens' Councils for the attack on Cole, and the Ku Klux Klan.[22]

By contrast, violent local resistance to attempted desegregation of education led the Baptist General Convention of Texas to issue a strong law and order statement in the same year. After Governor Allan Shivers had used Texas Rangers to prevent federal court-ordered desegregation at Texarkana Junior College and Mansfield High School, when white mobs surrounded the two institutions, the Baptist General Convention of Texas unanimously approved a recommendation from its Christian Life Commission that severely criticized resistance to the courts. It read: "[W]e recommend that our people consistently refuse to take part in lawlessness, mob rule, and the resistance of constituted authority and that they commit themselves unreservedly in this racial crisis to the Christian attitude of nonviolence and to an insistence that the due processes of law be observed for all citizens."[23]

Unlike Shivers, who defended Jim Crow, Governor Frank G. Clement of Tennessee restored order in Clinton, Anderson County, when a segregationist mob appeared, and he allowed the desegregation of Clinton High School to continue. Clement sent the National Guard to the town in September 1956 after hostile whites, inspired by visiting segregationist agitator John Kasper, attacked adult blacks and intimidated twelve African-American students who had desegregated the school. The day after the Guard arrived, the Reverend Paul Turner devoted part of his sermon to the need for Christian citizens to support law and order. As pastor of the 1300-member First Baptist Church for eight years in a town that had a population of only 3,700, Turner wielded considerable influence. With his support, but scarcely dependent upon it, the National Guard restored order.[24]

After the Guard left, Kasper and his sympathizers resumed their activities. Harassment of African-American students continued, and by November each of them had withdrawn from school. Alarmed both by their withdrawal and the failure of established community leaders to speak out in their defense, Turner offered to lead the black children back to school. He later explained: "As long as the law is the law and Negro children wish to go to school—as they have a moral right to do—then they should be able to go unheckled and unhindered." Turner escorted the children to school on December 4, accompanied by a deacon from his church and a Methodist layman. Returning to his church alone, he was beaten by a gang of whites. That same day, the town held elections for mayor and alderman. News of Turner's beating swept the community and gave its leaderless, moderate majority a cause to rally around. In a high turnout, Clinton's voters defeated Citizens' Council candidates by a five-to-one majority. The militants would probably have lost anyway, but Turner's beating ensured that their defeat was overwhelming.[25]

After the crisis, Turner claimed that his congregation had been "98 per cent in total sympathy with what I did." The Clinton Baptist Association Pastors' Conference commended him for his actions. It also praised "the school authorities, city officials, [and] the majority of the citizens of Clinton, who have stood for law and order and against mob violence. . . . " Although Turner received support from his church and other pastors in East

Tennessee, his convention preferred to ignore the desegregation problem. In its original report to the Tennessee Baptist Convention, the Social Service Committee, responding to "recent events in Anderson County," endorsed the *Brown* decision as the law of the land. However, segregationist pressure forced the committee to withdraw its endorsement.[26]

Richard N. Owen, editor of the *Baptist and Reflector,* also ignored the Clinton crisis, but he later welcomed the jury trial conviction in Knoxville of John Kasper and six others for violating a permanent injunction, issued by Federal District Judge Robert Taylor, against interference with school desegregation in Clinton. He explained that "The trial issue was not segregation versus desegregation. The issue was the authority of the court and the upholding of law and order in this land."[27]

As in Tennessee, segregationist sentiment forced the Georgia Baptist Convention to retreat from making an endorsement of *Brown*. Its Social Service Commission recommended in 1956 that the convention recognize the Court's ruling as lawful and "in harmony with the Constitution." After an hour-long debate the messengers voted, by a margin of three to one, to reject the recommendations, but they retained a section of the commission's report that warned against violence and lawlessness.[28]

The Florida Baptist Convention also appealed for order. It adopted a Social Service and Temperance Committee report in 1956 that called on Baptists to obey civil law. The committee warned that "Our careless discussions that are reflected in ugly words, un-Christlike actions, heated arguments, and disrespect for law and those in authority, are posing this hour not the problem of integration, but disintegration." The report admonished Baptists to reject violence and mob resistance to desegregation. It declared that "Baptist people . . . who believe in the New Testament as their guide, can never be recruited, nor would we make fit candidates for any mob organization such as the Ku Klux Klan, Night Riders, or Vigilantes, or any others whose goal is to defeat and set aside the laws of our land, regardless of what our own personal interpretation of that law may be."[29]

Segregationist pressure inhibited all the Baptist state conventions from discussing the merits of integration. The Baptist State Convention of North Carolina, which had recognized the validity of the *Brown* decision in 1954, retreated two years later to the less controversial ground of deploring "the revived activity of the Ku Klux Klan" in the state.[30]

As segregationist resistance hardened within and outside the church, the SBC's Christian Life Commission felt impelled to include race relations in its annual report in 1957. However, the commission presented its report as information, rather than for adoption, to placate segregationists, who believed, erroneously, that it endorsed integration. The report argued that neither "the laws of segregation or non-segregation" could make peace and appealed for understanding between the races. It protested against "the violence in all its ugly forms that is being used against the Negro people in the current segregation issue" and called on "the law enforcement agencies of local, state, and national governments" to protect African Americans. The report also expressed opposition to "vocal minorities who are able to arouse sufficient opposition to force the resignation of pastors and to incite retaliation against peaceful citizens who speak or act according to their convictions on racial justice and interracial goodwill."[31]

A few months after the convention met, Governor Orval Faubus defied court-ordered desegregation in Little Rock, Arkansas. Although the Arkansas Baptist State Convention refused to comment on the controversy, Erwin L. McDonald, editor of the *Arkansas Baptist,* and some of the city's Southern Baptist pastors championed law and order. Only one Southern Baptist minister, the Reverend Wesley Pruden, pastor of Broadmoor Baptist Church and president of the Capital Citizens' Council, publicly opposed desegregation.[32]

On September 1, the Sunday before school desegregation was due to begin, Dale Cowling, pastor of the 2,585-member Second Baptist Church, delivered a sermon in which he argued that school desegregation was the law and "Christians ought to be obedient to civil authority and to abide by the laws of the land." Cowling concluded by appealing for a "peaceful solution of the problem." The following day, Governor Orval Faubus called out the National Guard to prevent desegregation of Central High School.[33]

In response, sixteen Protestant Little Rock ministers, including Cowling, W. O. Vaught Jr., of Immanuel Baptist Church, and Harold Hicks, of Pulaski Heights Baptist Church, released a statement that condemned Faubus's action for defying national law and undermining respect "for proper constitutional authority." Erwin McDonald refused to take a "stand either for or against integration," but he insisted that "we want to be counted with those who stand for law and order, for clear, cool thinking, and for lives motivated by the love of Christ."[34]

President Dwight D. Eisenhower federalized the National Guard and sent federal troops to insure desegregation. Brooks Hays, president of the SBC and congressman for the Fifth District, which included Little Rock, told the Little Rock Lions Club: "The enforcement of law is not limited to popular laws. Constitutional forms are maintained only when people are completely dedicated to the ideal of law and order without reference to its impingement upon some cherished practices of their own. . . . [L]et me emphasize that the issue is not integration or Federal authority in school matters, but rather how to deal with lawlessness." Hays and forty leading clergymen sponsored a day of prayer on October 12, Columbus Day. Eighty-four Little Rock churches and synagogues, including three of the city's four largest Southern Baptist churches, held services that called for law and order. Troops remained with the African-American children at desegregated Central High School for the rest of the academic year, but Faubus closed the capital's schools between 1958 and 1959. Throughout the crisis, the Arkansas Baptist State Convention did not address the divisive school issue.[35]

Only Alabama among the Baptist state conventions went on record against the federal government's actions in Little Rock. Leon Macon recoiled at the sight of "free people . . . faced with bayonets, and some even [allegedly] having their blood drawn by these weapons." Although he "thoroughly" supported "the principle of law and order," Macon claimed that the crisis demonstrated a growing centralization of power in Washington, which, if left unchecked, might create "a totalitarian system." His convention's Christian Life Commission also warned against the increasing power of the federal government. The commission declared: "Never in the history of the nation has a federal government by judicial decree attempted to enforce a law against the overwhelming and persistent opposition of the majority of the citizens of an area, as is being presently the case in the South. Then to add agony to pain the thoughtful Christian realizes that what is being called 'the law of the land' has never been passed by the law-making agency of the government; namely the Congress."[36]

However, no Baptist state convention endorsed resistance to desegregation. The Baptist General Association of Virginia did not comment when Governor J. Lindsay Almond temporarily closed some of the state's public schools in an unsuccessful attempt to prevent desegregation in 1958. While some state conventions and editors kept silent when their states experienced desegregation, most called for obedience to the law and condemned segregationist resistance.[37]

When the federal court-ordered desegregation of the University of Georgia in January 1961 led to a campus riot, John Jeter Hurt Jr. condemned the rioters as "anarchists" and appealed for a "return to law and order." As Atlanta officials prepared for school desegregation in the fall, the Atlanta Baptist Pastors Conference adopted a resolution in July that called on Georgians "to observe the law" and "orderly procedure" when the schools reopened. Hurt prayed that Atlanta "will be a model in law observance and Christian conduct." The schools desegregated without incident.[38]

After a riot, in which two people died, accompanied the desegregation of the University of Mississippi in 1962, Joe T. Odle, editor of the *Baptist*

Record, wrote that Mississippians "utterly disapprove of such acts." Odle also claimed that "The people want law and order maintained, and do not want mob violence or rule to be allowed anywhere in the state."[39]

The violence at the University of Mississippi led South Carolina's public officials to focus on peaceful compliance when a federal court ordered secular Clemson College to admit African American Harvey Gantt in January 1963. Horace G. Hammett, general secretary-treasurer of the Baptist State Convention, joined the leaders of South Carolina's other major denominations in issuing a plea that the state "not . . . be disgraced by violence." The convention's Christian Life and Public Affairs Committee issued a related statement that urged citizens to avoid violence, preserve order, and respect "constituted governmental authority."[40]

With desegregation imminent, S. H. Jones, editor of South Carolina's *Baptist Courier,* broke his usual silence about race. Jones wrote: "[T]here is not full agreement, even among Christians, on the question of race relations; however, there should certainly be agreement that law and order should prevail always. Also, Christians are motivated by good will toward all people and can never afford to approve violence." In Columbia, eighteen Southern Baptist pastors and denominational workers joined over one hundred white ministers in calling for "obedience . . . justice, and brotherhood." The college desegregated peacefully.[41]

Apart from calling for obedience to court orders, the SBC and most Baptist state conventions and editors condemned incidents of segregationist violence in the late 1950s and early 1960s. The SBC adopted a resolution in 1961 that rejected "mob violence" in race relations, a reference to the beating of the Freedom Riders by whites in Alabama as they tested desegregation of interstate bus terminals. Leon Macon also denounced the mob for undermining "law and order," and his convention adopted a recommendation in 1962 that rejected "violence or demonstrations of prejudice or hatred against anyone."[42]

After four African-American children died in the bombing of Birmingham's Sixteenth Street Baptist Church in September 1963, Leon Macon deplored racial violence. "Although we have never endorsed integration," he wrote, "we certainly do endorse law and order, for when these break down we have anarchy." Prompted by the incident, the SBC's Executive Committee adopted a resolution that expressed "deepest sympathy to those families who have lost loved ones and to others who have been victimized by such racial strife." The resolution made no reference to Birmingham. It represented a compromise between an original draft offered by Charles A. Trentham of Knoxville, Tennessee's First Baptist Church that specifically mentioned the Birmingham church bombing and an alternative resolution from Leon Macon, who objected to "singling out Birmingham when it [violence] is a problem all across the country."[43]

Racial violence especially plagued Mississippi. Joe Odle condemned the assassination of Medgar Evers, field secretary of the Mississippi chapter of the NAACP, in 1963. Over forty African-American churches were burnt by whites in the state during the summer of 1964 in the mostly unfounded belief that they were acting as meeting places for a black voter registration drive organized by the Council of Federated Organizations (COFO). During COFO's Freedom Summer project, civil rights workers suffered eighty beatings, thirty-five shooting incidents, thirty house bombings and six murders. In August 1964, Odle condemned the church burnings as "atrocious" and applauded local white efforts to fund their rebuilding. He wrote: "Christians of both races in Mississippi want these problems of racial conflict solved peaceably and justly. They know that lawless acts of any nature . . . murder, rioting, bombing, arson, threats, mob action, or any other . . . will not solve Mississippi's problems."[44]

Odle's editorial had a profound influence on the Mississippi Baptist Convention. Odle, Chester L. Quarles, the convention's executive secretary-treasurer, and William P. Davis, director of its Department of Negro Work, persuaded the convention's executive committee to solicit donations to rebuild the burned churches. The effort widened into an interracial cooperative enterprise with all of Mississippi's denominations, under the title the Committee of Concern. Chaired by Davis, the committee raised $128,766.67 and rebuilt forty-two churches and missions that had been destroyed between 1964 and 1965.[45]

The seventy-seven member Mississippi Baptist Convention Board passed a resolution in October 1964 that deplored "all acts of violence and all expressions of anarchy" and commended "the work of the Committee of Concern." A month later, the convention's messengers adopted a resolution that condemned "every act of violence and lawlessness." It also insisted that Mississippians had to be left to solve the state's racial problems and that their final solution could not be achieved "through federal intervention, the actions of outside groups coming into the state, or by radical or lawless action within the state." That the resolution did not discuss the grievances held by African Americans and dismissed federal intervention on their behalf demonstrated that the convention was concerned more with peace and order than with justice.[46]

Most Southern Baptists, like the Mississippi Baptist Convention, objected to the tactics of the civil rights movement. They regarded demonstrations and other forms of direct action as disorderly and, often, illegal. The SBC's resolution concerning the Freedom Rides in 1961 rejected "unwarranted provocation" by civil rights activists. Predictably, committed segregationists strongly condemned the protestors. Leon Macon wrote: "Outsiders announced beforehand that they were coming to Alabama to violate the state laws. . . . The willful breaking of the law will tear down respect for the state and when law and order are done away with the result is anarchy and all peoples suffer." James F. Cole, editor of the *Baptist Message,* called the protestors irresponsible. "The freedom riders . . . ," wrote Cole, "divorce freedom from responsibility and . . . do not attach to every right a duty and to every privilege an obligation." Opinion polls indicated that a nationwide white majority also opposed direct action. A survey conducted in 1961 found that 64 percent of Americans opposed the Freedom Rides and only 24 percent approved of them. Two years later, another survey discovered that 78 percent of southern whites and 59 percent of northern whites opposed the actions of the civil rights movement.[47]

Only the Baptist State Convention of North Carolina and the Baptist General Convention of Texas recognized the crucial role played in desegregation by direct action protests. Even Baptists who sympathized with the aims of the movement usually rejected its methods. A report by the Christian Life Committee of the Baptist General Association of Virginia observed that "Group or individual demonstrations that are in violation of the public law and are contrary to a Christlike approach to human relations, regardless of the virtue espoused in the ultimate objective of such efforts, should not be condoned." Erwin McDonald personally opposed segregation, but he warned that "no resorting to force, threats, or any other illegal means will make any constructive contribution, whether this be applied for or against integration." J. Marse Grant, editor of the *Biblical Recorder,* defended the right to protest within the limits of the law, but he argued that more could be achieved by relying on "governmental leadership in this state." Richard Owen objected to demonstrations as attempts "to try to settle problems in the streets" rather than "in deliberative assemblies by duly elected representatives."[48]

Although he respected Martin Luther King Jr. as "a qualified Negro speaker," E. S. James, the integrationist editor of the *Baptist Standard,* objected in the early 1960s to King's "pressure tactics" of direct action which he maintained had not "helped the cause of colored people very much." He insisted that African Americans did not need to protest since desegregation would be accomplished through the courts, yet he continued to criticize the NAACP which instigated many of the lawsuits that made the courts order desegregation. James believed that desegregation should be achieved by compliance with the law, rather than by force or pressure and, if this failed, by court order. He did not understand that black protests were necessary to make the courts enforce existing nondiscriminatory legislation in some cases and to force the federal government to overturn discriminatory laws so that the courts could act in other cases.[49]

The desire for voluntarism, as well as respect for property rights, united most Southern Baptists, whatever their views about Jim Crow, in opposition to the civil rights bill that proposed to outlaw segregation in public accommodations. In early 1964, one opinion poll found that "72 percent of the South" opposed the proposed legislation. George E. Bagley, executive secretary of the Alabama Baptist State Convention, and Leon Macon, serving as convention president, issued a joint statement that attacked the bill. They declared that "Our President is obviously trying to coerce the people in the nation into backing his move to enlarge power to the point where our freedom to choose our associates and neighbors will be placed in the hands of bureaucrats."[50]

In editorials, Macon attacked the bill as a step towards "an all-powerful centralized Federal government" that would "out-socialize the Socialists" and "make the Attorney General a dictator in large segments of our lives." Some integrationist Baptist editors also assailed the proposed legislation as impinging on the rights of businessmen. Erwin McDonald explained: "As I see it, there is a distinction to be drawn between desegregation by law of *public* institutions and facilities and that which is private. . . . I do not agree that the government should try to tell private businesses who their employees or customers must be." Initially skeptical about the proposed legislation, by 1964 both McDonald and Richard Owen recognized its necessity. "We must translate Christian concern for the rights of others, . . . " wrote Owen, "into laws that will uphold those rights within a framework of freedom for all."[51]

After the Civil Rights Act became law in July 1964, Baptist state convention editors called for obedience. Leon Macon argued that Baptists should obey the new act because it was "the law of the land and God's Word instructs us to be obedient to the powers which be." Although he believed that parts of the act were unconstitutional, Macon told his readers "we are not to take the law into our own hands but can take recourse through the courts." Both W. G. Stracener, editor of the *Florida Baptist Witness,* and Reuben Alley had criticized the bill before its passage as a threat to individual freedom, but, once it was enacted, they not only called for obedience to the law but argued, as Alley wrote, that "most citizens will agree that the time had arrived when Congress faced the necessity of enacting legislation to cover many of the conditions set forth in the Civil Rights Bill. . . . " Erwin McDonald joined the Arkansas State Advisory Committee of the U.S. Commission on Civil Rights.[52]

Despite the call of most Baptist editors for obedience to the Civil Rights Act, only the North Carolina and Virginia conventions endorsed it in 1964. The SBC, by a narrow margin, refused to endorse civil rights legislation when it met a few weeks before the passage of the civil rights bill. After the bill's passage, Wayne Dehoney, the SBC's president, told his Tennessee congregation that "As citizens, let every one of us give voluntary, peaceful, orderly obedience to law and to the orders of public officials."[53]

The SBC approved a resolution in 1965 that called for "peaceful compliance with laws assuring equal rights for all." Its annual meeting occurred two months after African Americans had been beaten as they demonstrated in Selma, Alabama, for their voting rights, and President Lyndon B. Johnson had responded by proposing a voting rights act. The Selma marches were marred by segregationist and state trooper violence, which some Southern Baptists blamed on provocation by the civil rights movement. Consequently, the resolution included an amendment that deplored unlawful demonstrations and violence. The amendment only passed by a close margin, 1,667 to 1,487, which indicated Southern Baptist division concerning the causes of the violence at Selma.[54]

Leon Macon argued that if everyone followed Martin Luther King Jr.'s example at Selma and ignored laws that did not agree with their conscience then "law and order would be completely broken down and we would have bedlam." Macon also claimed that "there are strong evidences that Communism is either sitting in the driver's seat or next to the driver." He condemned violence by segregationist white hoodlums, but he also excused a vicious attack by state troopers on the demonstrators as they attempted to cross the Edmund Pettus Bridge. The protestors, Macon claimed, were law breakers who should not "expect the law enforcement officers not to use force when they are disobeyed as officers." Editors of Baptist state convention newspapers typically called on African Americans to refrain from direct action, but surprisingly, given that a 1965 opinion poll found that 51 percent of the nation's white population believed that communism had played a significant (and 27 percent a minor) role in civil rights demonstrations, they did not, like Macon, redbait the movement.[55]

Predictably, the editors condemned the summer riots that broke out between 1964 and 1968, mainly in the urban African-American ghettoes of the North and West. Leon Macon blamed the riots on the federal government, which, he claimed, had generated unrealistic expectations among African Americans, since it had "gone entirely too fast in granting what it thinks are rights due minority groups. . . . " W. G. Stracener attacked the riots as "a wild and flagrant disregard for the rule of law and an open rebellion against the authority of government." With scarcely a consideration for unemployment and other social ills, he argued that they were largely an outgrowth of "the effects of the preaching of 'civil disobedience' by numerous Negro leaders and no small number of well-intentioned but misguided white ministers" and the tendency of recent Supreme Court decisions to protect "the 'legal rights' of the law violator. . . . " Although the Baptist General Convention of Texas recognized that the riots, which it regretted, grew out of unjust social conditions, many conventions and editors simply condemned them as lawless and violent.[56]

Some progressive Baptists, hitherto unenthusiastic or critical of the civil rights movement's direct action tactics, belatedly and cautiously accepted their necessity in the wake of the riots, which made nonviolent protest appear comparatively moderate and restrained. In 1965, E. S. James wrote: "Had it not been for them [religious leaders of the civil rights movement] the docile marches in the South might have become violent race riots like those in other areas. Some of the sit-ins, lie-ins, and other 'ins' are rather absurd and disgusting. Frequently they hurt the cause they seek to promote. We need to remember, however, that 20 million human beings had to find some method of protesting the second class status imposed on them by the white people."[57]

The assassination of Martin Luther King Jr. in April 1968 and the riots which followed across the nation also led Erwin McDonald and Reuben Alley to reassess the civil rights movement. McDonald praised King warmly "as one of the great men of his day" and defended his record of civil disobedience, which he had criticized in King's lifetime. He condemned riots but balanced his condemnation of them with a concern to address and rectify their causes. McDonald declared that "We cannot heal the sickness of our society by rioting and pillaging and burning and killing. . . . [L]et us use our influence and our means positively to break down the walls of inhuman discrimination and to help people to come into their full rights and privileges as fellow human beings." Reuben Alley, once a critic of demands for immediate integration, praised King's "Christian philosophy" of nonviolence. He observed that "Violence . . . may easily have found expression by many more than the small minority had it not been for the restraining influence of the doctrine of nonviolence which followers of Martin Luther King proclaimed continuously during the period of crisis."[58]

Whatever their views about King, Baptist state convention editors condemned his murder, but many Baptists remained critical of his methods. John E. Roberts, editor of the *Baptist Courier,* claimed that "Violence often dogged his [King's] steps and at times he did little or nothing to discourage it." Pastors and lay people often shared Roberts's view. Vaughn W. Denton, pastor of Crossett, Arkansas's Magnolia Baptist Church, claimed that "He

[Dr. King] talked peace with his lips, but his actions resulted in violence. He openly defied the law and caused his followers to do likewise." Militant segregationists condemned King as a communist. Mrs. Walter C. Dean of Birmingham, Alabama, complained that "It's bad enough that leaders of our nation have bowed down to this Communistic leader, resulting in complete chaos and disregard for law as a result of his 'nonviolent'—extremely violent movement, but to have our Southern Baptist colleges and leaders promote and allow it to infiltrate our literature is unforgiveable [*sic*]."[59]

A minority of Southern Baptists defended King, although some shared the critics' reservations about his strategy. Carel G. Norman, pastor of Mount Ida, Arkansas's First Baptist Church, explained: "I did not always agree with Dr. Kings [*sic*] methods nor his results but I have for a long time been sympathetic with his aims. . . . " A few Baptists praised King's approach. "If it had not been for the leadership of Dr. King," wrote Louisianan A. B. Short Jr. to the *Baptist Record,* "we white people would still have the Negro sitting in the back of the public buses." Influenced by King's death, the SBC's annual meeting overwhelmingly adopted a statement in June 1968 that supported equal human and legal rights, and acknowledged "our share of responsibility for creating in our land conditions in which justice, order, and righteousness can prevail."[60]

Concerned by the slow pace of justice in educational provision, Supreme Court rulings in 1969 and 1971 ordered the South to complete segregation and allowed the use of busing to achieve it. Although many Baptists opposed desegregation and some withdrew their children into private schools, most did not countenance illegal resistance. Instead, many of its opponents advocated minimal compliance with desegregation and no more. R. M. Sullivan, a Baptist layman from Hattiesburg, wrote to the *Baptist Record* that "school administrators and teachers . . . should follow the letter of the Court's Order and this only." The Baptist General Association of Virginia criticized busing as disruptive. Many Baptist editors agreed, and some, particularly in the Deep South, also argued that courts were unfairly targeting the South. Nevertheless, the editors counselled obedience. John Jeter Hurt Jr., E. S. James's successor as editor of the *Baptist Standard,* wrote: "We share in a determination to do all possible to maintain the concept of neighborhood schools. We share the anxiety of parents about busing into strange and remote areas. . . . The concerned Christian will not scream at the inequity of court decisions, even if he believes them wrong. Instead, he will carry the appeal to the highest court and, if still dissatisfied, work for the political leverage which changes the law. Always to be deplored are those blind and selfish who seek to destroy by enlisting mobs for violence."[61]

Respect for the law influenced some of busing's most determined opponents. In April 1969, federal district judge James B. McMillan ordered the busing of students to desegregate Charlotte-Mecklenburg schools in North Carolina. When busing began in September 1970, white parents organized a school boycott and 3,500 white children entered private schools. Charlotte's Southern Baptists divided over the issue. Gene Owens, pastor of Charlotte's Myers Park Baptist Church, publicly supported busing, but his congregation included prominent anti-busing leader Tom Harris. In its April 1971 ruling, *Swann v. Charlotte-Mecklenburg Board of Education,* the Supreme Court upheld the use of busing to integrate the district's public schools. Harris responded: "We've got to stand where the law is, not just where we would like it to be." Although many Baptists opposed busing and school desegregation, most did not resort to illegal means to prevent them.[62]

Baptist leaders and editors consistently urged their coreligionists to reject force and violence in response to desegregation mandated by federal authorities. Fear of disorder and social chaos helped to motivate all but a progressive minority of integrationists to counsel obedience to court-ordered desegregation as an issue of law, rather than justice. While some Baptists joined the Ku Klux Klan, the Citizens' Councils and mobs that sought to prevent school and university integration, they did so without the support of and often in direct opposition to the pronouncements of their conventions. Baptists often regarded segregationist mobs and nonviolent civil rights protestors as equally disrespectful of law and social peace, and they condemned them in equal measure. They insisted that African Americans should pursue their grievances through the courts, without recognizing the role of direct action in creating a climate for legislative change. Although some Baptists sought to evade school desegregation, their leaders counselled obedience to the courts, and they cautioned that protests should be directed through the legal system, instead of being taken to the streets.

8

"The Great Commission": Evangelism at Home and Abroad

T HE "GREAT COMMISSION," the duty to evangelize all peoples outlined in *Matthew* 28:19–20, first led to the creation of Southern Baptist associations and conventions in the nineteenth century and lies at the heart of Baptist life. Until the civil rights era, most Baptists saw no conflict between their desire to evangelize nonwhite peoples and their support for racial segregation in the South. Southern white resistance to desegregation and the civil rights movement drew national and international attention to the region's racism and undermined the missionary endeavor. As the movement and the federal government made inroads against legal segregation in the 1950s, some denominational leaders sought to steer the SBC away from addressing racial issues for fear of alienating the segregationist majority and thereby leading to a reduction in the gift-giving necessary to fund missionary activity. However, increasing pressure from missionaries, who protested that the South's racial crisis hampered their efforts, and from concerned leaders in the convention's missions agencies encouraged Baptist conventions and editors to address race relations in the late 1950s and early 1960s. As they became aware of the growing incompatibility between support for Jim Crow laws and the evangelistic imperative, increasing numbers of Baptists either repudiated segregation or, at least, acquiesced in its elimination.

Baptists believed that the born again were witnesses who had a duty to serve as missionaries for Christ in their everyday lives. Churches, associations, state conventions and the SBC all had as their purpose the carrying out of missionary responsibilities. Article II of the SBC's Constitution stated that "It shall be the design of the Convention to promote foreign and home missions. . . . " The chief responsibility for fulfilling this goal lay with the HMB and the FMB, which appointed the SBC's missionaries, supported with funds from the denomination's Cooperative Program and contributions from the WMU. The Brotherhood Commission, focused on men and boys, promoted missions in Baptist churches.[1]

In 1943, the HMB and the FMB finally retired the debts that had undermined their activities and cut their missionary numbers since the 1920s.
As World War Two ended, both boards sought to reinvigorate their programs and win new converts in the postwar world. In June 1945, the FMB
adopted a program to increase its missionaries from 550 to 750. M. Theron
Rankin, the board's executive secretary, warned Baptists that "More and
more, the sincerity of our missionary interests in the colored peoples in
their native lands will be judged by our actions toward the people of those
lands who live among us." The issue grew in importance when in 1948 the
board adopted, and the SBC supported, a Program of Advance that targeted new missions fields and sought the appointment of 1,750 missionaries. On the eve of the *Brown* school desegregation ruling, the expansion
program had already secured 908 missionaries in thirty-three countries,
many of them in Asia and Africa.[2]

The HMB had over six hundred missionaries in 1945, whose work included evangelistic outreach to African Americans, Native Americans and
Appalachian whites, and new programs in the West. The board increased
its budget for racial work to $109,000 in 1945, and by 1947 Southern Bap-
tists, at the SBC and state convention levels, spent $206,000 a year on such
work, which focused on promoting black ministerial training.[3]

Aware of the need to promote improved race relations if it were to further black evangelism, the HMB published a series of study books on race
for all age groups in 1946. T. B. Maston wrote *"Of One": A Study of Christian
Principles and Race Relations* for adults and young people. Maston drew
heavily on biblical teachings and on the reports and recommendations of
the SBC's Social Service Commission. He asked Baptists to support economic opportunity, equal pay and voting rights for African Americans. Maston dismissed southern white fears about miscegenation, and asked "Can
we not insist on social justice without social equality?" The book sold nearly
18,000 copies between 1946 and 1950. According to Foy Valentine, it "had
a vastly greater effect on Southern Baptists than any Convention resolution
on race has ever had."[4]

Despite the book's success, the HMB generally avoided civil rights issues
in the late 1940s, after southern whites reacted with hostility to President
Harry S. Truman's civil rights program. Articles on race in *Home Missions*,
the board's monthly magazine, focused on missions programs and black
ministerial education. The magazine adopted a paternalistic attitude towards African Americans. In May 1949, it contended that "White Baptists
of the South are the Negro's friends. Our best way to help the Negro is to
let him know we are his friends, and to make it possible for him to help
himself through his own channels." Despite the HMB's earlier efforts to

promote greater understanding between the races through its literature, by 1950 its only pamphlet concerning race focused on black ministerial training and had as its cover a picture of a horse-drawn carriage, with an African-American driver, carrying a wealthy white couple.[5]

Through the Annie Armstrong Offering, the WMU provided at least half of the funds used by the HMB in its work with African Americans. In the 1940s and early 1950s, the WMU addressed race relations in its publications more frequently and more progressively than the SBC's missions boards. Its evangelistic work prompted the WMU to urge its members to treat African Americans with respect and courtesy, although reassuring them that they need not fear social equality as a result. But increasingly concerned for the maintenance of segregation, in May 1946 *Royal Service,* the WMU's magazine for adults, described demands for its abolition as "frightening, difficult, dangerous, revolutionary, and unreasonable."[6]

However, WMU publications began to attack segregation in the late 1940s. The February 1948 edition of *World Comrades,* a magazine for boys and girls, included a story in which two pre-school girls, one black and one white, had become friends while travelling with their mothers on a train journey. They had to separate into Jim Crow carriages when the train reached the South. The African-American mother explained to her perplexed child that the system of segregation required them to move into an inferior carriage. The article illustrated in a practical manner the demeaning and harmful effects of segregation.[7]

Royal Service published articles in March 1949 that attacked the biblical defense of segregation, dismissed fears about the consequences of social equality and praised the autobiography of NAACP leader Walter White. Its February 1950 issue also focused on race. WMU publications for younger readers continued their criticism of southern racial practices. In 1950, Hermione Dannelly Jackson wrote in *The Window of Y.W.A.,* a magazine for young women: "We in the South have made the Negro what he is because of our segregation and treatment of him. Then we point to the product of our system and use it to justify the way we treat him. It is a vicious circle that the white man could not beat under the same circumstances. We must learn to live beside the Negro rather than by pushing him down to stand on top of him." The WMU took practical steps against segregation by integrating the Young Men's Mission Conference it sponsored at Ridgecrest, North Carolina, in 1949 and its training school at Louisville, Kentucky, three years later.[8]

At the state level, WMUs affiliated with Baptist conventions contributed to their budgets for missions work among African Americans. The Baptist General Convention of Texas created a Department of Interracial Cooperation in 1944, concerned with missions and improving race relations. The convention increased the department's budget from an initial $15,000 to $75,000 by 1950 and its workforce rose from 19 to 93. In 1943, the Baptist General Association of Virginia had only one field worker for its evangelistic work with blacks, but by 1946 it had three.[9]

The state conventions feared increasing Catholic competition for African-American converts. The Texas and Virginia conventions also recognized that segregation in the SBC and the South undermined the Southern Baptist appeal among nonwhites at home and abroad. In 1953, Virginia's Inter-Racial Committee observed that blacks were being attracted to Catholic churches because "They are not drawing race boundary lines." A. C. Miller, director of the Department of Interracial Cooperation, explained how Southern Baptist racism affected missions work in Texas: "One of the great handicaps retarding the evangelization of the minority groups is that of our attitude toward them and their attitude toward us. Many of our people have never accepted the Christian attitude toward peoples of other nationalities and races. Until we can extend a Christian hand of sympathetic understanding across the barrier of racial prejudice and hate, we are not going to lift the minority groups in Texas toward God as we should."[10]

Baptist state conventions in the Deep South recognized the Catholic threat, but they also regarded increased missions programs among African Americans as a means to deflect their attention and support away from the civil rights movement. When the Mississippi Baptist Convention Board increased its budget for "Negro Work" from $2,400 in 1944 to $4,000 in 1945, A. L. Goodrich, editor of the *Baptist Record,* argued that this was the way "to create better race relations." The convention steadily increased its allocation for missions among blacks, which by 1949 reached $13,500.[11]

It also agreed in 1944 to help fund the black-run Mississippi Union Baptist Theological Seminary for the education of African-American ministers. The convention placed the renamed Mississippi Baptist Seminary under the control of a biracial board of trustees, with the stipulation that there should always be a white majority of one. Heavily dependent on Southern Baptists for financial support, Herbert L. Lang, the seminary's black founder and president, appealed to them by arguing that religion encouraged black acceptance of segregation. He told the Mississippi Baptist Convention in 1949 that "In every community where there is a trained Negro preacher, there is a better Negro citizenry." A year later, he warned the messengers: "The Roman Catholic Church is offering all types of bids for the Negro. All cults are bidding for the Negro. The Negro minister is by far and large the most influential person of his race. If he is untrained, he is easily deceived and misled. If he is trained, he can be the most powerful force for good in church and community. If the Negro can be led to act as a unit he can sway the balance of power. The Negro minister can do this leading. With a fair degree of training the Negro preacher is a mighty factor for God and country." Lang's appeal proved effective. The convention created a Negro Work Department in 1953, both to increase its support of the seminary and to coordinate its missions work.[12]

In neighboring Alabama, the state convention appointed a committee in 1945 to explore ways of aiding black Baptists, which became a standing Committee on Ways and Means of Helping Negroes. The convention voted in 1950 to establish a Department of Negro Work with a "white man" as full-time secretary. Alabama's Southern Baptists became increasingly alarmed about both the success of Catholic missions among African Americans and black support for civil rights, which they equated with Communism. In 1953, the Report on Ways and Means of Helping Negroes stated that "It is a well known fact that the Catholics are vigorously striving to reach the negro with money, education and social propaganda. In this they are succeeding for [sic] beyond the knowledge of many. For many years we have been saying, the negro is naturally Baptist in belief. Most of us also believed that communism was of no special significance and our lesson has been bitterly disappointing. . . . [W]e must inaugurate a far more vigorous program among the negroes or learn another bitter lesson." The Georgia Baptist Convention expanded its work among blacks for the same reasons. In 1950, it budgeted $4,000 to employ an executive secretary for the Negro Georgia Missionary and Educational Convention.[13]

Denominational editors in the Deep South shared the concerns of their conventions. S. H. Jones, editor of the *Baptist Courier,* warned that African Americans might "become victims of Romanism and every sort of cult and 'ism,'" unless Southern Baptists helped to educate black preachers so that they could guide blacks away from such dangers. Jones wrote: "Negroes are peculiar in some respects, but they are like all other people in that they respond to the right sort of leadership. Negro preachers have great influence, and they must be properly taught if that influence is to be good and constructive." Finley W. Tinnin, editor of the *Baptist Message,* also discerned a key role for black ministers. He declared that "Adequate facilities for educating young Negro preachers in the South would prove a blessing to white Baptists, and, indeed, to all Christian white people in the South. The South needs a great many young Negro ministers who understand the South and the relationship between whites and colored people in the South. Failure on our part to make possible thorough theological education to the young Negro preachers of the South will result in lowering the bars to enemies of the South to reach them and to inflame their minds and hearts against their white neighbors." Ironically, the concern of Southern Baptists to improve African-American ministerial education actually brought about the end of the whites-only policies of their seminaries.[14]

The HMB had helped to fund the American Baptist Theological Seminary for the training of black ministers since its opening in 1924. L. S. Sedberry, the seminary's executive secretary, reassured Southern Baptists in 1950 that "The American Seminary is doing the job that needs to be done—training Negro ministers, without raising the issue of race or stirring up the prejudices and animosities of either whites or Negroes." However, the school was poorly financed and provided an inferior education, despite significant increases in funding from the SBC in the second half of the 1940s.[15]

Southern Baptist seminaries did not admit blacks as regular students, although, in recognition of the inadequacy of black ministerial training, both Southern and Southwestern Baptist Theological seminaries had offered them tuition through extension classes since the war years. The abandonment of racial discrimination in the admissions policies of their seminaries offered Southern Baptists a practical method of advancing black ministerial education which, given the small numbers of African Americans qualified to take advantage of them, would lead to no more than token integration. Hence, three of the four Southern Baptist seminaries in the eleven southern states, Southern, Southwestern and New Orleans, agreed to operate nondiscriminatory admission policies commencing in 1951 and 1952. Dr. Gaines S. Dobbins, acting president of The Southern Baptist Theological Seminary, told the press that "This action was taken after long study and much careful thought. It came out of a deep sense of obligation to our fellow Negro Baptists in helping to provide more adequate advantages for the training of qualified Negro students for whom provision is lacking and who would therefore be compelled to go outside the bounds of the Convention for their training in a Baptist seminary."[16]

Despite the opening up of Southern Baptist seminaries to African Americans, many black Baptist clergymen remained excluded from seminary level education by poverty and lack of educational preparedness. The HMB conducted a survey of its mission work among African Americans in 1952. It urged that the work be expanded for three reasons: "(1) The soul-need of the Negro people, saved and unsaved. (2) The unprecedented pressure of the Federal Government to force a program on the South which we think can best be met by whole-hearted cooperation between the white and Negro citizenship, spearheaded by Christian leaders in both groups. (3)

The Catholic leadership in the United States has met a definite long-range program designed to lead the Negroes to the Catholic faith and principle." A year later, the board adopted the recommendation of its Survey Committee to set-up programs of black missions, in cooperation with Southern Baptist state conventions, in states which had large black populations. On January 1, 1954, the Louisiana Baptist Convention became the first state to establish a Department of Negro Work in cooperation with the HMB.[17]

While the HMB sought to deflect attention away from civil rights, the FMB continued to warn of the dangers that American racism posed for its missionaries. The race relations agencies of both the Virginia and Texas conventions published the anguished pleas of missions leaders in their reports. In 1953, the Inter-Racial Committee in Virginia quoted the claim of Cornell Goerner, a missions professor at The Southern Baptist Theological Seminary, that "In some parts of the world we cannot go much further in foreign mission work until we go much deeper in adjusting race relations back in our own home country."[18]

In one case, the missions theme had a direct bearing on church integration. Oak Grove Baptist Church, near Paragould, Arkansas, admitted ten African-American members in April 1954, because they did not have a church of their own. The Reverend Amos Greer, a missionary for the Greene County Baptist Association to which the church belonged, claimed that the congregation acted because "we would look funny talking about foreign missions if we could not do something like this in our own community." Here was an early indication that the demands of missions and segregation might come into conflict. In this instance, however, Greer indicated that the congregation hoped that its new black members might join a black mission planned by the church.[19]

The *Brown* ruling, a month later, highlighted the problem of racial discrimination in the South. Courts Redford, executive secretary of the HMB, responded with caution. "We should seek," said Redford, "to so implement the decision as to conserve and improve the great gains already made in racial understanding and co-operation." By contrast, L. S. Sedberry declared "it is an opportunity to help fifteen million colored people, and several million of other minority races now in America, to become not only good citizens of the United States, but also good citizens of the kingdom of God." Baker James Cauthen, who had recently succeeded Rankin as the FMB's executive secretary and shared his commitment to the Advance program, welcomed the ruling as beneficial to the worldwide missionary enterprise. Some Baptist clergymen also recognized the link between missions and desegregation. John G. Clark, pastor of Pulaski, Virginia's First Baptist

Church, told his congregation in defense of *Brown* that "Everywhere our missionaries go they must try to explain segregation in the U.S. They must apologize for it."[20]

In its report to the SBC in June 1954, the Christian Life Commission reminded Baptists that "Our treatment of minority peoples in our citizenship weakens the witness of our missionaries in other lands even more than in our own." Although the SBC adopted the commission's report and its recommendation in support of *Brown*, it did not adopt any further resolutions regarding segregation during the remainder of the decade as Southern Baptist hostility to desegregation intensified.[21]

The WMU also became cautious in its treatment of race. Alma Hunt, the auxiliary's executive secretary, recalled that "When the Supreme Court ruled in favor of school desegregation, WMU supported the idea and encouraged our members to facilitate adjustment." However, the WMU soon faced opposition from segregationist women and men to its efforts. In 1954, the organization tabled the proposed integration of the Young Woman's Auxiliary Conference. *Royal Service* stepped back from dealing with racial issues in the mid-1950s, although the WMU's publications for younger readers continued to address race relations. "We had to stay ahead of the people," Hunt remembered, "but not be like the engine that uncoupled itself from the train cars."[22]

However, it became increasingly impossible to separate missions from American race relations. The attempt of white mobs to prevent school desegregation in Mansfield and Texarakana, Texas, and Clinton, Tennessee, during 1956 and again in Little Rock, Arkansas, the following year generated adverse national and international publicity that undermined the efforts of Southern Baptist missionaries abroad. Missionaries sent reports and letters describing their dilemma to convention newspaper editors and denominational officials. Buford L. Nichols, a missionary in Indonesia, wrote to each state convention paper in 1956. He declared: "When some one [*sic*] in a leadership position makes statements or writes sanctioning segregation, his statements are played up in the papers as examples of the hypocrisy of what is called democracy in America. . . . We want the people, all people everywhere, to know that Christianity does not sanction racial segregation. . . . What we do and say in the homeland will directly help or hinder our worldwide missionary effort."[23]

Some denominational leaders responded to the anguished pleas of their missionaries. Theodore F. Adams, pastor of Richmond, Virginia's First Baptist Church and president of the Baptist World Alliance, told the SBC's annual meeting in 1956 that "We need to take care lest our actions in one land should jeopardize our witness in others." C. C. Warren's presidential address to the SBC warned Baptists that defiance of *Brown* threatened the success of foreign missions.[24]

Southern race relations had a particularly strong effect on the convention's missionaries in Africa, who numbered 248 by 1956. The SBC's Christian Life Commission issued a strong denunciation of racial violence and intimidation in its annual report to the convention in 1957 because, as its executive secretary A. C. Miller explained, "pressure began to mount from various Convention leaders, and more especially from our foreign missionaries on furlough and from some on their fields" for a statement on race. In that year, Southern Baptist missionaries in Nigeria adopted a resolution in which they stated that "racism is inconsistent with, and a hindrance to, the world mission task to which Southern Baptists have committed themselves." As part of its educative role, the Christian Life Commission also published a pamphlet, *Race Relations: A Factor In World Missions* by Cornell Goerner, for distribution to the SBC's denominational leaders and pastors. Goerner wrote: "[T]he report of an instance of racial discrimination or persecution seems to spread with unusual speed. An incident which occurs in Chicago or Atlanta today will be in the headlines in Cairo, Hong Kong, Tokyo, and Lagos tomorrow. . . . [T]hese news items may quickly destroy good will and understanding which the missionary has laboriously built up over the years, and may create embarrassments and problems which greatly hinder his work."[25]

The missions theme also influenced some Baptist state convention editors. In January 1957, Richard N. Owen, editor of the *Baptist and Reflector,* referred to a letter he had received from an unnamed Baptist missionary in Nigeria about the disturbances in Clinton and warned that "the task of Southern Baptist missionaries in Africa has been made more difficult as the people of Africa have learned of racial troubles in America." Erwin L. McDonald, editor of the *Arkansas Baptist,* reprinted the front page of the *Buenos Aires Herald,* sent to him by Baptist missionary James O. Watson during the Little Rock school desegregation crisis. Stories about Little Rock dominated the page. Watson commented: "You can imagine how this helps Baptist Mission work."[26]

Some Baptist state conventions warned that violence adversely affected foreign missions. In 1958, segregationist extremists in Florida dynamited a synagogue in Miami and a black school in Jacksonville. At the Florida Baptist Convention's annual meeting in November, Julius H. Avery, the convention's president, claimed that racial terrorism constituted a "serious handicap to the struggling efforts of our few missionaries in many foreign countries." R. B. Culbreth, pastor of Miami Springs Baptist Church, preached to the convention about "The Racial Problem." Culbreth stated:

"In Jordan, the children of our missionaries were pelted with stones and the Arab children cried the only American words they knew, "Little Rocks." There is absolutely no way to avoid the race factor in world missions, except by rising above it in Christian love." So impressed were the messengers by Culbreth's words that they instructed editor W. G. Stracener to publish the sermon in the *Florida Baptist Witness*.[27]

Segregationists bombed Nashville's Jewish Community Center in March 1958. A few months later, the Tennessee Baptist Convention adopted the report of its Christian Life Committee that urged Baptists to work in behalf of improved race relations. The report warned that "Our missionaries plead with us from abroad that we must find a solution to racial misunderstanding or our gospel will lose its power among the races of the earth. May we with all the grace, courage, and understanding of God's spirit do our part in this very real issue in our state." Georgia also experienced violence. Segregationists dynamited the Atlanta Temple in October 1958. SBC president Brooks Hays declared in an address to the Georgia Baptist Convention, a few weeks later, that "The word of our missionaries in foreign lands is that we must seek a peaceful settlement to the race issue. . . . We must recognize the dignity and worth of man."[28]

Baptist conventions in the Deep South were the most resistant to the pleas of missionaries. When the Mississippi Baptist Convention elected William P. Davis as director of the Department of Work with Negroes in 1957, Chester Quarles, the convention's executive secretary, warned him that "The people are not ready, don't push us." In the same year, the Resolutions Committee of the Louisiana Baptist Convention refused to report out a mild resolution on race relations proposed by emeritus missionaries Greene W. and Martha K. Strother. The Strothers' resolution maintained that there was but one race, the human race, called for equal rights and opportunities for African Americans, and urged the Supreme Court to slow down public school desegregation in areas that had large black populations. The Resolutions Committee proposed, and the convention approved, an alternative resolution that regretted that "certain of our missionaries have difficulties arising out of publicity given to racial problems" but maintained that African Americans preferred segregation. An unnamed participant commented "We would have preferred to remain silent."[29]

Although the FMB and its missionaries impressed on Baptists some awareness of the impact of racial incidents at home on foreign missions, the HMB continued to take a cautious approach to race relations for fear of jeopardizing Baptist support for its activities. Under pressure from two Baptist state convention secretaries in the Deep South, the board decided in 1958 to withdraw *The Long Bridge,* a new study book commissioned six years before for use by local WMUs. The book discussed the board's program of work with African Americans, but it did not question segregation and included statements from black Baptists, who claimed that African Americans preferred to remain in black churches. Nevertheless, the HMB considered any discussion of racial issues too controversial in view of the white South's resistance to school desegregation. Courts Redford explained: "Your Home Mission Board is not willing to inject into the life of our churches and their organizations a study that is so fraught with the possibility of harmful debate and divisive discussion."[30]

An editorial by J. Marse Grant of the North Carolina Southern Baptist paper *Charity and Children* protesting that withdrawal of the book violated local church autonomy produced sufficient protest to secure a commitment that it would be returned to Baptist book stores. However, the HMB stuck by its decision not to use *The Long Bridge* as a study book and, rather than returning it to the book stores, the board destroyed the remaining copies.[31]

While the HMB avoided racial issues as divisive and therefore a hindrance to its efforts, foreign missionaries continued to call on Baptists to speak out on race. The SBC's Christian Life Commission cited the concerns of missionaries in its report to the convention in 1958. The commission declared that "Our missionaries have pled with us through the years to overcome our racial antipathy which hinders them in their work. Now their pleadings have turned to warnings that a gospel that does not lead its advocates to reconcile racial differences in their own land will not be heard by the people of various races in other lands." Adiel J. Moncrief, the commission's chairman, also drew attention to the missions theme in his address to the SBC. He quoted one missionary as saying "If the people in the U.S.A. could only know how handicapped our missions are!"[32]

When Georgia faced a choice in 1960 and 1961 between closing down its public schools to avoid desegregation under federal court order or repealing its massive resistance legislation, Virginia Cobb, a Georgian missionary serving in Lebanon, wrote in the *Christian Index* that "You have sent us out to proclaim Christ and then you tie our hands and our witness by your actions on the homefront." Some readers also recognized that the racial crisis threatened missions. "The attitude of the Baptist people in Georgia toward the race question," wrote layman Howard L. Rhodes of St. Simon's Island, "is doing untold harm to the work of our missionaries in colored countries. . . . "[33]

Students at Wake Forest College in North Carolina used the missions theme to end the college's ban on black student admissions. They created a scholarship fund to educate an African student. Harris Mobley, a Southern Baptist missionary in Ghana, then arranged for Edward Reynolds to apply to Wake Forest. However, the college's trustees refused to admit the Ghanaian. Instead, funded by Wake Forest students, he entered Shaw University, a black institution in Raleigh. Over seven hundred Wake Forest students declared Reynolds to be an honorary student of their college, and they continued to lobby its trustees to admit him. In April 1961, the trustees yielded to the pressure and agreed to desegregate graduate, but not undergraduate, classes in September. A year later, they voted to desegregate regular undergraduate programs, having enrolled a black student, Kernard C. Rockette, in summer school in 1961. Reynolds finally gained admittance in 1962.[34]

The adoption of direct action protests on a large scale by the civil rights movement in the early 1960s generated national and international publicity that increased the pressure on Southern Baptist missionaries. Furthermore, the peoples of the newly independent countries of Africa and Asia, who had thrown off white colonial rule, were particularly sensitive to racism. At the SBC's annual meeting in 1961, Arkansas missionary Josephine Skaggs, on furlough from Nigeria, made a widely reported speech about the damage done to missions by domestic racial violence and discrimination. Skaggs asked: "What good can the Peace Corps do as they say in effect, 'I (Americans) hate Negroes at home, but love them in Africa?'" She also pointed to the hypocrisy of those who financed missions in Africa but would not allow American or African blacks to enter or join their Southern Baptist churches. E. S. James, editor of the *Baptist Standard,* wrote: "I doubt that anyone who heard Missionary Josephine Skaggs at St. Louis will ever again be a strong advocate of segregation." The SBC adopted a resolution that criticized the Freedom Riders and those who had attacked them during their journey through Alabama, and warned of the dangers that domestic racial strife had on the missions program.[35]

In the early 1960s, missionaries at home and abroad and leaders in the Home and Foreign Mission Boards, spoke more frequently and more forcefully against racial discrimination in America than they had ever done before. "As a mission volunteer, . . . " wrote Joe James Watkins to the *Baptist Standard* in 1961, "I feel that there is . . . no reason why Negroes should not be admitted to institutions of higher education. . . . " Mississippi missionary Antonia Canzoneri complained to the *Baptist Record* in 1962 from Nigeria about the effects that the violent opposition of whites to the desegregation of the University of Mississippi was having on Southern Baptist missions. She wrote: "You are closing the door of Africa in our faces. The Communists do not need to work against the preaching of the gospel here by Americans; you are doing it quite adequately."[36]

The WMU gave extensive coverage to civil rights in its publications. In

1962, it adopted T. B. Maston's 1959 work *The Bible And Race,* which challenged the biblical defense of segregation, as a study book for its members in Southern Baptist churches. Although Courts Redford discouraged the HMB from addressing racial issues, some members of its staff did so nevertheless. C. E. Autrey, director of the board's Division of Evangelism, declared in 1961: "The denomination should not oppose integration but should let it take its due course. . . . The whole process of integration must come. The church is being tested. In this crucial hour, the church should stand up and be counted, otherwise it is failing its mission in the 20th century." Walker L. Knight, who had become editor of *Home Missions* in 1959, began to address race relations in the early 1960s. In March 1961, Knight editorialized against tuition grants by state governments to pay for students to go to private schools as a means to avoid attendance at integrated schools. Knight argued that such grants might lead to many denominational parochial school systems and so undermine the public school system and the separation of church and state. Asked by a reader whether he took a stand on integration itself, Walker replied in September 1962 that although he took no editorial position, he did favor open access to schools, churches, and businesses for all.[37]

Concern about missions created pressure on Baptist institutions to desegregate. The trustees of Ouachita Baptist College in Arkadelphia, Arkansas, voted in April 1960 to accept qualified students from foreign mission fields should they apply. Ouachita admitted its first black students, Michael and Mary Makasholo from Rhodesia, in January 1962. Ralph A. Phelps Jr., the college's president, explained that "We have taken this step with the conviction it is an essential part of our world mission program. Our missionaries in Africa and other parts of the world have told us the communists are 'beating them to death' with the fact that mission converts are not permitted to come to the school that sent out the missionaries." Arkadelphia's First Baptist Church, which included many faculty and students from the college, voted two-to-one in a secret ballot to "look with favor" on membership applications from foreign black students at Ouachita. Under the policies of the church and college, American blacks remained barred from entry but concern for missions had made a dent in segregation.[38]

Missions also influenced the desegregation of Macon, Georgia's Mercer University. Its trustees voted unanimously in October 1962 to appoint a committee charged with examining desegregation. Although the trustees had independent authority, they sought advice from the Georgia Baptist Convention, which appointed five members of its Executive Committee to study the issue. In February 1963, Sam Jerry Oni, a Ghanaian converted by Baptist missionaries, applied for admission to Mercer in the fall. John Jeter

Hurt Jr., editor of the *Christian Index,* argued that the university had to separate Oni's application, as a foreign mission convert, from the issue of desegregation. Hurt declared that "We either admit him or we should have the courage to call home all of our missionaries and go out of the business. We either admit him or we are in greater need of missionary preaching than Ghana." The overwhelming majority of letters to the newspaper supported Hurt's editorial and most cited the missionary imperative as their reason. Layman Jack Carpenter declared: "If one soul be lost to our missionaries by excluding this young man and I do not speak my heart, I have blood on my hand. . . . "[39]

The Georgia Baptist Convention's special committee, which had not considered the issue of admitting Oni, advised in March against integrating the university because the "time is not quite right." However, Mercer University's study committee recommended that its trustees end racial discrimination in student admissions. They did so by a vote of thirteen to five, with three abstentions and ten absent from the meeting. John Jeter Hurt Jr. welcomed the decision as both "Christian" and "wise." Mercer admitted Oni and two black Americans in September.[40]

Anxiety about missions appeared among a broad spectrum of denominational leaders and opinion makers as civil rights direct action protests peaked in 1963. In widely reported comments, Baker James Cauthen warned that the FMB, which had recently exceeded the Advance Program's target of 1,750 missionaries, might have to withdraw its missionaries from some of the fifty-three countries they operated in. He also wrote in *The Commission,* the FMB's magazine, "In recent months missionaries have repeatedly called attention to the bearing of racial disturbances upon the witness they seek to give. One able servant of God wrote, 'As far as I am aware nothing has ever occurred to so tarnish the image of America.'" The editors of Baptist state convention newspapers in Arkansas, Georgia, North Carolina, Tennessee, Texas and Virginia drew their readers' attention to the missions issue, and some published testimonies from missionaries about the damaging effects of segregation and American race relations on their efforts.[41]

In *Home Missions,* Walker Knight endorsed the SBC's decision to include Race Relations Sunday, a commitment to improved race relations observed annually by pastor exchanges between black and white churches and sometimes by joint services, on its calendar beginning in 1965. He also called for racially inclusive policies in Southern Baptist churches, schools, hospitals and agencies, and a recognition that African Americans had been deprived of their civil rights. Knight reported in September 1963 that he had received a large correspondence concerning his editorial and that slightly more of the comments were favorable. Courts Redford reprimanded the editor and, in reference to the board's newly appointed African-American office secretary, told him that "We've got all of the integration we can take here."[42]

The Brotherhood Commission engaged T. B. Maston to write the pamphlet *The Christian and Race Relations* for use by Baptist men in monthly church Brotherhood meetings, retreats with their pastors and associational Brotherhood gatherings. In the pamphlet, published in 1963, Maston quoted from missionaries and appealed to Baptists to obey the law, reject prejudice, and treat African Americans in accordance with "the gospel of love."[43]

In a speech to the SBC in 1963, Foy Valentine, executive secretary of the Christian Life Commission, echoed Josephine Skaggs' comments of two years before when he noted "the immensely absurd spectacle of loving the souls of Negroes in Africa and hating their guts in Nashville. . . . " Valentine also told Southern Baptists that "We need to abolish racial discrimination in our country and in our churches. . . . " The commission continued to emphasize the missions theme in its literature by publishing the pamphlet *Missions and Race* by Ross Coggins, a former missionary to Indonesia.[44]

Southern Baptists in the peripheral South remained more receptive to the foreign missions message than many in the Deep South. The Southeast Texas [Baptist] Association adopted a resolution in 1963 that urged Baptists to "face the racial crisis realistically" so as "not [to] impede the winning of lost persons here or in the mission fields." It asked churches to accept members "regardless of personal, social, political, economic, cultural, racial, or any other discriminatory consideration."[45] Howard W. Lee wrote to the *Religious Herald:* "How can missionaries in far off countries and pastors in strife-torn cities explain to people that we dismiss teachers who find difficulties in Genesis but we honor those who explain away the plain teachings of the New Testament?" By contrast, Louisianian B. R. Lawson complained to the *Baptist Standard* that "I personally don't see how our race problem here would hinder their [missionaries'] work any more than colored people in the Congo killing and discriminating against white people." However, a few Baptists in the Deep South responded positively to the missions issue. Monroe Crosby of Georgia urged Baptists to desegregate. He wrote: "If charity (love) begins at home, and it does, let's start tearing down these barriers at home first, then extend this offer to others. If we can't love these at home how can we say we will love the foreign."[46]

The desegregation of Furman University, a Baptist institution in Greenville, South Carolina, illustrated Baptist divisions about segregation and the saliency of the missions theme. Encouraged by their students and faculty, the trustees of Furman voted in October 1963 to admit qualified black applicants. Although the trustees had independent authority, the General Board of the Baptist State Convention of South Carolina asked them to defer action until the convention could study its implications and adopt a policy for all of its colleges. The board presented its recommendation for further study to the convention's annual meeting in November.[47]

Progressives and hard-line segregationists clashed at the convention over the General Board's recommendation. In a substitute motion Julian Cave Sr. urged the convention to disapprove of any Baptist college desegregation. James Browder declared, in reply, that "it is foolish to send missionaries to non-white areas if we pass this substitute motion which disapproves of integrating our colleges." The convention's moderate segregationist majority adopted the middle ground of accepting the General Board's recommendation requesting a delay by Furman, pending further study and a report to the convention's next meeting. The university complied with the recommendation.[48]

At the convention's meeting in 1964, the messengers, by a narrow margin of 943 votes to 915, rejected the General Board's recommendation that they leave college admissions policies to the discretion of trustees. In a vote taken after "many of the messengers" had left, they expressed their disapproval of college integration by a margin of 905 votes to 575. Desegregation, the ballots suggested, split Baptists almost evenly. Furman's trustees defied the convention by reaffirming their nondiscriminatory admissions policy. J. Wilbert Wood, chairman of the Board of Trustees, explained that "a nondiscriminatory admissions policy for Furman University is necessary because it is right, it is Christian, . . . and it is in accord with our denomination's great worldwide program of missions." The university admitted African-American students in January 1965.[49]

Despite opposition, particularly from Baptists in South Carolina and other parts of the Deep South, the SBC's missions organizations placed increasing emphasis on racial equality in their publications. The WMU became bolder and more outspoken in 1964 as it tried to prepare Baptist women to accept the pending civil rights bill. In March of that year, *Royal Service* included an article by Mary Allred that dismissed fears that desegregation would lead to interracial marriage or to a decline in educational or moral standards. Allred also wrote: "You know, I don't worry about sitting next to a Negro on a bus, or at the lunch counter. . . . I'm not even excited over the possibility of a Negro worship[p]ing in the church I happen to be in!" Predictably, Allred's article led to criticism from segregationists, but it also received some support.[50]

In September 1964, the WMU gave extensive coverage to race relations in its publications, which led to some subscription cancellations. The cover of the *Window,* a magazine for young women, pictured a black hand and arm pointing upward. Underneath the picture the magazine carried a brief thematic statement: "The cry of the Negro American reaching for first-class citizenship is heard across the land and Southern Baptist young people must involve themselves positively—under God's leadership—in this modern revolution. That's what this month's issue is about." *Tell,* a publication for girls, included an extensive list of program suggestions designed to undermine racial prejudice. "The Woman's Missionary Union," T. B. Maston wrote in 1966, "has generally made and continues to make the most directly challenging approach in the whole area of race." The WMU's efforts were important because its magazines enjoyed wide circulation and were used by local church WMU's for training purposes, especially training for girls. The *Brotherhood Commission,* the WMU's male counterpart, also emphasized race relations in 1964. The commission published articles on race in the *Brotherhood Journal,* its magazine for men, and in three successive issues of *Ambassador Life* for boys.[51]

Promotion of Race Relations Sunday and the passage of the Civil Rights Act of 1964 drew the HMB and *Home Missions* into a greater emphasis on race relations. Arthur Rutledge, who had succeeded Courts Redford as the board executive secretary, also encouraged support for racial equality. In January 1965, Victor Glass, Secretary of the Department of Work with National Baptists, wrote a lengthy insert in *Home Missions* in which he described the HMB's work with black Baptists and included suggestions for interracial cooperation. The piece brought howls of protest from segregationists, mainly in the Deep South, as did another article that month by W. T. Moore, director of the North Tulsa [Oklahoma] Baptist Center for Negroes, who spoke out strongly in favor of the Civil Rights Act. Moore asked "If its [*sic*] right to back legislation against liquor and gambling why isn't it right to back legislation against discrimination because of race?" In May 1966, Walker Knight called for open churches in an editorial. Two months later, Glass wrote an impassioned defense of the civil rights movement: "The law is on the side of the Negro. . . . World opinion is on the Negro's side. . . . Group protest is a strategy employed for documentation and establishing eyewitnesses to police and public brutality. This is a spiritual movement. It is [led] by preachers and has the support and prayers of the churches. . . . "[52]

In addition to their regular articles on race relations *Home Missions, Royal Service* and the *Window* ran special issues on the subject. Some articles were merely informative but others explained and defended the African-American struggle for equality. Mrs. Ralph Gwin wrote in the July 1967 issue of *Royal Service:* "People seeking to improve their lot have historically had to resort to various forms of protest. . . . Men no longer are willing to live as second-class persons in our revolutionary world. . . . Peaceful protests have won sympathy for the Negro cause and helped alter opinions of many white people." Gwin also defended the 1964 Civil Rights Act and the 1965 Voting Rights Act as proper and necessary.[53]

Although both the HMB and WMU publications generated protest and lost thousands of readers, the magazines nevertheless played an important educative role and received praise from many readers, including some residents of the Deep South. In 1967, Earle F. Stirewalt of Atlanta, Georgia, commended *Home Missions* for its coverage of race. "Several of my friends," wrote Stirewalt, "have also expressed their appreciation of the forthright manner in which you and your staff present the live issues in our troubled, changing society."[54]

The HMB, thirteen state conventions' departments of work with National Baptists and the SBC's Christian Life Commission released statements in January 1968 that urged Baptists to tackle the causes of riots, which they listed as injustice, poverty, unemployment, crime and family breakdown. They also asked churches to drop racially discriminatory admissions policies and SBC agencies to employ qualified African Americans at all levels. A few months earlier the FMB had appointed Sue Thompson, its first black missionary since the 1880s, and in 1968 the HMB appointed its first black employee to exercise genuine authority when Emmanuel L. McCall became Victor Glass's associate.[55]

McCall contributed to the drafting of "A Statement of Christian Concern," drawn up after Victor Glass, Porter Routh, executive secretary of the SBC's Executive Committee, and H. Franklin Paschall, president of the SBC, called an informal conference of Baptist leaders in the wake of Martin Luther's King Jr.'s assassination and the subsequent riots. Signed by seventy-one executives of SBC agencies, including Baker James Cauthen, Alma Hunt and Arthur Rutledge, state convention leaders, and Baptist state convention newspaper editors, the statement confessed Baptist complicity in the racial crisis, called on Baptists to address the crisis and sought the creation of a task force to coordinate their efforts.[56]

The statement received wide publicity in the Baptist press before it was presented on June 4 to the SBC's Executive Committee, which had to decide whether to recommend it for approval by the SBC that opened its annual meeting the same day. The Executive Committee debated the statement at length in the teeth of considerable opposition. According to J. Marse Grant, editor of the *Biblical Recorder,* the "turning point" came when Baker James Cauthen reported that 197 missionaries on furlough had requested the SBC to take action. The statement that finally won approval from the Executive Committee, after several revisions, contained a weakened Baptist confession of guilt and assigned the job of coordinating Baptist efforts to deal with the racial crisis not to a new task force but to the HMB. It also claimed that the SBC had endeavored to affirm "God's love for all men of all continents and colors" and would continue to do so through the evangelistic enterprise.[57]

The SBC overwhelmingly approved the statement, now renamed "A Statement Concerning The Crisis In Our Nation," with one major amendment that urged "all leaders and supporters of minority groups to . . . respect . . . the person and property of others and to manifest the responsible action commensurate with individual dignity and Christian citizenship." In its final form, the statement declared Baptist commitment to securing "opportunities in matters of citizenship, public services, education, employment, and personal habitation that every man may achieve his highest potential as a person," and open churches. Erwin McDonald welcomed the statement. He wrote: "It is significant that the action is not in the form of a resolution but now stands as a statement of Convention policy. The fact that the Convention has called on one of its agencies—the Home Mission Board—to implement the new policy is real evidence that the Convention is taking a decisive, new turn." H. Franklin Paschall was less sanguine. He described the statement as "a public show of concern for racial problems in our country" and predicted that "its greatest effect will be in the press and not in practical programs." Events largely justified Paschall's prediction.[58]

Through its Department of Work with National Baptists, the HMB did its best to foster cooperation between black and white Baptists, but, like the convention, it had no power to bring about church integration. The board also coordinated action by SBC agencies regarding implementation of the crisis statement. Victor Glass expressed disappointment that the convention did not create a new agency to carry out the statement, and he regretted that the HMB was unable to achieve more in the task. Although the board promoted the hiring and appointment of African Americans to positions of influence in the convention and its agencies, even as late as 1973 the total number of blacks employed by SBC agencies stood at 132 and only ten of these held staff jobs. The remainder were employed in clerical posts.[59]

The HMB sponsored films and publicity about black problems, but some agencies ran into trouble when they undertook related efforts. As a result of the crisis statement, the WMU and the Brotherhood Commission decided to produce a mission action guide for churches about ministering to African Americans. The resulting product was "too strong" and apparently not used. Despite setbacks, the board made some advances. It authorized a $1 million church loan fund for ethnic groups, deposited $100,000 from its reserve funds in a minority bank and gave a $10,000 grant to the Opportunities Industrialization Centers of America, sponsored by Philadelphia black Baptist minister, Leon H. Sullivan, for job training of the long-term unemployed. The HMB also created scholarships for trainees in Chicago's Urban Training Center and supported Professor Henlee H. Barnette's efforts to start a black studies program at The Southern Baptist Theological Seminary, which bore fruit in 1970.[60]

At the committee's own request, the HMB dismantled the committee on national crisis in 1971 and transferred its responsibilities to the board's programs and standing committees. The committee reported at its final meeting that "There is still a crisis in our nation. We have far from finished the job." The real significance of the crisis statement was that it marked a break with the paternalism with which the SBC and its agencies had previously treated African Americans, and a recognition of the serious problems that blacks faced.[61]

Several developments in 1971 indicated that an attempt to move from paternalism to fraternalism increasingly characterized many of the Baptist state conventions' policies toward African Americans. An interracial meeting of Texas Baptists in Houston's Astrodome, organized by Jimmy Allen, president of the Baptist General Convention of Texas, brought together 41,777 people from six of the eight black, white and Hispanic conventions in the state. It constituted the largest gathering of Baptists in history. The Baptist State Convention of North Carolina and the black Baptist General Convention of North Carolina agreed to set up a joint committee to ensure greater understanding and cooperation between them. Even in the Deep South, there were signs of change. For the first time, an African-American minister delivered a major address at the annual meeting of the Louisiana Baptist Convention. The Baptist State Convention of South Carolina established a Department of Cooperative Ministries with National Baptists. The convention's Christian Life and Public Affairs Committee also called on Baptists to transform their relationship with National Baptists from paternalism to fraternalism, and, in subsequent years, convention committees held meetings with South Carolina's black Baptist leaders.[62]

At the end of World War II few Southern Baptists, outside the FMB and its missionary contingent, perceived any conflict between segregation and evangelism. The civil rights movement and southern white resistance to its protests, alongside the desegregation demands of the federal government and courts, generated pressure from missionaries and FMB officials for the

SBC and its leaders to speak out against racism, which, they warned, hurt their efforts, particularly in the newly independent countries of Africa and Asia. Progressives in the WMU and the Christian Life Commission publicized missionaries' concerns. Some Baptist leaders, especially in the HMB and the Deep South, feared that convention pronouncements on race would alienate the segregationist majority, and they sought to avoid the subject. However, the direct action phase of the civil rights movement in the early 1960s generated international publicity and increased the pressure on Southern Baptist leaders and opinion makers to condemn racism. By 1963, Baptist state convention and SBC editors often informed their readers of the threat posed to missions by southern race relations. Concern for evangelism and the Baptist image abroad led some Baptist colleges, even in the Deep South, to admit African and African-American students. Baptist lay people in the peripheral South proved most receptive to the arguments of missionaries, but these arguments also made an impact on some in the Deep South. The evangelistic imperative played an important role in facilitating Baptist adjustment to desegregation.

9

The Variety of the Southern
Baptist Experience in Desegregation

Dıversıty marked Southern Baptist responses to desegregation. Across the South, Baptists divided between biblical segregationists, moderate segregationists and progressives. Those most opposed to desegregation tended to live in the black belt, and in rural and urban areas with relatively high numbers of African-American inhabitants. Consequently, given demographic patterns, the intensity of Baptist support for Jim Crow peaked in the Deep South, became less marked in the Mid-South states of Arkansas and Tennessee and lessened further in the peripheral South, notwithstanding militant segregationist pockets in areas that had high proportionate black populations. The pace of Baptist college and church desegregation broadly reflected the tripartite cleavage of opinion. Despite the progressive views of WMU leaders, both sexes shared the same range of opinion toward Jim Crow and in equal proportion. To a considerable extent ministers shared the views of their parishioners about segregation, but they also exhibited a diversity that reflected more than their geographical position. By contrast, Baptist students, regardless of their location in the South's subregions, took more progressive, or, at least, less reactionary, positions regarding segregation than their state conventions and their elders in church.[1]

Although most white southerners opposed desegregation in the civil rights era, they did not do so equally across the South. In the Deep South, 90 percent of whites expressed opposition to school desegregation in 1956 and only one out of seventeen approval. By contrast, in Arkansas, Florida, North Carolina and Virginia 20 percent of whites favored *Brown* and in Texas and Tennessee nearly 25 percent did so. Men and women did not significantly differ in their view of segregation. A 1958 survey of Baptist women in east Tennessee, where African Americans formed lower percentages of the population than in the state's western half, found that only 20 percent of them favored school desegregation. Other opinion poll evidence suggested that across the South, white men and women shared similar views concerning Jim Crow. Among southern white parents, 46 percent of men supported strict school segregation in 1965 and 16 percent endorsed full school desegregation, compared with 42 percent and 14 percent of women respectively on these issues. WMU leaders at the regional and state convention levels tended to be more progressive than their female constituency. There were many examples of Baptist women outside the leadership who supported Jim Crow in letters to the denominational press.[2]

Aside from a few progressives, denominational officials within the SBC and Baptist state conventions frequently sought to avoid the divisive issue of desegregation at convention meetings. Convention messengers tended to reflect the geographical spread of opinion generally found among southern whites. In the 1950s and 1960s, messengers from the Deep South frequently sought to prevent the SBC from speaking out on race and, when they could not, to dilute the strength of its pronouncements and undermine the Christian Life Commission. Their task became increasingly difficult as southerners acquiesced in desegregation and the SBC admitted conventions organized in the North and West, most of them after 1939, whose messengers tended to be progressive concerning race relations.[3]

Without success, Montague Cook, pastor of Moultrie, Georgia's Trinity Baptist Church, objected to a section of the SBC's Christian Life Commission report in 1958 that advised "restoration of communication and fellowship with people of every race," because he thought that it could be interpreted as approval of integration. Neither did Jack Trammel, pastor of Sardis, Alabama's Shiloh Baptist Church, have any more success in seeking to force the commission to refund a grant for its race relations work from the Ford Foundation's Fund for the Republic. Trammel used a common segregationist tactic when he accused the Fund of giving aid to Communism and claimed that its grant money was therefore "tainted." The messengers overwhelmingly rejected Trammel's motion to return the grant, but, for the sake of unity and to avoid further controversy, the commission decided not to accept any further grants from the Fund.[4]

On other occasions, malcontents from the Deep South enjoyed more success. Alabamians led by A. Hamilton Reid, executive secretary of the state convention, Leon Macon, editor of the *Alabama Baptist,* and some black-belt pastors succeeded in blocking a resolution commending Brooks Hays for a presidential address to the SBC in 1959 that criticized segregation. Five years later, the SBC narrowly rejected a Christian Life Commission recommendation in support of open churches and civil rights legislation, and instead adopted a substitute prepared by messengers from Louisiana, Mississippi and Alabama that emphasized the autonomy of the local church and defended the Southern Baptist record in race relations. Thereafter, messengers from the Deep South lacked the influence to secure rejection of race relations recommendations and resolutions and could only manage, at best, to amend or qualify them.[5]

When the SBC overwhelmingly adopted a crisis statement in 1968 that supported open churches and racial equality, opposition to it came mostly from the Deep South. Messengers from the other southern states felt that the convention needed to respond positively to racial problems and those from non-southern churches supported them. The decisive influence came from southern-based Baptists, since non-southern churches remained a small minority of overall SBC membership.[6]

At the state level, the Texas and North Carolina conventions consistently issued the most advanced pronouncements and reports concerning race relations and desegregation. Behind them stood the Baptist General Association of Virginia; its record marred only by its silence at the peak of the state's massive resistance to school desegregation in the 1950s. The Arkansas and Tennessee conventions generally avoided pronouncements on race, while the Florida Baptist Convention called for adjustment to desegregation when resistance in the state threatened Baptist primary commitments to education, law and order, and evangelism. By contrast, only the Alabama and Louisiana conventions publicly defended Jim Crow.[7]

With a few exceptions, Baptist college and church desegregation usually occurred first and least slowly in the peripheral South, with Texas at the forefront. Austin, Texas's University Baptist Church accepted its first African-American member in 1950. A year later, Wayland Baptist College in Plainview, Texas, became the first and, until 1961, the only Southern Baptist college or university in the South to accept black students. When the college accepted African Americans, two Southern Baptist churches in the area followed suit. In the 1950s, a few Southern Baptist churches in some other states also agreed to admit blacks. After the first *Brown* decision, Birmingham, Alabama's First Baptist Church voted to admit African Americans to services should they visit. However, Texas continued to lead the way. Two black Baptist churches, Ebenezer Baptist Church and Nineteenth Street Baptist Church, joined the Austin Association in 1955, although they still retained their membership of a black Baptist convention. They were the first African-American churches in the South to join an association affiliated with the SBC.[8]

The rise of massive resistance in the South during the second half of the 1950s halted further progress toward desegregation of Baptist institutions. In November 1955, the Baptist State Convention of North Carolina recommended by a vote of 816 to 285 that the trustees of its institutions, over which the convention had no authority, consider "their responsibility and opportunity to open doors of knowledge . . . to qualified applicants regardless of race." However, no Baptist college desegregation occurred in the state. Indeed, made aware by the convention that their charters did not prohibit African Americans from admittance, two colleges, Chowan in Murfreesboro and Gardner-Webb in Boiling Springs, adopted policies that barred blacks.[9]

Not until the early 1960s, with massive resistance over, did incremental desegregation of Baptist colleges and churches resume in the peripheral South, influenced by secular educational desegregation in the region. In some cases, colleges and churches desegregated in response to applications for admission from Africans converted by Baptist missionaries abroad. Mars Hill College in North Carolina admitted Oralene Graves, an African-American undergraduate in 1961, and Wake Forest College at Winston-Salem desegregated its graduate programs in the same year and its undergraduate classes in 1962. Meredith College for women at Raleigh and Gardner-Webb College also abolished discriminatory admissions policies. Ouachita Baptist College in Arkadelphia, Arkansas, admitted two foreign black missionary converts in 1962, while continuing to bar African Americans from admission. In Texas, Hardin-Simmons University in Abilene, the University of Corpus Christi and Baylor University adopted integration policies in the early 1960s. Mercer University in Macon, Georgia, admitted Sam Oni, a missionary convert, and two African Americans in 1963.[10]

Texas Southern Baptist churches continued to pioneer desegregation, but they did not adopt open admissions policies to any significant degree until 1963. In that year, the Baptist General Convention of Texas mailed a questionnaire to 4,500 member churches and received replies from 1,259. Two hundred and thirty-four churches answered that they would accept African-American members and 178 said that they would refuse blacks membership. Seven hundred and forty-seven churches claimed that they would permit black attendance and 147 said they would deny blacks admittance to services.[11]

Many of the Texas churches surveyed had no official policy on church attendance (63 percent) or membership (74 percent) for African Americans but most of these churches had adopted some kind of informal policy on the issue during 1963. They did so, in part, because that year witnessed numerous civil rights demonstrations in the South which led some Texas Baptists to reconsider their attitude to blacks, and, more immediately, because prestigious Southern Baptist churches in the state's cities had been subject to picketing by African Americans after these churches had refused blacks admittance. In the most famous incident, blacks picketed Houston's First Baptist Church, pastored by K. Owen White, the SBC's president, after it had refused to accept an African American into membership. Embarrassed by the affair and also wanting to avoid a similar confrontation, some Texas churches voted to accept blacks should they request membership.[12]

A national survey conducted in 1963 found that almost 90 percent of the SBC's 32,892 churches would not admit African Americans to membership. It revealed that church desegregation, although small, was more pronounced in the peripheral than in the Deep South. Texas far exceeded the other ten southern states in the number of its churches open to blacks. North Carolina had four churches with black members, while Arkansas and Georgia had one each, in both cases to accommodate foreign mission converts studying at Baptist colleges. In addition, Nashville, Tennessee's First Baptist Church admitted two Nigerian students under watchcare while they attended a local college. Florida had twenty-five churches willing to admit African Americans to services, but none of its churches had black members.[13]

Church desegregation usually occurred, if it happened at all, after secular desegregation, which in 1963 remained confined mainly to parts of the urban South, thereby excluding most of the Deep South, except for a few cities. A 1964 survey revealed that "In Southern districts where considerable integration of schools has taken place 54 percent of white adults favor integration; in districts where token integration has occurred, 38 percent express favorable attitudes, and in segregated districts 28 percent favor integration." Eight years earlier, only 31 percent of southern whites in areas with some school desegregation had approved of the idea. Whites became more accepting of desegregation once it had occurred, and this helps to explain why church desegregation tended to follow integration of schools and public accommodations.[14]

Before the Civil Rights Act of 1964 mandated the desegregation of public facilities, only one other Baptist university in the Deep South besides Mercer, Furman University, voted to abandon racially discriminatory admissions. However, opposition from the Baptist State Convention of South Carolina to the decision of Furman's trustees, who acted from Christian conviction and a concern for missions, delayed desegregation until 1965.[15]

The year 1965 marked a pivotal point in Baptist college desegregation since Title VI of the Civil Rights Act required educational institutions to pledge that they were in compliance with desegregation if both they and their students were to remain eligible for federal grants and loans. A survey by *Baptist Press*, the SBC's news agency, concluded that by April 1965 over 70 percent of junior and senior colleges related to the SBC had agreed to comply with the act. Only one Baptist college in the peripheral South, North Carolina's Wingate College, refused to sign the compliance pledge.

The four Baptist colleges in Virginia refused to accept federal loans for themselves or their students on the grounds of the separation of church and state. However, in the aftermath of the act, they adopted racially non-discriminatory admissions policies to conform with those of secular educational institutions.[16]

In most cases, colleges desegregated only to maintain their students' eligibility for federal aid. Having admitted African Americans to graduate classes eighteen months previously, the trustees of Ouachita Baptist College voted in August 1964 to admit blacks to undergraduate programs. To secure the acquiescence of moderate segregationists, Ralph A. Phelps Jr., the college's president, presented the decision as a pragmatic response to altered circumstances that would enable students to continue their education. Phelps explained: "The Board felt that it had no other choice but to comply. Failure to do so would have meant losing our R.O.T.C. [Reserve Officer Training Corps program], the oldest in the state, and denying our students participation in such programs as the National Defense Loan Program, on which some 200 of them are now attending Ouachita."[17]

The financial need of their students also prompted some Baptist colleges in the Deep South that had hitherto barred African Americans to sign the compliance pledge. Four of the Georgia Baptist Convention's five Baptist colleges and already desegregated Mercer University signed the required civil rights compliance pledge, and the fifth college, Norman College, secured permission from the convention to change its whites-only admissions charter. Only one of the Mississippi Baptist Convention's four colleges, William Carey, located at Hattiesburg, signed the pledge in 1965. The college had not previously been open to black students. The Mississippi Baptist Convention's three remaining colleges preferred to forfeit federal loans for buildings and their students, both of which they had previously accepted, in order to keep their institutions strictly segregated. The same was also true of the Alabama Baptist State Convention's three colleges, Howard College, Birmingham, Judson College, Marion, and Mobile College. Of the colleges in South Carolina and Louisiana, only Furman University signed the compliance pledge.[18]

Mississippi College in Clinton established a scholarship drive to fund its students, who had formerly been dependent on federal aid. However, Baptists and their conventions proved unable to compensate students for the loss of federal assistance. By 1969, all of the Mississippi Baptist Convention's colleges had signed the compliance pledge and by the following year, every Baptist college in the South had done so.[19]

Federal guidelines also required Baptist hospitals to comply with desegregation or forfeit federal aid for themselves and their patients. Initially,

some hospitals located in the Deep South and in more militant segregationist areas of the peripheral South refused. They included Jacksonville,
Florida's Baptist Memorial Hospital and Mississippi Baptist Hospital in
Jackson. However, by 1969, most hospitals had, under financial pressure,
also signed the compliance pledge so that their patients could receive Medi-
care or Medicaid. Adoption of an open admissions policy, however, did
not always lead to its ready implementation. Meeting in New Orleans in
1969, the SBC felt compelled to pass a resolution that urged the Southern
Baptist Hospital in the city to bring its practice into line with its stated
non-discriminatory policy.[20]

Just as the Deep South proved to be a laggard in college and hospital
desegregation, so it also remained in opening churches to African Americans. A HMB survey in 1968 recorded 433 churches in Texas willing to
admit African Americans to membership, 131 in Florida, ninety-two in
North Carolina, fifty-one in Tennessee, forty-two in Virginia, seventeen in
Georgia, six in Mississippi, four in South Carolina, two in Arkansas, and
none in Alabama and Louisiana. The division between the peripheral and
Deep South also held true in the number of churches that had at least one
African-American member: Texas seventy-nine, Florida fourteen, Tennessee twelve, North Carolina nine, Virginia seven, Mississippi three, Georgia
two and South Carolina one. Black churches affiliated with Southern Baptist associations existed only outside the Deep South, numbering eight in
Texas, six each in Florida and North Carolina, and two in Tennessee. The
number of Southern Baptist churches open to African Americans increased
during the second half of the 1960s, but, at the same time, some urban
churches relocated to the suburbs with their parishioners as blacks moved
into their neighborhoods. Established nearly sixty years, Birmingham, Alabama's Calvary Baptist Church closed for this reason in 1966. The phenomenon of church relocation to the suburbs occurred across the urban
South.[21]

Although the Deep South was a militant segregation bastion throughout
the civil rights era, hard-line segregationists existed beyond the region, and
even within it there was a diversity of opinion among Southern Baptists
regarding segregation. V. O. Key Jr. argued in 1949 that opposition to
African-American progress was greatest in the South's rural black belt
counties that existed in every state but were most numerous in the Deep
South. In the black belt, where African Americans comprised upwards of
forty percent of the population, whites were the most resistant to change,
because they felt under greatest threat from the prospect of school desegregation and black enfranchisement. Subsequent studies have, with occasional qualifications, confirmed the substance of Key's hypothesis.[22]

Biblical segregationist letters to the denominational press came most frequently from Southern Baptists in rural black-belt areas, whether they were in the Deep South or the peripheral South. Thus outside the Deep South, militant segregationists were most numerous in east Texas, the plantation counties of Arkansas that adjoined the Mississippi River, the northern panhandle of Florida, the eastern Piedmont of North Carolina and its coastal plain, plantation counties in west Tennessee and the Southside and Tidewater regions of Virginia. Although a minority among urban Baptists, biblical segregationists could also be found in towns and cities with a substantial black presence, such as Birmingham, Alabama, and Jacksonville, Florida.[23]

Despite warnings and condemnations from some Baptist state conventions and denominational officials and editors, Baptist segregationists sometimes joined the Ku Klux Klan and the Citizens' Councils. Klansmen accepted an invitation from Atlanta, Georgia's Inman Yards Baptist Church to attend worship services in January 1949. Seven years later, Klansmen marched into services in some Alabama churches and left donations. In the early 1960s, Robert Lee "Wild Bill" Davidson, Imperial Wizard of the United Klans, Knights of the Ku Klux Klan of America, the largest Klan group in the nation, served as director of the Baptist Training Union in his hometown Southern Baptist church in Macon, Georgia. Louis W. Hollis, a deacon of Jackson, Mississippi's First Baptist Church, served as secretary of the Citizens' Council Association and executive director of the Jackson Citizens' Council.[24]

Some Southern Baptist clergymen, such as Charles C. Jones, pastor of Mississippi's Mendenhall Baptist Church, joined the Citizens' Councils and played prominent roles. Marion A. Woodson, pastor of Olanta, South Carolina's Bethel Baptist Church, told the Lake City Citizens' Council that "We must strive to leave our children a constitutional form of government and a segregated society that works in harmony." Henry L. Lyon Jr., pastor of Montgomery, Alabama's Highland Avenue Baptist Church and a frequent speaker on biblical segregation at Citizens' Council meetings, gave the prayer of invocation at the inaugural of Governor George C. Wallace, a Methodist, in January 1963. Although Lyon did not mention segregation, he praised the Confederacy for defending states' rights.[25]

Clergymen who defended segregation as Christian sometimes led local Citizens' Council chapters or their equivalents. During the Little Rock school desegregation crisis, only one of the city's Southern Baptists ministers, Wesley Pruden, pastor of Broadmoor Baptist Church, publicly opposed desegregation. Pruden served as the president of the Capital Citizens' Council, which never exceeded five hundred members and drew its main support from the working class and from Missionary Baptist clergymen. William T. Bodenhamer, pastor of Ty Ty Baptist Church, in Tift County, served as a state legislator and became executive director of the white supremacist States' Rights Council of Georgia, Inc., in 1955, which peaked at fewer than ten thousand members. Bodenhamer resigned and ran for state governor in 1958 but lost heavily to Lieutenant Governor S. Ernest Vandiver.[26]

Biblical segregationists were also among those who founded the Baptist Laymen of Alabama in May 1957 and its sister organization the Baptist Laymen of Mississippi. Formed as religious equivalents of the Citizens' Councils to which many of their members also belonged, the two groups sought to prevent any dissent from massive resistance within the churches or by their respective state conventions and the SBC. Claiming an initial membership of 160, primarily from the black belt and Montgomery County, the Alabama organization soon "attracted an impressive following," according to historian Numan V. Bartley. Its literature frequently advanced the biblical defense of Jim Crow.[27]

Pastors who defended segregation as biblical tended to have relatively little education. They could be found in both rural and urban churches, but they were more commonplace in the former. In urban areas, they tended to pastor the less prestigious churches that, like themselves, comprised the working class and the less educated. Segregationist pastors of larger, urban churches generally defended Jim Crow on practical, rather than religious, grounds. They argued that while they, of course, supported equal rights, they opposed the civil rights movement because it created disorder, frequently violated laws, and was, some suggested, subject to Communist influence. Gwin T. Turner, pastor of Vicksburg, Mississippi's Bowmar Avenue Church, conceded in the *Baptist Record* that "the Negro" desired and deserved equal rights but, with the implication that African Americans were not yet ready to receive them, asserted that "he has the responsibility of showing that he treats these rights with respect and regards them as a trust." Turner viewed the civil rights movement as a sinister plot, devised by unspecified conspirators. He wrote: "There are many who are seeking to agitate us into a fit of anger, and thus throw us into total confusion, preparing us to be manipulated by others. The designers of this plot have been able to sweep into their movement many well intentioned but misguided people."[28]

Small in number, progressive pastors who called for adjustment to secular desegregation and, in some cases, for integration of their churches, tended to occupy the pastorates of the prestigious First Baptist churches which had large, middle class memberships. In May 1957, Nolan P. Howington, pastor of Little Rock, Arkansas's First Baptist Church, delivered a sermon that condemned racial prejudice and biblical segregation as a "perversion of the Scriptures." After the sermon, Howington declared his support for the city's school desegregation plan. Many pastors of urban First Baptist churches had, like Howington, been seminary educated, and they reflected the influence of their progressive professors.[29]

Urban pastors sometimes called for compliance with desegregation in statements issued by local ministerial groups or associations, both Baptist and interdenominational. They preferred the feeling of unity, security and comparative anonymity afforded by collective action. In March 1954, the Gainesville Ministerial Association, composed of the city's Protestant clergymen, called on Georgians to support public education, whatever the decision of the Supreme Court in the forthcoming *Brown* case. The ministers affirmed their "faith in continued constitutional government and in the public school system as two of the great cornerstones on which our democracy rests." In anticipation that the federal courts would order school desegregation in their cities, over three hundred ministers of various denominations in Dallas, Texas, and Atlanta, Georgia, signed statements in 1958 that called for compliance with school desegregation. In the summer of 1961, fifty-three Baton Rouge, Louisiana, clergymen, including thirteen Southern Baptists, called on the city's residents to support the public schools even if they desegregated. Their statement declared that "discrimination on account of race or religion is a violation of the divine law of love."[30]

Just as there were urban progressive pastors, so there were also some, but probably fewer, rural progressive pastors. Many rural and some urban progressive pastors lost their pulpits for expressing their views. The congregation of Fortune Baptist Church, Parkin, east Arkansas, dismissed the Reverend E. Jones in March 1955 for denouncing Jim Crow as unchristian in a sermon. Jones remembered: "I was called before a special meeting of the congregation and given the choice of not preaching on the subject or being dismissed." Harassment eventually led each of the Baptist signatories of the Baton Rouge statement to leave their pastorates.[31]

However, it would be incorrect to assume that most lay Baptists were always or necessarily unyielding segregationists. Cases studies of urban churches indicate that many Baptists did not support hard-line segregationist resistance. Although Tallahassee, Florida's First Baptist Church voted in February 1964 not to accept the recommendation of its pastor, C. A. Roberts, and deacons to overturn a one hundred-year-old policy of excluding African Americans, they did so by the narrow margin of 640 votes to 626. A few months after the passage of the Civil Rights Act in July 1964, First Baptist allowed blacks to attend worship services.[32]

By the second half of the 1960s, with public accommodations desegregated under federal law, Baptists became increasingly receptive to church desegregation. After a protracted, acrimonious struggle Richmond, Virginia's First Baptist Church admitted two Nigerian members in January 1965 and later overturned a ban on black membership dating back to 1841. Despite their initial opposition to an open admissions policy advocated by their pastor, Theodore F. Adams, and young lay people, the deacons relented and recommended that a committee study the policy. In a mail vote, seventy percent of the congregation approved the committee's desegregation recommendation. In the meantime, six segregationist deacons had filed a lawsuit to block desegregation, but they lost their case on a technicality.[33]

In April 1965, Alexandria's Belle View Baptist Church became the first church in the Baptist General Association of Virginia to admit African-American members. Segregationists in Belle View called for the dismissal of its pastor, Norman Alexander Yance, when he urged the church to admit a black couple to membership, but the congregation gave him an overwhelming vote of confidence. Yance later recalled that "Half of those who voted for my dismissal were not at all active in the church; most made no financial contribution to the church. Only two or three could be called active members."[34]

Surprisingly, perhaps, a similar pattern even appeared in some rural, black-belt churches. When Plains Baptist Church, near Americus, Georgia, voted to bar African Americans in 1965, over two hundred people attended the meeting. Yet, fewer than seventy people voted, and the church adopted the policy by only fifty-four votes to six. Several dozen people told future U.S. President Jimmy Carter, one of those who had voted for an open policy, that "they agreed with my stand, but did not want to vote openly in the church conference." The abstainers realized that those who took a stand for equal rights faced social ostracism and retribution from organized segregationists. Carter, who ran a peanut farm, had been subjected to a boycott after refusing to join the local Citizens' Council chapter.[35]

Several rural and urban churches split over the question of desegregation in the second half of the 1960s and during the early 1970s. Committed segregationists usually comprised older members of the congregation and sporadic churchgoers. Irregular attenders were less subject to the influence of progressive Baptist clergymen and the educational message disseminated by progressives in the SBC's agencies, while progressives found older members harder to wean away from their long-held support for Jim Crow. Irregular churchgoers and nonmembers often attended and voted for the exclusion of African Americans when churches considered admissions policies.

Macon, Georgia's Tattnall Square Baptist Church dismissed the Reverend Thomas J. Holmes in September 1966, after he had publicly stated his opposition to a closed door policy toward blacks which the church had adopted by 289 votes to 109. Holmes estimated that at least one hundred people voted in the ballot who had not previously attended church and that most, if not, all of these were diehard segregationists. After Holmes's dismissal, approximately one hundred church members left Tattnall Square to form a new, open door church.[36]

J. Herbert Gilmore Jr. resigned the pastorate of Birmingham, Alabama's First Baptist Church in October 1970, after a majority had voted to receive two African Americans into membership, but still short of the two-thirds majority required under the church's by-laws. He took almost his entire staff and 255 church members, over a third of First Baptist's regular attendance, with him to establish a new, open church, the Church of the Covenant. Gilmore noted that many of those who voted against accepting the two applicants "had not been in the church for years" and that at least 80 percent of those who chose to remain in First Baptist after the split were aged sixty-five or over.[37]

Opinion polls confirmed that each generation of white southerners tended to be more accepting of desegregation than the preceding generation. A survey in 1956 found that 19 percent of those aged 21–24 approved of school integration, 15 percent of the 25–44 age group, 12 percent of the 45–64 group and 10 percent of those aged 65 and over. Polls conducted in the second half of the 1960s and the early 1970s confirmed that the young had the highest pro-integration scores among white southerners.[38]

Surveys taken between the 1950s and the 1970s also indicated that approval ratings for school integration rose with the educational levels of those interviewed, which, in part, explained why the young, with greater access to education, tended to be more accepting of integration than preceding generations. In 1956, 28 percent of white southerners with a college education approved of school integration, 15 percent of high school graduates and 5 percent of those with eight years or less of education. Eight years later, the figures for the same groups stood at 48 percent, thirty-two percent and 20 percent, respectively. Aside from increasing education levels, the young tended to be more approving of school integration than previous generations because, by the 1960s and 1970s, they had "been [more] exposed to different values in race relations" as a result of the desegregation of public facilities and also increasingly of public education.[39]

Among Southern Baptists, college and seminary students and BSUs consistently proved to be the most progressive elements during the civil rights era. BSUs, sponsored by the Sunday School Board, provided an on-campus ministry to Baptist students in both secular and religious institutions and linked them to local Baptist churches. Regardless of their location in the South, BSUs adopted more liberal positions on race than their respective state conventions, and they often urged their conventions forward in race relations. When polled during the 1950s and 1960s on the question of desegregating the Baptist educational institutions they attended, students usually voted in favor. Their education influenced the progressive views of many Baptist students by exposing them to ethics and race relations courses in seminaries and also in some colleges and universities. Furthermore, throughout the civil rights era, Southern Baptist educational materials for the young, published by the Sunday School Board and the WMU, addressed race relations much more frequently and forcefully than those directed at adults.[40]

The sympathy of many Baptist students with the African-American struggle for equality was apparent even in the immediate postwar period. A meeting of representatives of six hundred Baptist youth organizations in Georgia during February 1947 adopted a "minimum bill of rights" for blacks, which called for voting rights, equal pay for equal work, equal education, and employment opportunities, although it did not condemn Jim Crow. The meeting also asked that African Americans be appointed to serve on juries in cases involving black people.[41]

Some young Baptists rejected the biblical defense of segregation. In 1948, T. Gilbert Butler and T. Howard Johnson Jr., both students at Alabama's Auburn Polytechnic Institute, wrote a lengthy article in the *Alabama Baptist* that refuted every major segregationist "proof text." Although they believed that "it is best for the two races to remain ethnologically distinct," the students argued that Jim Crow was not "the Christian way" to prevent miscegenation. They declared: "Segregation in the past has not prevented intermingling of the races. It has been only the source of discrimination, injustice and misunderstanding." Other students also rejected white supremacy. When the Ku Klux Klan held a rally in Macon, Georgia, in 1949, students from Mercer University attended wearing white cards that read "I am here in protest against the Klan and all its principles."[42]

Some Baptist students directly challenged segregated meetings. The BSU held an annual week-long retreat at Ridgecrest Baptist Assembly in North Carolina, which often included seminars and discussions about race relations. During the 1946 retreat, the students voted overwhelmingly for African Americans to be included, but the Sunday School Board, which ran

Ridgecrest, denied their request. In the same year as they challenged racial exclusivity at Ridgecrest, Southern Baptist students helped to organize the first Southwide Conference of Baptist Theological Students, an interracial meeting of Baptist theological students designed to promote fellowship and cooperative efforts to spread the gospel.[43]

In 1947, the state BSU held an interracial revival in Texas, while North Carolina's BSU invited twenty-five black students to attend its convention, where they mixed freely with whites. The North Carolina students intended to repeat the experiment at their next convention in 1948, but the host church in Gastonia voted to segregate the meeting. Consequently, African Americans refused to attend. The convention itself "voted unanimously to have all future state-wide Baptist student meetings on an interracial fellowship basis." The students also decided to include a black student on their officers' council, and in April 1949 the BSU elected an African American, William Worley, as extension vice president of its officers' council.[44]

Southern Baptist Theological Seminary students presented a petition to the seminary's trustees in April 1950 that urged them to approve the admission of qualified African Americans. A student survey revealed that 94.7 percent of the student body approved of a nondiscriminatory admissions policy. Of the 754 people polled, 714 favored desegregation, thirteen objected and twenty-seven expressed no opinion. Among those from the eleven states of the former Confederacy, 493 students endorsed desegregation, twelve opposed it and twenty-two abstained. Their petition indicated that the students were concerned primarily with racial injustice. It declared: "The Negro is the only race not allowed to attend Southern Seminary and we do not feel that true Christian principles are being carried out with this discrimination." The seminary desegregated in 1951.[45]

Students also played an important role in desegregating Wayland Baptist College in the same year. The student body voted unanimously that black students should be admitted. According to Wayland student Leon McBeth, "This student vote was part of the persuasion by which the president convinced the trustees to go along." Even before the *Brown* school desegregation decision, then, some Baptist students endorsed desegregation.[46]

More students endorsed desegregation after the Supreme Court's ruling. Although the Louisiana Baptist Convention ignored *Brown* at its annual meeting in November 1954, its BSU unanimously approved the ruling at its annual convention, which also included representatives from two black colleges, Southern University in Baton Rouge and Leland Baptist College in Baker. In addition, the BSU voted to continue to hold integrated annual meetings.[47]

Baptist students in North Carolina also took a progressive approach to integration, and they exerted pressure on the Baptist State Convention to act. Initially, the state convention took no position on school desegregation at its annual meeting in 1954. In response, the state BSU presented a resolution to the messengers "recognizing the validity" of *Brown*, and they urged the convention to desegregate Baptist institutions in "all haste commensurate with sound judgment and Christian love." The Resolutions Committee removed the word "haste" and suggested that the convention appoint a committee to study institutional desegregation. The messengers consented.[48]

The experience of Southern Baptists in Tennessee mirrored that of North Carolina. The Tennessee Baptist Convention ignored the *Brown* ruling at its annual meeting in 1954. When it met a year later, Mia Canariis, Secretary of the Tennessee Baptist Student Convention, presented a resolution that the students had adopted in October which called for the Tennessee Baptist Convention's four educational institutions to be open "to all races regardless of color." Unwilling to take a stand on the issue, the Resolutions Committee recommended that the convention refer the resolution "to the Trustees of such institutions to work out according to their charters and to the best interests of all concerned." The messengers agreed. Baptist colleges in the state remained all white.[49]

Even in states that adopted massive resistance to school desegregation, Baptist students spoke out against Jim Crow. In October 1957, at the height of the Little Rock school desegregation crisis, the Arkansas BSU's annual convention adopted a statement that affirmed "the equal worth of all individuals," supported "the law of the land," and condemned "violence in the settlement of any difficulty." Only one of the 360 delegates attending voted against the declaration. Yet when the Arkansas Baptist State Convention held its annual meeting in November, it made no pronouncements on the crisis.[50]

In the wake of the Little Rock crisis, Virginia elected J. Lindsay Almond Jr. as governor on the promise that he would resist desegregation. While the Baptist General Association of Virginia proved unwilling to address segregation, Virginia BSU members on a spring retreat passed a resolution in April 1958 that condemned racial discrimination. The students expressed concern at "the irreparable harm" done to "the foreign mission program among colored people" by racism at home. They called for Baptist Assembly Grounds, and religious and secular colleges and universities to be desegregated.[51]

Southern Baptist students played a role in desegregating several Baptist colleges in the early 1960s. Students at Mercer University voted for desegregation by a margin of three-to-two in a campus poll during February

1961. Their opinion encouraged Rufus C. Harris, the university's president, to ask its trustees to authorize the admission of African-American students.[52] Two months later, Texas BSU leaders adopted a resolution that did not call for integration of Baptist schools, but stated the willingness of Baptist students to cooperate with desegregation and also expressed concern about the effects of racial discrimination on foreign missions. A year later, the student congress of Baylor University, a Baptist institution in Waco, passed a resolution, by thirty votes to five, that urged the trustees to integrate the university. The move followed a straw poll of Baylor students in which they had indicated a desire to see the university opened to blacks. The following November, Baylor trustees voted to eliminate race as a consideration in admissions.[53]

Baptist students acted as a progressive influence in the Baptist State Convention of South Carolina. In November 1961, the convention rejected a resolution to instruct its institutions to desegregate. A month later, South Carolina's BSU voted 117 to 25 to adopt a resolution which suggested that the trustees of Baptist institutions consider their "responsibility" to desegregate them. A few days later, in an informal, unofficial poll the faculty of Furman University voted 68 to 12 for desegregation and their students concurred by 512 votes to 434. After the Baptist State Convention had voted in 1964 against desegregating Furman University, the state BSU, in effect, rebuked the convention by voting 121 to 57 in favor of integrating its statewide activities. Four years later, the BSU presented a statement to the convention in support of open churches. It announced that "We do not see how a stand of racial prejudice or segregation can be derived from Christianity. Can we afford the vice of mental isolation that permits us to send missionaries to Kenya and Nigeria to establish Baptist churches among the black men there while we will not open membership in our churches to black men here?" Militant segregationist resistance led the messengers to receive the statement as "information only."[54]

In the neighboring state of North Carolina, Baptist students continued to exert a progressive influence. They formed Baptist Students Concerned in 1968 to encourage discussion in the SBC of racial problems, poverty and the Vietnam War. When the SBC met in June, they held a vigil outside the convention hall in support of the crisis statement on race relations that the messengers later adopted. Inspired by the crisis, 1,300 students attending the annual Leadership Training Conference of the Texas BSU unanimously adopted a statement in which they promised to work to end "every trace of racial discrimination in our Baptist Student Unions, sororities, fraternities, and clubs, as well as in matters of student housing and employment."[55]

As the crisis statement had urged, Baptists students in South Carolina continued to press for open churches. In September 1971, Due West Baptist Church voted by a margin of three-to-one to maintain its ban on admitting African Americans, after its pastor, Don Stevenson, had invited an interracial BSU chapter to use the church's facilities for its meetings. The next month, church deacons cancelled the service because a black student was present, and the congregation voted forty-seven to thirty-six to dismiss Stevenson. However, fear of adverse publicity also led the church to end its discriminatory admissions policy. In response to the Due West incident, the BSU successfully called on the Baptist State Convention of South Carolina to adopt a resolution supporting a day of Reconciliation and Prayer by its churches, so that they might "re-examine their position on the racial issue." The BSU also sponsored the resolution in protest at the decision of the Sunday School Board to withdraw an issue of *Becoming* for promoting church desegregation.[56]

Other Baptist students also objected to the *Becoming* affair. The BSU convention in North Carolina approved a resolution that deplored "the timidity" shown by the Sunday School Board's action. The Student Congress at Baylor University adopted a resolution that expressed "extreme disappointment" and warned of the affair's "unfortunate reprecussions [*sic*] among fellow Christians in the black community."[57]

In common with other Baptists, students gave less attention to race relations after the early 1970s. Anecdotal evidence suggests that some progressive Baptists left the denomination in the 1960s and 1970s, frustrated by what they saw as a denomination unwilling or too slow to change. Those who left for other denominations often chose Episcopal or Methodist churches, while some abandoned organized religion entirely. The SBC thereby lost some of the progressive voices that might have, at least partially, offset its growing apathy toward racial issues after 1971.[58]

Often seen as a socially conservative and even reactionary religious group, Southern Baptists, in fact, defy simple classification. They presented a wide range of responses to the issue of desegregation. Baptist acceptance of change in race relations tended to increase with education, urban habitation and location in areas where African Americans formed a relatively small proportion of the population. It also increased with each new generation. Sex had no appreciable influence on racial attitudes. Less educated, older, rural, and especially black-belt Baptists tended to be the most hostile to racial change. However, even these generalizations cannot always be sustained, as is seen in the examples of those black-belt churches in the Deep South which included substantial numbers who favored desegregation but felt intimidated into keeping silent. The response of Southern Baptists to racial change has to be seen in its local, regional and national context, with an awareness of change over time as some Baptists came to relinquish seg-regationist views and new, increasingly progressive generations gradually replaced their forebears. A comparison with other leading national and regional denominations also places the SBC's record in race relations in relief.

10

The Major White Denominations and Race Relations, 1945–1971

If the responses of Southern Baptists to desegregation are to be understood, they must be seen in the context of those of the other major southern, northern, and national Christian denominations and their members. This chapter presents a comparison between Southern Baptists and the Presbyterian Church in the United States (PCUS), the Presbyterian Church in the United States of America (PCUSA), the Disciples of Christ, the Methodist Church, the Protestant Episcopal Church and Catholic bishops in the South. During the civil rights era, the SBC consistently lagged behind large northern and southern Christian denominations in both the number and content of its pronouncements on race relations. To a lesser extent, Baptist state conventions in the peripheral South also trailed behind their Protestant and Catholic counterparts. However, in the Deep South, where whites proved most opposed to desegregation, Baptist state conventions defended segregation no more than many other major denominations in the region. Across the South, Protestant and Catholic lay people often proved as reluctant to desegregate their churches, colleges and denominational life as Southern Baptist laity. Lay sentiment, rather than denominational polity or even theological beliefs, played the crucial role in determining the pace at which the major Christian bodies tackled desegregation at the local and state level.

With few, if any, African-American members of Southern Baptist churches and the SBC's training of black ministers confined to the American Baptist Theological Seminary and to extension classes in some of its seminaries, desegregation of Baptist life seemed of little immediate relevance to most Southern Baptists in 1945. However, other major white Christian denominations already had a black presence. At the end of World War II, most African Americans who were members of predominantly white denominations attended black, rather than integrated, churches in both the North and the South. The Methodist Church had 330,600 blacks among its 8,046,129 members, followed by the Protestant Episcopal Church with 60,326 blacks among 2,227,524 members, the Disciples of Christ with 60,000 blacks among 1,672,354 members, the Northern Baptist Convention with 45,000 blacks among 1,555,914 members, the PCUSA with 40,581 blacks among 2,040,399 members, and the PCUS with 3,132 blacks among 565,853 members. There were approximately 500,000 black Catholics in America. In the postwar era, non-SBC denominations faced a growing demand from their black members for racial equality and integration in church life that made it difficult for denominational meetings to ignore, especially as the civil rights movement developed.[1]

In theory, denominations that were hierarchical in nature, such as the Catholic and Protestant Episcopal churches, could desegregate their schools and churches by order of their bishops. The Methodist Church was also hierarchical and made policy in the General Conference, which met quadrennially. Denominations that possessed congregational polities, such as the SBC and the Disciples of Christ, were much less likely to desegregate their southern churches since they were governed by their parishioners. Presbyterians operated a halfway house between episcopal and congregational polities, in which a series of hierarchically constituted church courts from the local court, or session, to the presbytery and synod, and, ultimately, the General Assembly, the highest court, made policy decisions.[2]

In practice, regardless of polity, all denominations were constrained, to some degree, in the formation and implementation of their race relations policies by the sentiment of their members. Denominational organizations at the national, regional and state levels often staked out more progressive positions on racial issues than those shared by most of their coreligionists. They also took into account the strength of local segregationist sentiment before making decisions and pronouncements about race relations or the desirability and speed at which desegregation should occur in their institutions.[3]

Although Catholic, Episcopalian, Methodist and Presbyterian clergymen were, in theory, less subject to the whims of their congregations than ministers of congregational churches, in practice they often felt similar pressures from hostile members of their congregations, if they took unpopular positions in favor of desegregation. Furthermore, ministers of all denominations shared a concern to demonstrate their worth and achieve upward mobility by efficiently managing and enlarging their churches, without alienating their parishioners by advocating controversial or divisive views about race relations. Despite being protected from dismissal by their congregations, Catholic priests were, nevertheless, subject to organizational constraints on their outspokenness similar to those operating on Southern

Baptist ministers. Historian William A. Osborne explained that "Promotion to the pastorate in most dioceses is geared to what might be called organizational welfare. Seniority plays a major role, as does ability to 'run a parish'—that is, to administer an organization."[4]

In terms of its racial composition and geographical location, the PCUS or Southern Presbyterians most closely approximated the SBC among the major denominations. Comprising a membership that was 98 percent white (and one percent Hispanic), the denomination was entirely southern. The PCUS confined most of its African-American churches, accounting for a mere one percent of its total membership, to the Snedecor Memorial Synod, created in 1916, after an attempt to establish an Afro-American Presbyterian Church had failed. Its sister denomination, the predominantly northern PCUSA respected southern customs by maintaining all-black synods and presbyteries in the South, whereas outside the region its black churches belonged to general synods and presbyteries.[5]

In 1939, the Methodist Church tackled the problem of a large African-American membership, located mostly in the South, by placing most of its black churches in an all-black Central Jurisdiction. The arrangement was the price paid to reunify Methodism's northern and southern branches, which had split in 1844 as a consequence of the sectional tensions that eventually led to the Civil War. However, reunification in 1939 also assured blacks of representation in the General Conference, which included each of its jurisdictions.[6]

Unlike the Methodist and Presbyterian denominations, the Protestant Episcopal Church had not fractured over sectional tensions before the Civil War. In the civil rights era, most black Episcopalians lived in the North. By 1945, all of the denomination's black churches, including those in the South, participated in regional organizations, although South Carolina still denied them full voting rights in diocesan conventions. In theory the Disciples of Christ also ignored race in its organizational structures, but, in practice, the Disciples organized their work with black churches separately from that with white churches. Unlike the Disciples, the Northern Baptist Convention had no black churches in the South. Its African-American churches participated in Baptist associations, state conventions and annual regional conventions.[7]

Like the Protestant denominations, the Catholic Church observed local etiquette in the South and tended to minister to blacks in segregated institutions. Separate parochial schools and churches catered to blacks and whites in the region, although sometimes African Americans sat in church galleries and received communion after whites. During the civil rights era, black Catholic numbers increased from a small base in the South. The expansion in part reflected and, at the same time, influenced a growing commitment by the Catholic Church to racial equality.[8]

The civil rights movement's fight against racism during World War Two, wartime race riots and disturbances, and America's commitment to defeat racist Nazi Germany encouraged the country's major denominations to study the racial problem afresh and to reconsider their policies toward minority groups. Another impetus came from increased efforts after the war, particularly by the PCUS, the Catholic Church and the SBC, to evangelize African Americans and the world's non-white majority.[9]

Northern white denominations far outpaced their southern counterparts in supporting civil rights in the immediate postwar years. The Federal Council of Churches, comprised of twenty-five Protestant denominations with a combined membership of over twenty-five million people, made a non-binding declaration in 1946 that condemned segregation as "a violation of the Gospel of love and human brotherhood" and called on its member bodies to "work for a non-segregated church and a non-segregated society." The statement was soon adopted by the PCUSA and the Disciples of Christ, while the Northern Baptist Convention and the Protestant Episcopal Church also condemned segregation. In 1948, the Methodists denounced "racial discrimination" as "unchristian" and recommended that "every Methodist, and every Methodist church, conference, and institution accept the achievement of full fellowship in our churches as a vital responsibility." However, the PCUS did not endorse the attack on Jim Crow and, unlike the Southern Presbyterians, the SBC was not a member of the Federal Council of Churches. The gap between northern and southern religion on race widened as some northern Protestant denominations went on to support fair employment practices legislation and several, including the Northern Baptist Convention, condemned residential segregation.[10]

Unwilling to alienate their segregationist parishioners by condemning Jim Crow, southern white denominations criticized inequities within segregation, commissioned studies on racial issues, and focused on educating their members in Christian attitudes toward minorities. In 1945, the PCUS expressed disapproval of racial discrimination in employment, education, housing and the ballot. The denomination also created an Ad Interim Committee on Negro Work which recommended in 1946 that greater effort be expended on evangelism among African Americans, Stillman College (its institution for black ministerial training) upgraded and blacks given a greater say in running their own activities. Subsequently, Southern Presbyterians promoted the creation of new black churches within the denomination, and in 1952, they launched a $2 million appeal to fund black evangelism and improve Stillman College. The PCUS also transformed its low-budget Permanent Committee on Social and Moral Welfare into a $20,000 Department of Christian Relations with a full-time secretariat in 1946. The department's task was to "produce suitable literature for informational and instructional purposes," to "speak to the churches" on social issues and to "speak for the churches when commissioned to do so, or when the Assembly's pronouncements are to be carried out."[11]

The SBC's appointment of a Committee on Race Relations in 1946 and its decision a year later to allocate the Social Service Commission with a $10,000 budget mirrored the actions of the PCUS. Like the Southern Presbyterians, the convention also criticized employment and voting discrimination and claimed that equal rights could be divorced from segregation. Furthermore, the SBC instructed its agencies and colleges to develop an educational program in race relations, and in 1947 it adopted a Charter of Principles in Race Relations that called for equal opportunities and justice but ignored segregation. Its charter marked the convention as being as advanced on race relations as any other major southern white denomination. At their General Assembly in 1947, Southern Presbyterians, much like the SBC, urged their parishioners to support the civil rights of minorities, but, unlike the convention, they specifically criticized the Ku Klux Klan.[12]

Northern denominations continued to outpace their southern counterparts in the late 1940s by attacking segregation. While the SBC's Social Service Commission endorsed the desire of President Harry S. Truman's Committee on Civil Rights to rectify racial discrimination, it did not discuss its legislative recommendations. Similarly, the PCUS supported civil rights for African Americans, noted their absence and recognized, in general terms, "the role of both education and legislation" in "safeguarding human rights." By contrast, the Northern Baptist Convention praised Truman's civil rights program. It also called for "the ending of all racial segregation in employment, the armed forces and housing" and condemned segregation in its own churches.[13]

The SBC's Social Service Commission did not advocate open churches, but it urged Southern Baptist seminaries to consider desegregation. The commission noted that the Southern Presbyterians' Union Theological Seminary in Richmond, Virginia, had admitted black graduate students since 1935. By 1951, three of the SBC's four seminaries in the South had desegregated and all of the Southern Presbyterian seminaries had ended racial discrimination in admissions policies. Both denominations acted to promote black ministerial training as the black seminaries they supported proved inadequate to the task. Although theological schools at other Methodist universities remained all white, the Perkins School of Theology at Southern Methodist University also desegregated in 1951, as did the Protestant Episcopal Church's Virginia Theological Seminary in Alexandria. In practice, seminary desegregation, regardless of denomination, did not exceed tokenism.[14]

The SBC kept pace with other denominations in desegregating its seminaries, but it did not otherwise attack Jim Crow. However, even more active and outspoken denominations made little progress in undermining segregation in their institutions. The General Assembly of the PCUS voted in 1951 to gradually eliminate the Snecedor Memorial Synod. White synods in the Deep South received its presbyteries, but the denomination's churches remained segregated and black churches continued to be treated as a separate entity, the Snecedor Region, in PCUS programs. Although the PCUSA had adopted a policy of cultivating interracial churches in the 1940s, few had developed in the North by the early 1950s. Methodists declared in 1952 that "there is no place in The Methodist Church for racial discrimination or racial segregation," yet both remained enshrined in the continued existence of the Central Jurisdiction.[15]

In the same year, the General Convention of the Protestant Episcopal Church, which met triennially, adopted a resolution that declared Christianity to be "incompatible with every form of discrimination based on color or race." However, its trustees refused to desegregate the School of Theology at the University of the South, an Episcopalian institution in Sewanee, Tennessee. A year later, after widespread criticism and an offer of resignation by the dean of the school and seven of its eight faculty members, the trustees reversed their decision. By 1954, all Episcopalian seminaries were desegregated and in that year, the Diocese of South Carolina accorded blacks full voting rights at diocesan meetings, the last Episcopal diocese to do so.[16]

The Catholic Church also began to attack southern segregation but with limited results. The Catholic Committee of the South, a small group founded in 1939 with the support of many of the region's bishops to promote social justice, passed a resolution in 1951 that favored "ultimate integration" of blacks into all spheres of American life. Two years later, at the end of the committee's convention, the Bishops of the South issued a statement that "deplored the practice of racial segregation and the injustices that flow from it. . . . "[17]

As members of a hierarchical institution, Catholic bishops could order their churches, schools and hospitals to desegregate. In some peripheral southern states, where segregationist sentiment was less militant than in the Deep South, Catholic bishops issued desegregation orders before the *Brown* decision. Robert E. Lucy, Archbishop of San Antonio, where some Catholic schools had been integrated for some years, stated in April 1954 that all Catholic educational institutions had to integrate fully. A month later, Vincent S. Waters, Bishop of Raleigh, North Carolina, ordered Catholic churches and high schools to desegregate, and he urged Catholic elementary schools and hospitals to follow suit. Peter L. Ireton, Bishop of Richmond, Virginia, also ordered Catholic high schools under his control to admit African-American students, as did William Adrian, Bishop of Nashville, Tennessee. St. Anne's Catholic school in Rock Hill, South Carolina, desegregated in 1954, the only parochial school in the Deep South to do so. With the partial exception of Louisiana, other bishops deferred to local segregationist sentiment among whites and Jim Crow remained in place in their dioceses.[18]

Louisiana contained over half of the South's Catholic population and 20 percent of the nation's black Catholics. Notre Dame Seminary in New Orleans admitted two African Americans in 1948. A year later Joseph F. Rummel, Archbishop of the Diocese of New Orleans, desegregated the annual Holy Name parade in the city and then cancelled the event when local authorities refused to allow an integrated march. Rummel also ordered the city's churches to remove "white" and "colored" signs. Loyola University in New Orleans admitted two black graduate students in 1952. Both Rummel and Bishop Jules Jeanmard of Lafayette ordained black priests in 1953. Rummel also issued a pastoral letter that urged churches to end segregation. However, Catholic officials continued to tolerate separate Catholic schools for blacks and whites.[19]

The PCUS, like some Catholic bishops, began to reassess its view of segregation prior to the Supreme Court's ruling. In 1953, the Presbyterian General Assembly discussed segregation within the denomination, but, in place of making any decisions, referred the matter to its Council on Christian Relations. A year later, just after the *Brown* decision, the General Assembly adopted the council's report, which supported the Supreme Court's ruling and affirmed that "enforced segregation of the races" was "out of harmony with Christian theology and ethics. . . . " The report, approved by 239 votes to 169, also urged Presbyterian churches, synods, higher education institutions and governing bodies to desegregate. Although the SBC endorsed the *Brown* decision as constitutional and Christian, it did not explicitly condemn segregation, nor did it urge desegregation upon its churches and other institutions.[20]

In contrast to the PCUS, the Council of Bishops of the Methodist Church adopted a position closer to that of the SBC. The council declared that the Supreme Court's ruling was "in keeping with the attitude of The Methodist Church," and, as the convention had done, welcomed the gradual nature of its implementation as a means to foster adjustment.[21]

The other major denominations made more forceful pronouncements on race. The American Baptist Convention, as the Northern Baptist Convention had renamed itself in 1950, commended the Supreme Court's desegregation ruling and urged "American Baptists to increase their opposition to other areas of segregation—housing, employment, recreation, [and] church participation." At their General Assembly, Northern Presbyterians expressed "thanksgiving" for the *Brown* decision and urged their coreligionists to take an active part in securing its effective implementation. The International Convention of Disciples of Christ commended the Supreme Court's ruling and urged its churches, agencies and institutions to "initiate and encourage voluntary" integration. The General Convention of the Protestant Episcopal Church stated in 1955 that "discrimination and segregation are contrary to the mind of Christ and the will of God" and urged Episcopalians to "accept and support" the *Brown* decision.[22]

State level organizations, particularly in the peripheral South, sometimes supported their denominations' pronouncements concerning *Brown* or the principle of desegregation. They included Southern Baptist conventions in North Carolina and Virginia, PCUS synods in Arkansas, Texas and Virginia, and Methodist conferences in Florida, Little Rock, North Arkansas, North Carolina, North Texas and Southwest Texas. In the Deep South, the major Protestant denominations exhibited a range of responses from calls for calm and lawful obedience to silence. Unlike Southern Baptist state conventions, in 1954 some Presbyterian groups openly expressed hostility to desegregation. The Synod of Mississippi called on the PCUS to rescind its support for *Brown* and desegregation within the church, while the Synod of Alabama tabled a resolution that supported desegregation and the Synod of South Carolina voted 125 to eighty to retain Jim Crow in its institutions. C. C. J. Carpenter, the Episcopal Bishop of the Diocese of Alabama, denounced the court's ruling as a "set back" in race relations. The Mississippi Conference of the Methodist Church endorsed segregation within the church.[23]

Opposition to *Brown* mounted in the South between 1955 and 1956. Accordingly, the SBC adopted no recommendations or resolutions concerning race relations again until 1961, and between 1957 and 1961 its Christian Life Commission presented annual reports to the convention as information rather than for adoption. By contrast, the other major white denominations continued to adopt forthright and increasingly progressive resolutions and pronouncements on the subject during the second half of the 1950s. The Disciples of Christ, the American Baptist Convention and the PCUSA called on their churches to select their staff without regard to race and to support efforts to end discrimination in education, housing and public facilities. In 1956, the Methodist Church declared that there was no place within it "for racial discrimination or enforced segregation." It recommended that where they existed "by any method or practice, whether by conference structure or otherwise," they should "be abolished with reasonable speed." However, the action had little impact since the General Conference also determined that black churches and conferences in the Central Jurisdiction could only transfer into other administrative structures upon a two-thirds majority vote of the conferences involved. Segregation remained largely intact because it could not be relinquished without overwhelming support from whites.[24]

A year later, the Southern Presbyterian General Assembly, in contrast to the silence of the SBC, approved a 4,000 word pronouncement that denounced the Ku Klux Klan and the Citizens' Councils, as well as racial discrimination in politics, employment, education and the church. The document also defended interracial Koinonia Farm in southwest Georgia, which had been repeatedly attacked by members of the local white community. Even though the farm was organized and run by Southern Baptist Clarence Jordan, his denomination said nothing in his support.[25]

In the same year, the American Baptist Convention called for Baptist church membership, pastorates, and "each Baptist organization, school, home, and hospital" to be open to all regardless of race. The convention also urged Baptists not to align themselves "with any organized group or movement that works to retain segregation . . . , the Ku Klux Klan, White Citizens Councils, and all exclusive groups that deny membership to others on the basis of race." The highest ranking leaders of the United Presbyterian Church in the USA, formed a year earlier from the merger of the PCUSA and the United Presbyterian Church, issued a statement in September 1958 that supported the use of federal troops "if necessary" to enforce school desegregation in Little Rock. The Catholic Church also attacked racism. The Roman Catholic Bishops of the United States released a statement in 1958 that condemned segregation laws and called for equal economic and educational opportunity for all.[26]

Although the Catholic Bishops and the major white Protestant denominations, except the SBC, issued strong statements in the second half of the 1950s, they had little practical impact on segregation within the church, and they aroused opposition from many lay people and some ministers, particularly in the Deep South. State and district religious groups, clergymen and lay people were generally no more willing to desegregate in the South than Southern Baptists, whatever the statements of their leading southern or national bodies.

State level religious organizations in the peripheral South, which had, in some cases, endorsed desegregation of their institutions or the public school system in 1954 and 1955, often fell silent as massive resistance to school desegregation mounted, while those in the Deep South either opposed desegregation, made platitudinous calls for peace and calm, or simply ignored the issue. Among Southern Baptists, only the state conventions in Louisiana and Alabama endorsed segregation, but even then they did not do so on biblical grounds. Few state organizational meetings of the other mainstream denominational bodies defended Jim Crow as Christian either. However, there were exceptions. The Protestant Episcopal Diocese of South Carolina adopted a resolution at its annual convention in 1956 which declared "that there is nothing morally wrong in a voluntary recognition of racial differences and . . . voluntary alignments can be both natural and Christian."[27]

Some clergymen and lay people, particularly in the Deep South, organized groups to pressure their state bodies into silence about desegregation and to oppose its implementation within religious institutions. The Association of Methodist Ministers and Laymen, founded in December 1954 to resist attempts to dismantle the Central Jurisdiction, had its largest membership in Alabama and Mississippi, and its successor, the Laymen's Union, formed in 1959, also attracted support from adjacent states. Segregationists from other denominations organized the Baptist Laymen of Alabama, the Baptist Laymen of Mississippi, and another Deep South group, the Presbyterian Laymen for Sound Doctrine and Responsible Leadership, Inc., in the second half of the 1950s. Individual churches sometimes sent their denominations resolutions that opposed race relations statements made by their social action agencies.[28]

Southern Baptist lay people and clergy from the Deep South attempted in vain to curtail the activities of the Christian Life Commission and to secure its abolition, but they succeeded in restricting its budget. Similarly, presbyteries in Mississippi, Alabama, and South Carolina asked the General Assembly of the PCUS in 1958 to abolish the denomination's Council on Christian Relations, but without success.[29]

Although segregationists usually could not stop their regional or national denominational gatherings from speaking out on race, they were largely successful in preventing or restricting desegregation of denominational institutions in the South during the second half of the 1950s. At its General Conference in 1956, the Methodist Church chose to retain the Central Jurisdiction. The PCUSA made slow progress in obeying the order of its General Assembly in 1954 to begin desegregation of its synods and presbyteries. Since the 1940s, the denomination had adopted a policy of fostering integration churches, but again progress was very limited. A survey conducted between 1956 and 1957 found that only 13 percent of its predominantly white churches had at least one African American involved in their activities, while in the South only three such churches had any black participation. Historian David M. Reimers contends that the Protestant Episcopal Church and the American Baptist Convention shared a similar record to Northern Presbyterians, while the Methodist Church "undoubtedly had proportionately fewer racially inclusive congregations" than the PCUSA. The Disciples of Christ fared better than most Protestant groups in its policy of church desegregation, but even so, the denomination's achievements lagged far behind its aspirations. By 1956, only 464 churches of the seven thousand surveyed in forty states had integrated to some extent.[30]

Southern Baptist churches were little different from other white Protestant churches in the South in neither including nor welcoming African Americans. However, Baptists trailed behind other denominations in making progress towards desegregating their colleges. By 1956, 55 of 188 Protestant colleges and universities in the South, most of them in the peripheral states, had relinquished Jim Crow, with Wayland Baptist College in Texas the SBC's sole representative. Its record of desegregating thirty-five of its forty-five higher education institutions in the South helped to establish the progressive reputation of the Catholic Church in attacking segregation. However, in terms of desegregating its churches and parochial schools the Catholic record in the South was much closer to that of the major white Protestant denominations in the region.[31]

There was little difference between southern white Protestant and Catholic lay people in their preference for segregation. According to a survey of southern white Christians conducted by the *Catholic Digest* in 1956, only 17 percent of Protestants and 19 percent of Catholics supported desegregation. Catholic bishops, supposedly more immune to parishioner pressure than Protestant leaders, often bowed to segregationist sentiment. Desegregation of denominational institutions which had begun in some parts of the upper South came to a virtual halt after 1955 with the rise of massive resistance. Apart from an occasional exception, Catholic dioceses did not resume desegregation until 1962. Journalist Hodding Carter III reported that in the 1950s "The Roman Catholic Church, although committed to integration, did not advocate integration in its parochial schools in Mississippi, nor did its priests often exhort their congregations on the subject of segregation."[32]

The experience of Archbishop Rummel in Louisiana illustrates the significant impact of lay segregationist sentiment on Catholic officials in the South. Rummel personally opposed Jim Crow. After the *Brown* decision, his private letter of objection to state Governor Robert Kennon prevented a bill that would have permitted local school boards to give tuition grants to children attending private schools from coming to a vote in the state assembly. Following the second *Brown* ruling, Rummel issued a pastoral letter which indicated that Catholic schools would not desegregate before September 1956 but implied, rather than stated, that they might then do so.[33]

In February 1956, Rummel condemned segregation as "morally wrong and sinful" in a pastoral letter. The message stimulated growing lay Catholic opposition to Rummel's integrationist sympathies into open rebellion as malcontents formed the Association of Catholic Laymen. Although the association disbanded in April after Rummel threatened its members with excommunication, they simply transferred their efforts to the rapidly expanding Citizens' Councils. Faced with popular lay and clerical opposition to desegregation, Rummel announced in July 1956 that parochial school desegregation would be delayed "at least" until September 1957. In the event, he continued to procrastinate until finally desegregating parochial schools in 1962, two years after public schools in New Orleans had, by federal court order, become the first to integrate in the state. Rummel and Catholic officials worried that if they acted in advance of public school desegregation, white parents might remove their children from parochial schools. Furthermore, Catholic authorities feared that the staunchly segregationist Louisiana state assembly might retaliate by withdrawing from Catholic schools the free text books, school buses and lunches it provided them with.[34]

Rummel excommunicated Leander H. Perez, the political boss of the parishes of Plaquemines and St. Bernard and a leader in the Citizens' Council, and two other segregationist leaders, Jackson G. Ricau and B. J. Galloit Jr., in 1962 for persistent criticism of the archbishop's policy of parochial school desegregation. Catholics in Louisiana were as likely as Protestants to support the Citizens' Councils. While Catholic clergy, subject to the authority of their bishops, did not officiate at Council meetings, historian Neil R. McMillen writes that across the South "a sizeable proportion of the movement's leadership came from the Protestant clergy." The Reverend James P. Dees, rector of Statesville, North Carolina's Trinity Episcopal Church, served on the editorial board of *The Citizens' Council,* the movement's magazine. The Reverend L. B. McCord, an ordained Southern Presbyterian clergyman, also served on the board and was the executive secretary of the South Carolina Association of Citizens' Councils. Protestant ministers acted as Council chaplains. The movement's membership, like its leadership, comprised a cross section of lay people drawn from the largest Protestant denominations, as well as Catholics in Louisiana.[35]

Although it seems likely that, as Howard Dorgan argues, a majority of Protestant clergymen in the Deep South favored segregation in the 1950s, a minority criticized Jim Crow and, just like Southern Baptist ministers who spoke out, some lost their pulpits for doing so. Robert McNeil, pastor of Columbus, Georgia's First Presbyterian Church wrote an article on race relations for *Look* magazine in 1957 that called for a dialogue between the races and freedom for African Americans. The article, his subsequent meeting with Ralph McGill, the moderate editor of the *Atlanta Constitution*, and McNeil's support for Koinonia Farm led segregationists to force his dismissal as pastor by the Southwest Georgia Presbytery in 1959.[36]

Some ministers spoke out for compliance in the midst of local desegregation crises. Marion A. Boggs, pastor of Second Presbyterian Church (PCUS), like Southern Baptist ministers Nolan P. Howington and Dale Cowling, appealed in 1957 for adherence to court-ordered school desegregation in Little Rock, Arkansas. Dunbar H. Ogden Jr., pastor of the city's Central Presbyterian Church (PCUS), and Will D. Campbell, an ordained Southern Baptist minister now working for the Department of Racial and Cultural Relations of the National Council of Churches, led Central High School's first African-American students to class in defiance of the mob, as Baptist minister Paul Turner had done during Clinton, Tennessee's school desegregation crisis a year earlier. When Governor Orval Faubus closed Little Rock's schools in 1958, an interdenominational group that included Boggs, Robert R. Brown, the Episcopal Bishop of Arkansas, and Paul E. Martin, Bishop of the Methodist Church, called for them to be reopened.[37]

In the late 1950s and early 1960s, ministers in large southern cities, including Southern Baptists, often signed interdenominational statements that appealed for calm adherence to school desegregation. When Dallas, Texas, faced a school desegregation order in 1958, three hundred of the city's Protestant ministers, led by Bishop William C. Martin of the Methodist Church, Bishop C. Avery Mason of the Protestant Episcopal Church, John F. Anderson, pastor of First Presbyterian Church, and Foy Valentine, director of the Christian Life Commission of the Baptist General Convention of Texas, declared that "enforced segregation is morally and legally wrong" and urged acceptance of integration. A year later, 125 ministers and rabbis in Greater Miami responded to imminent school desegregation in the city by appealing for preservation of public education and condemning "hatred and scorn for those of another race."[38]

Encouraged by public school desegregation, Protestant denominations slowly resumed desegregation of a few of their colleges in the peripheral South during the early 1960s. The Baptist State Convention of North Carolina experienced its first college desegregation in 1961, when Wake

Forest College integrated its graduate programs and Mars Hill College desegregated undergraduate classes. A year later, Wake Forest and Meredith colleges admitted African-American undergraduates. Davidson College (PCUS) and Duke University, both in North Carolina, and Southern Methodist University also desegregated their undergraduate programs in 1962. Catholic dioceses desegregated parochial schools in much of the South during 1962 but, usually, only in areas that had already begun public school desegregation. They included Houston-Galveston, New Orleans, Atlanta, Miami, St. Augustine, Savannah, Charleston, Little Rock, Amarillo, Austin, Corpus Christi and El Paso.[39]

Pressure for college desegregation often came from denominational officials charged with evangelism and missions, and from missionaries in the field. The direct action phase of the civil rights movement that began with the sit-ins of 1960 and the Freedom Rides, a year later, exposed southern racism to the world and embarrassed the region's denominations. The SBC condemned racist violence by resolution in 1961, but it also denounced civil rights protests. In the same year, the American Baptist Convention reaffirmed its support for desegregation of all its churches, institutions and offices, as well as housing. Furthermore, the convention commended the civil rights movement for using "nonviolent methods to break the patterns and injustices of segregation and discrimination in public places and in public transportation."[40]

Civil rights demonstrations and marches peaked in 1963. Aware of Southern Baptist hostility to the movement, the SBC avoided civil rights at its annual meeting. A resolution from the floor of the convention that expressed support for civil rights protesters jailed in Birmingham, Alabama, and called on Southern Baptists to eliminate "all discriminatory custom from our communities" was buried in the Resolutions Committee. The *Christian Century* commented: "So far as official action is concerned the Southern Baptist Convention at Kansas City ignored completely the oppressed Negro and the racial strife in that part of the nation where Southern Baptists are the predominant Christian body."[41]

By contrast, in May 1963 Arthur Lichtenberger, Presiding Bishop of the Protestant Episcopal Church, urged Episcopalians to involve themselves in race relations issues and to support the civil rights movement financially. Lichtenberger said in reference to the demonstrators, "We must support and strengthen their protest in every way possible, rather than give support to the forces of resistance by our silence." Eugene Carson Blake, the highest official in the United Presbyterian Church, Bishop Daniel Corrigan of the National Council of the Protestant Episcopal Church, Monsignor Austin J. Healy of the Roman Catholic Archdiocese of Baltimore and Rabbi Morris

Lieberman of Baltimore were arrested for their participation in a civil rights march in Baltimore, Maryland, on July 4. Blake also lobbied hard in support of the civil rights bill, appearing before a congressional committee and as a speaker at the March on Washington for Jobs and Freedom in August 1963, representing the National Council of Churches.[42]

Although many lay people remained critical of direct action and participation in it by denominational leaders, most of the major religious groups, apart from the SBC, spoke out on behalf of civil rights. The United Presbyterian Church in the USA's General Assembly unanimously voted $500,000 in 1963 to fund a Commission on Religion and Race to fight racial discrimination. Furthermore, the American Baptist Convention commended Martin Luther King Jr., Ralph Abernathy, "and others who are in the forefront of the non-violent struggle for justice and peace and assure[d] them of our support." In its strongest statement thus far, the General Assembly of the PCUS urged "every Presbyterian institution, whether church, school, orphanage, home for the aged, or conference center, boards and agencies of the Church [to] abolish all racial barriers and references. . . . " Progressive Southern Baptists lamented their convention's timidity. "Other denominations in our section," wrote E. S. James, editor of the *Baptist Standard,* in June 1963, "have far outstripped [Southern] Baptists in preaching and teaching that the colored man is entitled to every opportunity that is ours."[43]

Yet, despite their rhetorical commitment to civil rights, the major Protestant denominations achieved little more desegregation of their institutions in the South during the early 1960s than the SBC. Almost 90 percent of the churches in the SBC refused to admit African Americans to membership in 1963 and the ones that did, with the exception of those in Texas, were nearly all outside the South. Approximately ten Baptist colleges in the region operated nondiscriminatory admissions policies. A survey of 1,178 Southern Presbyterian churches in the same year found that 623 would welcome African Americans at services, albeit sometimes on a segregated basis. Two hundred and ninety-five churches would not admit blacks. Only twenty-eight churches had black members. Nine of the denomination's twenty-three junior and senior colleges had desegregated.[44]

Although non-SBC Protestant denominations remained slow to desegregate, they, unlike the SBC, which rejected a recommendation in 1964 that endorsed open churches, maintained pressure on their institutions to act. In the same year, the General Assembly of the PCUS "instructed" relevant synods to abolish all-black presbyteries and integrate their churches into geographic presbyteries. It forbade segregation in member churches, subject to the approval of a majority of the denomination's presbyteries. The

General Assembly also requested Southern Presbyterian agencies to help ministers and congregations "on how we can effectively contribute to the elimination of segregation and racial discrimination."[45]

The General Conference of the Methodist Church voted in 1964 to abolish its all-black Central Jurisdiction within the next four years. It left the question of what to do with the seventeen black conferences in the Central Jurisdiction to the jurisdictional and annual conferences, both black and white. Although in the North, black churches from the Central Jurisdiction began to be immediately integrated into the white annual conferences, white conferences in the southern states took no action to integrate black Methodist churches and left them in black conferences.[46]

Predominantly northern denominations also acted against segregation. The United Presbyterian Church in the USA adopted a more progressive position on racial issues than the SBC. The Presbyterian General Assembly elected its first black moderator, Dr. Edler G. Hawkins, in 1964. Its commissioners also voted to seek presbytery approval to eliminate a provision from the denomination's Form of Government that permitted segregation in presbyteries, and approved a timetable to integrate segregated southern presbyteries by January 1, 1967. At its annual meeting, the American Baptist Convention advocated withholding loans to racially exclusive Baptist churches, declared that the "membership, leadership, ministry and staff" of the convention and its churches should be open to all "regardless of race," and suggested that churches include fair-employment practice clauses in their contracts with builders.[47]

Catholic bishops in the Deep South also began to exert pressure on behalf of desegregation. In April 1964, Thomas J. Toolen, Bishop of Mobile-Birmingham, announced that all parochial schools in the diocese, which included eleven north Florida counties, would desegregate in September, a year after token public school desegregation had commenced in a few of Alabama's cities. Richard O. Gerow, Bishop of Natchez-Jackson, desegregated parochial schools in the fall of 1964 to coincide with token public school desegregation in Mississippi.[48]

The major denominations, with the exception of the SBC, felt able and emboldened to take increased action against segregation partly because the civil rights bill, enacted in July 1964, mandated the desegregation of public accommodations. The SBC refused to endorse civil rights legislation at its annual meeting in June 1964. Convention president K. Owen White informed U.S. Senators that he objected to the bill, and he expressed the hope that other Southern Baptists would do the same.[49]

Subject to southern white cultural influences the PCUS, like the SBC, refused to lobby for the civil rights bill or to support civil rights demonstrations. Its commissioners rejected a proposal that the denomination send an official representative to Washington, D.C., to participate in a prayer convocation, sponsored by the National Council of Churches, in support of the civil rights bill. Instead, they approved a resolution that, in an obvious but unspecified reference to the Birmingham civil rights demonstrations of 1963, deplored the "defiance of court orders and the unlawful manipulation and use of children of juvenile age . . . in the advancement of local or national programs regardless of the nature or purpose of such programs." When questioned, the resolution's sponsor, Talbott Ellis, a Birmingham judge, claimed, somewhat incongruously, that his resolution was concerned in part with white parents who kept their children out of schools desegregated under court order. Despite its large southern white membership, the General Conference of the Methodist Church endorsed orderly, non-violent civil rights demonstrations in 1964, although delegates refused to go specifically on record in support of civil disobedience.[50]

Denominations with a large northern membership took the strongest stand in support of direct action. In 1963, the House of Bishops of the Episcopal Church called on the U.S. Congress to enact civil rights legislation. At its triennial convention in 1964, the church offered "unwavering material and moral support" to Episcopalians involved in the civil rights struggle, and it adopted a resolution that approved interracial marriage. The American Baptist Convention called on its members to "contact their senators requesting them to pass a strong civil-rights bill." The convention not only expressed support for non-violent civil rights demonstrations and presented an award to Martin Luther King Jr., himself an American Baptist, it also urged its members to participate in the demonstrations.[51]

The Selma, Alabama, protest in 1965 for voting rights, and white violence against the demonstrators, saw clergymen, mostly from the North, accept Martin Luther King Jr.'s invitation to participate. The Reverend Arthur E. Walmsley, executive secretary of the Protestant Episcopal Church's Department of Christian Social Relations, headed a contingent of Episcopal priests at the march. Catholic priests from fifty dioceses, nuns, and lay Catholics joined the Selma demonstrations. Some Southern Presbyterians, including leading figures such as Ernest Trice Thompson and James L. Mays of Union Theological Seminary and Malcolm Calhoun of the denomination's Board of Christian Education, also marched. Furthermore, at its General Assembly in 1965 the PCUS endorsed civil disobedience, providing that those who engaged in it accepted responsibility for their actions and the judgements of the courts.[52]

Leading progressive Southern Baptists did not take part in the Selma demonstrations or, with the exception of W. R. Grigg, in other civil rights protests. Although the SBC finally supported civil rights legislation at its 1965 meeting, its resolution also condemned civil disobedience. Despite the widening gap between SBC statements and those of the other major Protestant denominations, including its closest counterpart the PCUS, in practice each Protestant body continued to experience similar difficulties in trying to desegregate their institutions in the Deep South.[53]

Desegregated Southern Presbyterian colleges, like Southern Baptist institutions, remained largely confined to the peripheral South. The nondiscrimination compliance pledge required by the Civil Rights Act for colleges and their students to maintain eligibility for federal monies, led many Presbyterian, Methodist and Southern Baptist colleges to desegregate in 1965. In both denominations, the holdouts were mainly located in the Deep South. In 1966, Belhaven College in Jackson, Mississippi, became the last Southern Presbyterian college to relinquish segregation. By 1970, all Southern Baptist colleges had abandoned racial discrimination in admissions.[54]

Both Southern Presbyterians and Methodists continued to encounter resistance from the Deep South to the desegregation instructions that they had issued in 1964. Although the Presbyterian General Assembly reiterated its call for black churches to be included in white presbyteries, by March 1966 twenty-two black churches had still to be received by seven presbyteries in the Deep South. Southern Presbyterian, Methodist and Southern Baptist ministers sometimes lost their pastorates in the region for speaking out about race relations. Despite its many pronouncements against segregation, the Disciples of Christ still maintained parallel African-American and white conventions in six states. Even many Episcopalian lay people continued to oppose desegregation in the Deep South. The congregation of Savannah, Georgia's St. John's Episcopal Church voted 700 to 45 in 1965 to withdraw from the Protestant Episcopal Church, rather than admit African Americans to services. By contrast, journalist George McMillan claimed that "a Negro will find himself welcomed at any Catholic church in the South, even those in Mississippi and Alabama" and Harold R. Perry became the first black American Catholic bishop in 1965, when he was appointed auxiliary bishop of New Orleans.[55]

Despite setbacks in achieving integration, the major Protestant denominations, except the SBC, continued to make pronouncements that challenged their members to integrate and to support the African-American struggle for equality. The convention did not pass any resolutions or make any recommendations on race at its 1966 and 1967 meetings, despite race riots in American cities and increasing numbers of young blacks adopting Stokely Carmichael's call, first made in 1966, for Black Power.[56]

However, the American Baptist Convention passed resolutions in 1966 that favored open housing legislation and federal rent subsidies for the poor. A few months later, the convention's General Council endorsed Black Power insofar as it referred to blacks organizing and uniting with others to achieve inclusion "in the decision making or power structures of our society. . . . " Although it was not about to endorse Black Power, even the Southern Presbyterian Assembly called on the church to "continue to support and regard with compassion those who practice civil disobedience when no legal recourse has been left open to them and who act in Christian conscience and allegiance to Almighty God." The Southern Presbyterians Assembly's support of civil disobedience in 1966 represented a stronger version of the endorsement it had given a year earlier.[57]

Many denominations also became actively involved in efforts to improve life for African Americans. In May 1966, the General Assembly of the United Presbyterian Church in the USA authorized four of its high-ranking officials to take part in and support a school desegregation suit in Wilcox County, Alabama. Six months later, the Methodist Board of Missions appropriated $70,000 for the National Council of Churches' Delta Ministry program, designed to uplift poor blacks in Mississippi. Indeed, all the major Protestant denominations, except the SBC, helped finance the Delta Ministry in some degree, while the Catholic Diocese of Natchez-Jackson developed its own program, Systematic Training and Redevelopment Inc., to help Mississippi's largely African-American poor into employment.[58]

In addition to supporting the Delta Ministry, the Protestant Episcopal Church developed the largest race relations program of any single denomination, when it created the General Convention Special Program (GCSP) in 1967 with an initial budget of $3.9 million. The program sought to empower the poor and excluded, and to support anti-racist church and community groups. During its first year, the GCSP, under its African-American director Leon Modeste, distributed grants in excess of $1 million to a wide range of groups.[59]

While the Episcopalians supported activism, the assassination of Martin Luther King Jr. in 1968 and the ensuing riots finally led the SBC to address race relations once more, by adopting a statement that supported open churches and equal rights. Between 1968 and 1971, the HMB, charged with coordinating the convention's efforts to further racial equality, authorized a $1 million church loan fund for ethnic groups and made several grants to African-American organizations.[60]

Although the SBC's statement marked a significant advance on its previous efforts in race relations, the other major denominations responded equally and, often, more strongly to the nation's racial crisis. The Southern Presbyterians, like the SBC, endorsed open housing but, unlike the convention, they also made financial contributions to a civil rights organization, the Southern Christian Leadership Conference (SCLC), and to Memphis refuse collectors, who supported by the SCLC, were on strike for higher wages and union recognition. A year later, the PCUS gave $15,000 to help organize the Black Presbyterian Leadership Conference (BPLC) to promote black concerns within the denomination. The BPLC used some of its subsequent denominational grants to promote black economic development.[61]

The American Baptist Convention's General Council agreed to many of the demands of the newly-formed Black Churchmen of the American Baptist Convention that focused on means to ensure greater black representation in the convention's agencies and offices, and the eradication of any vestiges of racism in the convention's communications and publishing activities. However, the convention refused to create a million-dollar crisis fund for blacks.[62]

Other denominations did offer African Americans financial assistance. The Disciples of Christ set a target in 1968 of raising $2 million over two years to alleviate urban problems. The United Presbyterian General Assembly asked the denomination to double the $100,000 target for its annual fund for freedom, devoted to black causes, with half of the funds going to the SCLC. Furthermore, it instructed its boards and agencies to adopt buying and contracting policies favoring businesses with equal employment practices, and to invest 30 percent of available funds in low-income housing and minority businesses in the inner city. The assembly also called for "eventual elimination of the present welfare system and for the establishment of an adequate income for all. . . . "[63]

The newly formed United Methodist Church appropriated $680,000 for ecumenical, Methodist, and community groups that addressed racial and poverty issues. Its mission board created a $3 million fund for loans to ghetto enterprises. The denomination also allocated $35 million between 1968 and 1971 for "minority group empowerment and self-determination." Less generous, the Catholic bishops of the United States voted $25,000 to establish an urban task force to work with the National Council of Churches and the Synagogue Council on racial problems. The bishops also called for the "total eradication of any elements of discrimination in our parishes, schools, hospitals, homes for the aged and similar institutions."[64]

Despite its adoption of the crisis statement, the SBC still remained more cautious on racial and social issues than most other denominations. However, all the major Protestant groups continued to meet opposition to desegregation from their southern churches. Surveys revealed that although the numbers of Southern Baptist churches with African-American members grew across the South between 1963 and 1968, in relative terms only slightly more churches, 11 percent of all SBC churches in America, were willing to receive black members in 1968 than there had been in 1963. Only in 1968 did the PCUS finally succeed in ending segregated presbyteries, but its churches still remained largely segregated.[65] The year should also have marked the end of the Central Jurisdiction in the United Methodist Church. However, some white Methodist conferences in the Deep South continued to resist merger with African-American conferences, and the Central Jurisdiction did not disappear entirely until the last of them acquiesced in 1973.[66]

James Forman, a veteran civil rights activist, became less concerned with desegregation and more focused on improving the economic position of African Americans. The National Black Economic Development Conference (BEDC) adopted Forman's Black Manifesto in April 1969, which demanded that the nation's white denominations pay blacks $500 million (later raised to $3 billion) in reparations for past injustices. In rejecting the Black Manifesto by resolution, the SBC stood in the mainstream of national public opinion, since a Gallup poll revealed that only 2 percent of whites supported and 94 percent opposed the proposal. African-American opinion divided between 21 percent in favor of the proposition, 52 percent opposed and 27 percent undecided. The General Board of the National Council of Churches expressed understanding of the spirit of the Black Manifesto but rejected its Marxist ideology. Consequently, the board urged its member denominations to pledge $500,000 to African-American organizations detached from the radical BEDC, and some responded by increasing their funding of black groups. One year after Forman had made his initial demand for $500 million, the Black Manifesto had raised only $300,000 for the BEDC, $200,000 of which had come from the Protestant Episcopal Church.[67]

Many Episcopal parishes reduced their financial contributions to the church in protest at its support for the BEDC. The loss of funds and the GCSP's provision of a few of its grants to groups that endorsed violence led the General Convention to tighten control over the program and significantly reduce its budget. By 1973, the GCSP was defunct, its functions absorbed into other programs by order of the General Convention.[68]

The late 1960s and the early 1970s saw the major denominations' interest in and commitment to racial equality peak. The American Baptist Convention elected its first black president, Thomas Kilgore Jr., in 1969. A year later, John M. Burgess became the first African American in the Protestant Episcopal Church to be elected diocesan bishop for a largely white diocese, Massachusetts. Neither the SBC nor its state conventions in the South had any elected black officials, although two of its state conventions in the North elected African Americans to office in 1969. The Baptist Convention of Oregon-Washington chose Irene James as second vice president, and the Utah-Idaho Baptist Convention elected Ira Martin to its Executive Board.[69]

Sometimes the denominations adopted positions considerably at odds with those of many of their members and also with national opinion. The Council on Church and Race of the United Presbyterian Church generated substantial lay opposition, when in 1971 it contributed $10,000 to the defense fund of Angela Davis, a black Communist indicted as an accessory in a violent incident in a California court. Although 83 percent of white Americans opposed busing school children to ensure racial balance in the public schools, both the American Baptist Convention and the General Assembly of the United Presbyterian Church passed resolutions in 1972 that favored busing, and the National Catholic Conference for Interracial Justice attacked "anti-busing" as "a code word for racism."[70]

By contrast, the more cautious SBC assumed positions increasingly closer to the American mainstream, if still ahead of the more conservative elements of its own constituency. The convention did not take a position on the controversial subject of busing, but as full school desegregation came to the Deep South in 1970 and 1971, it adopted resolutions in support of public education and against the creation of private schools as a means of evading integration. Baptist state convention leaders in the Deep South often endorsed public schools, sometimes in joint statements with leaders of other denominations. Unlike Catholic and Episcopalian bishops, such as Episcopalian John M. Allin and Catholic Joseph B. Brunini, both in Mississippi, Baptists in the region focused on education and law and order, rather than on the desirability of integration. Across the South, some members from each denomination responded to school and residential desegregation and busing by joining white flight to the suburbs and to private education. White Protestant churches, located in inner cities that became increasingly African American, sometimes sold their property and joined their parishioners in the suburbs.[71]

After the early 1970s, the SBC's annual meetings, like those of other major denominations, evidenced little interest in racial issues. The phenomenon reflected a combination of factors. Apathy, exhaustion, alienation arising from the growth of separatism among some blacks, a belief that racial issues had been effectively addressed or paradoxically that the attempt had been made and failed, and the rise of new issues, such as the role of women, ageing and refugees, all played a part.[72]

Predominantly northern mainline denominations, regardless of polity or theology, consistently made the strongest pronouncements on race relations and desegregation, followed by the Methodist Church, which contained a large southern contingent. While the Catholic Church opposed racial discrimination, its southern bishops pushed for desegregation of schools and churches only when local conditions seemed favorable. Some Catholic bishops in the peripheral South ordered parochial school desegregation shortly before or after the *Brown* decision. However, Catholic bishops largely ceased further desegregation during massive resistance. They resumed it in line with local public school integration in the 1960s. After 1953, the SBC's record of pronouncements on race became increasingly less progressive than that of the PCUS. Southern Presbyterians also achieved church and college desegregation, however limited, a little faster than Southern Baptists in the 1960s. But whatever the resolutions of their denominations, religious white southerners shared the same sentiments toward segregation as other whites among whom they lived, with the most marked opposition coming from those in the Deep South. Consequently, denominations with a southern presence faced substantial resistance to desegregation, and they moderated implementation of their policies accordingly. As the largest denomination in the South, the SBC proved, not surprisingly, to be the most cautious in race relations, yet its caution was only different in degree, not in kind, from that of other denominations operating in the region. And by the early 1970s, its positions on race appeared increasingly closer to those of mainstream national white opinion.

11

An Overview: Southern Baptists and African Americans, 1972–1995

I N AN ECHO of the national mood, Southern Baptist denominational meetings exhibited a declining interest in race relations in the early 1970s, until the issue had virtually disappeared from SBC and Baptist state convention resolutions and newspapers by the middle of the decade. New issues arose to displace race on both the Baptist and national agenda. Yet, at the same time, more and more Baptist churches abandoned racial discrimination in admissions and, despite resistance, the pattern extended into the Deep South. Creeping token desegregation marked the SBC's agencies and its churches, while many churches and their parishioners continued to relocate to the suburbs to escape black migration to the cities and some Baptist parents withdrew their children from the public education system to secular and Baptist schools. In the mid-1970s, increasing numbers of black churches became dually aligned with Southern Baptist associations. This development continued and intensified during the period of fundamentalist resurgence within the SBC that began in 1979. The growing black presence within the SBC seemed, on the surface, to be at odds with fundamentalist dominance which had arisen, in part, as a consequence of antipathy toward support for civil rights, women's rights and other liberal positions by the SBC's Christian Life Commission and Baptist progressives.

In its annual meeting, held in December 1971, the SBC's Christian Life Commission recognized that "our racial prejudices have not been wiped out, that complacency threatens to mute our witness" and that "there is a tendency for some within the Southern Baptist Convention to withdraw from the struggle for reconciliation." It was symptomatic of the problem that the trustees of the Sunday School Board, in their semiannual meeting two months later, approved guidelines for dealing with race in curriculum materials for church usage, which warned writers and editors not to promote church integration.[1]

The Sunday School Board had always been reluctant to tackle integration and race relations in the educational literature that it produced for the churches, but, in the 1970s, the convention contained fewer voices calling attention to them. Many of the Southern Baptist pastors and lay people most sympathetic to civil rights had left the denomination, frustrated by what they saw as its timidity on racial issues. Partly in consequence, the SBC seldom addressed racial issues after 1971, and, when it did, it refused to support corrective measures against racism and merely reaffirmed its general commitment to racial justice in well-worn platitudes. The Southern Baptist declension from racial issues also reflected national trends. Both Presidents Richard Nixon and Gerald Ford opposed busing. Its use led to widespread opposition from white parents in the North as well as the South. Influenced by white disapproval and affected by Nixon's appointment of strict constructionist judges, the Supreme Court rendered decisions, beginning in 1974, that restricted the use of busing. In another move popular with many whites, the Supreme Court's 1978 *Bakke* ruling rejected racial quotas as a means to rectify past discrimination against African Americans.[2]

The SBC refused to take sides on either busing or affirmative action because of the hostility these issues aroused among many Southern Baptists. Busing weakened the commitment of some Baptists to public education. As it came into effect in Memphis, Tennessee, in January 1973, many white parents relocated to the suburbs to escape its reach or transferred their children into the rapidly expanding number of private schools. During the first six months of busing, white parents withdrew 6,700 children from the public school system. Southern Baptist churches provided most of the buildings for private schools in the city. Ten Memphis churches combined their facilities to form the Southern Baptist Educational Center, thirteen churches on the northside created Frayser Baptist Schools, and East Park Baptist Church developed the Briarcrest complex, the largest private school system in the nation, with thirteen elementary schools and one high school.[3]

In some cases, congregations pressured their pastors into accepting private schools, but, frequently, pastors led in their establishment. Bob Agee, pastor of Ardmore Baptist Church, initially resisted his congregation's demand for a private school, but once convinced that such schools were inevitable he decided to cooperate in forming the Frayser system in order to ensure quality private education. By contrast, Wayne Allen, pastor of East Park Baptist Church, served as the driving force behind the creation of the Briarcrest system. Some pastors frankly admitted that they had started church schools to evade busing. Floyd Simmons, pastor of Elliston Baptist Church, declared: "I would never have dreamed of starting a school, hadn't it been for busing." A few pastors denied any connection between busing and the founding of their churches' private schools. The Reverend Wayne Allen claimed that he had long dreamed of creating a Baptist school. The rapid proliferation of Southern Baptist schools in the wake of court-ordered busing strongly suggests that, usually, opposition to busing and full school desegregation were important motives behind their creation.[4]

The founders of church schools denied that they opposed the principle of desegregation. The Reverend Floyd Simmons explained: "Integration wasn't it. We've been integrating in Memphis for years. Our kids were the first to be bused, that's what it was about." The Reverend Wayne Allen pointed out that the Briarcrest system had an open admissions policy, and he claimed that he had tried to recruit African-American students, faculty and administrators but without success.[5]

Other cities across the South also experienced private school expansion, often in Baptist churches, in response to busing and desegregation. Most Baptist state conventions, like the SBC, ignored busing. Only the Texas and North Carolina conventions endorsed the measure. The Baptist General Convention of Texas defended busing in 1973 as a necessary corrective to years of defiance of court-ordered school desegregation, and it urged Baptists to stay in racially changing communities and to obey the law. The Baptist State Convention of North Carolina, which had witnessed a successful use of busing to integrate Charlotte's schools after initial difficulties, expressed support in 1974 for "reasonable techniques, including those presently employed" to achieve desegregation.[6]

Just as the SBC ignored the busing issue, so it also refused to condemn or support affirmative action. Instead, the messengers adopted a resolution in 1973 that commended ethnic representation on The Southern Baptist Theological Seminary Board of Trustees, the Annuity Board, and the Christian Life Commission and urged further ethnic representation on the denomination's agencies and boards. The convention passed a similar resolution in 1974 and rejected resolutions that would have established quota systems and rights for minorities and women.[7]

Despite its two resolutions in favor of minority representation, tokenism continued to prevail across the SBC. More and more churches, including some in the urban Deep South, adopted open policies, but few blacks joined them. A random survey of America's Southern Baptist pastors, conducted by the HMB in 1973, found that 91 percent of their churches were willing to receive African-American members. However, only 559 of the 2,000 pastors questioned returned the survey, which, in consequence, probably presented an exaggerated picture of Southern Baptist progress in race relations. Presumably, many pastors opposed to integration did not reply.

The survey revealed that only 731 predominantly white Southern Baptist churches actually had African-American members, with an average of only five per church. Greater interracial religious activity occurred in areas outside the South, especially Oregon, Michigan, and California. Although 191 predominantly black churches existed throughout the SBC, with twenty-eight of these in Texas, only seven were located in seven southeastern states. Since 68 percent of the churches that replied to the survey indicated that they were actively seeking African Americans, they were clearly having difficulty in attracting them.[8]

The unwillingness of African Americans to join white Southern Baptist churches can be attributed to white hostility, different styles of worship, loyalty to traditional black denominations, and to a growing affinity among some blacks for separatism because of the failure of the civil rights movement to achieve large-scale integration and their disillusionment with the small benefits that limited integration had brought. Residential segregation, class differences, and the tendency of Southern Baptist churches to join white flight to the suburbs also served to reduce the number of blacks that Southern Baptist churches could reach.[9]

Tokenism prevailed in SBC agencies as it did in the churches. Although the HMB promoted the hiring and appointment of African Americans to positions of influence in the SBC, even as late as 1973 the total number of blacks employed by convention agencies stood at 132, and only ten of these held staff jobs. The remainder occupied clerical posts. When Emmanuel L. McCall succeeded Victor Glass as head of the Department of Cooperative Ministries with National Baptists in January 1975, he became the first African American to head a department of an SBC agency. The WMU did not employ its first black national staff member until January 1978.[10]

The SBC elected its first African American to office, seventy-eight year old Charles King, in 1974, when it made him a second vice president, but no other blacks followed King into elective office in the 1970s. By the middle of the decade, African Americans in other white Protestant denominations had lost some of the high-ranking posts that they had secured in the late 1960s and early 1970s. With the exception of Texas and the Upper South, most Baptist state conventions did not even achieve tokenism within their staff. The messengers to the Baptist General Convention of Texas passed a resolution in 1972 that urged the convention to do all it could to achieve representation for minorities, women, and youth on its boards, commissions, and committees. The convention elected its first African American to office in 1973, choosing Harold T. Branch as second vice president, but it did not appoint its first black executive staff member until 1976, when it made Vernon Hickerson consultant for work with African Americans.[11]

Apathy toward race relations dominated the SBC and the other major denominations. At a Christian Life Commission conference on race relations in 1973, speaker after speaker inveighed against Southern Baptist indifference and a new racism among African Americans and whites that served to prevent further integration within the denomination's churches and other efforts to improve race relations. Cecil Sherman, the progressive pastor of Asheville, North Carolina's First Baptist Church, said of Southern Baptist efforts to effect racial reconciliation: "Most of the people feel, 'We've tried, and it didn't work. And I told you so!'" Larry McSwain, assistant professor of church and community at The Southern Baptist Theological Seminary, put Baptist neglect of race relations into a national perspective. "Much of the apathy and inactivity in racial affairs," McSwain commented, "is the result of the widespread belief by white America that since the riots have stopped, the problems are solved."[12]

Most African-American and white lay Baptists had little contact with each other. Corbin L. Cooper, director of the Baptist State Convention of North Carolina's Department of Cooperative Ministries with General Baptists, observed in 1973: "We just have to get together with personal contacts. You can pray about it all night long, but unless someone goes out and visits the next morning, it's not going to solve much." That same year Cesar Scott, black associate in campus ministries for the Baptist General Association of Virginia, claimed that personal relationships were rare between black and white students in his state. African-American and white BSUs tended to remain mutually exclusive. "One of the reasons," observed Scott, "is because of peer group pressure; blacks stay with blacks and whites stay with whites." White Baptist students had lost the idealism of the 1960s, and African-American students, influenced by separatism, found whites "more or less incidental to their lives."[13]

In its report to the SBC in 1974, the Christian Life Commission lamented that "A fatigue both of heart and of will grips the church today at the point of race relations." The commission attempted to revive Baptist interest in race relations by recommending that Baptists "work earnestly for racial justice in public education, employment, health care, housing, consumer concerns, and citizen participation in the political process." It also urged SBC agencies to attack racism in their program assignments and to avoid it in their employment practices. Although the SBC approved the commission's recommendation, it had no significant impact on either Southern Baptists, the convention, or its agencies.[14]

Even the Christian Life Commission fell prey to the apathy toward race relations that it decried. The commission's literature on race relations was old and dated and, as a result, sold poorly. After 1974, the commission neglected race relations in its reports and recommendations to the SBC. It became preoccupied with new social issues, such as women's rights, homosexuality, world hunger, pornography, morality on television, and drugs. Indeed, the SBC did not pass or approve another resolution or recommendation that involved a race relations component until 1978, and even that resolution was merely part of a universal Declaration of Human Rights with no specific suggestions regarding African Americans.[15]

The SBC's other agencies covered African Americans and their problems with decreasing frequency in their magazines after 1973. Although primarily concerned with missions work among blacks and whites, the HMB and the WMU necessarily continued to be involved with efforts to improve interracial understanding. In 1975, they collaborated on a series of study guides for all ages under the rubric *Ministering in Changing Ethnic Patterns* that presented America's racial groups positively. The HMB also produced *Crossing Barriers Through Ministries with National Baptists,* which concentrated on Southern Baptist relations with black Baptists. The board held the first of an annual series of conferences for black and white Baptists in 1977 on "The Church in the Racially Changing Community."[16]

Baptist state conventions played an expanding role in improving relations between black and white Baptists by holding joint meetings of their respective conventions or engaging in combined evangelistic enterprises. Biracial, joint convention meetings occurred in North Carolina (1974), Virginia (1975) and Arkansas (1976). The Mississippi Baptist Convention's Department of Work with National Baptists brought black and white pastors together for the first of an annual series of human relations conferences in 1973. Five thousand of Alabama's Baptists, drawn from five different conventions, black and white, came together for a joint United States Bicentennial session in Birmingham in 1976.[17]

African Americans became more directly involved in the SBC, as the total number of black churches affiliated with Southern Baptist associations grew dramatically. Between 1973 and 1976, the number of predominantly black churches in the SBC rose by 76 percent, from 191 to 340. They were mostly located in inner-city areas, whereas most white Southern Baptists lived in the suburbs and rural areas. Furthermore, with the exception of Texas, the vast majority of the growth in black SBC churches and in black membership of predominantly white SBC churches occurred in the states bordering the South and beyond. Black churches joined the SBC primarily because of the educational literature and financial resources it offered, and because of a "desire to participate in the ideal of a multiracial fellowship." Some black Southern Baptist churches were dually aligned with one of the National Baptist conventions, while others were affiliated solely with the SBC. In the southern states, especially the Deep South tier, white Southern Baptists were still reluctant to welcome African Americans into their associations or churches, and consequently blacks and black churches did not seek to join them.[18]

Southern Baptist churches, like those of the other major denominations both North and South, mostly remained wholly white or wholly African American, with little mixture of the races. Historian Martin E. Marty estimated in 1976 that even in the North less than one percent of whites went to church with African Americans. Between 1972 and 1975, five Southern Baptist churches closed in Birmingham, Alabama, because African Americans had moved into their vicinity. Some churches continued to maintain racially discriminatory policies. Tuscaloosa, Alabama's Alberta Baptist Church turned away African-American students from its services in April 1975. Influenced by adverse publicity, its deacons soon voted to adopt an open-door policy. In 1976, the twenty-four member Selma Baptist Association refused to admit the Good News Church, which had three black members. Ed Cruce, pastor of Sardis' Shiloh Baptist Church and the association's moderator, admitted that most of its churches had either official or unofficial policies excluding African Americans.[19]

The deacons of Plains Baptist Church, Georgia, home church of Democratic presidential nominee Jimmy Carter, enforced its closed-door policy against the Reverend Clennon King and three other blacks, who sought admission in 1976. They also voted eleven to one to ask their pastor, Bruce Edwards, to resign, because he had supported King's admission. The congregation rebuffed their deacons by voting 121 to 66 to adopt an open policy and 107 to 84 to retain Edwards. Approximately forty of the negative votes came from inactive members who had not attended the church in many years. In February 1977, after Jimmy Carter, who was then President, had transferred his membership to a church in Washington, D.C., vengeful segregationists, including many inactive members, packed the church and voted to dismiss Edwards, who then resigned. Twenty-eight members left the congregation and established the Maranatha Baptist Church, with an open admissions policy.[20]

It is indicative of the continuing problem of racism that Baptist state conventions in Florida (1975 and 1976) and South Carolina (1976) adopted resolutions that urged their churches to desegregate and congratulated those which already had. Although more and more Baptist churches rejected racial discrimination, some churches continued to found private schools, often with the intent of enabling whites to evade school desegregation. By 1976, there were 189 schools associated with Baptist churches across the nation, which included thirty-six in Tennessee, twenty-six in both Florida and Texas and twenty-two in Alabama. Three years later, they numbered at least 300 and had an estimated 50,000 students. Influenced by private school growth, the SBC, against the advice of the Christian Life Commission, overwhelmingly adopted a resolution in 1979 that opposed an IRS proposal to deny tax exempt status to private schools, including church schools, unless they could prove that they did not discriminate on the basis of race in their admissions policies. In effect, the convention gave its approval to Southern Baptist schools for whites only. Furthermore, the Sunday School Board reversed its policy and supplied Baptist church schools with Bible curriculum materials and training in administration.[21]

Despite the resolution, Southern Baptists had made significant strides away from segregation and discrimination, although the denomination was still not free of them. Corbin L. Cooper's 1977 dissertation surveyed racism among church Sunday School directors, deacon chairmen, Brotherhood Commission directors and WMU directors in North Carolina. Although they agreed that African Americans had rights, 17.6 percent of the respondents also agreed that "it is best to keep them in their own districts and schools and to prevent too much contact with whites." Of these, 8.4 percent strongly agreed with the statement. The more racially prejudiced church leaders were found in rural areas and small churches. They tended to be older and less educated. A "large majority" of lay leaders did not make racist responses to Corbin's questions. Opinion polls found that by 1979, 60 percent of white southerners supported integration, and another poll in 1980 found that only 5 percent objected to token school desegregation. Few Baptists defended segregation as biblical and the vast majority rejected segregation in principle. Most Southern Baptist churches, including many in the Deep South, no longer operated all-white admissions policies.[22]

Both the SBC and the Baptist state conventions promoted cooperation with black Baptist denominations. Black and white Baptists cooperated in joint evangelistic campaigns in Mississippi and Alabama during 1979 and such activities became routine across the South. Harper Shannon said in his presidential address to the Alabama Baptist State Convention in November 1979: "This is the most significant thing that Alabama Baptists (both black and white) have ever attempted to do together in the history of our denomination. We can never go back to the dark ages of estranged relationships, blatant prejudices, sheer racism and all the rest of the things that are the result of suspicion, animosity, misinformation and lack of Christian love."[23]

By 1980, there were six hundred black Southern Baptist churches, with 100,000 members, and 50,000 African Americans in 2,900 predominantly white Southern Baptist churches. Although most black Southern Baptists and their churches were located outside the South, they also featured within the region, and they had begun to appear in small numbers even in the Deep South. Louisiana Baptist associations admitted their convention's first African-American churches in 1978. When the Ku Klux Klan underwent a revival in the late 1970s and early 1980s, some Baptist state conventions condemned it, and the SBC's Christian Life Commission finally began to update its literature on race relations. In 1980, the Southern Baptist foundation, which invested the funds of SBC agencies, prohibited investment that supported racial discrimination.[24]

Nevertheless, a remnant of segregationist sentiment remained among Southern Baptists, particularly in the black belt and in some urban churches located in areas with substantial African-American populations. In 1980, six of the Montgomery (Alabama) Baptist Association's forty-five churches admitted to operating policies that excluded blacks. In some churches, open door policies were merely symbolic of Christian acceptance of all worshippers, and they had been adopted with the expectation that they would not need to be enforced. Most white Southern Baptists had little contact with African Americans either in church or socially. Whites tended to live in the suburbs, while many blacks remained in the city or lived in different suburban areas. A minority of white Southern Baptists sent their children to the expanding Baptist school sector. Emmanuel McCall remained the only African American to head an SBC agency in 1980, and black employment within the SBC remained token. The SBC promoted black church development but defended private schools against IRS nondiscrimination regulations. It no longer provided leadership on racial issues. In the second half of the 1970s, Baptist state conventions also focused on other issues, such as the economy, welfare, poverty, migrant workers, hunger, drugs, pornography, morality on television, abortion, women's rights, divorce, homosexuality and prayer in the public schools, with only occasional attention to race.[25]

By the end of the 1970s, a new and ultimately successful drive by fundamentalists to wrest control of the SBC from those they perceived, generally erroneously, as theologically liberal began to enjoy success. The conflict generated by fundamentalist advocacy of biblical inerrancy and school prayer, and opposition to women's ordination, abortion and homosexuality increasingly dominated SBC meetings. The convention elected a fundamentalist, Adrian Rogers, as president in 1979. Fundamentalists elected more of their number to the presidency during the next twenty years. Using the appointive powers of the president, they gradually secured control of SBC agencies, boards and seminaries and forced their opponents from positions of influence. Although self-identified fundamentalists were a minority within the SBC, they succeeded because they were well organized, had a clear cut program and faced a divided and ill-prepared opposition.[26]

Fundamentalist control of the SBC did not seem to augur well for further progress on race relations within the denomination. Motivation and support for the fundamentalist drive for power had, in part, derived from objections to the tolerant positions advocated by the Christian Life Commission, the HMB and some denominational leaders regarding social issues, including race. Their critics charged that fundamentalist support for the family and law and order, and opposition to welfare were code words for racism. Indeed, in private Adrian Rogers told Cecil Sherman, "If we had slavery today, we would not have this welfare mess." Prominent fundamentalist leaders, such as Rogers, Charles Stanley and James Draper Jr., were connected to New Christian Right organizations, such as the American Coalition for Traditional Values. During the 1980s, many Southern Baptist pastors switched from the Democratic to the Republican Party, and they often agreed with the conservative Moral Majority, led by independent Baptist preacher Jerry Falwell. Furthermore, a minority of fundamentalists held segregationist views. Curtis W. Caine Sr., a trustee of the SBC's Christian Life Commission from Mississippi, defended South African apartheid as beneficial at a commission meeting in 1988. He also attacked Martin Luther King Jr. as a fraud. Robert Parham, who opposed the fundamentalists, claimed that "many" trustees "nodded in agreement" and none "challenged Caine's statement." *Baptist Press* reported that Caine's words had met with silence.[27]

Although segregationist fundamentalists, such as Caine, attracted press headlines, fundamentalists could not be easily categorized. Many fundamentalist pastors, such as Fred Lackey of Jasper, Alabama's Westside Baptist Church, had encouraged their churches to desegregate in the 1970s. Fundamentalist SBC presidents often pastored desegregated churches. Jerry Vines, president of the SBC in 1989, declared that "Southern Baptists have grown in our understanding that the Gospel is for all people everywhere. To integrate is consistent with the Gospel I have always preached." Richard Land, the fundamentalist executive director of the SBC's Christian Life Commission, advocated racial justice and under his leadership the commission organized a race relations conference in 1989. It was simplistic and misleading to assume that the conservative economic and social views of fundamentalists and many other Southern Baptists and Americans were necessarily and always code words for racism. Fundamentalists were, however, divided about the civil rights movement. Random polls of Southern Baptist pastors and lay leaders in the mid and late 1980s found that 55 percent of "self-identified fundamentalists" disagreed or were unsure that the civil rights movement had led the nation in the right direction.[28]

Walker L. Knight, a progressive on race and an opponent of the fundamentalists, argues that after they took control of the SBC in 1979, it "regressed in making racial changes." Fundamentalist leaders, he claims, did not provide leadership on race. The SBC, Knight asserts, passed just two resolutions on civil rights between 1980 and 1992 and each sought to exempt religious organizations from civil rights legislation. Although a 1986 resolution encouraged "agencies and committees to increase the involvement of blacks and other minorities in employment, missions and programs," with the exception of developing churches in African-American communities, the opposite occurred. According to Knight, "Fewer blacks served as trustees of boards and agencies. Fewer blacks were in leadership roles."[29]

Baptist progressives, who had championed civil rights and integration within the denomination, focused on trying to stem the fundamentalist extension of control over the SBC, and, when they lost the battle, they found themselves unable to influence the convention on race. Following their defeat, progressives founded parallel organizations, such as the Southern Baptist Alliance in 1987 and the Cooperative Baptist Fellowship in 1991, to promote their views and rally their supporters. However, they paid far more attention to women's rights and female ordination than to racial issues, and their organizations had few African-American members.[30]

Overall, Baptists were split between the fundamentalist wing, a smaller group of theological moderates and a broad middle of theological conservatives who rejected the dogmatism of the fundamentalists. In political terms, fundamentalists supported right-wing Republicans, theological moderates included political liberals and conservatives, and the theologically conservative middle divided almost evenly between conservatives and liberals on issues such as abortion, defense policy and welfare. Although Southern Baptist ministers and many lay people became increasingly Republican and right-wing in the 1980s, many lay Baptists, although politically conservative, did not follow them in a rightward shift.[31]

Opinion poll evidence gathered between 1980 and 1988 (1984–1988 for Southern Baptists) placed Southern Baptists as the least progressive of all America's mainline religious groups regarding integrated housing and interracial socializing. Fifty-two percent of Southern Baptists did not object to an African-American dinner guest, and 45 percent believed that whites had no right to exclude blacks from their neighborhoods, but 53 percent favored laws that prohibited interracial marriage. However, Baptists trailed only a little behind other southern white Protestants. Forty-five percent of United Methodists in the South also favored legal prohibition of interracial marriage. The majority of southern whites among the Disciples of Christ, Episcopalians, Presbyterians, Southern Baptists and United Methodists believed that the federal government had no obligation to improve black living standards, and they also believed homeowners had the right to sell to whomever they chose, including the right to refuse African-American buyers.[32]

Despite its growing conservatism, by the early 1980s the SBC claimed to be "the most integrated denomination in America." Furthermore, a huge growth in black membership occurred as a consequence of an aggressive SBC campaign of establishing black churches, adopted in 1989. By 1990, the denomination had 14.9 million members and 37,700 churches nationwide, including 300,000 African Americans in 1,500 black churches and 6,000 integrated churches. However, blacks and whites largely remained in separate churches. Many black churches joined the SBC because it offered financial support and educational materials. Approximately one-third of black SBC churches adopted dual alignment with the SBC and a black denomination. Although the SBC employed more full-time black professionals than any other denomination, their posts limited their duties to liaising with other African Americans. In 1991, the convention's nine hundred office holders included only eight blacks.[33]

Critics charged that the SBC passed resolutions on race in 1989, 1993 and 1995 with an eye to African-American recruitment. In 1989, the SBC declared, "We repent of any past bigotry and pray for those who are still caught in its clutches." Four years later, the convention endorsed civil rights laws and urged Baptists "to redouble their efforts . . . to reach across racial and ethnic boundaries to establish both wholesome friendships and mutually beneficial ministry relationships." In 1995, the SBC adopted a resolution by a 95 percent majority that apologized to African Americans for Baptists' complicity in slavery and "for condoning and/or perpetuating individual and systematic racism in our lifetime . . . ," and asked for their forgiveness. When questioned, Charles Carter, chairman of the Resolutions Committee, denied that the resolution grew out of a desire to maintain the SBC's numerical growth by attracting African Americans. Carter also claimed that black Southern Baptists, who now numbered 800,000 of the denomination's 15.6 million members, "did not put any pressure on us to do this." However, unnamed denominational officials were reported as saying that the resolution would primarily serve the cause of attracting more black churches to the convention. Furthermore, its origins lay in a "Declaration of Repentance," drafted "by the directors of SBC associations from the 12 major American cities where more than 42 percent of the total U.S. black population lives."[34]

Nevertheless, the resolution indicated that more and more Southern Baptists had repudiated the SBC's racist past in a denomination that retained between 82 and 86 percent of its membership in the South. Richard Land declared: "I know of very few people who would claim to be Southern Baptists who would overtly make racist or segregationist comments. There is no impediment to African-American participation at state convention or association levels. In fact, it is actively encouraged. That is different, however, from having significantly integrated congregations. It has not filtered down to the local-congregation level." With some justice, Land attributed limited church integration to different worship styles between whites and African Americans. However, Don Sharp, the African-American pastor of Chicago's Faith Tabernacle Baptist Church, commented that "It's really a neo-racist attitude that blacks are alright, and there is a place for them if they speak the white language." Another black Southern Baptist minister, Eddie Jones, observed that white pastors understood the need for racial reconciliation, yet still faced the problem of "getting it down to their congregation in a way in which they won't lose their job[s]." Southern Baptists still had a long way to go before they integrated their churches, and many white Baptists remained wary of religious and social interaction with blacks. But the nation's other major white Protestant denominations also remained largely all white or all black, with few mixed churches.[35]

By the early 1970s, with the civil rights movement moribund and urban riots over, Southern Baptists and most American whites turned their attention away from black America. Apathy and indifference to African-American problems characterized most Baptists and Americans for the rest of the decade, except in their unwillingness to countenance busing and affirmative action to compensate blacks for past discrimination. Baptists did not seek residential or school integration, and some actively sought to escape them by joining white flight to the suburbs and private schools. Nevertheless, by the end of the decade, most Southern Baptists rejected racist stereotypes and enforced segregation in principle. Their churches were largely open to African Americans, but whether most Baptists would have welcomed black members remained a question. Significant social and religious interaction with African Americans and black Baptists remained rare among white Southern Baptists at the local level, but no rarer than among other white southerners. Fundamentalist control of the SBC in the 1980s and 1990s did not significantly alter the situation. However, the convention began to establish black churches and, despite the segregationist views of some fundamentalists, it passed several resolutions deploring racism, which culminated in its 1995 apology for Baptist involvement in slavery and racism.

12

Conclusion

As suggested by the sociology of religion, the SBC, Baptist state conventions and the editors of denominational newspapers tended to support the existing order of society. Lay Baptists, clergymen and denominational officials held primary commitments to law and order, peace and stability, public education, and evangelism at home and abroad. In 1945, most Baptists did not see any contradiction between their commitments and segregation. When a contradiction became apparent in the 1950s and 1960s as the federal government outlawed segregation and white southerners responded with defiance and violence, the SBC, Baptist state conventions and denominational editors, except in some cases when under extreme pressure from segregationists in the second half of the 1950s, called for law and order, peace, and public education. The denominational leadership proved to be adaptive and often more attuned to social change than most of its members.

Some historians hold that the SBC and state conventions have been the captives of southern white racist culture and limited in their social commentary by the Southern Baptist belief in the primacy of evangelism and a loosely-structured, democratic, congregational polity. Although this is partly true, the story is more complicated. The conventions and their members were influenced tremendously by their culture, but they also influenced that culture. Throughout the civil rights era, the SBC and Baptist state conventions did not simply support southern race relations as they were. A progressive elite in the Social Service and Christian Life commissions and the seminaries pushed Baptists forward in race relations. Although progressives followed behind secular developments, it was nevertheless important that they did follow them, despite the opposition of most Southern Baptists to desegregation.

Progressives passed through three stages. In their first stage, between 1945 and 1953, they urged white southerners to institute a genuine separate-but-equal policy in race relations. In sum, progressives called for equality in job opportunities, employment, voting rights and the dispensation of justice. In their second stage, between 1954 and 1963, they called for adherence to the *Brown* decision and attacked the biblical defense of segregation. Progressives developed a non-segregationist argument that, without calling for integration, refuted the arguments put forward by segregationists. In their third stage, progressives called for integration. Clearly, at every turn, progressives followed behind secular developments inaugurated by the civil rights movement and the federal government, but, nevertheless, they played a vital role in helping Southern Baptists to adjust to and accept the demise of legal segregation.

By attacking the biblical defense of segregation, progressives weakened the linchpin of the hard-line segregationist defense. They called into question the legitimacy of Jim Crow and, over time, undermined the plausibility structure of the segregationist world-view. By emphasizing the damage done to law and order, public education and foreign missions by segregationist resistance, progressives encouraged moderate segregationists, who believed that the Bible neither sanctioned nor condemned segregation, to accept change, however reluctantly. Progressives exercised significant influence over the SBC through editorial writing, sponsorship of resolutions, Christian Life Commission reports, recommendations and conferences, and non-segregationist and integrationist literature. At key moments in the civil rights struggle, the SBC approved resolutions or statements (1954, 1965, and 1968) in support of progressive change. In each case, the messengers adopted the resolutions more because they wanted to preserve law and order and prevent damage to Southern Baptist missionary efforts abroad than because they supported the goals of the civil rights movement.

At times, however, segregationist pressure and sentiment became so strong in the SBC that the convention refused to take a progressive stance in race relations, even at the cost of neglecting core commitments. At the height of massive resistance, in the second half of the 1950s, the convention kept quiet about racial issues, and it did not pass any race-related resolutions until 1961. Popular Baptist hostility to school desegregation and the threat that segregationists might withhold financial support from the convention forced it into silence.

The Baptist state conventions were equally subject to popular sentiment. The response of the state conventions to racial issues after 1945 fell into one of three categories. The North Carolina, Virginia and, especially, Texas conventions followed a progressive course, which sometimes exceeded the positions adopted by the SBC. Contrary to the expectations of sociological theory, the Arkansas, Tennessee and Florida conventions, for the most part, ignored racial issues and offered Baptists little or no guidance. Although sometimes openly hostile to the civil rights movement and desegregation, the Deep South conventions did not simply kowtow to popular hard-line segregationist sentiment. They followed a path dictated, above all, by a commitment to law and order, peace, public education and missions. Faced with the reality of public school desegregation initially in the early 1960s and more widely ten years later, virtually every convention came out in favor of preserving the public school system, even on a desegregated basis. In general, the greater the proportion of whites to African Americans in a state the more progressive was the state and its Baptist convention. In other words, the conventions tended to share the racial mores of the culture in which they operated. Biblical segregationists were most numerous in the black belt that stretched across much of the South, in plantation counties and in urban areas with substantial African-American populations.

The approach of Baptist editors to race relations tended to correlate with that of their respective state conventions, although some editors were more reactionary and others more progressive. Editors who addressed racial issues shared the same core commitments regardless of state or region, even if they differed over segregation. Committed to law and order, they attacked civil rights demonstrations and segregationist violence alike. As the federal government outlawed segregation, even segregationist editors called for obedience to civil rights laws as a Christian duty, regardless of their personal opinion of them. The combined effects of *most* of the editors' efforts throughout the post-1945 period was to ease adjustment to racial change by opposing violent or unlawful segregationist opposition, upholding the law, and supporting public education in the face of desegregation.

However, neither the Baptist state conventions nor editors were immune to extreme pressure from segregationists and some editors, especially in the Deep South, openly supported continued segregation, if only as a voluntary social system. Although the Baptist General Association of Virginia and its newspaper editor, Reuben E. Alley, had called for obedience to *Brown* in 1954, both wilted under the strain of the state's massive resistance to desegregation in the second half of the 1950s. The General Association ceased to discuss racial issues, and Alley became critical of the Supreme Court's decision. Massive resistance drove both the Alabama and Louisiana conventions into declaring their support for segregation, although, significantly, they did not endorse diehard opposition to desegregation. Alabama's Christian Life Commission also criticized the Citizens' Councils.

The conventions and editors sought to guide both pastors and the laity, but they were also subject to their influence. Despite the existence of outspoken segregationist and non-segregationist Baptists, most Baptist clergymen simply ignored racial issues in the civil rights era. Some pastors believed in the primacy of evangelism and argued that involvement in social issues detracted from saving individuals, the only sure way to save society. For others, evangelism served as a convenient excuse not to discuss the controversial and divisive issue of desegregation. Progressive ministers often feared to speak out lest they lose their pulpits or divide their churches and hinder financial contributions from their congregations. At the mercy of Baptist democracy, such clergymen mostly kept silent or delivered their message on race relations in coded language. Only a few ministers delivered sermons that overtly attacked Jim Crow.

Pastors and lay people usually reflected the racial views of their state and region, with the most committed and outspoken segregationists in the Deep South. Despite the segregationist sentiment of most Southern Baptists for much of the post-1945 era, there was always and in all regions, including the Deep South, a minority of progressive Baptists and lay people. Their numbers grew in response to biblical non-segregationist arguments, progressive statements and resolutions by Baptist conventions and, moreover, in response to secular change. Their norms changed as those of society altered in the aftermath of the intervention of the federal government prompted by the civil rights movement.

Case studies of local churches and their congregations suggest common themes applicable to all areas of the South. Seminary-educated ministers tended to be more progressive or, at least, less crude in their defense of segregation than uneducated pastors. Only educated ministers usually held the bigger, urban pastorates, and for this reason, as well as a more tolerant environment, urban churches tended to be more progressive than those in rural areas. Young Baptists, especially students, were more open to progressive change in race relations than older age groups and, at least in the 1950s and 1960s, each new generation of Baptists tended to be less committed to segregation than their parents. Less tied to traditional southern race relations because of their youth, the young and students with inquiring minds were more receptive to calls for equality made by the civil rights movement that emerged in their formative years. Significantly, by the late 1960s and early 1970s, most of the few remaining outspoken diehard segregationists were old. When churches split over integration, the old formed the majority of those who favored discriminatory admissions policies.

Church divisions over integration also reveal that, in most cases, an active minority of committed segregationists could block the adoption of open policies by their churches. Older and hence more wealthy and entrenched in positions of power within the local church, segregationists exerted considerable and often determinative influence. Moreover, they could mobilize segregationist church members, typically less active in church affairs, for crucial votes on church integration and the tenure of an integrationist pastor. That irregular churchgoers often outvoted regular attendees on church desegregation motions also suggests that committed Baptists were more progressive than backsliders. Backsliders by definition, unlike regular churchgoers, paid little attention to their pastor's sermons, editorials in Baptist papers and convention resolutions and reports. Hence, they were not exposed either to the views of progressives or to the chastening influence of Baptist editors, who, at the very least, opposed illegal segregationist defiance and, at the most, supported the goals, if not the tactics, of the civil rights movement.

Had the SBC been less democratic and more hierarchical and thus not subject to intervention by segregationist backsliders or regular Baptist segregationists, it might have moved faster and further on race relations under the influence of the progressive elite. Although the democratic polity of Southern Baptists allowed segregationists to vote down progressive resolutions and actions and to exert pressure by threatening to withdraw financial support, other major denominations in the South were also constrained, albeit to a slightly lesser degree, by the South's traditional system of race relations. Catholic bishops rarely desegregated parochial schools ahead of public school desegregation, and Catholic churches followed local mores when it came to integration. In the late 1960s, Southern Presbyterian and Methodist assemblies and conferences encountered as much difficulty in desegregating their churches in the Deep South as the SBC.

That predominantly northern denominations adopted more progressive positions on race relations than their southern counterparts only reinforces the evidence that southern white culture exerted tremendous influence over southern denominations, regardless of polity. Furthermore, since the northern-based American Baptist Convention passed more progressive resolutions on race-related issues than the SBC, despite a shared commitment to evangelism and personal redemption, it cannot be said that Southern Baptist theology determined the reluctance of its adherents to support progressive racial change. Although almost every major denomination had an agency that promoted progressivism in race relations and adjustment to change, in each case they did not move ahead of secular developments. Southern white Christians adjusted to racial change primarily because the federal government gave them little choice. Their denominations played a significant but secondary and supporting role in the process of adjustment.

The adoption of open policies by Baptist churches and colleges tended to follow local, school and college desegregation, and the Civil Rights Act of 1964. By the early 1970s, most Southern Baptists, even in the Deep South, accepted the end of legal discrimination even though some joined white flight to the suburbs and private schools to escape its results. Although more Southern Baptist associations accepted African-American churches and more Baptist churches admitted black members, Baptists in the South, for the most part, had little contact with African Americans residentially, religiously or socially. Tokenism prevailed in Baptist churches, and in SBC offices and those of the more progressive Baptist state conventions.

In effect, Southern Baptists joined the American mainstream in the 1970s. Across America, blacks inhabited the inner city and whites the suburbs. A smaller percentage of African Americans than whites lived in the suburbs, belonged to the middle class or occupied positions of power. Furthermore, both Southern Baptists and other white Americans believed that with the demise of legal discrimination and the cessation of riots, blacks had received all they had wanted and deserved. Americans, including Baptists, became concerned with other issues, such as abortion and women's rights. Progressives also had less influence in the SBC in the 1970s, as many of their number had left for other denominations dissatisfied with the convention's record in race relations. Conversely, some Baptists believed that the SBC and its agencies had become too liberal on social issues and liberal in theology. They helped to sustain a successful fundamentalist drive for power that began with the election of the first of a series of fundamentalist SBC presidents in 1979.

Despite the convention's internal struggles, in the decades after the civil rights movement more and more Baptist churches abandoned racially discriminatory admissions policies, and black churches increasingly joined Southern Baptist associations. Even in the 1990s, integrated Baptist congregations remained rare in the South, and tokenism still prevailed at the SBC and Baptist state convention levels. However, overt racism and a belief in forced segregation had virtually disappeared among white Baptists. The SBC's adoption of a resolution in 1995 that condemned and apologized for the role of Southern Baptists in slavery and racism demonstrated that many white Baptists were coming to terms with one of the most unfortunate aspects of their past.

Appendix

BAPTIST STATE CONVENTION NEWSPAPERS: CIRCULATION

	1945	1954	1970
Alabama Baptist	27,000	66,004	150,000
Arkansas Baptist*	23,300	45,000	60,000
Baptist & Reflector (Tennessee)	36,304	61,450	70,000
Baptist Courier (South Carolina)	41,024	88,500	106,000
Baptist Message (Louisiana)	20,500**	48,200	55,000
Baptist Record (Mississippi)	50,376	83,794	110,000
Baptist Standard (Texas)	135,000**	278,849	376,567
Biblical Recorder (North Carolina)	31,552	56,798	92,000
Christian Index (Georgia)	35,049	74,246	130,000
Florida Baptist Witness	20,000	34,834	67,505
Religious Herald (Virginia)	13,000	24,500	31,000

*Renamed the *Arkansas Baptist Newsmagazine* on January 21, 1960.
**1944 circulation figures.

Source: *Annual*, SBC, 1945, 47; 1954, 428; 1971, 242; *ESB*, vol. 3, s.v. "Arkansas Baptist Newsmagazine," by Erwin L. McDonald.

Notes

ABBREVIATIONS

BJC Baptist Joint Committee
BSSBA Baptist Sunday School Board Archive
ESB Encyclopedia of Southern Baptists
NCBHC North Carolina Baptist Historical Collection
SBHLA Southern Baptist Historical Library and Archives

1. THE SOUTHERN BAPTIST CONVENTION AND AFRICAN AMERICANS, 1845–1944

1. John Lee Eighmy, *Churches in Cultural Captivity: A History of the Social Attitudes of Southern Baptists*, with revised introduction, conclusion, and bibliography by Samuel S. Hill (Knoxville: University of Tennessee Press, 1987), 10–17, 21–25, 31–32, 38–39; Rufus B. Spain, *At Ease In Zion: A Social History of Southern Baptists, 1865–1900* (Nashville: Vanderbilt University Press, 1967), 32–33, 38–40, 45, 118–20, 210–11; *ESB*, vol. 4, s.v. "Black Southern Baptists," by Sidney Smith.

2. H. Shelton Smith, *In His Image, But . . . Racism in Southern Religion, 1780–1910* (Durham: Duke University Press, 1972), 47–55; Paul Harvey, *Redeeming the South: Religious Cultures and Racial Identities among Southern Baptists, 1865–1925* (Chapel Hill: University of North Carolina Press, 1997), 8–10.

3. Eighmy, *Churches in Cultural Captivity*, 26–28; Harvey, *Redeeming the South*, 9–11, 34.

4. Eighmy, *Churches in Cultural Captivity*, 10–16; Nancy Tatom Ammerman, *Baptist Battles: Social Change and Religious Conflict in the Southern Baptist Convention* (New Brunswick: Rutgers University Press, 1990), 31–32.

5. Eighmy, *Churches in Cultural Captivity*, 21–24; Bill J. Leonard, *God's Last and Only Hope: The Fragmentation of the Southern Baptist Convention* (Grand Rapids, Mich.: William B. Eerdmans, 1990), 19 (first quotation); Harvey, *Redeeming the South*, 18 (second and third quotations); Spain, *At Ease in Zion*, 13–16, 32–33.

6. Eighmy, *Churches in Cultural Captivity*, 24–25; Charles Reagan Wilson, *Baptized in Blood: The Religion of the Lost Cause, 1865–1920* (Athens: University of Georgia Press, 1980), 4–5, 7–11 (first quotation on pp. 7–8), 13–14, 16, 23, 28, 34, 37–38, 40–41, 46, 57–81 (second quotation on p. 75).

7. Wilson, *Baptized in Blood*, 12, 40–41, 43–46, 68–69, 100, 102–103; Spain, *At Ease in Zion*, 72–74; Harvey, *Redeeming the South*, 38.

8. Harvey, *Redeeming the South*, 31–38 (quotation on p. 34), 45–52, 61–65.

9. Kenneth K. Bailey, "The Post-Civil War Racial Separations in Southern Protestantism: Another Look," *Church History* 46 (December 1977): 455–57, 467–70; *ESB*, vol. 4, s.v. "Black Southern Baptists," by Sidney Smith.

10. Harvey, *Redeeming the South*, 38 (first quotation); Spain, *At Ease in Zion*, 52–53 (second quotation on p. 52), 56–57, 67, 97–99.

11. Eighmy, *Churches in Cultural Captivity*, 32–36 (quotation on p. 34).

12. Spain, *At Ease in Zion*, 54–55 (quotation on p. 55), 81; Eric Foner, *Reconstruction: America's Unfinished Revolution, 1863–1877* (New York: Harper & Row, 1988), 66–67, 239, 251–61, 446–49.

13. Spain, *At Ease in Zion*, 88–90, 96–102, 117–21.
"And he [Noah] said, Cursed *be* Canaan; a servant of servants shall he be unto his brethren.

And he said, Blessed *be* the LORD God of Shem; and Canaan shall be his servant.

God shall enlarge Japheth, and he shall dwell in the tents of Shem; and Canaan shall be his servant." *Genesis* 9:25–27.
As the verse indicates, Noah, not God, had pronounced the curse and directed it at Canaan, not Ham. Furthermore, there is no mention of black skin.

14. Spain, *At Ease in Zion*, 109–11; Wilson, *Baptized in Blood*, 113.

15. Spain, *At Ease in Zion*, 82–84, 107, 113 n.52; Xi Wang, *The Trial of Democracy: Black Suffrage and Northern Republicans, 1860–1910* (Athens: University of Georgia Press, 1997), 53–68, 78–102, 118–59, 180–81, 212–13.

16. Spain, *At Ease in Zion*, 83–89, 92–93, 108 (quotations), 113–114; Harvey, *Redeeming the South*, 219–20; Eighmy, *Churches in Cultural Captivity*, 38, 42.

17. Joel Williamson, *The Crucible of Race: Black-White Relations in the American South Since Emancipation* (New York: Oxford University Press, 1984), 117–18; Spain, *At Ease in Zion*, 111–13.

18. Spain, *At Ease in Zion*, 60–64, 66; Eighmy, *Churches in Cultural Captivity*, 36–40 (quotations on p. 40); Harvey, *Redeeming the South*, 70–74, 183–84.

19. Catherine B. Allen, *A Century to Celebrate: History of Woman's Missionary Union* (Birmingham: Woman's Missionary Union, 1987), 242–44; Harvey, *Redeeming the South*, 240–41.

20. Harvey, *Redeeming the South*, 30–31, 46, 203; Eighmy, *Churches in Cultural Captivity*, 55, 74 n.7, 77; Spain, *At Ease in Zion*, 125–26 (quotation on p. 125).

21. Foy Dan Valentine, "A Historical Study Of Southern Baptists And Race Relations, 1917–1947" (Th.D. diss., Southwestern Baptist Theological Seminary, 1949), 22–23, 36 (first quotation); David M. Reimers, *White Protestantism and the Negro* (New York: Oxford University Press, 1965), 45 (second quotation); Kenneth K. Bailey, *Southern White Protestantism in the Twentieth Century* (New York: Harper & Row, 1964), 40 (third and fourth quotations); Arthur B. Rutledge, *Mission to America: A Century and a Quarter of Southern Baptist Home Missions* (Nashville: Broadman Press, 1969), 134–35; Allen, *A Century to Celebrate*, 245–46.

22. Bailey, *Southern White Protestantism*, 41–42; Eighmy, *Churches in Cultural Captivity*, 81–83, 93–108; Leon McBeth, "Origin of the Christian Life Commission," *Baptist History and Heritage* 1 (October 1966): 31–33.

23. Valentine, "A Historical Study Of Southern Baptists And Race Relations, 1917–

1947," 29, 31–32 (first quotation on p. 31); John Lee Eighmy, "Recent Changes in the Racial Attitudes of Southern Baptists," *Foundations* 5 (October 1962): 354 (second quotation).

24. George Brown Tindall, *The Emergence of the New South, 1913–1945* (Baton Rouge: Louisiana State University Press, 1967), 146–57.

25. *Annual*, SBC, 1920, 97 (quotations); Harry Emerson Byrd, "An Analysis of Pronouncements on Major Issues by the Social Service Commission of the Southern Baptist Convention From 1914–1946" (Th.M diss., Southeastern Baptist Theological Seminary, 1959), 155.

26. Allen, *A Century to Celebrate*, 246–47.

27. Reimers, *White Protestantism and the Negro*, 45; *Annual*, *SBC*, 1944, 101; Harvey, *Redeeming the South*, 185–86. In 1915, the National Baptist Convention experienced a schism and divided between the National Baptist Convention, U.S.A., Inc., and the National Baptist Convention of America. *ESB*, vol. 2, s.v. "Negroes, Southern Baptist Relations To," by Courts Redford.

28. Byrd, "An Analysis of Pronouncements on Major Issues by the Social Service Commission of the Southern Baptist Convention From 1914–1946," 151–55, 160–61; Tindall, *The Emergence of the New South*, 171–75, 550–54.

29. Allen, *A Century to Celebrate*, 247–48; Tindall, *The Emergence of the New South*, 550–51, 554.

30. Harvard Sitkoff, *The Struggle for Black Equality, 1954–1992* rev. ed. (New York: Hill and Wang, 1993), 10–11, 18–19; Tindall, *The Emergence of the New South*, 561–64.

31. Robert Moats Miller, *American Protestantism and Social Issues, 1919–1939* (Chapel Hill: University of North Carolina Press, 1958), 309; *Annual*, SBC, 1944, 97–101; Edward L. Wheeler, "An Overview of Black Southern Baptist Involvements," *Baptist History and Heritage* 16 (July 1981): 8.

32. *Annual*, SBC, 1939, 129, 141 (quotations); Tindall, *The Emergence of the New South*, 550–54.

33. *Annual*, SBC, 1940, 80, 84–85 (quotations on p. 85), 95.

34. Ibid., 1941, 126–27 (first quotation on p. 126); 1944, 132 (second and third quotations); Mark Newman, "The Baptist General Association of Virginia and Desegregation, 1931–1980," *Virginia Magazine of History and Biography* 105 (Summer 1997): 260.

35. Sitkoff, *The Struggle for Black Equality*, 11–12.

36. Brooks Hays, *A Southern Moderate Speaks* (Chapel Hill: University of North Carolina Press, 1959), 196–97 (quotation on p. 197); Allen, *A Century to Celebrate*, 253.

37. Sitkoff, *The Struggle for Black Equality*, 12, 16; David R. Goldfield, *Black, White, and Southern: Race Relations and Southern Culture 1940 to the Present* (Baton Rouge: Louisiana State University Press, 1991), 33, 36.

38. Eighmy, *Churches in Cultural Captivity*, 95, 131, 151–53; *Annual*, SBC, 1943, 107–109 (quotations on p. 107).

39. Ibid., 1944, 133 (quotation), 135–36; Goldfield, *Black, White, and Southern*, 33–34.

40. Davis C. Hill, "Southern Baptist Thought and Action in Race Relations, 1940–1950" (Th.D. diss., Southern Baptist Theological Seminary, 1952), 189, 199–201; Eighmy, *Churches in Cultural Captivity*, 109–113, 115–17.

41. Eighmy, *Churches in Cultural Captivity*, 82–83, 86–88, 109, 115–16.

42. *Annual*, Virginia, 1933, 70–71; 1938, 79; 1939, 87–91; 1941, 128–31; 1942, 120–22; 1943, 102–103 (quotations on p. 102), 117; 1944, 117–19; 1946, 82; 1951, 76;

Numan V. Bartley, *The New South, 1945–1980* (Baton Rouge: Louisiana State University Press, 1995), 29–30.

43. *Annual,* North Carolina, 1942, 44 (first quotation); 1943, 34 (second and third quotations); 1944, 44 (fourth quotation).

44. *Proceedings,* Texas, 1941, 86–87; 1943, 67–70; 1944, 187; John W. Storey and Ronald C. Ellison, *Southern Baptists of Southeast Texas: A Centennial History, 1888–1988* (Beaumont, Tex.: Golden Triangle Baptist Association, 1988), 136–37.

45. *Proceedings,* Texas, 1944, 188–189 (quotation on p. 188); 1945, 193.

46. *Annual,* Alabama, 1941, 147 (quotations); 1942, 106–107; 1943, 126–130; 1944, 108–110; *Annual,* Arkansas, 1940, 88–91; 1941, 82–84; 1942, 92–94; 1943, 86; 1944, 87–88; *Annual,* Mississippi, 1941, 144–53; 1942, 128–46; 1943, 131–50; 1944, 117–130; *Proceedings,* Tennessee, 1941, 93–95; 1942, 112–13; 1943, 102–103; 1944, 112–13.

47. *Annual,* Louisiana, 1940, 40–43; 1941, 20–22, 46, 51 (first and second quotations), 56, 58; 1942, 23–24; 1943, 33–34; 1944, 11, 39–40 (third quotation on p. 39); *Annual,* SBC, 1944, 135–36.

48. *Minutes,* Georgia, 1941, 30, 32–33 (first quotation on p. 32; second quotation on p. 33); 1944, 34, 36–37 (third quotation on p. 36).

49. *Minutes,* South Carolina, 1941, 28, 136–137 (first, second, third and fourth quotations on p. 136; fifth quotation on p. 137).

50. *Annual,* Florida, 1942, 83–84 (quotations on p. 84).

51. Ibid., 1943, 74 (first quotation); *Minutes,* South Carolina, 1943, 23, 133 (second quotation).

52. *Annual,* Florida, 1944, 85, 87 (first and fourth quotations); *Minutes,* South Carolina, 1944, 19, 20 (fifth quotation), 138 (second and third quotations).

53. Neil R. McMillen, *The Citizens' Council: Organized Resistance to the Second Reconstruction, 1954–64* (Urbana and Chicago: University of Illinois Press, 1971), 5–7.

54. Valentine, "A Historical Study Of Southern Baptists And Race Relations," 8, 225–27 (quotations on p. 226), 229–30; *Annual,* SBC, 1960, 274; Ammerman, *Baptist Battles,* 236–37.

55. Valentine, "A Historical Study Of Southern Baptists And Race Relations," 7, 65, 231–32 (quotations on p. 232).

56. Allen, *A Century to Celebrate,* 251–53 (first quotation on p. 251); Leon McBeth, "Southern Baptists and Race Since 1947," *Baptist History and Heritage* 7 (July 1972): 162; *Annual,* Louisiana, 1941, 46, 51 (second quotation), 56, 58; *Minutes,* South Carolina, 1942, 141 (third quotation); 1943, 114–15; 1944, 27, 147; *Annual,* Mississippi, 1944, 35 (fourth quotation), 61 (fifth quotation); 1945, 90; *Minutes,* Georgia, 1941, 22; *Annual,* Alabama, 1945, 96–97; *Annual,* Virginia, 1939, 88–90; 1941, 129–30; 1942, 54, 120–22; 1943, 65–66; *Annual,* North Carolina, 1942, 44; 1944, 43–44; *Annual,* Texas, 1943, 67–70; 1944, 187–89.

57. "Race Relations And Home Missions," *Home Missions* 14 (April 1943): 3 (first quotation); Emmanuel L. McCall, "Home Mission Board Ministry in the Black Community," *Baptist History and Heritage* 16 (July 1981): 34–35; "Résumé of Significant Events in the History of the Home Mission Board of the SBC," 132 (second quotation), Box 63, Folder 7, Herschel H. Hobbs Papers, SBHLA.

58. *Annual,* Florida, 1943, 74 (first and second quotations); *Annual,* Alabama, 1944, 19 (third quotation); *Annual,* Virginia, 1943, 92; Valentine, "A Historical Study Of Southern Baptists And Race Relations," 174 (fourth quotation).

59. Valentine, "A Historical Study Of Southern Baptists And Race Relations," 165–

78, 229; Herbert H. Hyman and Paul B. Sheatsley, "Attitudes toward Desegregation," *Scientific American* 211 (July 1964): 16–20.

2. AN OVERVIEW: SOUTHERN BAPTISTS AND DESEGREGATION, 1945–1971

1. Nancy Tatom Ammerman, *Baptist Battles: Social Change and Religious Conflict in the Southern Baptist Convention* (New Brunswick: Rutgers University Press, 1990), 52; Phillip Baron Jones, "An Examination of the Statistical Growth of the Southern Baptist Convention" in *Understanding Church Growth and Decline: 1950–1978*, eds. Dean R. Hoge and David A. Roozen (New York: Pilgrim Press, 1979), 162, 177; John Shelton Reed, *The Enduring South: Subcultural Persistence in Mass Society* (Chapel Hill: University of North Carolina Press, 1986 [1972]), 57–59.

2. Numan V. Bartley, *The Rise of Massive Resistance: Race and Politics in the South During the 1950's* (Baton Rouge: Louisiana State University Press, 1969), 12–14 (quotation on p. 13); John Shelton Reed and Merle Black, "Jim Crow, R.I.P.," in John Shelton Reed, *Surveying the South: Studies in Regional Sociology* (Columbia: University of Missouri Press, 1993), 96–98.

3. George D. Kelsey, *Social Ethics Among Southern Baptists, 1917–1969* (Metuchen, N.J.: Scarecrow Press, 1973), 245–46, 249.

4. Ibid., 231–40, 247, 249–54; W. T. Moore, *His Heart is Black* (Atlanta: Home Mission Board, 1978), 73–92.

5. *Annual*, Alabama, 1961, 146–47 (quotation on p. 146); Leon Macon, "We Must Be Law-Abiding," *Alabama Baptist*, July 30, 1964. "Go ye therefore, and teach all nations, baptizing them in the name of the Father, and of the Son, and of the Holy Ghost: Teaching them to observe all things whatsoever I have commanded you; and, lo, I am with you alway, *even* unto the end of the world. Amen." (*Matthew* 28:19–20). "Let every soul be subject unto the higher powers. For there is no power but of God: the powers that be are ordained of God. Whosoever therefore resisteth the power, resisteth the ordinance of God: and they that resist shall receive to themselves damnation" (*Romans* 13:1–2). "Put them in mind to be subject to principalities and powers, to obey magistrates, to be ready to every good work" (*Titus* 3:1).

6. "Criswell Raps Racism, Segregation in Broadcast," *Baptist & Reflector*, July 25, 1968.

7. "Southern Baptist Leader Opposes Civil Rights Program," *Baptist Message*, June 3, 1948 (first quotation); E. D. Solomon, untitled editorial, *Florida Baptist Witness*, February 28, 1946 (second quotation). "And [God] hath made of one blood all nations of men for to dwell on all the face of the earth. . . ." (*Acts* 17:26).

8. *Annual*, North Carolina, 1946, 43, 49 (quotation); Mark Newman, "Getting Right with God: Southern Baptists and Race Relations, 1945–1980" (Ph.D. diss., University of Mississippi, 1993), chaps. 4–5; Anthony Lake Newberry, "Without Urgency or Ardor: The South's Middle-Of-The-Road Liberals and Civil Rights, 1945–1960" (Ph.D. diss., Ohio University, 1982), 15–17, 27.

9. *Annual*, North Carolina, 1946, 49–50; *Proceedings*, Texas, 1950, 173–74, 186; 1951, 202, 204; *Annual*, Virginia, 1952, 76, 79; Katherine Parker Freeman, "Christ The Answer To Racial Tension," *Royal Service* 43 (March 1949): 20–28; D. Elton Trueblood, "Make Brotherhood Real," *Light* 3 (February 1950): 1.

10. L. L. Carpenter, "United and Spirit of Progress Mark Convention in Chicago," *Biblical Recorder,* May 27, 1950 (first quotation); "SBC Seminaries To Enrol Negroes," *Baptist Courier,* April 5, 1951; Lee Porter, "Southern Baptists and Race Relations, 1948–1963" (Th.D. diss., Southwestern Baptist Theological Seminary, 1965), 53–54 (second quotation on p. 54); *Annual,* SBC, 1952, 55.

11. "Southern Baptist Leaders Urge Calm Appraisal of Court Ruling," *Florida Baptist Witness,* May 27, 1954 (first and third quotations); "SBC President's Statement on Supreme Court Decision," *Florida Baptist Witness,* May 27, 1954 (second quotation); Alma Hunt, *Reflections from Alma Hunt* (Birmingham: Woman's Missionary Union, 1987), 71.

12. "Southern Baptist Leaders Urge Calm Appraisal of Court Ruling," *Florida Baptist Witness,* May 27, 1954 (quotation). The Social Service Commission became the Christian Life Commission in 1953. Most state conventions also adopted the name change for their commissions. *Annual,* SBC, 1953, 53.

13. *Annual,* SBC, 1954, 56 (third quotation), 403–404 (first and second quotations on p. 404); "Ruling On Segregation Endorsed," *Christian Index,* June 10, 1954.

14. *Annual,* North Carolina, 1954, 55–57, 70; *Annual,* Virginia, 1954, 83, 88; Newman, "Getting Right with God," 376–78, 453, 486, 494–96.

15. David M. Gardner, "Segregation's Problems," *Baptist Standard,* June 10, 1954 (quotation); A. L. Goodrich, "The SBC Convention," *Baptist Record,* June 10, 1954; Finley W. Tinnin, "Non-Segregation," *Baptist Message,* June 3, 1954; Newman, "Getting Right with God," 412–13, 457–58, 517, 519–20.

16. Bartley, *The Rise of Massive Resistance,* 60 (quotation), 74–79.

17. Ibid., 82–107, 116 (quotations), 131, 251–92.

18. Ibid., 296–302.

19. Newman, "Getting Right with God," 327–39, 341–44.

20. *Minutes,* Georgia, 1956, 35, 39 (quotation); *Annual,* Alabama, 1956, 33, 143; *Annual,* Louisiana, 1957, 72–73; Newman, "Getting Right with God," 328–39, 379–96, 453–54, 496–97.

21. "An Appeal For a Christian Spirit in Race Relations," *Biblical Recorder,* April 21, 1956; Porter Routh to Owen Cooper, May 7, 1956, "Supreme Court's Decision on Segregation [Folder 1]," SBC Executive Committee Records, SBHLA.

22. *Annual,* SBC, 1956, 72.

23. A. C. Miller, "Speaking The Truth In Love," *Christian Life Bulletin* 1 (January-February 1958): 3; *Annual,* SBC, 1957, 362; Maxwell Baker to A. C. Miller, December 4, 1956, Box 1, Folder 7, SBC Christian Life Commission Papers, SBHLA; Moore, *His Heart is Black,* 17–18; Newman, "Getting Right with God," 119–27, 129–31, 327–28, 331–34.

24. *Annual,* Alabama, 1956, 33, 134–36, 143; Bartley, *The Rise of Massive Resistance,* 251–75, 283, 285–86, 320–31; "Virginia Baptists Refuse To Endorse Gov. Almond," *Religious News Service,* November 14, 1958 (quotation).

25. Richard N. Owen, "Segregation and Its Alternative," *Baptist and Reflector,* February 2, 1956; Erwin L. McDonald, "The Way Out," *Arkansas Baptist,* October 10, 1957; Bartley, *The Rise of Massive Resistance,* 146–47; Newman, "Getting Right with God," 416–18, 458–62, 526–27.

26. Kenneth K. Bailey, *Southern White Protestantism in the Twentieth Century* (New York: Harper & Row, 1964), 148–50; Mark Newman, "The Tennessee Baptist Convention and Desegregation, 1954–1980," *Tennessee Historical Quarterly* 57 (Winter 1998): 241–42.

27. Reed Sarratt, *The Ordeal of Desegregation: The First Decade* (New York: Harper &

Row, 1966), 14–21, 29–30, 106–110, 354; Neil R. McMillen, "Development of Civil Rights, 1956–1970," in *A History of Mississippi,* ed. Richard Aubrey McLemore (Hattiesburg: University & College Press of Mississippi, 1973), vol 2, 162; Harvard Sitkoff, *The Struggle For Black Equality, 1954–1992,* rev. ed. (New York: Hill and Wang, 1993), 61–183.

28. *Annual,* SBC, 1961, 84 (first and second quotations); Sitkoff, *The Struggle For Black Equality,* 88–103; Porter, "Southern Baptists and Race Relations," 151–55, 157; John Jeter Hurt, Jr., "Missions Forces Reform At Home," *Christian Index,* July 4, 1963 (third quotation).

29. "Appeal For Open Public Schools," *Christian Index,* November 24, 1960; *Annual,* North Carolina, 1960, 44, 68, 175–76; 1961, 144–45, 176; 1963, 76; *Proceedings,* Texas, 1963, 24, 94; "Survey of Racial Picture," *Baptist Messenger,* December 12, 1963; Newman, "Getting Right with God," 400–401, 404–407, 430–33, 505–507, 512–16, 559 n. 59, 755–56.

30. Leon Macon, "Law And Order," *Alabama Baptist,* September 5, 1963; John Jeter Hurt, Jr., "World Watches As Georgia Acts," *Christian Index,* January 19, 1961; Newman, "Getting Right with God," 527–29.

31. Richard N. Owen, "Racial Strife," *Baptist & Reflector,* May 30, 1963; E. S. James, "Desegregation, Yes—by Legislation, No," *Baptist Standard,* July 24, 1963; Sitkoff, *The Struggle For Black Equality,* 118–35; Newman, "Getting Right with God," 420–26, 462.

32. Grace Bryan Holmes to the *Christian Index,* September 22, 1960; "How Whites Feel About Negroes: A Painful American Dilemma," *Newsweek* 62 (October 21, 1963): 45.

33. *Annual,* SBC, 1964, 73 (first quotation), 74 (second quotation), 229; Ross Coggins, "The Law And The Gospel," *Baptist Program,* August 1964, 3; "Deep South Bloc Kills Commission Race Statement," *Biblical Recorder,* May 30, 1964; " . . . And This One Passed by Close Margin," *Biblical Recorder,* May 30, 1964; Foy Valentine, "Baptist Polity and Social Pronouncements," *Baptist History and Heritage* 14 (July 1979): 57–58.

34. "Civil Rights Law Viewed As A Test," *Baptist Press,* July 8, 1964.

35. *Annual,* SBC, 1965, 90–92 (quotations on pp. 91–92).

36. *Annual,* North Carolina, 1964, 151–52, 174; *Proceedings,* Texas, 1964, 29–31; *Annual,* Virginia, 1964, 66, 69; Richard N. Owen, "Obey The Law," *Baptist & Reflector,* July 16, 1964; E. S. James, "Southern Baptists and the Civil Rights Law," *Baptist Standard,* July 15, 1964; Leon Macon, "This Is Our Answer," *Alabama Baptist,* July 23, 1964; W. G. Stracener, "Liberty and the Pursuit of Happiness," *Florida Baptist Witness,* July 2, 1964; Reuben E. Alley, "Civil Rights Legislation," *Religious Herald,* July 9, 1964.

37. Ross Coggins, "A Strategy for Southern Baptists in Race Relations," in *Christianity and Race Relations: Addresses From Conferences At Glorieta and Ridgecrest* (Nashville: Christian Life Commission, 1964), 142–45; Newman, "Getting Right with God," 593–98, 685–89, 725–27; Mrs. S. A. Williams to *Royal Service* 58 (December 1964): 34–35; Reed and Black, "Jim Crow, R.I.P.," 98.

38. John Lee Eighmy, *Churches in Cultural Captivity: A History of the Social Attitudes of Southern Baptists,* with a revised introduction, conclusion, and bibliography by Samuel S. Hill (Knoxville: University of Tennessee Press, 1987), 195; "A Long Hot August," *Baptist Program,* August 1965, 5 (quotation).

39. "Most Schools Sign U.S. Compliance," *Baptist Record,* April 15, 1965; Moore, *His Heart is Black,* 80.

40. "Leaders Deplore Assassination and White Racism," *Biblical Recorder,* April 13, 1968; "Editors Urged to Fight Racism," *Florida Baptist Witness,* May 2, 1968; "SBC Execu-

tive Committee Urged To Deal With Crisis," *Baptist Press,* April 10, 1968; "A Statement of Christian Concern," *Biblical Recorder,* May 25, 1968 (quotations); Andrew M. Manis, "Silence or Shockwaves: Southern Baptist Responses to the Assassination of Martin Luther King, Jr.," *Baptist History and Heritage* 15 (October 1980): 19–27, 35; Sitkoff, *The Struggle for Black Equality,* 184–209.

41. *Annual,* SBC, 1968, 67–69 (quotations), 73; Billy Keith, *W. A. Criswell: The Authorized Biography* (Old Tappan, N.J.: Fleming H. Revell, 1973), 175.

42. "Report of Survey of Superintendents of Missions Concerning Racial Representation of Southern Baptist Church Memberships," Box 2, Folder 155, Wendell R. Grigg Papers, NCBHC; *Annual,* SBC, 1970, 78–79; 1971, 78–79; Hudson Baggett, "A Plea for Patience," *Alabama Baptist,* March 5, 1970; Newman, "Getting Right with God," 676–78, 771–75, 800–802; David R. Goldfield, *Black, White, and Southern: Race Relations and Southern Culture 1940 to the Present* (Baton Rouge: Louisiana State University Press, 1991), 257–60.

43. *Annual,* SBC, 1969, 79–80; 1970, 79–80; 1971, 79; Jim Newton, "Revision of Becoming Prompts Record Response Toward BSSB," *Baptist Press,* November 24, 1971; James L. Sullivan, *God Is My Record* (Nashville: Broadman Press, 1974), 125–26.

44. Sitkoff, *The Struggle for Black Equality,* 210–14, 216.

45. *Annual,* SBC, 1969, 79–80 (quotations); "Manifesto receives little support," *Baptist Standard,* August 13, 1969; James F. Findlay, Jr., *Church People in the Struggle: The National Council of Churches and the Black Freedom Movement, 1950–1970* (Oxford: Oxford University Press, 1993), 199–225.

46. *Annual,* SBC, 1969, 76 (first quotation), 79–80; "Convention News," *Baptist Message,* June 19, 1969 (second quotation); Alonzo L. Hamby, *Liberalism and Its Challengers: F.D.R. to Reagan* (New York: Oxford University Press, 1985), 343–44.

47. *Annual,* SBC, 1970, 80–81 (quotation on p. 80); Adam Fairclough, "A Study of the Southern Christian Leadership Conference and the Rise and Fall of the Non-Violent Civil Rights Movement" (Ph.D. diss., Keele University, United Kingdom, 1978), 409–11; Manning Marable, *Race, Rebellion and Reform: The Second Reconstruction in Black America, 1945–1990,* 2d ed. (Houndmills, England: Macmillan, 1991), 108–13.

3. The Sociology of Religion and Social Change

1. Kenneth K. Bailey, *Southern White Protestantism in the Twentieth Century* (New York: Harper & Row, 1964), 2 n. 3; Charles Reagan Wilson, *Baptized in Blood: The Religion of the Lost Cause, 1865–1920* (Athens: University of Georgia Press, 1980), 2–4.

2. Ernst Troeltsch, *The Social Teaching of the Christian Churches,* with an introduction by H. Richard Niebuhr, tr. Oliver Wyon (London, England: George Allen & Unwin, 1931; repr., Chicago: University of Chicago Press, 1976), vol 1, 331 (quotations); Rhys Isaac, *The Transformation of Virginia, 1740–1790* (Chapel Hill: University of North Carolina Press, 1982); John Lee Eighmy, *Churches in Cultural Captivity: A History of the Social Attitudes of Southern Baptists,* with revised introduction, conclusion, and bibliography, 1987, by Samuel S. Hill (Knoxville: University of Tennessee Press, 1987), xviii.

3. Emile Durkheim, *The Elementary Forms of the Religious Life: A Study in Religious Sociology,* tr. Joseph Ward Swain (London, England: George Allen & Unwin, 1915; repr., Glencoe, Ill.: Free Press, 1947), 47; Michael W. Hughey, *Civil Religion and Moral Order: Theoretical and Historical Dimensions* (Westport, Conn.: Greenwood Press, 1983), xiii, 22;

Bill J. Leonard, *God's Last and Only Hope: The Fragmentation of the Southern Baptist Convention* (Grand Rapids, Mich.: William B. Eerdmans, 1990), 11–15, 18–20.

4. Charles Y. Glock and Rodney Stark, *Religion and Society in Tension* (Chicago: Rand McNally, 1965), 170, 183, 227 (first quotation), 228, 239 (third quotation); F. Ernest Johnson, "Do Churches Exert Significant Influence on Public Morality?," *Annals of the American Academy of Political and Social Science* 280 (March 1952): 127 (second quotation).

5. Glock and Stark, *Religion and Society in Tension*, 239; *Annual*, SBC, 1954, 56 (first quotation); "SBC President's Statement On Supreme Court Decision," *Florida Baptist Witness*, May 27, 1954 (second quotation).

6. *Minutes*, Georgia, 1954, 61.

7. Glock and Stark, *Religion and Society in Tension*, 234, 239; *Christian Principles Applied to Race Relations* (Nashville: Christian Life Commission, n.d. [1965]).

8. Meredith B. McGuire, *Religion: The Social Context*, 2d ed. (Belmont, Calif.: Wadsworth Publishing Co., 1987), 121, 129.

9. *The Clarion-Ledger/Jackson Daily News* [Mississippi], July 1, 1984 (quotation); Peter L. Berger, *Invitation To Sociology: A Humanistic Perspective* (Garden City, N.Y.: Doubleday, 1963; repr. Harmondsworth, England: Pelican Books, 1966), 132.

10. Edward L. Queen II, *In the South the Baptists are the Center of Gravity: Southern Baptists and Social Change, 1930–1980* (Brooklyn: Carlson Publishing, 1991), 77–78; James F. Burks, "Integration Or Segregation," *Religious Herald*, May 3, 1956; H. M. Stroup to W. R. Grigg, April 28, 1956, Box 1, Folder 34, Wendell R. Grigg Papers, NCBHC.

11. M. A. Webb to Porter Routh, October 14, 1955, "Supreme Court's Decision on Segregation [Folder 1]," SBC Executive Committee Records, SBHLA; Niebuhr quoted in Barry Hankins, "Southern Baptists and Northern Evangelicals: Cultural Factors and the Nature of Religious Alliances," *Religion and American Culture* 7 (1997): 281.

12. W. Levon Moore, "Why Don't Southern Ministers Speak Out?" *Baptist Record*, June 25, 1964.

13. Ibid.; Eighmy, *Churches in Cultural Captivity*, 124–25; James J. Thompson, Jr., *Tried as by Fire: Southern Baptists and the Religious Controversies of the 1920s* (Macon, Ga.: Mercer University Press, 1982), 53–56, 58, 145–46, 149.

14. Henlee Hulix Barnette, "The Southern Baptist Theological Seminary and the Civil Rights Movement: The Visit of Martin Luther King, Jr., Part Two," *Review and Expositor* 93 (Winter 1996): 77, 93; Leonard, *God's Last and Only Hope*, 43–44.

15. McGuire, *Religion*, 235 (first quotation), 237 (second quotation).

16. Peter L. Berger, *The Sacred Canopy: Elements of a Sociological Theory of Religion* (Garden City, N.Y.: Doubleday, 1967), 147.

17. "Southern Ministers Speak Their Minds," *Pulpit Digest* 39 (December 1958): 13–17; Howard Dorgan, "Response of the Main-line Southern White Protestant Pulpit to *Brown* v. *Board of Education*, 1954–1965," in *A New Diversity in Contemporary Southern Rhetoric*, eds. Calvin M. Logue and Howard Dorgan (Baton Rouge: Louisiana State University Press, 1987), 46.

18. *The Clarion-Ledger/Jackson Daily News*, July 1, 1984 (first quotation); John R. Bodo, "The Pastor and Social Conflict" in *Religion and Social Conflict*, eds. Robert Lee and Martin E. Marty (New York: Oxford University Press, 1964), vii, 168 (second quotation).

19. Thomas J. Holmes in collaboration with Gainer E. Bryan, Jr., *Ashes for Breakfast* (Valley Forge, Pa.: Judson Press, 1969), 65, 72, 93–95.

20. Tim Nicholas, "White Baptist Recalls Danger of Black Civil Rights Stance," *Baptist Press*, November 6, 1973 (quotations); Owen Cooper, interviewed by Graham Lee Hales,

Jr., December 11, 1972, The Mississippi Oral History Program of the University of Southern Mississippi, vol. 17 (1975), 26; "Minister's Home Explosion Scene," *Alabama Baptist*, July 24, 1958.

21. E. J. Kearney, "The Church's Responsibility In Race Relations," sermon preached at Seventh and Main Baptist Church, Bonham, Texas, September 15, 1957, Box 13, Folder 5, SBC Christian Life Commission Papers, SBHLA; Holmes, *Ashes for Breakfast*, 48–50.

22. Wayne Flynt, *Alabama Baptists: Southern Baptists in the Heart of Dixie* (Tuscaloosa: University of Alabama Press, 1998), 474–75.

23. Benjamin B. Ringer and Charles Y. Glock, "The Political Role of the Church as Defined by Its Parishioners," *Public Opinion Quarterly* 18 (Winter 1954–1955): 337–47; G. Jackson Stafford, "It Happened in a Baptist Church," in "Supreme Court's Decision on Segregation [Folder 1]," Executive Committee Records, SBHLA.

24. T. B. Maston, "Southern Baptists and the Negro (Part 1)," *Home Missions* 37 (July 1966): 19; Ernest Q. Campbell and Thomas F. Pettigrew, *Christians in Racial Crisis: A Study of Little Rock's Ministry* (Washington, D.C.: Public Affairs Press, 1959), 90–92.

25. Campbell and Pettigrew, *Christians in Racial Crisis*, 93, 97 (first quotation); Maston, "Southern Baptists and the Negro (Part 1)," 19 (second quotation); Flynt, *Alabama Baptists*, 428–32.

26. Ernest White, "Baptist Churches and Race Problems," *Baptist Program*, October 1964: 4; Colbert S. Cartwright, "What Can Southern Ministers Do?," *Christian Century* 73 (December 26, 1956): 1505; "The World Around Us," *Christian Century* 84 (March 1, 1967): 285.

27. *The Clarion-Ledger/Jackson Daily News*, July 1, 1984.

28. Ross Coggins, "A Strategy For Southern Baptists In Race Relations," in *Christianity and Race Relations: Addresses from Conferences at Glorieta and Ridgecrest* (Nashville: Christian Life Commission, 1964), 142; G. Avery Lee, *Some Quiet Thoughts on a Turbulent Issue* (Nashville: Christian Life Commission, n.d. [1956]).

29. Andrew Michael Manis, *Southern Civil Religions in Conflict: Black and White Baptists and Civil Rights, 1947-1957* (Athens: University of Georgia Press, 1987), 70; Glock and Stark, *Religion and Society in Tension*, 241.

30. "Racial Integrity Through Free Choice," *Christian Century* 74 (November 11, 1957): 1387 (first and second quotations); Campbell and Pettigrew, *Christians in Racial Crisis*, 100 (third quotation); Johnny Jackson, "A Christian Appraisal of School Integration," (fourth quotation), Box 11, Folder 6, SBC Christian Life Commission Papers, SBHLA.

31. Campbell and Pettigrew, *Christians in Racial Crisis*, 102 (first and third quotations); Lee, *Some Quiet Thoughts on a Turbulent Issue*, 5 (second quotation); Ernest Q. Campbell and Thomas F. Pettigrew, "Racial and Moral Crisis: The Role of Little Rock Ministers," *American Journal of Sociology* 64 (March 1959): 515 (fourth quotation).

32. Campbell and Pettigrew, *Christians in Racial Crisis*, 103–104.

33. Campbell and Pettigrew, "Racial and Moral Crisis," 515–16.

34. "Creative Church in Georgia," *Christian Century* 74 (March 6, 1957): 285. "Will ye steal, murder, and commit adultery, and swear falsely, and burn incense unto Baal, and walk after other gods whom ye know not;

And come and stand before me in this house, which is called by my name, and say, We are delivered to do all these abominations?" *Jeremiah* 7:9–10

35. Maston, "Southern Baptists and the Negro (Part 1)," 19.

4. SOUTHERN BAPTISTS AND THE BIBLICAL
DEFENSE OF SEGREGATION

1. Edward L. Queen II, *In the South the Baptists are the Center of Gravity: Southern Baptists and Social Change, 1930–1980* (Brooklyn: Carlson Publishing, 1991), 93.

2. Peter L. Berger, *The Sacred Canopy: Elements of a Sociological Theory of Religion* (Garden City, N.Y.: Doubleday, 1967), 29 (first quotation), 32–34 (third quotation on p. 33; second quotation on p. 34), 37 (fifth quotation), 52; Andrew Michael Manis, *Southern Civil Religions in Conflict: Black and White Baptists and Civil Rights, 1947–1957* (Athens: University of Georgia Press, 1987), 88 (fourth quotation).

3. Berger, *The Sacred Canopy,* 98 (first quotation); Meredith B. McGuire, *Religion: The Social Context,* 2d ed. (Belmont, Calif.: Wadsworth Publishing Co., 1987), 199 (second quotation).

4. Berger, *The Sacred Canopy,* 47 (first quotation), 49–50 (second quotation on p. 49; third quotation on p. 50).

5. Rufus B. Spain, *At Ease in Zion: A Social History of Southern Baptists, 1865–1900* (Nashville: Vanderbilt University Press, 1967), 45–46, 56–57, 98–99.

6. Wayne Flynt, *Alabama Baptists: Southern Baptists in the Heart of Dixie* (Tuscaloosa: University of Alabama, 1998), xvi, 458, 477–78, 480, 526, 543, 566–67, 569.

7. Leon Macon, "This Is Our Answer," *Alabama Baptist,* July 23, 1964; O. W. Taylor, "All Races of Men From One Man," *Baptist & Reflector,* January 16, 1947; David M. Gardner, "Racial Equality Demanded," *Baptist Standard,* October 4, 1945.

8. Resolution of the Cameron Baptist Church, Cameron, South Carolina, October 20, 1963, Folder "Race Relations—1963–1964," Executive Committee Records, SBHLA; Mrs. Sam Fowler Stowers to the *Baptist Standard,* January 25, 1958.

9. "Race Problem Resolutions Adopted By Mendenhall Church," *Baptist Record,* September 26, 1946; A. Mims Wilkinson, Jr., to the *Christian Index,* August 1, 1968.

10. E. D. Estes to Brooks Hays, February 13, 1958, Box 2, Folder 7, Brooks Hays Papers, SBHLA; the Reverend James F. Burks, "Integration Or Segregation," *Religious Herald,* May 3, 1956.

11. H. T. Sullivan, "The Christian Concept Of Race Relations," *Baptist Message,* October 10, 1957; Mrs. Roy McCaa to the *Baptist Message,* October 17, 1957; E. R. McCorthy to the *Arkansas Baptist Newsmagazine,* September 10, 1964.

12. "A Resolution Relating to the Issue of Segregation-Integration," *Baptist Message,* December 5, 1957.

13. Humphrey K. Ezell, *The Christian Problem of Racial Segregation* (New York: Greenwich, 1959), 14–15; Carey Daniel, *God the Original Segregationist* (N.p., n.d.), 2–5; T. J. Preston to the *Christian Index,* January 6, 1955.

14. Daniel, *God the Original Segregationist,* 5–6.

15. Resolutions passed by Manning Baptist Church, South Carolina, July 17, 1957, and Summerton Baptist Church, Summerton, South Carolina, October 13, 1957, Box 11, Folder 9, SBC Christian Life Commission Papers, SBHLA; Resolution of the Hermitage Baptist Church of Camden, South Carolina, September 1, 1957, Box 2, Folder 6, Brooks Hays Papers, SBHLA.

16. Mrs. Dave Miles to the *Baptist Standard,* October 22, 1958; A. A. Kitchings to H. Franklin Paschall, undated letter, Box 14, Folder 457, H. Franklin Paschall Papers,

BSSBA. *Deuteronomy* 7:1–4 describes the destruction of Israel's armies but says nothing of God separating mankind by race. *Ezra* chapters 9 and 10 concerned groups whom God had forbidden the Jews to marry. Religious, not racial, differences accounted for the prohibition.

17. Don Keleg to the *Baptist Standard,* December 10, 1955 (first quotation); Bob Weems to the *Baptist Record,* November 30, 1972 (second quotation); J. D. Butler to A. C. Miller, April 30, 1956, Box 1, Folder 3, SBC Christian Life Commission Papers, SBHLA (third quotation); Mrs. J. R. Patterson to the *Baptist Standard,* December 9, 1954 (fourth quotation).

18. George Bell Timmerman, Sr., to the Reverend G. Jackson Stafford, July 29, 1955, "Supreme Court's Decision on Segregation [Folder 2]," Executive Committee Records, SBHLA (first quotation); Virginia Molett to *Home Missions* 38 (March 1967): 3 (second quotation); Mrs. Hoyt S. Haynes to *Home Missions* 39 (June 1968): 2 (third quotation); J. D. Butler to A. C. Miller, February 19, 1956, Box 1, Folder 3, SBC Christian Life Commission Papers, SBHLA (fourth quotation).

19. Leon Macon, "The Way of Christ," *Alabama Baptist,* March 18, 1965.

20. Leon Macon, "Baptists and Social Action," *Alabama Baptist,* May 1, 1958; Hugh Cantrell, "Arkansas Baptist Convention Annual Sermon," *Arkansas Baptist,* November 21, 1957; James J. Thompson, Jr., *Tried as by Fire: Southern Baptists and the Religious Controversies of the 1920s* (Macon, Ga.: Mercer University Press, 1982), 38–41; Samuel S. Hill, Jr., *Southern Churches in Crisis* (New York: Holt, Rinehart and Winston, 1967), xiv.

21. James F. Burks, "Integration Or Segregation," *Religious Herald,* May 3, 1956; Thompson, *Tried as by Fire,* 62, 73–76, 108–110.

22. Virginia Barker to *Home Missions* 38 (March 1967): 3; O. P. Bazer to *Home Missions* 40 (April 1969): 2; Mr. and Mrs. R. W. Scarborough to *Home Missions* 36 (April 1965): 2.

23. Manis, *Southern Civil Religions in Conflict,* 93.

24. Finley W. Tinnin, "A Sane View On Segregation," *Baptist Message,* September 27, 1956; John Shelton Reed and Merle Black, "Jim Crow, R.I.P.," in John Shelton Reed, *Surveying the South: Studies in Regional Sociology* (Columbia: University of Missouri Press, 1993), 103; John J. Wicker, Jr., "Christianity and Race Relations," *Religious Herald,* August 29, 1963 (first quotation); *Annual,* Louisiana, 1957, 73 (second quotation); Leon Macon, "Integration," *Alabama Baptist,* May 3, 1956 (third quotation).

25. Manis, *Southern Civil Religions in Conflict,* 42–44; *Annual,* Arkansas, 1954, 87–88 (first quotation); W. H. Prescott to the *Baptist Standard,* March 29, 1961 (second quotation); the Reverend Harry E. Dawkins to G. Avery Lee, September 21, 1956 (third quotation), Box 1, Folder 8, SBC Christian Life Commission Papers, SBHLA; H. T. Sullivan, "Who Desires Integration?," *Baptist Message,* December 5, 1957 (fourth and fifth quotations).

26. William T. Bodenhamer to "Eighty Ministers who signed Racial Manifesto in Atlanta, Georgia," November 5, 1957, Box 11, Folder 9, SBC Christian Life Commission Papers, SBHLA; Neil R. McMillen, *The Citizens' Council: Organized Resistance to the Second Reconstruction, 1954–64* (Urbana and Chicago: University of Illinois, 1971), 84–89, 174–75.

27. Thompson, *Tried as by Fire,* 72–76; the Reverend J. M. Drummond to the *Alabama Baptist,* February 10, 1972; Resolution of Ridge Boulevard Baptist Church of Jacksonville, Florida, October 10, 1956, Box 1, Folder 8, SBC Christian Life Commission Papers, SBHLA.

28. W. I. Pittman quoted in Manis, *Southern Civil Religions in Conflict,* 44.

29. S. J. Thompson to the *Religious Herald,* January 6, 1955.

30. John G. Swafford to Ross Coggins, March 26, 1964, Box 21, Folder 21, Executive Committee Records, SBHLA; *An Address by Dr. W. A. Criswell, Pastor, First Baptist Church, Dallas, Texas, to the Joint Assembly, State of South Carolina, Wednesday, February 22, 1956, 12.30 P.M.* (N.p., n.d.).

31. Ezell, *The Christian Problem of Racial Segregation,* 25; G. C. Moore, Jr., to *Home Missions* 39 (September 1968): 2 (quotation); Mrs. B. R. Bannister to the *Christian Index,* September 8, 1960.

32. T. C. Hardman to the *Christian Index,* July 22, 1954 (first quotation); Francis M. Jessup to James L. Sullivan, January 23, 1956, Box 1, Folder 3, SBC Christian Life Commission Papers, SBHLA (second quotation).

33. "Racial Intergration [*sic*] Opposes The Purpose Of God," sermon by the Reverend Montague Cook, in Montague Cook, *Racial Segregation Is Christian: Two Sermons on Racial Segregation* (N.p., n.d.).

34. Leon Macon, "The Situation in Washington," *Alabama Baptist,* February 28, 1963; W. D. Malone to Dr. Duke McCall, July 5, 1961, Box 3, Folder 57, J. D. Grey Papers, SBHLA; the Reverend Billy G. Pierce to the *Arkansas Baptist Newsmagazine,* August 8, 1963.

35. M. R. Carpenter to Edward H. Pruden, June 1, 1966, Box 14, Folder 434, Paschall Papers, BSSBA.

36. Reed and Black, "Jim Crow, R.I.P.," 98.

37. David R. Goldfield, *Black, White, and Southern: Race Relations and Southern Culture 1940 to the Present* (Baton Rouge: Louisiana State University Press, 1991), 261–63; David Wilkinson, "2 + 2 = Who?," *Home Missions* 50 (September-October 1979): 15–21.

38. Goldfield, *Black, White, and Southern,* 257–61.

39. "Criswell Raps Racism, Segregation In Broadcast," *Baptist & Reflector,* July 25, 1968 (first and second quotations); "SBC President Says 'Committed Laymen Needed in Baptist Race Relations,'" *Baptist Press,* March 1, 1974 (third quotation); *Annual,* SBC, 1954, 56; 1965, 88–89; 1968, 66–69, 73.

40. Morris H. Gardner to the *Alabama Baptist,* October 10, 1974.

5. PROGRESSIVE SOUTHERN BAPTISTS AND CIVIL RIGHTS

1. Numan V. Bartley, *The Rise of Massive Resistance: Race and Politics in the South During the 1950's* (Baton Rouge: Louisiana State University Press, 1969), 305 (first quotation); Andrew Michael Manis, *Southern Civil Religions in Conflict: Black and White Baptists and Civil Rights, 1947–1957* (Athens: University of Georgia Press, 1987), 26–27, 64 (second quotation).

2. *Annual,* SBC, 1944, 129–31; John W. Storey, *Texas Baptist Leadership and Social Christianity, 1900–1980* (College Station: Texas A & M University Press, 1986), 4–5, 10, 13–14, 122–143, 149–55, 223–24; W. T. Moore, *His Heart is Black* (Atlanta: Home Mission Board, 1978), 42–71; Jesse C. Fletcher, *The Southern Baptist Convention: A Sesquicentennial History* (Nashville: Broadman & Holman, 1994), 243–44.

3. *The Bible Speaks On Race* (Nashville: Christian Life Commission, n.d.); R. Lofton Hudson, *Is Segregation Christian?* (Nashville: Christian Life Commission, n.d.). "So God

created man in his *own* image, in the image of God created he him; male and female created he them." *Genesis* 1:27. "But we see Jesus, who was made a little lower than the angels for the suffering of death, crowned with glory and honour; that he by the grace of God should taste death for every man." *Hebrews* 2:9.

4. *Annual,* North Carolina, 1969, 164 (first quotation); 1958, 103 (second quotation); Mark Newman, "The Baptist State Convention of North Carolina and Desegregation, 1945–1980," *North Carolina Historical Review* 75 (January 1998): 2; T. B. Maston, *Segregation and Desegregation: A Christian Approach* (New York: Macmillan, 1959), 163 (third quotation).

5. John J. Carey, *Carlyle Marney: A Pilgrim's Progress* (Macon, Ga.: Mercer University Press, 1980), 13–14, 19–20, 39, 48; Moore, *His Heart is Black,* 34, 37–38, 59; Storey, *Texas Baptist Leadership and Social Christianity,* 10–11, 124–25, 148.

6. Foy Valentine, "Reflections on a Journey Through the Racial Crisis," in *Proceedings of Southern Baptists and Race* (Nashville: Christian Life Commission, 1989), 10 (quotation); Moore, *His Heart is Black,* 6, 22–23, 34, 44–45, 65; Carey, *Carlyle Marney,* 20; Storey, *Texas Baptist Leadership and Social Christianity,* 124–25, 151–53.

7. G. McLeod Bryan, *Dissenter in the Baptist Southland: Fifty Years in the Career of William Wallace Finlator* (Macon, Ga.: Mercer University Press, 1980), ix, 9, 11, 41, 94–97, 112.

8. William Penn Davis, interviewed by Harold K. Gower, March 24, 1972, The Mississippi Oral History Program of the University of Southern Mississippi, vol. 15 (1973), 1, 12–14 (quotation on p. 13); Moore, *His Heart is Black,* 44, 46.

9. Moore, *His Heart is Black,* 22–23 (quotation), 34.

10. Dallas Lee, *The Cotton Patch Evidence* (New York: Harper & Row, 1971), 6–15; P. Joel Snider, *The "Cotton Patch" Gospel: The Proclamation of Clarence Jordan* (Lanham, Md.: University Press of America, 1985), 7–12; Moore, *His Heart is Black,* 23–24.

11. Moore, *His Heart is Black,* 65–66, 75–76; Storey, *Texas Baptist Leadership,* 11–12, 143, 153; Andrew S. Chancey, "'A Demonstration Plot for the Kingdom of God': The Establishment and Early Years of Koinonia Farm," *Georgia Historical Quarterly* 75 (Summer 1991): 321–53; Clarence Jordan, "Christian Community in the South," *Journal of Religious Thought* 14 (Autumn-Winter, 1956–1957): 27–36; Henlee H. Barnette, *Clarence Jordan: Turning dreams into deeds* (Greenville, S.C.: Smith & Helwys, 1992); Tracy Elaine K'Meyer, *Interracialism and Christian Community in the Postwar South: The Story of Koinonia Farm* (Charlottesville: University Press of Virginia, 1997).

12. *Chicago Defender,* July 19, 1952; "Billy Graham's address to Kansas City Convention 1956" (first and second quotations), Box 1, Folder 13, SBC Christian Life Commission Minutes 1956, SBHLA; Moore, *His Heart is Black,* 83–84 (third quotation on p. 83); "Dallas Pastor Stirs Controversy With Statements On Integration," *Baptist Message,* March 1, 1956; Joe E. Barnhart, "Billy Graham," in *Encyclopedia of Religion in the South,* ed. Samuel S. Hill (Macon, Ga.: Mercer University Press, 1984), 307–308.

13. Henlee Hulix Barnette, "The Southern Baptist Theological Seminary and the Civil Rights Movement: From 1859–1952. Part One," *Review and Expositor* 90 (Fall 1993): 531–50; Moore, *His Heart is Black,* 52–61, 74–75, 79.

14. Anthony Dale Roberts, "Jesse Burton Weatherspoon: The Ethics of Advocacy in a Southern Baptist Context" (Ph.D. diss., Southern Baptist Theological Seminary, 1983), 20–21, 196–209, 225–31; Jase Jones, "To Race Relations," and Charles Myers, "Race Relations," in *An Approach to Christian Ethics: The Life, Contribution and Thought of T. B. Maston,* comp. William M. Pinson, Jr. (Nashville: Broadman Press, 1979), 62–66, 168–75;

Moore, *His Heart is Black,* 52–61, 74–75; N. Larry Baker, "C. W. Scudder: Ethicist and Advocate for Kingdom Causes," *Baptist History and Heritage* 33 (Spring 1998): 19–33.

15. Clayton Sullivan, *Called to Preach, Condemned to Survive: The Education of Clayton Sullivan* (Macon, Ga.: Mercer University Press, 1985), iv, 3–6, 67–79, 141–43 (quotation on p. 143); "SBC To Enrol Negroes," *Baptist Courier,* April 5, 1951; Michael T. Irwin, "J. B. Weatherspoon: Christian Statesman," *Quarterly Review* 17 (April-June 1982): 48, 53; Storey, *Texas Baptist Leadership and Social Christianity,* 134.

16. Snider, *The "Cotton Patch" Gospel,* 10–11; Storey, *Texas Baptist Leadership,* 10, 123, 148–49; John Lee Eighmy, *Churches in Cultural Captivity: A History of the Social Attitudes of Southern Baptists,* with a revised introduction, conclusion, and bibliography by Samuel S. Hill (Knoxville: University of Tennessee Press, 1987), 89–91, 154–55; Robert Parham, "A. C. Miller: The Bible Speaks on Race," *Baptist History and Heritage* 27 (January 1992): 33.

17. *Annual,* SBC, 1945, 96–97; Fletcher, *The Southern Baptist Convention,* 175.

18. "A New Baptist Magazine Makes Its Appearance," *Biblical Recorder,* February 6, 1946; Davis C. Hill, "Southern Baptist Thought and Action in Race Relations, 1940–1950" (Th.D. diss., Southern Baptist Theological Seminary, 1952), 269 n. 165; Newman, "The Baptist State Convention of North Carolina and Desegregation," 6.

19. Hill, "Southern Baptist Thought and Action in Race Relations," 310 (quotation); "Baptist State Convention," *Biblical Recorder,* December 4, 1946; *Annual,* North Carolina, 1946, 48–50, 92; Walter Spearman, "Southern Baptists Act On The Race Problem," *Christian Frontiers* 2 (January 1947): 20; Newman, "The Baptist State Convention of North Carolina and Desegregation," 6.

20. Louis S. Gaines, "That Report on Social Service and Civic Righteousness!," *Biblical Recorder,* December 11, 1946; Spearman, "Southern Baptists Act On The Race Problem," 19–21; *Annual,* North Carolina, 1946, 50, 92; Numan V. Bartley, *The New South, 1945–1980* (Baton Rouge: Louisiana State University, 1995), 76; Newman, "The Baptist State Convention of North Carolina and Desegregation," 7.

21. *Annual,* SBC, 1946, 120, 124–25, 127 (first quotation); 1947, 47–48, 342–43 (third and fourth quotations on p. 342); Harold E. Fey, "Why They Behave Like Southern Baptists," *Christian Century* 64 (May 21, 1947): 649 (second quotation); *Race Relations: A Charter of Principles* (Louisville, Ky.: Social Service Commission, n.d).

22. *Annual,* SBC, 1947, 33–35, 47–48; 1948, 53, 337 (quotations); Jack Bass and Walter DeVries, *The Transformation of Southern Politics: Social Change and Political Consequence Since 1945* (New York: Basic Books, 1976), 5–6.

23. News releases in Box 1, Folder 8, SBC Christian Life Commission Minutes, SBHLA; "Southern Baptists Study Race Relations," *Religious Herald,* September 1, 1949; "Southern Baptists Denounce Klan," *Christian Century* 66 (September 14, 1949): 1059–60; Curtis Welton Gaddy, "The Christian Life Commission of the Southern Baptist Convention: A Critical Evaluation" (Th.D. diss., Southern Baptist Theological Seminary, 1970), 94–95; Mark Newman, "Getting Right with God: Southern Baptists and Race Relations, 1945–1980" (Ph.D. diss., University of Mississippi, 1993), 188–90, 202–204, 208–209.

24. L. L. Carpenter, "Social Service Commission Will Study Race Relations," *Biblical Recorder,* September 29, 1948; "Baptist Leader Encouraged On Attitude Toward Negro," *Alabama Baptist,* September 30, 1948; Finley W. Tinnin, "Dr. Brimm's Statement On Race Relation [*sic*]," *Baptist Message,* October 14, 1948; *Annual,* Virginia, 1946, 81–85; 1947,

72–76, 79; *Annual,* Florida, 1947, 72, 74–75; 1948, 20, 107–108; 1949, 31–35, 137; *Minutes,* South Carolina, 1947, 12–13, 118–19; 1948, 111–13, 1949, 21, 23, 138–39; *Annual,* Alabama, 1948, 25, 103; 1949, 28, 125; 1951, 19, 130–31; *Minutes,* Georgia, 1944, 34, 36–37; 1946, 33, 36; *Annual,* North Carolina, 1947, 37, 39–40; *Proceedings,* Tennessee, 1948, 36, 174–75.

25. J. B. Weatherspoon, *Southern Baptists and Race Relations* (Louisville: Social Service Commission, 1949), 4; *Proceedings,* Texas, 1950, 173–74; *Annual,* Virginia, 1952, 79.

26. G. Avery Lee, *Some Quiet Thoughts On A Turbulent Issue* (Nashville: Christian Life Commission, n.d. [1956]), 5–6.

27. A. C. Miller, "Don't Blame the Supreme Court," *Biblical Recorder,* January 16, 1954; "Southern Baptists Approve Decision," *Christian Century* 71 (June 9, 1954): 692 (quotation); Newman, "Getting Right with God," 412–13, 457–58, 517–20.

28. *Annual,* SBC, 1954, 56 (first quotation), 404 (second quotation); "Southern Baptists Support Court," *Christian Century* 71 (June 16, 1954): 723 (third and fifth quotations); L. L. Carpenter, "Southern Baptist Convention Meets in St. Louis," *Biblical Recorder,* June 19, 1954 (fourth quotation).

29. Reuben E. Alley, "A Week After The Convention," *Religious Herald,* June 17, 1954; Kenneth K. Bailey, *Southern White Protestantism in the Twentieth Century* (New York: Harper & Row, 1964), 144–45; Chester Molpus to the *Baptist Record,* July 22, 1954 (first quotation); *Annual,* North Carolina, 1954, 70; *Annual,* Alabama, 1954, 27, 123–24; *Minutes,* South Carolina, 1954, 21, 128 (second quotation); *Minutes,* Georgia, 1954, 61 (third quotation); *Proceedings,* Texas, 1954, 170, 172 (fourth quotation); Storey, *Texas Baptist Leadership and Social Christianity,* 150 (fifth and sixth quotations); "The Bible Speaks," *Baptist Standard,* February 12, 1955; W. R. Grigg, "What's Wrong," *Baptist Standard,* January 7, 1956; W. R. Grigg, "Separate but Equal," *Baptist Standard,* January 14, 1956.

30. Bartley, *The Rise of Massive Resistance,* 59–60 (quotation on p. 60), 64–65, 82–149, 251–92.

31. Newman, "Getting Right with God," 327–32, 336–39; Harold E. Fey, "Expansion Minus Comity," *Christian Century* 74 (June 12, 1957): 728; "Southern Baptists Cautious Over Race Integration Issue," *Religious News Service,* November 24, 1956.

32. *Annual,* SBC, 1957, 362 (quotation); Newman, "Getting Right with God," 332–33.

33. "The Southern Baptists," *Information Service,* 35 (December 1, 1956): 2.

34. A. C. Miller, "We Need More Light Than Heat," *Christian Life Bulletin,* April 1956, 4 (quotation); *The Bible Speaks on Race;* Dale Cowling, "A Pastor Looks at Integration in Little Rock," *Christian Life Bulletin,* November 1957, 3.

35. Hudson, *Is Segregation Christian?,* 2–3 (quotation on p. 2); *The Bible Speaks On Race* (quotation on p. 6).

36. Lee, "Some Quiet Thoughts on a Turbulent Issue," 8; Cornell Goerner, *Race Relations: A Factor in World Missions* (Nashville: Christian Life Commission, n.d. [1957]); T. B. Maston, *Integration* (Nashville: Christian Life Commission, 1956), 8; Cowling, "A Pastor Looks at Integration in Little Rock," 3–4.

37. Maston, *Integration,* 10; Lee, "Some Quiet Thoughts on a Turbulent Issue," 4.

38. T. B. Maston, "A Statement On 'Integration,'" *Baptist Message,* October 3, 1957 (first and second quotations); Maston, *Integration,* 14 (third quotation); Cowling, "A Pastor Looks at Integration in Little Rock," 4 (fourth quotation); J. B. Weatherspoon, *Race Relations—A Christian View* (Nashville: Christian Life Commission, n.d. [1957]), 6 (fifth quotation).

39. Francis E. Stewart to the Christian Life Commission, March 13, 1957 and Charles F. Sims to A. C. Miller, July 17, 1957, Box 11, Folder 6, SBC Christian Life Commission Papers, SBHLA; John Hall Jones, *The Unity of Humanity* (Nashville: Christian Life Commission, 1956).

40. James H. Fox, Jr., to A. C. Miller, December 19, 1957, W. E. Maring to A. C. Miller, November 21, 1957, Box 11, Folder 6, Richard A. Harris, Jr., to A. C. Miller, February 26, 1958, Box 13, Folder 5, A. C. Miller to Mary A. Holmes, April 29, 1958, Box 13, Folder 6, SBC Christian Life Commission Papers, SBHLA.

41. *Annual*, SBC, 1957, 363 (quotation); "Information on the Work of the Christian Life Commission of the Southern Baptist Convention in its meeting with the Advisory Council of Southern Baptists for Work with Negroes, Nashville, February 25–26, 1957," Box 11, Folder 4, SBC Christian Life Commission Papers, SBHLA.

42. *Annual*, SBC, 1959, 88 (first quotation), 78 (second quotation); "Racial Fight On Resolutions," *Christian Index*, May 28, 1959; Brooks Hays, *A Southern Moderate Speaks* (Chapel Hill: University of North Carolina Press, 1959), chapter 6.

43. *Annual*, SBC, 1959, 394 (first quotation); A. C. Miller to E. Butler Abington, December 12, 1957 (second quotation), and Miller to H. E. Carter, December 10, 1957 (third quotation), Box 11, Folder 9, SBC Christian Life Commission Papers, SBHLA.

44. A. C. Miller to Ralph E. Lattimore, September 27, 1956 (first quotation) and Eldie F. Hicks to A. C. Miller, October 2, 1956 (third quotation), Box 1, Folder 8, and A. C. Miller to Leon Macon, February 19, 1958 (second quotation), Box 13, Folder 6, SBC Christian Life Commission Papers, SBHLA.

45. Bartley, *The Rise of Massive Resistance*, 320–32; Harvard Sitkoff, *The Struggle for Black Equality, 1954–1992*, rev. ed. (New York: Hill and Wang, 1993), 61–82.

46. *Annual*, SBC, 1960, 72, 273 (first quotation); "Let's Show Christian Love Instead of Racist Hate, Valentine Says," *Biblical Recorder*, June 10, 1961 (second quotation).

47. *Annual*, North Carolina, 1960, 44, 175–76; 1961, 144–45, 176; *Annual*, Virginia, 1962, 81; *Proceedings*, Texas, 1963, 24, 94; Newman, "Getting Right with God," 349–50, 403–407, 423–25, 463–64.

48. *New York Times*, March 26, 1964; *Annual*, SBC, 1964, 73–74 (third quotation on p. 73), 229 (first and second quotations), 1965, 244; Henlee H. Barnette, "Southern Baptist Churches And Segregation," *Baptist and Reflector*, February 27, 1964; Ross Coggins, "A Strategy For Southern Baptists In Race Relations," in *Christianity and Race Relations: Addresses from Conferences at Glorieta and Ridgecrest* (Nashville: Christian Life Commission, 1964), 142–45; " . . . And This One Passed by Close Margin," *Biblical Recorder*, May 30, 1964.

49. *Annual*, SBC, 1965, 244 (first quotation); "Southern Baptists Tackle Race Problem," *Christian Century* 81 (September 23, 1964): 1164 (second quotation); T. B. Maston, "Southern Baptists and the Negro (Part 3)," *Home Missions* 37 (September 1966): 38; "Right Theology Needed For Racial Tension," *Home Missions* 36 (January 1965): 9 (third quotation).

50. *Annual*, Virginia, 1964, 66, 69; *Proceedings*, Texas, 1964, 29–31 (first quotation on p. 30); *Annual*, North Carolina, 1964, 151–52, 174; U.S. Commission on Civil Rights, *Justice In Jackson: Hearings Held in Jackson, Miss. February 16–20, 1965*, vol. 2 (New York: Arno Press, 1971), 400 (second quotation).

51. *Annual*, SBC, 1964, 72–74, 229; 1965, 85, 88–91, 247 (first and second quotations); "Editorial Opinion and the Dallas Convention," *Baptist Program*, August 1965, 18

(third and fourth quotations); "A New Climate Down South?," *Christian Century* 82 (July 21, 1965): 907–908 (fifth quotation on p. 907); J. Marse Grant, "Dallas Could Usher in New Day for Southern Baptists," *Biblical Recorder*, June 12, 1965; E. S. James, "The Convention in Retrospect," *Baptist Standard*, June 16, 1965; Erwin L. McDonald, "Dallas, 1965," *Arkansas Baptist Newsmagazine*, June 10, 1965; Richard N. Owen, "Convention Comments," *Baptist & Reflector*, June 24, 1965; W. G. Stracener, "Southern Baptists Turn the Corner," *Florida Baptist Witness*, June 17, 1965.

52. *Annual*, Florida, 1965, 35, 114; *Annual*, Alabama, 1966, 35, 130 (quotation); *Minutes*, South Carolina, 1967, 47, 151–52 (quotation on p. 152).

53. Newman, "Getting Right with God," 611–15, 650 n. 97, 670–71, 675, 690, 693, 722, 730–31, 767–68, 797; *Annual*, SBC, 1968, 66–69, 73; Erwin L. McDonald, "The new image," *Arkansas Baptist Newsmagazine*, June 13, 1968.

54. "SBC Leaders Discuss Progress In Race Statement Actions," *Baptist & Reflector*, September 26, 1968 (first quotation); Kathleen Hilton to H. Franklin Paschall, June 1, 1968, Box 14, Folder 445, H. Franklin Paschall Papers, BSSBA (second quotation); Donald Atkinson to the *Alabama Baptist*, July 25, 1968 (third quotation).

55. "Southern Baptists Pick Criswell as President," *Christian Century* 85 (June 19, 1968): 808 (first quotation); "Criswell Raps Racism, Segregation In Broadcast," *Baptist & Reflector*, July 25, 1968; Erwin L. McDonald, "Race not an SBC issue," *Arkansas Baptist Newsmagazine*, June 26, 1969 (second quotation).

56. *Annual*, SBC, 1969, 79–80 (quotation on p. 80); 1970, 78–80; 1971, 78–79.

57. A. Ronald Tonks, "Oral Memoirs of Lawrence Brooks Hays," Historical Commission of the Southern Baptist Convention, Nashville, Tennessee, 1985, SBHLA, 468 (first quotation); Storey, *Texas Baptist Leadership and Social Christianity*, 187–88; E. S. James reply to Don Keleg, *Baptist Standard*, December 10, 1955; Dillard Wilbanks to the *Christian Index*, August 7, 1969 (second quotation).

58. Moore, *His Heart is Black*, 80, 90–92.

6. Public School Desegregation

1. *Annual*, SBC, 1945, 97 (quotation); 1947, 342; 1948, 337; 1950, 376; *Annual*, North Carolina, 1946, 43, 50; 1947, 37, 40; 1952, 51, 55; *Annual*, Virginia, 1946, 70, 81–85; 1947, 72, 74–76; 1949, 63–64; 1952, 76–78; *Proceedings*, Texas, 1950, 173.

2. David M. Gardner, "Racial Equality Demanded," *Baptist Standard*, October 4, 1945; *Annual*, Alabama, 1948, 25, 103; 1949, 28, 125; 1950, 28, 104; *Minutes*, Georgia, 1949, 56, 60; 1950, 47, 51–52; *Minutes*, South Carolina, 1947, 117, 119; 1948, 15, 113; 1949, 138 (quotations).

3. *Annual*, South Carolina, 1953, 127–28; *Minutes*, Georgia, 1949, 56, 60 (first and second quotations); 1950, 47, 51–52 (third quotation); Carl D. Bennett to the *Christian Index*, December 17, 1953; *Annual*, South Carolina, 1953, 22; Numan V. Bartley, *The Rise of Massive Resistance: Race and Politics in the South During the 1950's* (Baton Rouge: Louisiana State University Press, 1969), 37–38; Mark Newman, "The Georgia Baptist Convention and Desegregation, 1945–1980," *Georgia Historical Quarterly* 83 (Winter 1999): 689–90.

4. *Annual*, SBC, 1954, 56 (first quotation); *Annual*, Virginia, 1954, 83, 88 (second quotation); *Annual*, North Carolina, 1954, 70.

5. *Annual*, South Carolina, 21, 126–28 (quotation on pp. 126–27); Mark Newman,

"The Baptist State Convention of South Carolina and Desegregation, 1954–1971," *Baptist History and Heritage* 34 (Spring 1999): 57–59.

6. A. L. Goodrich, "The SBC Convention," *Baptist Record,* June 10, 1954; Finley W. Tinnin, "Non-Segregation," *Baptist Message,* June 3, 1954; Reuben E. Alley, "End of Segregation," *Religious Herald,* May 27, 1954; David M. Gardner, "Segregation's Problems," *Baptist Standard,* June 10, 1954.

7. Leon Macon, "Convention Issues," *Alabama Baptist,* June 17, 1954; Abe C. Jones to the *Biblical Recorder,* July 3, 1954; T. C. Hardman to the *Christian Index,* July 22, 1954.

8. John Jeter Hurt, Jr., "Keep Public Schools," *Christian Index,* October 28, 1954; Bartley, *The Rise of Massive Resistance,* 54–55, 68; R. Ray McCain, "Reactions to the United States Supreme Court Segregation Decision of 1954," *Georgia Historical Quarterly* 52 (December 1968), 381; Newman, "The Georgia Baptist Convention and Desegregation," 693.

9. Bartley, *The Rise of Massive Resistance,* 60. The 1950 census gave the percentage of African Americans in the peripheral south as Arkansas 22.4, Florida 21.8, North Carolina 26.6, Tennessee 16.1, Texas 12.8 and Virginia 22.2. In the Deep South, the figures were Alabama 32.1, Georgia 30.9, Louisiana 33, Mississippi 45.4 and South Carolina 38.9. Robert Howard Akerman, "The Triumph of Moderation in Florida Thought and Politics: A Study of the Race Issue from 1954 to 1960" (Ph.D. diss., The American University, 1967), 56.

10. Bartley, *The Rise of Massive Resistance,* 138–41.

11. Ronnie Dugger, "Texas Christians Stem the Tide," *Christian Century* 74 (July 31, 1957): 914 (quotation).

12. James M. Dunn, "The Ethical Thought of Joseph Martin Dawson" (Th.D. diss., Southwestern Baptist Theological Seminary, 1966), 161–62 (first quotation on p. 162); Dugger, "Texas Christians Stem the Tide," 913 (second quotation).

13. Dugger, "Texas Christians Stem the Tide," 912 (quotation); John J. Carey, *Carlyle Marney: A Pilgrim's Progress* (Macon, Ga.: Mercer University Press, 1980), 34; Bartley, *The Rise of Massive Resistance,* 141.

14. *Proceedings,* Texas, 1958, 19, 82 (quotations); Bartley, *The Rise of Massive Resistance,* 141.

15. L. L. Carpenter, "The Question of Segregation," *Biblical Recorder,* July 9, 1955; William Bagwell, *School Desegregation in the Carolinas: Two Case Studies* (Columbia, S.C.: University of South Carolina Press, 1972), 87–88; William H. Chafe, *Civilities and Civil Rights: Greensboro, North Carolina, and the Black Struggle for Freedom* (New York: Oxford University Press, 1981 [1980], 49–50; Mark Newman, "The Baptist State Convention of North Carolina and Desegregation, 1945–1980," *North Carolina Historical Review* 75 (January 1998): 12–13.

16. Bagwell, *School Desegregation in the Carolinas,* 90–92; Chafe, *Civilities and Civil Rights,* 51–52; Newman, "The Baptist State Convention of North Carolina and Desegregation," 13.

17. Numan V. Bartley, *The New South, 1945–1980* (Baton Rouge: Louisiana State University Press, 1995), 198; Tony Badger, "The Southern Manifesto," paper presented at the annual meeting of the Southern Historical Association, Orlando, Florida, November 11, 1993, pp. 2, 14–18; Newman, "The Baptist State Convention of North Carolina and Desegregation," 13–14.

18. Bartley, *The New South,* 195 (first quotation); Bagwell, *School Desegregation in the Carolinas,* 94–96; Chafe, *Civilities and Civil Rights,* 53–54, 58; L. L. Carpenter, "We Must

Not Allow Our Public Schools to be Destroyed," *Biblical Recorder,* July 21, 1956 (second quotation); Newman, "The Baptist State Convention of North Carolina and Desegregation," 14–15.

19. Chafe, *Civilities and Civil Rights,* 56, 59; Bruce E. Whitaker and Wendell G. Davis letters to the *Biblical Recorder,* September 1, 1956; Newman, "The Baptist State Convention of North Carolina and Desegregation," 15.

20. L. L. Carpenter, "Let Us Pray, Vote, and Hope," *Biblical Recorder,* September 1, 1956; Bagwell, *School Desegregation in the Carolinas,* 96–106, 117–18; Reed Sarratt, *The Ordeal of Desegregation: The First Decade* (New York: Harper & Row, 1966), 353; Newman, "The Baptist State Convention of North Carolina and Desegregation," 16.

21. *Annual,* Florida, 1955, 34–36 (quotations on p. 35); Tom R. Wagy, *Governor LeRoy Collins of Florida: Spokesman of the New South* (Tuscaloosa: University of Alabama Press, 1985), 60–61; Mark Newman, "The Florida Baptist Convention and Desegregation, 1954–1980," *Florida Historical Quarterly* 78 (Summer 1999): 6–7.

22. W. G. Stracener, "The Extremists Can't Settle It," *Florida Baptist Witness,* March 15, 1956 (quotations); Wagy, *Governor LeRoy Collins of Florida,* 61–72; Bartley, *The Rise of Massive Resistance,* 142, 278; Newman, "The Florida Baptist Convention and Desegregation," 7–8.

23. David R. Colburn and Richard K. Scher, "Race Relations and Florida Gubernatorial Politics Since the *Brown* Decision," *Florida Historical Quarterly* 55 (October 1976), 155–56; David R. Colburn, "Florida's Governors Confront the *Brown* Decision: A Case Study of the Constitutional Politics of School Desegregation, 1954–1970," in *An Uncertain Tradition: Constitutionalism and the History of the South,* eds. Kermit L. Hall and James W. Ely, Jr. (Athens: University of Georgia Press, 1989), 332–33; Newman, "The Florida Baptist Convention and Desegregation," 8. Collins received 434,274 votes and Lowry, his closest opponent, 179,019. Wagy, *Governor LeRoy Collins of Florida,* 72, 74–75.

24. *Annual,* Florida, 1957, 51, 52–53 (quotation on p. 53); Wagy, *Governor LeRoy Collins of Florida,* 79–83, 87–89; Newman, "The Florida Baptist Convention and Desegregation," 9–10.

25. Sarratt, *The Ordeal of Desegregation,* 98–99, 113–15.

26. Lee Seifert Greene, *Lead Me On: Frank Goad Clement and Tennessee Politics* (Knoxville: University of Tennessee Press, 1982), 195–98; Mark Newman, "The Tennessee Baptist Convention and Desegregation, 1954–1980," *Tennessee Historical Quarterly* 57 (Winter 1998): 239.

27. Richard N. Owen, "Segregation and Its Alternative," *Baptist & Reflector,* February 2, 1956; Newman, "The Tennessee Baptist Convention and Desegregation," 240–41.

28. Richard N. Owen, "Peace And Quiet," *Baptist & Reflector,* September 26, 1957; Hugh Davis Graham, *Crisis in Print: Desegregation and the Press in Tennessee* (Nashville: Vanderbilt University Press, 1967), 91–113, 154–58, 171–72; Newman, "The Tennessee Baptist Convention and Desegregation," 241–42.

29. Neil R. McMillen, *The Citizens' Council: Organized Resistance to the Second Reconstruction, 1954–64* (Urbana and Chicago: University of Illinois Press, 1971), 93–94, 94 n. 4; Bartley, *The Rise of Massive Resistance,* 131–32, 144 n. 61, 260–61; *Annual,* Arkansas, 1956, 86; Mark Newman, "The Arkansas Baptist State Convention and Desegregation, 1954–1968," *Arkansas Historical Quarterly* 56 (Autumn 1997): 296, 299–300.

30. Bartley, *The Rise of Massive Resistance,* 251–68; Newman, "The Arkansas Baptist State Convention and Desegregation," 300–303.

31. Bartley, *The Rise of Massive Resistance,* 268–69, 273–75, 275 n. 23; *Annual of the*

Pulaski County Baptist Association, 1958, 33, 48 (quotation); "Baptists Approve Little Rock Academy," *Religious News Service,* October 17, 1958; Newman, "The Arkansas Baptist State Convention and Desegregation," 305.

32. "400 Register at Little Rock Baptist High School," *Religious News Service,* October 21, 1958 (first quotation); Ralph Phelps, Jr., "Baptist High School in Little Rock," *Arkansas Baptist,* October 30, 1958; Erwin L. McDonald, "Ouachita Opens Temporary Academy," *Arkansas Baptist,* October 30, 1958 (second quotation); Newman, "The Arkansas Baptist State Convention and Desegregation," 305–306.

33. *Annual,* Arkansas, 1958, 32, 73; Erwin L. McDonald, "An Appraisal of The 105th State Convention," *Arkansas Baptist,* December 4, 1958; Erwin L. McDonald, "Our Public Schools Indispensable," *Arkansas Baptist,* February 12, 1959 (quotation); Newman, "The Arkansas Baptist State Convention and Desegregation," 306–307.

34. "Little Rock Clergymen Join Group Protesting Teachers' Ousting," *Religious News Service,* May 13, 1959; Erwin L. McDonald, *Across the Editor's Desk: The Story of the State Baptist Papers* (Nashville: Broadman Press, 1966), 39; Bartley, *The Rise of Massive Resistance,* 328–330; Newman, "The Arkansas Baptist State Convention and Desegregation," 307.

35. "Operation Ceased," *Baptist Standard,* July 29, 1959; Bartley, *The Rise of Massive Resistance,* 330–31; McMillen, *The Citizens' Council,* 281–82; Newman, "The Arkansas Baptist State Convention and Desegregation," 307–308.

36. Bartley, *The Rise of Massive Resistance,* 331–32; McMillen, *The Citizens' Council,* 97–98, 285; Sarratt, *The Ordeal of Desegregation,* 352–53; Newman, "The Arkansas Baptist State Convention and Desegregation," 308.

37. Bartley, *The Rise of Massive Resistance,* 80–81, 109–10; *Annual,* Virginia, 1955, 81, 83 (quotation); Reuben E. Alley, "For The Sake Of Free Public Schools," *Religious Herald,* December 8, 1955; Reuben E. Alley "Cause For Anxiety," *Religious Herald,* December 22, 1955; Mark Newman, "The Baptist General Association of Virginia and Desegregation, 1931–1980," *Virginia Magazine of History and Biography,* 105 (Summer 1997): 268–69.

38. Bartley, *The Rise of Massive Resistance,* 109–14; James W. Ely, Jr., *The Crisis of Conservative Virginia: The Byrd Organization and the Politics of Massive Resistance* (Knoxville: University of Tennessee Press, 1976), 38–39, 44–46; Benjamin Muse, *Virginia's Massive Resistance* (Bloomington: Indiana University Press, 1961), 15–16, 19, 28–34; Newman, "The Baptist General Association of Virginia and Desegregation," 269–70. The vote was fifty-nine to thirty-nine in the House of Delegates and twenty-one to seventeen in the state Senate. Ralph Eisenberg, "Virginia: The Emergence of Two-Party Politics," in *The Changing Politics of the South,* ed. William C. Havard (Baton Rouge: Louisiana State University Press, 1972), 51–52.

39. Muse, *Virginia's Massive Resistance,* 19–23 (quotation on p. 22); Bartley, *The Rise of Massive Resistance,* 113–14; *Annual,* Virginia, 1956, 85; Newman, "The Baptist General Association of Virginia and Desegregation," 270.

40. *Annual,* Virginia, 1957, 96 (first and second quotations); "134th Meeting of General Association," *Religious Herald,* November 21, 1957; Reuben E. Alley, "General Association In Review," *Religious Herald,* November 28, 1957; Ely, *The Crisis of Conservative Virginia,* 51–69; Reuben E. Alley, "Stop Pronouncements," *Religious Herald,* September 26, 1957 (third and fourth quotations); Newman, "The Baptist General Association of Virginia and Desegregation," 270–71.

41. Muse, *Virginia's Massive Resistance,* 54–57, 62–75, 86 (quotation); Paul L. Stagg, "To Friends Who Have Written," October 10, 1958, "Baptists and race problems—

Virginia," File BT734.2.B2V8, BJC; Newman, "The Baptist General Association of Virginia and Desegregation," 271–73.

42. Paul L. Stagg, "To Friends Who Have Written," October 10, 1958 (quotation), "Baptists and race problems—Virginia," File BT734.2.B2V8, BJC; Muse, *Virginia's Massive Resistance*, 112–13; "Segregated Private School Permitted At Another Virginia Church," *Religious News Service*, October 14, 1958; Newman, "The Baptist General Association of Virginia and Desegregation," 273.

43. *Annual*, Virginia, 1958, 61, 63–67 (quotations on p. 64); "Virginia Baptists Refuse To Endorse Gov. Almond," *Religious News Service*, November 14, 1958; Bartley, *The Rise of Massive Resistance*, 320–26; Newman, "The Baptist General Association of Virginia and Desegregation," 273–75.

44. Akerman, "The Triumph of Moderation in Florida Thought and Politics," 56; Bartley, *The Rise of Massive Resistance*, 14, 60.

45. *Annual*, Louisiana, 1960, 43, 89–90 (quotation); Bartley, *The Rise of Massive Resistance*, 335–38; Sarratt, *The Ordeal of Desegregation*, 100–103.

46. Raymond R. McCain, "A Description and Analysis of Speaking by Atlanta Ministers on Public School Desegregation from February, 1961, to August 30, 1961" (Master's thesis, Louisiana State University, 1962), 15–18 (first quotation on p. 18); "Protestant Leaders Attack Georgia Private School Plan," *Alabama Baptist*, February 16, 1956 (second and third quotations); Bartley, *The Rise of Massive Resistance*, 42; Paul E. Mertz, "'Mind Changing Time All Over Georgia': HOPE, Inc. and School Desegregation, 1958–1961," *Georgia Historical Quarterly* 77 (Spring 1993): 42; Newman, "The Georgia Baptist Convention and Desegregation," 684, 694.

47. *Atlanta Journal and Constitution*, November 3, 1957 (quotation); McCain, "A Description and Analysis of Speaking by Atlanta Ministers," 19–20; Newman, "The Georgia Baptist Convention and Desegregation," 695–96.

48. John Jeter Hurt, Jr., "Time Now for Leadership," *Christian Index*, October 16, 1958 (quotation); John Jeter Hurt, Jr., "Progressing Toward Solution," *Christian Index*, December 4, 1958; Mertz, "Mind Changing Time All Over Georgia," 43–44; McCain, "A Description and Analysis of Speaking by Atlanta Ministers," 25–29, 33–38, 135–38; Newman, "The Georgia Baptist Convention and Desegregation," 697–98.

49. *Minutes*, Georgia, 1959, 44, 121–22 (quotations on p.122); McCain, "A Description and Analysis of Speaking by Atlanta Ministers," 38–41; Newman, "The Georgia Baptist Convention and Desegregation," 698–99.

50. "Atlanta Clergymen Ask Preservation of Public Schools," *Religious News Service*, February 9, 1960 (quotation); McCain, "A Description and Analysis of Speaking by Atlanta Ministers," 41–44; Mertz, "Mind Changing Time All Over Georgia," 52–53, 55–56; Newman, "The Georgia Baptist Convention and Desegregation," 699.

51. *Minutes*, Georgia, 1960, 105; John Jeter Hurt, Jr., "Must Convention Avoid the Issue?," *Christian Index*, August 11, 1960; A. T. Fleming to *Christian Index*, August 25, 1960; Charles G. Johnson to the *Christian Index*, September 22, 1960; letters to the *Christian Index*, September 1, 8, 22, 1960; Newman, "The Georgia Baptist Convention and Desegregation," 699–700.

52. John Jeter Hurt, Jr., "Defeat Social Service Report," *Christian Index*, November 10, 1960; *Minutes*, Georgia, 1960, 33 (quotation), 104–105; "Appeal for Open Public Schools," *Christian Index*, November 24, 1960; McCain, "A Description and Analysis of Speaking by Atlanta Ministers," 44–48, 59–60; Newman, "The Georgia Baptist Convention and Desegregation," 700–701.

53. Bartley, *The Rise of Massive Resistance*, 132 (second quotation), 135 (first quotation), 282–86; Mark Newman, "The Alabama Baptist State Convention and Desegregation, 1954–1980," *Alabama Baptist Historian* 35 (July 1999): 5–8.

54. *Annual*, Alabama, 1956, 33, 142–43 (first quotation on p. 143); 1957, 31, 128–30 (second quotation on p. 130); Leon Macon, "Freedom of Choice Amendment Needs Examination," *Alabama Baptist*, August 23, 1956; Bartley, *The Rise of Massive Resistance*, 135; Edward R. Crowther, "Alabama's Fight to Maintain Segregated Schools, 1953–1956," *Alabama Review* 43 (July 1990): 221; Newman, "The Alabama Baptist State Convention and Desegregation," 8–11.

55. *Annual*, Alabama, 1961, 43, 146–47 (quotations).

56. Dan T. Carter, *The Politics of Rage: George Wallace, The Origins of the New Conservatism, and the Transformation of American Politics* (New York: Simon & Schuster, 1995), 162–63, 168–74; Newman, "The Alabama Baptist State Convention and Desegregation," 17.

57. "Christian Life And Public Affairs Committee Issues Statement," *Baptist Courier*, January 31, 1963 (quotation); *Minutes*, South Carolina, 1963, 45, 163; Bagwell, *School Desegregation in the Carolinas*, 164–65.

58. *Annual*, SBC, 1970, 78–79 (first quotation on p. 79); 1971, 78–79 (second quotation on p. 79).

59. "Christian Life Committee Calls For Calm in the Face of Integration," *Baptist Courier*, January 29, 1970 (first and second quotations); "Action Group In 'School' Statement," *Baptist Record*, January 15, 1970 (third and fourth quotations); "State Religious Leaders Speak on Public Schools," *Church News*, January 1970; Newman, "The Baptist State Convention of South Carolina and Desegregation, 69; Mark Newman, "The Mississippi Baptist Convention and Desegregation, 1945–1980," *Journal of Mississippi History* 59 (Spring 1997): 1–31.

60. "Religious Leaders Support Public Education System," *Alabama Baptist*, February 5, 1970; Hudson Baggett, "Allies in Education," *Alabama Baptist*, September 3, 1970; Newman, "The Alabama Baptist State Convention and Desegregation," 25–27.

61. James F. Cole, "The Public School Crisis," *Baptist Message*, January 22, 1970; James F. Cole, "Advocates Of The Public School System," *Baptist Message*, February 5, 1970 (first quotation); James F. Cole, "A Favorable Court Decision," *Baptist Message*, November 5, 1970 (second quotation).

62. "Action Group In 'School' Statement," *Baptist Record*, January 15, 1970; "Alabama Baptists delay action," *Baptist Standard*, August 19, 1970; *Annual*, Alabama, 1970, 32, 123–24.

63. *Minutes*, Georgia, 1970, 94–95 (first quotation on p. 94); Jack U. Harwell, "Internal Revenue Service Hits Segregated Schools," *Christian Index*, September 9, 1971 (second quotation).

64. "16 Baptist Churches in Mississippi Push Segregation," *Religious Herald*, January 29, 1970; Charles E. Myers, "Why We Chose Not To Have A Parochial School," *Light*, December 1979: 6–7 (first quotation); Newman, "The Mississippi Baptist Convention and Desegregation," 26–27; *Annual*, Alabama, 1971, 40, 142 (second quotation).

65. Reuben W. Griffith, "The Public School, 1890–1970" and Neil R. McMillen, "Development of Civil Rights, 1956–1970," in *A History of Mississippi*, ed. Richard Aubrey McLemore (Hattiesburg: University & College Press of Mississippi, 1973), vol 2, 175, 413; Walter B. Edgar, *South Carolina in the Modern Age* (Columbia, S.C.: University of South Carolina Press, 1992), 124–28; Newman, "The Mississippi Baptist Convention and Desegregation," 27; Neal R. Peirce, *The Deep South States of America: People, Politics, and Power*

in the Seven Deep South States (New York: W. W. Norton, 1974), 176, 395; Adam Fairclough, *Race & Democracy: The Civil Rights Struggle in Louisiana, 1915–1972* (Athens: University of Georgia Press, 1995), 445–46.

66. David R. Goldfield, *Black, White, and Southern: Race Relations and Southern Culture 1940 to the Present* (Baton Rouge: Louisiana State University Press, 1991), 258–61; Jonathan Kelley, "The Politics of School Busing," *Public Opinion Quarterly* 38 (Spring 1974): 24 n. 8.

67. *Annual*, Virginia, 1971, 114–15, 117–18 (first quotation on p. 118); "Neighborhood Schools, No Busing Supported in Contested Resolution," *Religious Herald*, November 18, 1971; Julian H. Pentecost, "Thank God and Take Courage," *Religious Herald*, November 18, 1971 (second quotation); Newman, "The Baptist General Association of Virginia and Desegregation," 282.

68. *Proceedings*, Texas, 1971, 26, 31 (quotation).

69. John Shelton Reed and Merle Black, "Jim Crow, R.I.P.," in John Shelton Reed, *Surveying the South: Studies In Regional Sociology* (Columbia: University of Missouri Press, 1993), 98; David Nevin and Robert E. Bills, *The Schools That Fear Built: Segregationist Academies in the South* (Washington, D.C.: Acropolis Books, 1976), 1–4, 19–21, 29, 37–43, 56–59, 81–83, 86–87; Richard A. Pride and J. David Woodard, *The Burden of Busing: The Politics of Desegregation in Nashville, Tennessee* (Knoxville: University of Tennessee Press, 1985), 6–7, 9, 18, 83–84, 92–106, 122–25, 141–45, 147–48, 151–54, 158, 160–64, 167–68, 190–91, 282; Melvin J. Knapp and Jon P. Alston, "White Parental Acceptance of Varying Degrees of School Desegregation: 1965 and 1970," *Public Opinion Quarterly* 36 (Winter 1972–1973): 587.

7. Law and Order

1. Harvard Sitkoff, *The Struggle for Black Equality, 1954–1992*, rev. ed. (New York: Hill and Wang, 1993), 12–14; David R. Goldfield, *Black, White, and Southern: Race Relations and Southern Culture 1940 to the Present* (Baton Rouge: Louisiana State University Press, 1991), 33–37.

2. *Annual*, North Carolina, 1945, 48 (first quotation); *Proceedings*, Tennessee, 1946, 147; *Proceedings*, Texas, 1944, 187; 1945, 91 (second and third quotations); John W. Storey and Ronald C. Ellison, *Southern Baptists of Southwest Texas: A Centennial History, 1888–1988* (Beaumont, Tex.: Golden Triangle Baptist Association, 1988), 136–37.

3. *Annual*, SBC, 1947, 342 (quotation); *Annual*, Alabama, 1947, 34, 54; 1951, 19, 131; *Annual*, Florida, 1949, 35, 137; *Minutes*, Georgia, 1946, 33, 38; 1949, 56, 60; *Annual*, North Carolina, 1950, 62, 65–66; 1951, 66, 71; *Minutes*, South Carolina, 1946, 13–14; 1948, 15–16, 112; 1949, 21, 23; 1950, 16–17; 1951, 16, 143; 1952, 21, 130.

4. O. P. Gilbert, "Exaggeration," *Christian Index*, August 15, 1946; Donald L. Grant, *The Way It Was in the South: The Black Experience in Georgia* (New York: Birch Lane Press, 1993), 366; Mark Newman, "The Georgia Baptist Convention and Desegregation, 1945–1980," *Georgia Historical Quarterly* 83 (Winter 1999): 686; Reuben E. Alley, "Try Sympathetic Helpfulness," *Religious Herald*, August 5, 1948.

5. David M. Gardner, "Racial Equality Demanded," *Baptist Standard*, August 16, 1945; Finley W. Tinnin, "Church Segregation in the South Misrepresented," *Baptist Message*, August 3, 1950.

6. *Annual*, SBC, 1945, 97 (first quotation); 1947, 342; *Annual*, Alabama, 1945, 108–110 (third quotation on p. 109); 1948, 25, 103; *Annual*, Florida, 1947, 72, 74–75; 1948,

20, 107–108; *Minutes,* Georgia, 1949, 56, 60 (second quotation); *Annual,* North Carolina, 1947, 37, 39–40; 1948, 40, 46; 1949, 53, 57; *Minutes,* South Carolina, 1947, 118–19; 1948, 112–13; 1949, 21, 23, 138; *Proceedings,* Tennessee, 1948, 36, 174–75; *Annual,* Virginia, 1947, 72, 75–76, 79.

7. *Annual,* SBC, 1947, 341–42; *Proceedings,* Tennessee, 1946, 147; *Annual,* North Carolina, 1946, 49; *Annual,* Virginia, 1949, 65.

8. *Annual,* North Carolina, 1946, 43, 50; *Minutes,* South Carolina, 1949, 21, 23; Numan V. Bartley, *The New South, 1945–1980* (Baton Rouge: Louisiana State University Press, 1995), 76.

9. "Southern Baptist Leader Opposes Civil Rights Program," *Baptist Message,* June 3, 1948 (first quotation); *Annual,* SBC, 1948, 337 (second quotation); Harvard Sitkoff, "Harry Truman and the Election of 1948: The Coming of Age of Civil Rights in American Politics," *Journal of Southern History* 37 (November 1971): 600–601.

10. *Annual,* Alabama, 1948, 25, 102 (quotation); *Proceedings,* Texas, 1950, 174. The Baptist State Convention of South Carolina marked an exception. In its report, accepted as information by the convention, the Commission on Social Service did not mention Truman's proposals, but it recognized that "political, legislative, educational, [and] economic action" were "essential" to improve race relations. *Minutes,* South Carolina, 1948, 15, 113 (quotation).

11. John Jeter Hurt, Jr., "Christian Rights," *Christian Index,* March 4, 1948; L. L. Gwaltney, "Focal Points," *Alabama Baptist,* February 12, 1948; Finley W. Tinnin, "World Alliance President on Civil Rights Issue," *Baptist Message,* March 18, 1948; Mark Newman, "Getting Right with God: Southern Baptists and Race Relations, 1945–1980" (Ph.D. diss., University of Mississippi, 1993), 252–53.

12. Sitkoff, "Harry Truman and the Election of 1948," 601–603, 609, 613; Bartley, *The New South,* 77–97.

13. "Southern Baptist Leaders Urge Calm Appraisal of Court Ruling" and "Religious Faith Will Dictate Actions" (first quotation), *Florida Baptist Witness,* May 27, 1954; "Resolution Concerning Supreme Court Decision," *Religious Herald,* May 27, 1954 (second quotation); Reuben E. Alley, "End of Segregation," *Religious Herald,* May 27, 1954; Leon Macon, "Convention Issues," *Alabama Baptist,* June 17, 1954 (third quotation); John Jeter Hurt, Jr., "Time for Prayer," *Christian Index,* May 27, 1954 (fourth quotation); L. L. Carpenter, "Proud of the South," *Biblical Recorder,* June 5, 1954; David M. Gardner, "Segregation's Problems," *Baptist Standard,* June 10, 1954.

14. *Annual,* SBC, 1954, 56 (first quotation); *Proceedings,* Texas, 1954, 172 (second quotation); *Annual,* Arkansas, 1954, 33, 84; *Annual,* North Carolina, 1954, 55–56 (fourth quotation on p. 56), 70 (third quotation); *Annual,* Virginia, 1954, 83, 88 (fifth quotation).

15. *Minutes,* South Carolina, 1954, 15, 127 (first quotation); *Minutes,* Georgia, 1954, 59, 61 (second quotation); *Annual,* Alabama, 1954, 27, 124 (third quotation).

16. "Southern Baptist Leaders Urge Calm Appraisal of Court Ruling," *Florida Baptist Witness,* May 27, 1954.

17. "Memphis Pastor Calls for Prayer on Court Ruling," *Baptist & Reflector,* June 10, 1954 (quotation); *Star-Tribune* [Chatham, Virginia], May 24, 1979; George R. Stewart, "Birmingham's Reaction to the 1954 Desegregation Decision" (Master's thesis, Samford University, 1967), 86.

18. Lacy Williams to the *Biblical Recorder,* June 5, 1954; H. L. Baptist to the *Religious Herald,* July 29, 1954.

19. Wilson Record and Jane Cassels Record, eds., *Little Rock, U.S.A.: Materials for*

Analysis (San Francisco: Chandler Publishing, 1960), 7–9 (first quotation on p. 9); John Jeter Hurt, Jr., "Sanity Demands Caution," *Christian Index,* June 9, 1955 (second and third quotations); Newman, "The Georgia Baptist Convention and Desegregation," 693–94; Numan V. Bartley, *The Rise of Massive Resistance: Race and Politics in the South During the 1950's* (Baton Rouge: Louisiana State University Press, 1969), 82–107.

20. *Minutes,* Georgia, 1955, 64, 69–70 (first and second quotations on p. 69; third quotation on p. 70); Newman, "The Georgia Baptist Convention and Desegregation," 694; *Annual,* Alabama, 1954, 27; 1955, 30, 125, 131 (fourth and fifth quotations); Mark Newman, "The Alabama Baptist State Convention and Desegregation, 1954–1980," *Alabama Baptist Historian* 35 (July 1999): 7.

21. Neil R. McMillen, *The Citizens' Council: Organized Resistance to the Second Reconstruction, 1954–64* (Urbana and Chicago: University of Illinois Press, 1971), 43–45, 50, 54–55; Newman, "The Alabama Baptist State Convention and Desegregation," 8.

22. Leon Macon, "The Segregation Problems," *Alabama Baptist,* March 8, 1956 (first and second quotations); Leon Macon, "Integration," *Alabama Baptist,* May 3, 1956; *Annual,* Alabama, 1956, 33, 134–136 (third quotation on p. 134); Bartley, *The Rise of Massive Resistance,* 146; Newman, "The Alabama Baptist State Convention and Desegregation," 8–9.

23. *Proceedings,* Texas, 1956, 177; Bartley, *The Rise of Massive Resistance,* 146–47.

24. Paul W. Turner, "The Role Of Church Leadership In Communities Facing School Desegregation," in *Christianity and Race Relations: Messages from the Sixth Annual Christian Life Workshop* (Dallas: Christian Life Commission, 1962), 55–57, 59; George Barrett, "Study in Desegregation: The Clinton Story," *New York Times Magazine,* September 16, 1956; Margaret Anderson, *The Children of the South* (New York: Farrar, Strauss and Giroux, 1966); Hugh Davis Graham, *Crisis in Print: Desegregation and the Press in Tennessee* (Nashville: Vanderbilt University Press, 1967), 93–100; Mark Newman, "The Tennessee Baptist Convention and Desegregation, 1954–1980," *Tennessee Historical Quarterly* 57 (Winter 1998): 241.

25. Turner, "The Role Of Church Leadership In Communities Facing School Desegregation," 56–58; "Church Groups Back Minister Who Escorted Negro Students," *Alabama Baptist,* December 20, 1956 (quotation); Newman, "The Tennessee Baptist Convention and Desegregation," 241.

26. "Church Groups Back Minister Who Escorted Negro Students," *Alabama Baptist,* December 20, 1956, (first quotation); Victor Watts to *Baptist & Reflector,* January 10, 1957 (second quotation); *Proceedings,* Tennessee, 1956, 42, 154–56 (third quotation on p. 155); "Southern Baptists Cautious Over Race Integration Issue," *Religious News Service,* November 24, 1956; Robert L. McCan to Paul Turner, December 4, 1956, Box 1, Folder 7, SBC Christian Life Commission Papers, SBHLA; Mary L. Cleveland, "A Baptist Pastor and Social Justice in Clinton, Tennessee," *Baptist History and Heritage* 14 (April 1979), 22; Newman, "The Tennessee Baptist Convention and Desegregation," 241–42.

27. Richard N. Owen, "The Issue: Law and Order," *Baptist & Reflector,* August 8, 1957 (quotation); Graham, *Crisis in Print,* 108–11; Newman, "The Tennessee Baptist Convention and Desegregation," 242.

28. "Messengers Ban Specifics In Racial Issue," *Christian Index,* November 22, 1956 (quotation); *Minutes,* Georgia, 1956, 35, 38–39; Newman, "The Georgia Baptist Convention and Desegregation," 695.

29. *Annual,* Florida, 1956, 38, 104–105 (first quotation on p. 104; second quotation on p. 105).

30. *Annual,* North Carolina, 1956, 41, 47 (quotation).

31. *Annual,* SBC, 1957, 59, 367–68 (quotations).

32. Ernest Q. Campbell and Thomas F. Pettigrew, *Christians in Racial Crisis: A Study of Little Rock's Ministry* (Washington, D.C.: Public Affairs Press, 1959), 29–30, 35–38, 41; Bartley, *The Rise of Massive Resistance,* 251–69; Mark Newman, "The Arkansas Baptist State Convention and Desegregation, 1954–1968," *Arkansas Historical Quarterly* 56 (Autumn 1997): 300.

33. Dale Cowling, "A Sermon—A Pastor Looks at Integration in Little Rock," *Christian Life Bulletin,* November 1957, 3, 5 (first quotation), 6 (second quotation). Bartley, *The Rise of Massive Resistance,* 258–65; Newman, "The Arkansas Baptist State Convention and Desegregation," 301.

34. "Action of Arkansas Governor Draws Condemnation and Praise of Ministers," *Arkansas Baptist,* September 12, 1957 (first quotation); Erwin L. McDonald, "Sitting on the Fence," *Arkansas Baptist,* September 12, 1957 (second and third quotations); Newman, "The Arkansas Baptist State Convention and Desegregation," 302.

35. Campbell and Pettigrew, *Christians in Racial Crisis,* 26–27, 30–32; Robert R. Brown, *Bigger Than Little Rock* (Greenwich, Conn.: Seabury Press, 1958), 93–109; "Community and Church Action, October 1957," in Record and Record, *Little Rock, U.S.A.,* 80; Bartley, *The Rise of Massive Resistance,* 268, 273–74, 328–31; Brooks Hays, *This World: A Christian's Workshop* (Nashville: Broadman Press, 1958), 92–100 (quotation on pp. 97, 100); Newman, "The Arkansas Baptist State Convention and Desegregation," 302–308.

36. Leon Macon, "Time For Meditations," *Alabama Baptist,* October 31, 1957 (first through fourth quotations; *Annual,* Alabama, 1957, 31, 128–30 (fifth quotation on p. 130).

37. "Virginia Baptists Refuse to Endorse Gov. Almond," *Religious News Service,* November 14, 1958.

38. John Jeter Hurt, Jr., "World Watches As Georgia Acts," *Christian Index,* January 19, 1961 (first and second quotations); "Urge Restraint," *Christian Index,* July 13, 1961 (third and fourth quotations); John Jeter Hurt, Jr., "Atlanta Nearing Time of Decision," *Christian Index,* July 13, 1961 (fifth quotation); Bartley, *The Rise of Massive Resistance,* 332–35; Newman, "The Georgia Baptist Convention and Desegregation," 700–701.

39. Joe T. Odle, "God's Solution Must Be Found," *Baptist Record,* October 4, 1962 (first quotation); Joe T. Odle, "Christians In A Crisis Hour," *Baptist Record,* October 11, 1962 (second quotation); John Dittmer, *Local People: The Struggle for Civil Rights in Mississippi* (Urbana and Chicago: University of Illinois Press, 1995), 138–42; Mark Newman, "The Mississippi Baptist Convention and Desegregation, 1945–1980," *Journal of Mississippi History* 59 (Spring 1997): 10–11.

40. "Prepare For Orderly Desegregation," *Alabama Baptist,* January 31, 1963 (first quotation); "Christian Life And Public Affairs Committee Issues Statement," *Baptist Courier,* January 31, 1963 (second quotation); Mark Newman, "The Baptist State Convention of South Carolina and Desegregation, 1954–1971," *Baptist History and Heritage* 34 (Spring 1999): 65.

41. S. H. Jones, "For Law And Order," *Baptist Courier,* January 31, 1963 (first quotation); Newman, "The Baptist State Convention of South Carolina and Desegregation," 65; "Prepare For Orderly Desegregation," *Alabama Baptist,* January 31, 1963 (second quotation).

42. *Annual,* SBC, 1961, 84 (first quotation); Leon Macon, "On Obeying The Law," *Alabama Baptist,* June 8, 1961 (second quotation); *Annual,* Alabama, 1956, 33, 134; 1958,

38, 135; 1962, 44, 134 (third quotation); *Minutes*, Georgia, 1956, 35, 39; 1958, 44, 102–103; *Annual*, North Carolina, 1956, 41, 47; *Proceedings*, Tennessee, 1959, 130; Richard N. Owen, "Peace And Quiet," *Baptist & Reflector*, September 26, 1957; Newman, "Getting Right with God," 381, 398, 401, 453, 457, 459, 463, 528–29.

43. Leon Macon, "Bombing Churches," *Alabama Baptist*, September 19, 1963 (first quotation); Leon Macon, "The Nashville Resolution," *Alabama Baptist*, September 26, 1963 (second quotation); "Resolution offers racial sympathy," *Arkansas Baptist Newsmagazine*, September 26, 1963 (third quotation).

44. Joe T. Odle, "Smoke Over Mississippi," *Baptist Record*, August 6, 1964; Dittmer, *Local People*, 242–65; Newman, "The Mississippi Baptist Convention and Desegregation," 12–14.

45. Chester L. Quarles, "Mississippi's Committee of Concern," *Royal Service* 62 (July 1967), 30–32; Newman, "The Mississippi Baptist Convention and Desegregation," 14.

46. "Mississippi Board 'Deplores' Violence," *Baptist Press*, October 2, 1964 (first and second quotations); *Annual*, Mississippi, 1964, 43–45 (third and fourth quotations on p. 43); Newman, "The Mississippi Baptist Convention and Desegregation," 14–15.

47. *Annual*, SBC, 1961, 84; Leon Macon, "On Obeying The Law," *Alabama Baptist*, June 8, 1961; James F. Cole, "Freedom Riders," *Baptist Message*, June 29, 1961; Hazel Erskine, "The Polls: Demonstrations and Race Riots," *Public Opinion Quarterly* 31 (Winter 1967–68): 656.

48. *Annual*, North Carolina, 1963, 144, 180; *Proceedings*, Texas, 1963, 24, 93–94; *Annual*, Virginia, 1960, 66; Erwin L. McDonald, "One word more," *Arkansas Baptist Newsmagazine*, September 26, 1963; J. Marse Grant, "Suddenly, Birmingham Is Everywhere, Including N.C.," *Biblical Recorder*, June 1, 1963; Richard N. Owen, "America Must Decide," *Baptist & Reflector*, September 5, 1963.

49. E. S. James, "Sheltering Seminary Students," *Baptist Standard*, May 17, 1961 (first quotation); E. S. James reply to Joe Hopkins, *Baptist Standard*, September 20, 1961 (second and third quotations); E. S. James reply to O. I. Scholars, *Baptist Standard*, March 13, 1963.

50. David Alan Horowitz, "White Southerners' Alienation and Civil Rights: The Response to Corporate Liberalism, 1956–1965," *Journal of Southern History* 54 (May 1988): 182 (first quotation); Don McGregor, "Baptists divided on question of President's Civil Rights Bill," *Baptist Standard*, April 1, 1964 (second quotation); Reuben E. Alley, "Civil Rights And Human Rights," *Religious Herald*, April 2, 1964; W. G. Stracener, "The President's Appeal to Southern Baptists," *Florida Baptist Witness*, April 9, 1964. Another survey estimated that 80 percent of southern whites opposed the Civil Rights Act as the time of its passage. Earl Black and Merle Black, *Politics and Society in the South* (Cambridge, Mass.: Harvard University Press, 1987), 112.

51. Leon Macon, "President Seeks SBC Help," *Alabama Baptist*, April 2, 1964; Erwin L. McDonald, "One word more," *Arkansas Baptist Newsmagazine*, September 26, 1963; E. S. James, "Desegregation, Yes,—by Legislation, No," *Baptist Standard*, July 24, 1963; Richard N. Owen, "Help Put An End to Inequalities," *Baptist & Reflector*, April 9, 1964.

52. Leon Macon, "We Must Be Law-Abiding," *Alabama Baptist*, July 30, 1964; Reuben E. Alley, "Civil Rights Legislation," *Religious Herald*, July 9, 1964; Newman, "Getting Right with God," 685, 725–27.

53. *Annual*, North Carolina, 1964, 152, 174; *Annual*, Virginia, 1964, 66, 69; *Annual*, SBC, 1964, 72–74; "Civil Rights Law Viewed as a Test," *Baptist Press*, July 8, 1964 (quotation).

54. *Annual*, SBC, 1965, 91–92 (quotation on p. 92); Sitkoff, *The Struggle for Black Equality*, 174–82.

55. Leon Macon, "Bishop And Congressmen Speak," *Alabama Baptist*, March 25, 1965 (first quotation); Leon Macon, "Things Not Generally Known," *Alabama Baptist*, April 1, 1965 (second and third quotations); Erskine, "The Polls: Demonstrations and Race Riots," 664.

56. Leon Macon, "A National Problem," *Alabama Baptist*, August 26, 1965; W. G. Stracener, "Costly Chaos from Disrespect for Law," *Florida Baptist Witness*, August 26, 1965; *Proceedings*, Texas, 1967, 17; *Annual*, North Carolina, 1967, 161; *Annual*, Louisiana, 1967, 113, 180; *Annual*, Mississippi, 1969, 114; *Proceedings*, Tennessee, 1968, 125–26.

57. E. S. James, "Christian Concern in the Racial Turmoil," *Baptist Standard*, March 24, 1965; J. Marse Grant, "Is Christian Conscience Insensitive to Injustice?," *Biblical Recorder*, May 15, 1965; *Annual*, North Carolina, 1964, 152, 174.

58. Erwin L. McDonald, "A nation mourns," *Arkansas Baptist Newsmagazine*, April 11, 1968 (first and second quotations); Erwin L. McDonald, "Anti-King backlash," *Arkansas Baptist Newsmagazine*, May 23, 1968; Reuben E. Alley, "After A Week Of Crisis," *Religious Herald*, April 18, 1968 (third and fourth quotations).

59. John E. Roberts, "A Tragedy," *Baptist Courier*, April 11, 1968; Vaughn W. Denton to the *Arkansas Baptist Newsmagazine*, May 23, 1968; Mrs. Walter C. Dean to *Home Missions* 39 (August 1968): 2; Newman, "Getting Right with God," 729–30, 797–98.

60. Carel G. Norman to the *Arkansas Baptist Newsmagazine*, April 18, 1968 (first quotation); A. B. Short, Jr., to the *Baptist Record*, May 16, 1968 (second quotation); *Annual*, SBC, 1968, 67–69 (third quotation on p. 68), 73.

61. R. M. Sullivan to the *Baptist Record*, January 29, 1970; Hudson Baggett, "Signs of The Time," *Alabama Baptist*, January 22, 1970; John Jeter Hurt, Jr., "The Path to Decisions," *Baptist Standard*, August 11, 1971; Newman, "Getting Right with God," 678, 694–95.

62. Frye Gaillard, *The Dream Long Deferred* (Chapel Hill: University of North Carolina Press, 1988), xv–xvi, xix–xx, 51–52, 78–81, 93–94, 96–98, 107–108, 123, 146 (quotation), 185; Mark Newman, "The Baptist State Convention of North Carolina and Desegregation, 1945–1980," *North Carolina Historical Review* 75 (January 1998): 25.

8. "The Great Commission":
Evangelism At Home and Abroad

1. *Annual*, SBC, 1945, 12 (quotation); M. Wendell Belew, *A Missions People: The Southern Baptist Pilgrimage* (Nashville: Broadman Press, 1989), 21–23, 131–32.

2. Belew, *A Missions People*, 96; J. C. Bradley, "Profiles of Home Mission Board Executives," *Baptist History and Heritage* 30 (April 1995): 30; A. C. Miller, "God and Us in Race Relations," *Baptist Standard*, December 6, 1945 (quotation); Baker J. Cauthen et. al., *Advance: A History of Southern Baptist Foreign Missions* (Nashville: Broadman Press, 1970), 51–53, 312; William R. Estep, *Whole Gospel Whole World: The Foreign Mission Board of the Southern Baptist Convention, 1845–1995* (Nashville: Broadman & Holman, 1994), 319, 419–20.

3. *Annual*, SBC, 1947, 340–41; Jesse C. Fletcher, *The Southern Baptist Convention: A Sesquicentennial History* (Nashville: Broadman & Holman, 1994), 169–70; Leon McBeth, "Southern Baptists and Race Since 1947," *Baptist History and Heritage* 7 (July 1972): 162.

4. T. B. Maston, *"Of One": A Study of Christian Principles and Race Relations* (Atlanta: Home Mission Board, 1946), 91 (first quotation); Foy Valentine, "Baptist Polity and Social Pronouncements," *Baptist History and Heritage* 14 (July 1979): 59 (second quotation); Davis C. Hill, "Southern Baptist Thought and Action in Race Relations, 1940–1950" (Th.D. diss., Southern Baptist Theological Seminary, 1952), 322, 323 table IV.

5. "A Negro Editor Speaks," *Home Missions* 20 (May 1949): 4 (quotation); Hill, "Southern Baptist Thought and Action in Race Relations," 327; Guy Bellamy, *Negro Missions* (Atlanta: Home Mission Board, n.d. [1950]).

6. Catherine B. Allen, *A Century to Celebrate: History of Woman's Missionary Union* (Birmingham: Woman's Missionary Union, 1987), 253 (quotations).

7. J. W. Marshall, "I Wish I Had Not Waked Up," *World Comrades* 26 (February 1948): 2–4.

8. Katherine Parker Freeman, "The Pricks Of White Society" and "Christ The Answer To Racial Tension," and Una Lawrence Roberts, review of Walter White, *A Man Called White, Royal Service* 44 (March 1949): 4–5, 10, 20–28, 33; Hill, "Southern Baptist Thought and Action in Race Relations," 227 (quotation); Allen, *A Century to Celebrate,* 253–54.

9. *Proceedings,* Texas, 1944, 187; 1950, 170; *Annual,* Virginia, 1943, 66; 1946, 133.

10. *Annual,* Virginia, 1953, 92 (first quotation); *Proceedings,* Texas, 1946, 174–75 (second quotation).

11. A. L. Goodrich, "Bread Cast Upon The Waters," *Baptist Record,* January 25, 1945; *Annual,* Mississippi, 1949, 110.

12. *Jackson [Mississippi] Daily News,* November 17, 1949 (first quotation), July 6, 1953; *Annual,* Mississippi, 1950, 143 (second quotation); 1953, 63, 91; 1962, 94.

13. Avery Hamilton Reid, *Baptists in Alabama: Their Organization and Witness* (Montgomery: Paragon Press, 1967), 395; *Annual,* Alabama, 1945, 96–97; 1948, 20; 1950, 24, 107–108 (first quotation on p. 108); 1953, 32, 142 (second quotation); Lee Porter, "Southern Baptists and Race Relations, 1948–1963" (Th.D diss., Southwestern Baptist Theological Seminary, 1965), 39.

14. S. H. Jones, "Baptists Educating Negro Preachers," *Baptist Courier,* September 23, 1948; Tinnin quoted in Porter, "Southern Baptists and Race Relations," 49.

15. L. S. Sedberry, "Should the American Seminary be Maintained?," *Baptist Courier,* August 10, 1950 (quotation); Hill, "Southern Baptist Thought and Action in Race Relations," 411.

16. "SBC To Enrol Negroes," *Baptist Courier,* April 5, 1951 (quotation); Henlee Barnette, "Negro Students in Southern Baptist Seminaries," *Review and Expositor* 53 (April 1956): 207–209. The Southeastern Baptist Theological Seminary in Wake Forest, North Carolina, the lone exception, did not adopt an open admissions policy until 1958. H. Shelton Smith to A. C. Miller, June 25, 1957, Box 11, Folder 6, SBC Christian Life Commission Papers, SBHLA.

17. *ESB,* vol. 2, s.v. "Negroes, Southern Baptist Relations To," by Courts Redford; Glen Lee Greene, *House Built Upon a Rock: About Southern Baptists in Louisiana* (Alexandria, La.: Executive Board of the Louisiana Baptist Convention, 1973), 295; Porter, "Southern Baptists and Race Relations," 40–41 (quotation).

18. *Annual,* Virginia, 1953, 93–94 (quotation on p. 94); *Proceedings,* 1950, 172–73; Cauthen et al., *Advance,* 64.

19. "Arkansas Baptist Church Becomes Interracial," *Religious News Service,* April 26, 1954 (quotation); Mark Newman, "The Arkansas Baptist State Convention and Desegregation, 1954–1968," *Arkansas Historical Quarterly* 56 (Autumn 1997): 297.

20. "Southern Baptist Leaders Urge Calm Appraisal of Court Ruling," *Florida Baptist Witness*, May 27, 1954 (first and second quotations); John G. Clark, "Segregation and the Christian Conscience," *Religious Herald*, November 11, 1954 (third quotation).

21. *Annual*, SBC, 1954, 56, 404 (quotation).

22. Alma Hunt, *Reflections from Alma Hunt* (Birmingham: Woman's Missionary Union, 1987), 71 (first quotation), 74–75 (second quotation on p. 75); Allen, *A Century to Celebrate*, 254.

23. B. L. Nichols to the *Biblical Recorder*, June 30, 1956; Numan V. Bartley, *The Rise of Massive Resistance: Race and Politics in the South During the 1950's* (Baton Rouge: Louisiana State University Press, 1969), 146–47, 251–69.

24. "Quotes from Convention Speakers," *Florida Baptist Witness*, June 28, 1956 (quotation); Fletcher, *The Southern Baptist Convention*, 217; *Annual*, SBC, 1956, 72.

25. *Annual*, SBC, 1957, 366–68; A. C. Miller to C. C. Warren, November 19, 1957, Box 11, Folder 9, SBC Christian Life Commission Papers, SBHLA (first quotation); Porter, "Southern Baptists and Race Relations," 210 (second quotation); Victor Glass, "Southern Baptists and the Negro," Box 4, Folder 303, Wendell R. Grigg Papers, NCBHC; Cornell Goerner, *Race Relations: A Factor in World Missions* (Nashville: Christian Life Commission, n.d. [1957]), 5 (third quotation).

26. Richard N. Owen, "Attitudes Here—Missions There," *Baptist & Reflector*, January 10, 1957; Erwin L. McDonald, "The Way Out," *Arkansas Baptist*, October 10, 1957.

27. Raymond A. Mohl, "The Pattern of Race Relations in Miami since the 1920s," in *The African American Heritage of Florida*, eds. David R. Colburn and Jane L. Landers (Gainesville: University Press of Florida, 1995), 345; David R. Colburn and Richard K. Scher, "Race Relations and Florida Gubernatorial Politics since the *Brown* Decision," *Florida Historical Quarterly* 55 (October 1976): 163; "Baptist Leader Scores Christians For 'Immaturity'," *Religious News Service*, November 14, 1958 (first quotation); W. G. Stracener, "A Convention of Progress and Purpose," *Florida Baptist Witness*, November 27, 1958; R. B. Culbreth, "The Racial Problem," *Florida Baptist Witness*, December 4, 1958 (second and third quotations); Mark Newman, "The Florida Baptist Convention and Desegregation, 1954–1980," *Florida Historical Quarterly* 78 (Summer 1999): 11–12.

28. *Proceedings*, Tennessee, 1958, 36, 134 (first quotation); Jackson Toby, "Bombing in Nashville," *Commentary* 25 (May 1958): 385–89; James C. Bryant, "Georgia Baptists and the Integration Crisis," *Viewpoints: Georgia Baptist History* 13 (1992): 14 (second quotation); Melissa Fay Greene, *The Temple Bombing* (London: Jonathan Cape, 1996).

29. W. T. Moore, *His Heart is Black* (Atlanta: Home Mission Board, 1978), 48 (first quotation); Greene W. Strother to Brooks Hays, December 15, 1958, Box 2, Folder 8, Brooks Hays Papers, SBHLA; *Annual*, Louisiana, 1957, 72–73 (second quotation on p. 72); Bartley, *The Rise of Massive Resistance*, 303–304 (third quotation on p. 304).

30. Phyllis Woodruff Sapp, *The Long Bridge* (Atlanta: Home Mission Board, 1957), chap. 6; J. Marse Grant, "Was SBC Founded to Preserve Segregation? . . . ," *Biblical Recorder*, April 13, 1968; Courts Redford, "Withdrawal Of The Book *The Long Bridge*," *Home Missions* 29 (January 1958): 10 (quotation).

31. "Baptist Weekly Credited With Reinstating Withdrawn Book," *Religious News Service*, March 12, 1958; John Caylor to *Biblical Recorder*, March 8, 1958; Moore, *His Heart is Black*, 17.

32. *Annual*, SBC, 1958, 391; Adiel J. Moncrief, "Living the Christian Life," Box 1, Folder 15, SBC Christian Life Commission Minutes, SBHLA.

33. Virginia Cobb to the *Christian Index*, September 1, 1960; Howard L. Rhodes to the *Christian Index*, August 11, 1960.

34. "WF to Admit Negroes To Graduate Schools," *Biblical Recorder*, May 6, 1961; "Wake Forest Board Lifts New Race Bar," *Biblical Recorder*, June 17, 1961; "Wake Forest Enrolls First Negro Student," *Biblical Recorder*, June 24, 1961; "All Racial Bars Dropped at Undergraduate Levels," *Biblical Recorder*, May 5, 1962; Will D. Campbell, *The Stem of Jesse: The Costs of Community at a 1960s Southern School* (Macon, Ga.: Mercer University Press, 1995), 82.

35. "Missionary To Nigeria Points To Inconsistency . . . 'I Hate Negroes at Home, But Love Them in Africa,'" *Biblical Recorder*, June 3, 1961 (first quotation); E. S. James reply to Ricardo Pena, *Baptist Standard*, August 2, 1961 (second quotation); *Annual*, SBC, 1961, 84.

36. Joe James Watkins to the *Baptist Standard*, March 1, 1961; Antonia Canzoneri to the *Baptist Record*, November 15, 1962; Porter, "Southern Baptists and Race Relations," 152–55.

37. T. B. Maston, *The Bible and Race* (Nashville: Broadman Press, 1959); Jase Jones, "To Race Relations," in *An Approach to Christian Ethics: The Life, Contribution and Thought of T. B. Maston*, comp. William M. Pinson, Jr. (Nashville: Broadman Press, 1979), 63; Porter, "Southern Baptists and Race Relations," 157 (quotation); L. O. Griffith, "Welcome to Walker L. Knight," *Home Missions* 30 (August 1959): 9; Walker L. Knight, "Will Segregation Break Down the Wall?," *Home Missions* 32 (March 1961): 18; Walker L. Knight reply to Karl H. Moore, *Home Missions* 33 (September 1962): 3.

38. "Baptist College in Arkansas Accepts Rhodesian Students," *Biblical Recorder*, January 27, 1962 (first quotation); "Arkadelphia Church Adopts Entry Policy," *Biblical Recorder*, February 17, 1962 (second quotation); Foy Valentine, "Developments in Desegregation" in *Christianity and Race Relations: Messages from the Sixth Annual Christian Life Workshop* (Dallas: Christian Life Commission, 1962), 11; Newman, "The Arkansas Baptist State Convention and Desegregation," 308–309.

39. "Board Considers Negro Students," *Christian Index*, October 25, 1962; *Minutes*, Georgia, 1962, 41; John Jeter Hurt, Jr., "Separate Ghana Student From Integration Issue," *Christian Index*, February 21, 1963; Jack Carpenter to the *Christian Index*, April 11, 1963; "Majority of Letters Favor Admitting Ghanaian," *Christian Index*, March 7, 1963; Mark Newman, "The Georgia Baptist Convention and Desegregation, 1945–1980," *Georgia Historical Quarterly* 83 (Winter 1999): 701–702. See also Alan Scot Willis, "A Baptist Dilemma: Christianity, Discrimination, and the Desegregation of Mercer University," *Georgia Historical Quarterly* 80 (Fall 1996): 595–615.

40. "Call for Veto; Russell Retires," *Christian Index*, March 28, 1963 (first quotation); "Mercer Trustees Vote to Drop Racial Barriers," *Christian Index*, April 25, 1963; John Jeter Hurt, Jr., "Mercer Took Christian Action; Let Us Do Same," *Christian Index*, April 25, 1963 (second and third quotations); "Admit Three Negroes," *Christian Index*, September 12, 1963; Newman, "The Georgia Baptist Convention and Desegregation," 702.

41. John Jeter Hurt, Jr., "Mission Forces Reform At Home," *Christian Index*, July 4, 1963; Erwin L. McDonald, "Christ or Chaos," *Arkansas Baptist Newsmagazine*, July 11, 1963; Jean and Gene Phillips to *Biblical Recorder*, November 16, 1963; Jesse C. Fletcher, *Baker James Cauthen: A Man for All Nations* (Nashville: Broadman Press, 1977), 193–94, 239; Moore, *His Heart is Black*, 83 (quotation); Mark Newman, "Getting Right with God: Southern Baptists and Race Relations, 1945–1980" (Ph.D. diss., University of Mississippi, 1993), 421–22, 424–25, 463–64, 531–32.

42. Walker L. Knight, "Race Relations Proposal For Southern Baptists," *Home Missions* 34 (July 1963): 3; Walker L. Knight, "Race Relations Reaction," *Home Missions* 34 (Sep-

tember 1963): 3; David M. Reimers, *White Protestantism and the Negro* (New York: Oxford University Press, 1965), 161; Walker L. Knight, "Race Relations: Changing Patterns and Practices" in *Southern Baptists Observed: Multiple Perspectives on a Changing Denomination,* ed. Nancy Tatom Ammerman (Knoxville: University of Tennessee Press, 1993), 172 (quotation).

43. T. B. Maston, *The Christian and Race Relations* (Memphis: Brotherhood Commission, n.d. [1963]), 10–12 (quotation on p. 11).

44. Foy Valentine, "You Can't Go Home Again," May 9, 1963 (quotation), Box 2, Folder 3, SBC Christian Life Commission Minutes, SBHLA; Ross Coggins, *Missions and Race* (Nashville: Christian Life Commission, n.d. [1963]).

45. *Annual,* Virginia, 1962, 81; *Proceedings,* Texas, 1962, 30; *Annual,* North Carolina, 1964, 152; John W. Storey and Ronald C. Ellison, *Southern Baptists of Southeast Texas: A Centennial History, 1888–1988* (Beaumont, Tex.: Golden Triangle Baptist Association, 1988), 189 (first, second and third quotations).

46. Howard W. Lee to the *Religious Herald,* July 4, 1963; B. R. Lawson to the *Baptist Standard,* April 10, 1963; Monroe Crosby to the *Christian Index,* April 4, 1963.

47. "Furman Trustees Adopt Policy On Applications," *Baptist Courier,* October 17, 1963; "Board Asks Delay," *Baptist Courier,* October 24, 1963; S. H. Jones, "General Board Meets," *Baptist Courier,* October 24, 1963; Mark Newman, "The Baptist State Convention of South Carolina and Desegregation, 1954–1971," *Baptist History and Heritage* 34 (Spring 1999): 65–66.

48. *Minutes,* South Carolina, 1963, 3, 36, 40–42 (quotation on p. 41), 51, 89–91; Newman, "The Baptist State Convention of South Carolina and Desegregation," 66–67.

49. *Minutes,* South Carolina, 1964, 3, 42–44 (first quotation on p. 44), 96; Erwin L. McDonald, "Courageous Furman," *Arkansas Baptist Newsmagazine,* February 18, 1965 (second quotation); "South Carolina college admits Negro applicants," *Baptist Standard,* February 17, 1965; Newman, "The Baptist State Convention of South Carolina and Desegregation," 67.

50. Mary Allred, "Using God's Eyes," *Royal Service* 58 (March 1964): 37–38 (quotation on p. 38); Dorothy B. Robinson to *Royal Service* 59 (October 1964): 15; Mrs. S. A. Williams to *Royal Service,* 59 (December 1964): 34–35; Gladys M. McLain to *Royal Service* 59 (February 1965): 12–13.

51. T. B. Maston, "Southern Baptists and Race Relations (part three)," *Home Missions* 37 (September 1966): 38 (quotations); "Junior Meetings" and "Intermediate Meetings," *Tell* 12 (September 1964): 20–37; Allen, *A Century to Celebrate,* 254–55. The circulation of *Royal Service,* which had grown from 245,645 in 1954 to 476,380 in 1964, dropped to 469,599 in 1965. Elaine Dickson, "Here's How Royal Service Subscribers Look in Statistics," *Royal Service* 59 (June 1965): 11; William M. Tillman, Jr., "Representative Actions and Statements Among Southern Baptists Concerning Black-White Relations, 1964–1976" (Ph.D. diss., Southwestern Baptist Theological Seminary, 1978), 107.

52. Victor T. Glass, "Working With National Baptists," and W. T. Moore, "Southern Baptists and Race Relations," *Home Missions* 36 (January 1965): 14–15 (first quotation on p. 15), 16-A-P; Knight, "Race Relations," 172; letters to *Home Missions* 36 (April 1965): 2, *Home Missions* 36 (June 1965): 2, *Home Missions* 36 (July 1966): 2; Walker L. Knight, "Changing with the Changes," *Home Missions* 37 (May 1966): 3; Victor Glass, "Missionary Implications of Racial Tensions," *Home Missions* 37 (July 1966): 16–17 (second quotation on p. 17).

53. Mrs. Ralph Gwin, "Developing Race Relations," *Royal Service* 62 (July 1967): 41–

44 (quotation on pp. 41–42); *Home Missions* 38 (January 1967), 39 (January 1968); *Royal Service* 62 (July, August 1967), 63 (July 1968); *Window* 38 (July 1967), 40 (August, September 1968).

54. Earle E. Stirewalt to *Home Missions* 38 (March 1967): 3; Hunt, *Reflections from Alma Hunt,* 75; Emmanuel L. McCall, "Home Mission Board Ministry in the Black Community," *Baptist History and Heritage* 16 (July 1981): 39. The Brotherhood Commission also continued to cover race relations, but it did so less frequently than the HMB or the WMU. Tillman, "Representative Actions and Statements Among Southern Baptists Concerning Black-White Relations," 96–99, 124.

55. "Baptists Urged To Act In Race Relations Area," *Alabama Baptist,* January 25, 1968; "An Open Letter," *Home Missions* 39 (January 1968): 7; *Christianity Today* 11 (May 26, 1967): 45; "Southern Baptists Elect First Negro Staff Member," *Baptist Press,* May 10, 1968.

56. Knight, "Race Relations," 173; "A Statement of Christian Concern," *Biblical Recorder,* May 25, 1968; Albert McClellan, *The Executive Committee of the Southern Baptist Convention, 1917–1984* (Nashville: Broadman Press, 1985), 211.

57. J. Marse Grant, "Victory for Moderation, Tolerance and Understanding," *Biblical Recorder,* June 15, 1968 (first quotation); *Annual,* SBC, 1968, 67–69 (second quotation on p. 68).

58. *Annual,* SBC, 1968, 66–69 (first and second quotations on p. 66; third quotation on p. 68), 73; Erwin L. McDonald, "The new image," *Arkansas Baptist Newsmagazine,* June 13, 1968 (fourth quotation); H. Franklin Paschall to Samuel H. Crowder, June 13, 1968 (fifth and sixth quotations), Box 14, Folder 445, H. Franklin Paschall Papers, BSSBA.

59. Tim Nicholas, "Race Relations: Southern Baptists and Blacks Today," *Home Missions* 43 (November 1973): 22; Moore, *His Heart is Black,* 30.

60. "Southern Baptist Convention leaders map action on social issues," *Arkansas Baptist Newsmagazine,* June 27, 1968; "Mission Agency Discontinues National Crisis Committee," *Baptist & Reflector,* August 19, 1971; Moore, *His Heart is Black,* 88 (quotation); McCall, "Home Mission Board Ministry in the Black Community," 36.

61. "Minutes of the Home Mission Board Committee on the National Crisis, February 13–14, 1969," Box 5, Folder 465, Wendell R. Grigg Papers, NCBHC; "Mission Agency Discontinues National Crisis Committee," *Baptist & Reflector,* August 19, 1971 (quotation).

62. "Withdrawal Sparks Reaction," *Baptist Standard,* November 17, 1971; Edward E. Plowman, "Texas Togetherness," *Christianity Today* 16 (November 19, 1971): 46–47; *Annual,* North Carolina, 1971, 90, 107, 120; "Race Relations, Baptism Issues Dominate SBC State Conventions," *Baptist Press,* November 30, 1971; *Minutes,* South Carolina, 1971, 161; 1972, 156–58; 1973, 161–62; Moore, *His Heart is Black,* 3; Newman, "Getting Right with God," 681, 778–79.

9. THE VARIETY OF THE SOUTHERN BAPTIST EXPERIENCE IN DESEGREGATION

1. Mark Newman, "Getting Right with God: Southern Baptists and Race Relations, 1945–1980" (Ph.D. diss., University of Mississippi, 1993).

2. Numan V. Bartley, *The Rise of Massive Resistance: Race and Politics in the South During*

the 1950's (Baton Rouge: Louisiana State University Press, 1969), 13–14; Hugh Davis Graham, *Crisis in Print: Desegregation and the Press in Tennessee* (Nashville: Vanderbilt University Press, 1967), 13–22; "Tennessee Baptist Women Against School Integration," *Religious News Service*, December 11, 1958; Melvin J. Knapp and Jon P. Alston, "White Parental Acceptance of Varying Degrees of School Desegregation: 1965 and 1970," *Public Opinion Quarterly* 36 (Winter 1972–1973): 589; Catherine B. Allen, *A Century to Celebrate: History of Woman's Missionary Union* (Birmingham: Woman's Missionary Union, 1987), 250–57.

3. Nancy Tatom Ammerman, *Baptist Battles: Social Change and Religious Conflict in the Southern Baptist Convention* (New Brunswick: Rutgers University Press, 1990), 50–52, 57–59.

4. "Messengers Refuse [to] Weaken Report," *Christian Index*, May 29, 1958 (first quotation); C. W. Bazemore, "Baptists Hold Great Convention at Houston Largest Attendance in History," *Biblical Recorder*, June 7, 1958 (second quotation); A. C. Miller to Reuben E. Alley, June 19, 1958, Box 13, Folder 6, SBC Christian Life Commission Papers, SBHLA.

5. Leon Macon, "The Race Issue at the Convention," *Alabama Baptist*, June 4, 1959; *Annual*, SBC, 1959, 85–88; 1964, 72–74; 1965, 84–85, 90–92, 246–47; "Strong Statement Loses To Soft One," *Alabama Baptist*, May 28, 1964; "Christian Life Report Approved," *Baptist Press*, June 5, 1965.

6. *Annual*, SBC, 1968, 66–69, 73; Billy Keith, *W. A. Criswell: The Authorized Biography* (Old Tappan, N.J.: Fleming H. Revell, 1973), 175; Ammerman, *Baptist Battles*, 57–59.

7. Newman, "Getting Right with God," 230–304, 374–573, 661–851.

8. Joseph Martin Dawson, "I Belong to a Southern Baptist Integrated Church," *Christian Century* 75 (November 12, 1958): 1303; Leon McBeth, "Southern Baptists and Race Since 1947," *Baptist History and Heritage* 7 (July 1972): 164; J. Herbert Gilmore, Jr., *They Chose To Live: The Racial Agony of an American Church* (Grand Rapids, Mich.: Eerdmans, 1972), 17–18, 50; "Negroes Join Austin," *Baptist Standard*, October 22, 1955; Harold T. Branch, "Implications of Multiple Affiliation for Black Southern Baptists," *Baptist History and Heritage* 16 (July 1981): 41–42.

9. *Annual*, North Carolina, 1955, 60–61 (quotation on p. 61); "Chowan Trustees Vote Not to Accept Negro Students," *Biblical Recorder*, December 24, 1955; "Gardner-Webb Will Not Admit Negroes," *Biblical Recorder*, February 25, 1956; Mark Newman, "The Baptist State Convention of North Carolina and Desegregation, 1945–1980," *North Carolina Historical Review* 75 (January 1998): 13, 21 n. 61.

10. Foy Valentine, "A Summary of Race Relations in the Past Year," 11–15, in "Minutes of the 1962 Session of the Advisory Council of Southern Baptists for Work with Negroes," Box 4, Folder 423, Wendell R. Grigg Papers, NCBHC; "Baylor sees integration proceeding smoothly," *Baptist Standard*, November 6, 1963; "Admit Three Negroes," *Christian Index*, September 12, 1963; Will D. Campbell, *The Stem of Jesse: The Costs of Community at a 1960s Southern School* (Macon, Ga.: Mercer University Press, 1995), 80–82; Newman, "The Baptist State Convention of North Carolina and Desegregation," 19–21.

11. "Texas Baptists move toward desegregation with caution," *Baptist Standard*, September 18, 1963.

12. Ibid.; "More Southern Baptist Churches Admit Negroes To Membership," *Alabama Baptist*, August 1, 1963. Despite being picketed, White's church continued to deny membership to African Americans. Lee Porter, "Southern Baptists and Race Relations, 1948–1963" (Th.D. diss., Southwestern Baptist Theological Seminary, 1965), 191–93.

13. *New York Times,* November 4, 1963; "Survey of Racial Picture," *Baptist Messenger,* December 12, 1963; "Churches Vary on Racial Policy," *Christian Index,* November 14, 1963; T. B. Maston, "Southern Baptists and the Negro (Part 3)," *Home Missions* 37 (September 1966): 41.

14. Herbert H. Hyman and Paul B. Sheatsley, "Attitudes toward Desegregation," *Scientific American* 211 (July 1964): 20.

15. "Furman Trustees Adopt Policy on Applications," *Baptist Courier,* October 17, 1963; "Board Asks Delay," *Christian Index,* October 24, 1963; *Minutes,* South Carolina, 1963, 3, 40–42, 51, 89–91; 1964, 3, 42–44, 96; Erwin L. McDonald, "Courageous Furman," *Arkansas Baptist Newsmagazine,* February 18, 1965; "South Carolina college admits Negro applicants," *Baptist Standard,* February 17, 1965.

16. "Most Schools Sign U.S. Compliance," *Baptist Record,* April 15, 1965; *Annual,* Virginia, 1965, 64.

17. "Racial barriers down at Ouachita," *Arkansas Baptist Newsmagazine,* August 20, 1964 (quotation); Erwin L. McDonald's replies to Verlee Dickerson, *Arkansas Baptist Newsmagazine,* September 3, 1964 and Mrs. W. B. Miller, Jr., *Arkansas Baptist Newsmagazine,* September 17, 1964.

18. "Most Schools Sign U.S. Compliance," *Baptist Record,* April 15, 1965; Joe T. Odle, "The Coming Convention," *Baptist Record,* November 10, 1966; *Annual,* Alabama, 1965, 42; 1968, 29, 33.

19. "MC Establishes Own Student Loan Fund," *Baptist Record,* March 18, 1965; Mark Newman, "The Mississippi Baptist Convention and Desegregation, 1945–1980," *Journal of Mississippi History* 59 (Spring 1997): 21–23; *Annual,* Alabama, 1967, 44–45; 1968, 33; W. T. Moore, *His Heart is Black* (Atlanta: Home Mission Board, 1978), 80.

20. *Annual,* Florida, 1966, 143; Joe T. Odle, "A Constructive Convention," *Baptist Record,* November 20, 1969; *ESB,* vol. 3, s.v. "North Carolina, Baptist State Convention of," by Ben C. Fisher; Newman, "The Mississippi Baptist Convention and Desegregation," 21–23; *Annual,* SBC, 1969, 74.

21. "Report of Survey of Superintendents of Missions Concerning Racial Representation of Southern Baptist Church Memberships," Box 2, Folder 155, Wendell R. Grigg Papers, NCBHC; Jere Allen, "Alabama Baptists Respond To The Transitional Community Church Crisis," *Alabama Baptist,* February 17, 1977; *Proceedings,* Texas, 1965, 19; *Annual,* Virginia, 1968, 65; "Southern Baptist Soundings," *Christianity Today* 11 (October 28, 1966): 58.

22. V. O. Key, Jr., with the assistance of Alexander Heard, *Southern Politics in State and Nation* (New York: Vintage Books, 1949), 5–12, 665–71; Earl Black, *Southern Governors and Civil Rights: Racial Segregation as a Campaign Issue in the Second Reconstruction* (Cambridge, Mass.: Harvard University Press, 1976), 22–24, 132–40, 360–61 n. 25; James M. Glaser, "Back to the Black Belt: Racial Environment and White Racial Attitudes in the South," *Journal of Politics* 56 (February 1994): 21–41.

23. *Columbia [South Carolina] Record,* November 13, 1964; Mark Newman, "The Alabama Baptist State Convention and Desegregation, 1954–1980," *Alabama Baptist Historian* 35 (July 1999): 4, 9–10, 13–14; Mark Newman, "The Arkansas Baptist State Convention and Desegregation, 1954–1968," *Arkansas Historical Quarterly* 56 (Autumn 1997): 295; Mark Newman, "The Florida Baptist Convention and Desegregation, 1954–1980," *Florida Historical Quarterly* 78 (Summer 1999): 2–3; Mark Newman, "The Georgia Baptist Convention and Desegregation, 1945–1980," *Georgia Historical Quarterly* 83 (Winter 1999): 684; Newman, "The Mississippi Baptist Convention and Desegregation," 1–31;

Newman, "The Baptist State Convention of North Carolina and Desegregation," 2, 11; Mark Newman, "The Tennessee Baptist Convention and Desegregation, 1954–1980," *Tennessee Historical Quarterly* 57 (Winter 1998): 238; Mark Newman, "The Baptist General Association of Virginia and Desegregation, 1931–1980," *Virginia Magazine of History and Biography* 105 (Summer 1997): 257–58, 265–66, 268; John W. Storey, *Texas Baptist Leadership and Social Christianity, 1900–1980* (College Station: Texas A & M University, 1986), 12.

24. John Jeter Hurt, Jr., "Klan vs. Church," *Christian Index*, January 27, 1949; "Klansmen Visit Baptist Church," *Baptist Record*, November 1, 1956; Fletcher Knebel and Clark Mollenhoff, "Eight Klans bring new terror to the South," *Look* 21 (April 30, 1957): 63; James Graham Cook, *The Segregationists* (New York: Appleton-Century-Crofts, 1962), 77–81, 120–27.

25. Charles C. Jones to the *Jackson [Mississippi] Clarion-Ledger*, December 22, 1955 and April 20, 1956; *Jackson [Mississippi] State Times*, June 12, 1958; *The News and Courier* [Charleston, South Carolina], April 16, 1957; Howard H. Quint, *Profile in Black and White: A Frank Portrait of South Carolina* (Washington, D.C.: Public Affairs Press, 1958), 65 (quotation); "Inauguration of Governor George C. Wallace," *Alabama Baptist*, January 24, 1963; Dan T. Carter, *The Politics of Rage: George Wallace, The Origins of the New Conservatism, and the Transformation of American Politics* (Baton Rouge and London: Louisiana State University Press, 1995), 79, 137.

26. Ernest Q. Campbell and Thomas F. Pettigrew, *Christians in Racial Crisis: A Study of Little Rock's Ministry* (Washington, D.C.: Public Affairs Press, 1959), 35–38, 41–62; Newman, "The Arkansas Baptist State Convention and Desegregation," 300; Neil R. McMillen, *The Citizens' Council: Organized Resistance to the Second Reconstruction, 1954–64* (Urbana and Chicago: University of Illinois Press, 1971), 80–89, 96.

27. "Alabama Baptists Hit New Lay White Supremacy Group," *Baptist Record*, May 30, 1957; *Christian Layman* 1 (April 1958): 1–23; S. E. Rogers, *Christian Love and Segregation* (Montgomery: Baptist Laymen of Alabama, n.d.); Newman, "The Mississippi Baptist Convention and Desegregation," 9; Bartley, *The Rise Of Massive Resistance*, 301 (quotation).

28. "Church's Ouster from County Group Continues Little Rock Issue," *Religious News Service*, October 23, 1959; Gwin T. Turner, "A Dialogue On State Problems," *Baptist Record*, April 29, 1965.

29. *Washington Post*, May 21, 1957.

30. "Pastors Favor Public Schools," *Christian Index*, March 18, 1954 (first quotation); Kenneth K. Bailey, *Southern White Protestantism in the Twentieth Century* (New York: Harper & Row, 1964), 148; "Louisiana Ministers Move to Maintain Public Schools," *Baptist Standard*, June 7, 1961 (second quotation).

31. "Pastor Ousted For Condemning Segregation," *Religious News Service*, March 21, 1955 (quotation); Walker L. Knight, "Race Relations: Changing Patterns and Practices," in *Southern Baptists Observed: Multiple Perspectives on a Changing Denomination*, ed. Nancy Tatom Ammerman (Knoxville: University of Tennessee Press, 1993), 167–68.

32. "Tallahassee Baptist Church Votes To Bar Negroes," *Religious News Service*, January 27, 1964; "Segregation Was Jolting to Pastor," *Biblical Recorder*, June 12, 1965; Newman, "The Florida Baptist Convention and Desegregation," 14.

33. "First Church at Richmond," *Religious Herald*, January 14, 21, 28, 1965; Theo Sommerkamp, "Richmond Church Admits 2 Nigerians," *Baptist Press*, January 22, 1965; Sue Nichols, "Lawsuit in a Richmond Church," *Christian Century* 83 (January 5, 1966): 24; Sue Nichols, "Richmond Church Suit Dismissed," *Christian Century* 83 (March 30,

1966): 411–12; Newman, "The Baptist General Association of Virginia and Desegregation," 279.

34. Norman Alexander Yance, "Moment of Truth for Belle View," *Baptist Program*, June 1966, 4–5 (quotation on p. 5); Newman, "The Baptist General Association of Virginia and Desegregation," 278–79.

35. Jimmy Carter, *Why Not The Best?* (Nashville: Broadman Press, 1975), 66–68 (quotation on p. 68); Peter G. Bourne, *Jimmy Carter: A Comprehensive Biography from Plains to Postpresidency* (New York: Scribner, 1997), 146–47; Newman, "The Georgia Baptist Convention and Desegregation," 704.

36. "In the Wake of Tattnall Square," *Home Missions* 37 (December 1966): 4; "Crisis At Tattnall Square," *Baptist Men's Journal* 38 (April–June 1967): 1–2, 5; Thomas J. Holmes with Gainer E. Bryan, Jr., *Ashes for Breakfast* (Valley Forge, Pa.: Judson Press, 1969), 40–47, 64–65, 79–80, 92–94, 97; Newman, "The Georgia Baptist Convention and Desegregation," 704–705.

37. Gilmore, *They Chose To Live*, 19, 46–47, 120–26 (quotation on p. 121), 128, 137; "B'Ham First Rejects Blacks; Pastor, Youth Director Resign," *Alabama Baptist*, October 1, 1970; Newman, "The Alabama Baptist State Convention and Desegregation," 27.

38. Herbert H. Hyman and Paul B. Sheatsley, "Attitudes toward Desegregation," *Scientific American* 195 (December 1956): 38; Andrew M. Greeley and Paul B. Sheatsley, "Attitudes toward Racial Integration," *Scientific American* 225 (December 1971): 15–16; D. Garth Taylor, Paul B. Sheatsley and Andrew M. Greeley, "Attitudes toward Racial Integration," *Scientific American* 238 (June 1978): 32; John Shelton Reed, "How Southerners Gave Up Jim Crow," *New Perspectives* 17 (Fall 1985): 17, 19 n. 9.

39. Herbert H. Hyman and Paul B. Sheatsley, "Attitudes toward Desegregation," *Scientific American* 195 (December 1956): 36, 38; Herbert H. Hyman and Paul B. Sheatsley, "Attitudes toward Desegregation," *Scientific American* 211 (July 1964): 22; Taylor, Sheatsley and Greeley, "Attitudes toward Racial Integration," 32–33, 36 (quotation).

40. Davis C. Hill, "Southern Baptist Thought and Action in Race Relations, 1940–1950" (Th.D. diss., Southern Baptist Theological Seminary, 1952), 98–166, 206–47, 322–25, 327–33; Newman, "Getting Right with God," 596–600; William M. Tillman, Jr., "Representative Actions and Statements Among Southern Baptists Concerning Black-White Relations, 1964–1976" (Ph.D. diss., Southwestern Baptist Theological Seminary, 1978), 117–18.

41. L. L. Carpenter, "Editorial Brevities," *Biblical Recorder*, February 12, 1947 (quotation); Newman, "The Georgia Baptist Convention and Desegregation," 687.

42. T. Gilbert Butler and T. Howard Johnson, Jr., "Auburn Students Speak on Segregation," *Alabama Baptist*, March 4, 1948; "Mercer Students Protest the Klan," *Light* 2 (March 1949): 3; Newman, "The Georgia Baptist Convention and Desegregation," 689.

43. Hill, "Southern Baptist Thought and Action in Race Relations," 328–29, 363–64.

44. "N. C. Students to Invite Negroes," *Light* 1 (December 1948): 4; James W. Ray to *Light* 2 (October 1949): 2–3 (quotation on p. 2); Hill, "Southern Baptist Thought and Action in Race Relations," 332–33; Newman, "The Baptist State Convention of North Carolina and Desegregation," 7.

45. B. J. Murrie, "The Louisville Seminary And Race Relations: Meeting Seminary Problems," *Light* 3 (June 1950): 2; Lee Porter, "Southern Baptists and Race Relations, 1948–1963" (Th.D. diss., Southwestern Baptist Theological Seminary, 1965), 52 (quotation); "SBC To Enrol Negroes," *Baptist Courier*, April 5, 1951.

46. McBeth, "Southern Baptists and Race Since 1947," 164.

47. Finley W. Tinnin, "B.S.U. On Interracial Issue," *Baptist Message*, December 2, 1954.

48. *Annual*, North Carolina, 1954, 49 (quotations), 70; Newman, "The Baptist State Convention of North Carolina and Desegregation," 12.

49. *Proceedings*, Tennessee, 1955, 36, 40, 127 (quotations); "Tennessee Leaves Race Decision to Trustees," *Biblical Recorder*, December 10, 1955; W. Fred Kendall, *A History of the Tennessee Baptist Convention* (Brentwood, Tenn.: Executive Board of the Tennessee Baptist Convention, 1974), 349; Newman, "The Tennessee Baptist Convention and Desegregation," 239–40.

50. "Arkansas Baptist Students Uphold Equal Worth of All," *Religious News Service*, October 16, 1957 (quotations); Newman, "The Arkansas Baptist State Convention and Desegregation," 304. The students unanimously adopted an identical resolution at their next convention meeting in October 1958. "Arkansas Baptist Students Stress 'Equal Worth' of Individuals," *Religious News Service*, October 13, 1958.

51. "Resolution On Racial Discrimination As Adopted By A Majority Of The Members Of The Virginia Baptist Student Union Present At The Spring Retreat Of April 18–20, 1958," "Baptists and race problems—Virginia" BT 734.2.B2V8., BJC.

52. "Board Considers Negro Students," *Christian Index*, October 25, 1962. The *Christian Index* reported that "To the statement, 'I would be willing to attend college with a Negro,' there were 309 affirmative votes, 180 negative and 58 said they were undecided." "Integration Vote," *Christian Index*, February 9, 1961.

53. "BSU Leaders Adopt Resolution Favoring Texas College Integration," *Baptist Standard*, April 26, 1961; "Baylor University students seek racial integration," *Baptist Standard*, April 11, 1962; "Baylor sees integration proceeding smoothly," *Baptist Standard*, November 6, 1963.

54. Samuel Southard, "Are Southern Churches Silent?," *Christian Century* 80 (November 20, 1963): 1432 (first quotation); Valentine, "A Summary of Race Relations in the Past Year," 13–14; "S.C. Baptist Student Union Votes 'State Level' Desegregation," *Religious News Service*, December 9, 1964; "Baptist Students Desegregate," *Christian Century* 81 (December 23, 1964): 1582; *Minutes*, South Carolina, 1968, 36–37 (second and third quotations); Mark Newman, "The Baptist State Convention of South Carolina and Desegregation, 1954–1971," *Baptist History and Heritage* 34 (Spring 1999): 68–69.

55. "Students Plan Houston Demonstration Over Convention's Silence on Issues," *Baptist Courier*, May 30, 1968; Edward E. Plowman, "Southern Baptists Take Sides," *Christianity Today* 12 (July 5, 1968), 1000; "Texas Students to Work Against Race Discrimination," *Baptist Press*, April 22, 1968 (quotation).

56. John Roberts, "Due West Church Fires Pastor; Open Doors," *Baptist Courier*, November 4, 1971; Don Kirkland, "BSU Will Sponsor Statewide Day of Prayer," and Bill Bellinger to the *Baptist Courier*, November 18, 1971; *Minutes*, South Carolina, 1971, 65 (quotation); Newman, "The Baptist State Convention of South Carolina and Desegregation," 69.

57. Jim Newton, "Revision of Becoming Prompts Record Response toward BSSB," *Baptist Press*, November 24, 1971.

58. "American convention churches in South organize," *Baptist Standard*, March 31, 1971; Ammerman, *Baptist Battles*, 143; Samuel S. Hill, "The Story before the Story: Southern Baptists since World War II," in Ammerman, ed., *Southern Baptists Observed*, 41–42; Donald Cunnigen, "Men and Women of Goodwill: Mississippi's White Liberals" (Ph.D diss., Harvard University, 1987), 513–14, 518–20.

10. The Major White Denominations and Race Relations, 1945–1971

1. Frank S. Loescher, *The Protestant Church and the Negro: A Pattern of Segregation* (New York: Association Press, 1948), 52; John LaFarge, S.J., *The Catholic Viewpoint on Race Relations* (Garden City, N.Y.: Hanover House, 1956), 22.

2. "The Southern Churches and the Race Question," *Christianity and Crisis* 18 (March 3, 1958): 17–28; Joel L. Alvis, Jr., *Religion & Race: Southern Presbyterians, 1946–1983* (Tuscaloosa: University of Alabama Press, 1994), 2–3; James R. Wood, "Authority and Controversial Policy: The Churches and Civil Rights," *American Sociological Review* 35 (December 1970): 1060.

3. "The Southern Churches and the Race Question," 17–18.

4. William A. Osborne, *The Segregated Covenant: Race Relations and American Catholics* (New York: Herder and Herder, 1967), 241; "The Southern Churches and the Race Question," 17.

5. Alvis, *Religion & Race*, 6, 14–15, 22, 44; David M. Reimers, *White Protestantism and the Negro* (New York: Oxford University Press, 1965), 123, 137–39.

6. Reimers, *White Protestantism and the Negro*, 147–53.

7. Ibid., 126; Loescher, *The Protestant Church and the Negro*, 52–54.

8. James J. Hennesey, S.J., *American Catholics: A History of the Roman Catholic Community in the United States* (New York: Oxford University Press, 1981), 193, 304–305.

9. Reimers, *White Protestantism and the Negro*, 109–12; W. Edward Orser, "Racial Attitudes in Wartime: The Protestant Churches During the Second World War," *Church History* 41 (September 1972): 337–53.

10. Reimers, *White Protestantism and the Negro*, 112–13 (first and second quotations on p. 112), 136, 141; Loescher, *The Protestant Church and the Negro*, 17–18, 42–44, 132–33; Grover C. Bagby, "Race Relations and Our Concern," *Methodist Story*, January 1965: 3 (third, fourth and fifth quotations).

11. Orser, "Racial Attitudes in Wartime," 343–44; Reimers, *White Protestantism and the Negro*, 118–19; Alvis, *Religion & Race*, 16–21, 25, 30–31, 36, 43–44; Kenneth K. Bailey, *Southern White Protestantism in the Twentieth Century* (New York: Harper & Row, 1964), 135 (quotations).

12. *Annual*, SBC 1946, 120, 127; 1947, 35, 47–48, 340–43; Loescher, *The Protestant Church and the Negro*, 136–37.

13. *Annual*, SBC, 1948, 337; Ernest Trice Thompson, *Presbyterians in the South*, vol. 3: 1890–1972 (Richmond, Va.: John Knox Press, 1973), 532 (first and second quotations); Davis C. Hill, "Southern Baptist Thought and Action in Race Relations, 1940–1950" (Th.D. diss., Southern Baptist Theological Seminary, 1952), 24 (third quotation).

14. *Annual*, SBC, 1948, 337; 1950, 45; Henlee Barnette, "Negro Students in Southern Baptist Seminaries," *Review and Expositor* 53 (April 1956): 207–209; Reimers, *White Protestantism and the Negro*, 119, 127–32; David E. Sumner, *The Episcopal Church's History: 1945–1985* (Wilton, Conn.: Morehouse-Barlow, 1987), 34.

15. Alvis, *Religion & Race*, 22–25; Reimers, *White Protestantism and the Negro*, 142; Bagby, "Race Relations and Our Concern," 3 (quotations).

16. Sumner, *The Episcopal Church's History*, 31, 35–36, 179, 193 (quotation).

17. Katherine Martensen, "Region, Religion, and Social Action: The Catholic Committee of the South, 1939–1956," *Catholic Historical Review* 68 (April 1982): 249–61 (first

quotation on p. 261); "The Churches Speak," *New South* 9 (August 1954): 4 (second quotation).

18. LaFarge, *The Catholic Viewpoint on Race Relations*, 98–99; Osborne, *The Segregated Covenant*, 46–47; Howard H. Quint, *Profile in Black and White: A Frank Portrait of South Carolina* (Washington, D.C.: Public Affairs Press, 1958), 63–64.

19. *The State* [Columbia, South Carolina], March 4, 1956; Adam Fairclough, *Race & Democracy: The Civil Rights Struggle in Louisiana, 1915–1972* (Athens: University of Georgia Press, 1995), 171.

20. Ernest Q. Campbell and Thomas F. Pettigrew, *Christians in Racial Crisis: A Study of Little Rock's Ministry* (Washington, D.C.: Public Affairs Press, 1959), 157–61 (quotations on p. 160); Alvis, *Religion & Race*, 57; *Annual*, SBC, 1954, 56.

21. Campbell and Pettigrew, *Christians in Racial Crisis*, 154.

22. *Statements Adopted by Religious Groups Re Segregation in the Public Schools* (New York: Department of Racial and Cultural Relations, National Council of Churches of Christ in the U.S.A., 1954): 4–5 (first quotation on p. 5); "Protestantism Speaks On Justice and Integration," *Christian Century* 75 (February 5, 1958): 164–65 (second and third quotations); Sumner, *The Episcopal Church's History*, 37 (fourth and fifth quotations); Campbell and Pettigrew, *Christians in Racial Crisis*, 149.

23. "The Churches Speak," 2; Thompson, *Presbyterians in the South*, vol. 3, 540–41; Bailey, *Southern White Protestantism in the Twentieth Century*, 143–44; Reimers, *White Protestantism and the Negro*, 116; S. Jonathan Bass, "Not Time Yet: Alabama's Episcopal Bishop and the End of Segregation in the Deep South," *Anglican and Episcopal History* 63 (June 1994): 238 (quotation); Hodding Carter III, *The South Strikes Back* (Garden City, N.Y.: Doubleday, 1959), 165.

24. *Annual*, SBC, 1957, 59; 1958, 53; 1959, 81; 1960, 72, 273; 1961, 85; Campbell and Pettigrew, *Christians in Racial Crisis*, 140–41, 146–47, 149–51, 154–55 (quotations on p. 155), 162–63; W. D. Weatherford, *American Churches and the Negro: An Historical Study from Early Slave Days to the Present* (Boston: Christopher Publishing House, 1957), 255–56.

25. "Southern Presbyterians Issue Sharp Condemnation of Racial Discrimination," *Religious News Service*, May 1, 1957.

26. Campbell and Pettigrew, 140–41 (first and second quotations on p. 141), 165–67; "Church Backs Use of Troops in Little Rock," *Religious News Service*, September 11, 1958 (third quotation); Winfred E. Garrison, "The Year in Religion," *Biblical Recorder*, January 11, 1958.

27. *Annual*, Alabama, 1957, 31, 129–30; *Annual*, Louisiana, 1957, 73; *Florence [South Carolina] Morning News*, April 19, 1956 (quotation).

28. Roy V. Sims to L. U. Amason, November 14, 1958, Box 2, Folder 8, Brooks Hays Papers, SBHLA; Numan V. Bartley, *The Rise of Massive Resistance: Race and Politics in the South During the 1950's* (Baton Rouge: Louisiana State University Press, 1969), 300–301.

29. "Southern Presbyterians Reaffirm Anti-Segregation Stand," *Religious News Service*, April 30, 1958; "Messengers Refuse [to] Weaken Report," *Christian Index*, May 29, 1958; C. W. Bazemore, "Baptists Hold Great Convention at Houston Largest Attendance in History," *Biblical Recorder*, June 7, 1958.

30. Reimers, *White Protestantism and the Negro*, 123, 142, 156, 176–77 (quotation on p. 176); J. Oscar Lee, "Reporting on Race Relations in Some Churches," *Royal Service* 51 (May 1957): 23.

31. Bailey, *Southern White Protestantism in the Twentieth Century*, 147.

32. "An Interesting Survey," *Baptist Standard,* June 9, 1956; Osborne, *The Segregated Covenant,* 47; Carter, *The South Strikes Back,* 166.

33. Fairclough, *Race & Democracy,* 171–74.

34. Ibid., 200–204 (first quotation on p. 200; second quotation on p. 204), 234–62.

35. James Graham Cook, *The Segregationists* (New York: Appleton-Century-Crofts, 1962), 194–202, 242–43; Neil R. McMillen, *The Citizens' Council: Organized Resistance to the Second Reconstruction, 1954–64* (Urbana and Chicago: University of Illinois Press, 1971), 59–72, 80, 171–79 (quotation on p. 174), 293–96.

36. Howard Dorgan, "Response of the Main-line Southern White Protestant Pulpit to *Brown* v. *Board of Education,* 1954–1965" in *A New Diversity in Contemporary Southern Rhetoric,* eds. Calvin M. Logue and Howard Dorgan (Baton Rouge: Louisiana State University Press, 1987), 23–25, 46; Alvis, *Religion & Race,* 65–66.

37. Alvis, *Religion & Race,* 69, 107; Bailey, *Southern White Protestantism in the Twentieth Century,* 148–49; David L. Chappell, *Inside Agitators: White Southerners in the Civil Rights Movement* (Baltimore: Johns Hopkins Press, 1994), 107–108, 119–20.

38. Julian N. Hartt, "Dallas Ministers on Desegregation," *Christian Century* 75 (May 21, 1958): 619–20; Bailey, *Southern White Protestantism in the Twentieth Century,* 148–49 (quotations).

39. Mark Newman, "The Baptist State Convention of North Carolina and Desegregation, 1945–1980," *North Carolina Historical Review* 75 (January 1998): 19–21; Osborne, *The Segregated Covenant,* 47–48; Bailey, *Southern White Protestantism in the Twentieth Century,* 147–48.

40. *Annual,* SBC, 1961, 84; *Resolutions adopted by the American Baptist Convention: Portland, Oregon, June 17, 1961* (Valley Forge, Pa.: Division of Christian Social Concern, American Baptist Convention, 1961) (quotation).

41. Kyle Haselden, "Baptists in Travail," *Christian Century* 80 (May 22, 1963): 674.

42. "Statement by the Presiding Bishop of the Episcopal Church, May 26, 1963," *The Episcopal Society for Cultural and Racial Unity Newsletter,* August 6, 1963 (quotation); Robert Wuthnow, *The Restructuring of American Religion: Society and Faith since World War II* (Princeton: Princeton University Press, 1988), 146; R. Douglas Brackenridge, *Eugene Carson Blake: Prophet with Portfolio* (New York: Seabury Press, 1978), 92–96, 102–104.

43. *New York Times,* May 21, 1963; Wuthnow, *The Restructuring of American Religion,* 146–47; Brackenridge, *Eugene Carson Blake,* 96–102; "Appeal For End To Racial Bias," *Christian Index,* May 30, 1963 (first quotation); "End All Racial Barriers, Assembly Urges Southern Presbyterian Units," *Religious News Service,* April 30, 1963 (second quotation); E. S. James, "Distressed in White House Conference," *Baptist Standard,* June 26, 1963 (third quotation).

44. *New York Times,* November 4, 1963; "Survey of Racial Picture," *Baptist Messenger,* December 12, 1963; Newman, "The Baptist State Convention of North Carolina and Desegregation," 21 n. 61; Thompson, *Presbyterians in the South,* vol. 3, 549; Bailey, *Southern White Protestantism in the Twentieth Century,* 148.

45. "Southern Presbyterians Act To Speed Up Integration," *Religious News Service,* April 28, 1964 (first quotation); "Southern Presbyterians Tackle Race Issue at General Assembly," *Religious News Service,* April 27, 1964 (second quotation); *Annual,* SBC, 1964, 73–74.

46. Reimers, *White Protestantism and the Negro,* 156–57.

47. "United Presbyterians Elect Negro Leader As President," *Religious News Service,* May 22, 1964; "United Presbyterian Timetable Asks End of Segregated Synods," *Religious*

News Service, May 28, 1964; "American Baptists Favor Equality, Unity Moves," *Christian Index,* June 4, 1964 (quotations).

48. *Jackson [Mississippi] Daily News,* April 27, 1964; Osborne, *The Segregated Covenant,* 90; Neil R. McMillen, "Development of Civil Rights, 1956–1970," in *A History of Mississippi,* ed. Richard Aubrey McClemore (Hattiesburg: University of Southern Mississippi, 1973), vol. 2, 162.

49. *Annual,* SBC, 1964, 73–74, 229; K. Owen White to Mr. and Mrs. E. H. Harrell, April 1, 1964, Box 1, Folder 7, K. O. White Papers, SBHLA.

50. "Southern Presbyterians Tackle Race Issue At General Assembly," *Religious News Service,* April 27, 1964 (quotations); "Orderly Rights Demonstrations Endorsed By Methodists," *Religious News Service,* May 5, 1964.

51. Sumner, *The Episcopal Church's History,* 41–42 (first quotation on p. 42); "Separate and Unequal," *Newsweek,* June 1, 1964: 82 (second quotation); "American Baptists Favor Equality, Unity Moves," *Christian Index,* June 4, 1964.

52. Sumner, *The Episcopal Church's History,* 42–43; John T. McGreevey, "Racial Justice and the People of God: The Second Vatican Council, the Civil Rights Movement, and American Catholics," *Religion and American Culture* 4 (Summer 1994): 221; Alvis, *Religion & Race,* 111–13; *Minutes of the One-Hundred-Fifth General Assembly of the Presbyterian Church in the United States,* 1965, 83, 158–60.

53. *Annual,* SBC, 1965, 91–92; W. T. Moore, *His Heart is Black* (Atlanta: Home Mission Board, 1978), 37.

54. Thompson, *Presbyterians in the South,* vol. 3, 546.

55. Alvis, *Religion & Race,* 93–98; Thompson, *Presbyterians in the South,* vol. 3, 547; "The Disciples in Dallas," *Christianity Today* 11 (October 14, 1966): 52; "Racial Turmoil Batters the Church," *Christianity Today* 9 (June 4, 1965): 45; George McMillen, "Silent White Ministers of the South," *New York Times Magazine,* April 5, 1964: 22; "A Negro Bishop," *Christianity Today* 10 (October 22, 1965): 38.

56. Harvard Sitkoff, *The Struggle for Black Equality, 1954–1992,* rev. ed. (New York: Hill and Wang, 1993), 194–204.

57. "American Baptists In Midstream," *Christianity Today* 10 (June 10, 1966): 47; "Resolution on 'Power and Justice' Passed by the General Council of the American Baptist Convention, November 3, 1966 [first quotation]," "Baptists and Race Problems— American Baptist Convention, 1966–," File BT 734.2.B2A3, BJC; *Minutes of the One-Hundred-Sixth General Assembly of the Presbyterian Church in the United States,* 1966, 90–91 (second quotation on p. 91).

58. "Presbyterian Leaders Are Authorized To Press School Desegregation Suit," *Religious News Service,* May 20, 1966; "Integration: A Rough Road," *Christianity Today* 11 (October 14, 1966): 52; *Jackson Daily News,* June 13, 1967; James F. Findlay, Jr., *Church People in the Struggle: The National Council of Churches and the Black Freedom Movement, 1950–1970* (Oxford: Oxford University Press, 1993), 111–68.

59. Sumner, *The Episcopal Church's History,* 43–44, 46–49.

60. *Annual,* SBC, 1968, 66–69, 73; Sitkoff, *The Struggle for Black Equality, 1954–1992,* 207–208; "Mission Agency Discontinues National Crisis Committee," *Baptist & Reflector,* August 19, 1971.

61. Edward E. Plowman, "Southern Presbyterian, Reformed Churches Vote to Merge," *Christianity Today* 12 (July 5, 1968): 38; *Minutes of the One-Hundred-Eighth General Assembly of the Presbyterian Church in the United States,* 1968, 101; Alvis, *Religion & Race,* 123–25, 128–29.

62. "American Baptists Respond to Black Power Challenge," *Christian Century* 85 (July 3, 1968): 878–80; Edward E. Plowman, "Cleavages In A.B.C.," *Christianity Today* 12 (June 21, 1968): 40.

63. "Churches Confront Urban Crises," *Christianity Today* 12 (June 21, 1968): 46; Willmar L. Thorkelson, "United Presbyterian General Assembly," *Christian Century* 85 (June 19, 1968): 823; Arthur H. Matthews, "United Presbyterians Confront Change," *Christianity Today* 12 (June 7, 1968): 39 (quotation).

64. "Churches Confront Urban Crises," *Christianity Today* 12 (June 21, 1968): 46; *Christianity Today* 15 (June 4, 1971): 37 (first quotation); "Racial Agenda For Catholics," *Christianity Today* 12 (May 24, 1968): 39 (second quotation). The Methodist Church and the Evangelical United Brethren Church merged in 1968 to form the United Methodist Church. Adon Taft, "Racial Birth Pangs For United Methodists," *Christianity Today* 12 (May 10, 1968): 34.

65. *New York Times,* November 4, 1963; "Southern Baptists Survey Negro-White Co-operation," *Baptist Press,* October 18, 1968; Alvis, *Religion & Race,* 93–98; Thompson, *Presbyterians in the South,* vol. 3, 547.

66. *United Methodist Information,* June 27, 1972; Frederick A. Norwood, *The Story of American Methodism: A History of the United Methodists and Their Relations* (Nashville and New York: Abingdon Press, 1974), 432.

67. *Annual,* SBC, 1969, 79–80; "Manifesto receives little support," *Baptist Standard,* August 13, 1969; "Black Manifesto's Birthday: Frosting on the Cake?," *Christianity Today* 14 (May 22, 1970): 37; Findlay, *Church People in the Struggle,* 199–225.

68. Sumner, *The Episcopal Church's History,* 50–58.

69. "ABC Elects First Negro President," *Baptist Standard,* May 21, 1969; Sumner, *The Episcopal Church's History,* 39; "Baptists Elect Negro Pastor to Convention Executive Board," *American Baptist News Service,* December 23, 1969.

70. Findlay, *Church People in the Struggle,* 220; Frank A. Sharp, "The Church Speaks On Busing," *Alabama Baptist,* July 27, 1972 (quotations); Jonathan Kelley, "The Politics of School Busing," *Public Opinion Quarterly* 38 (Spring 1974): 24 n. 8.

71. *Annual,* SBC, 1970, 78–79; 1971, 78–79; *Delta Democrat-Times* [Greenville, Mississippi], January 5, February 1, 4, 1970; James F. Cole, "Advocates Of the Public School System," *Baptist Message,* February 5, 1970; Robert W. Prichard, *A History of the Episcopal Church* (Harrisburg, Pa.: Morehouse, 1991), 243.

72. Robert L. Johnson, "Church on racism? 'Disinterest deafening,'" *National Catholic Reporter,* September 26, 1975; Sumner, *The Episcopal Church's History,* 3, 58.

11. AN OVERVIEW: SOUTHERN BAPTISTS AND AFRICAN AMERICANS, 1972–1995

1. "Resolution on The Continuing Racial Crisis" (quotations), Box 2, Folder 11, SBC Christian Life Commission Minutes, SBHLA; "BSSB Trustees Approve Guidelines for Writers," *Baptist Press,* February 3, 1972.

2. Nancy T. Ammerman, "Southern Baptists and the New Christian Right," *Review of Religious Research* 32 (March 1991): 224; Harvard Sitkoff, *The Struggle for Black Equality, 1954–1992,* rev. ed. (New York: Hill and Wang, 1993), 211–14, 216–17; Jonathan Kelley, "The Politics of School Busing," *Public Opinion Quarterly* 38 (Spring 1974): 24 n. 8.

3. David Nevin and Robert E. Bills, *The Schools That Fear Built: Segregationist Academies in the South* (Washington, D.C.: Acropolis, 1976), 32–36; John Egerton, *Promise of Progress:*

Memphis School Desegregation, 1972–1973 (Atlanta: Southern Regional Council, 1973), 5, 14, 16, 23–24, 32; David Wilkinson, "2 + 2 = Who?," *Home Missions* 50 (September-October 1976): 15–17; Mark Newman, "The Tennessee Baptist Convention and Desegregation, 1954–1980," *Tennessee Historical Quarterly* 57 (Winter 1998): 249.

4. Nevin and Bills, *The Schools That Fear Built*, 29–30 (quotation on p. 30), 33–36; Newman, "The Tennessee Baptist Convention and Desegregation," 249–50.

5. Nevin and Bills, *The Schools That Fear Built*, 29–30 (quotation on p. 30); Wilkinson, "2 + 2 = Who?," 16; Newman, "The Tennessee Baptist Convention and Desegregation," 250.

6. Wilkinson, "2 + 2 = Who?," 15; *Proceedings*, Texas, 1972, 31; 1973, 27, 30; 1975, 20, 34; *Annual*, North Carolina, 1972, 78, 89–90; 1973, 163; 1974, 96–97 (quotation on p. 96); Frye Gaillard, *The Dream Long Deferred* (Chapel Hill and London: University of North Carolina Press, 1988).

7. *Annual*, SBC, 1973, 79; 1974, 71; *New York Times*, June 13, 1974.

8. W. T. Moore, *His Heart is Black* (Atlanta: Home Mission Board, 1978), 92; "Black Worshippers Accepted At Mississippi Church," *Religious News Service*, February 27, 1973; Tim Nicholas, "Baptist Survey Reveals Black-White Relations," *Baptist Press*, October 26, 1973; "75,000 Blacks in Southern Baptist Churches," *Baptist Standard*, November 28, 1973.

9. G. Willis Bennett, *Confronting A Crisis: A Depth Study of Southern Baptist Churches in Metropolitan Transitional Areas* (Atlanta: Home Mission Board, 1967), 41–42; Cecil Sherman, "As I See It," *Contempo* 5 (June 1975): 5, 25; Roy Edward Godwin, "The Role of the Church in Racial Integration in Urban Areas of Transition" (Th.M. thesis, Southern Baptist Theological Seminary, 1967), 37–40.

10. Tim Nicholas, "Race Relations: Southern Baptists and Blacks Today," *Home Missions* 43 (November 1973): 22; "'Outgrown Geographic Patterns'," *Biblical Recorder*, June 22, 1974; *ESB*, vol. 4, s.v. "Home Mission Board Program of Black Church Relations," by Emmanuel L. McCall; Catherine B. Allen, *A Century to Celebrate: History of Woman's Missionary Union* (Birmingham: Woman's Missionary Union, 1987), 256–57.

11. "SBC Names First Black Officer in 129-Year History," *Baptist Press*, June 13, 1974; "Segregation in Churches—Why It Still Thrives," *U.S. News & World Report* 81 (November 29, 1976): 16; *Proceedings*, Texas, 1972, 26; "Branch Elected Vice President," *Baptist Standard*, November 14, 1973; "Install Hickerson," *Baptist Standard*, April 28, 1976.

12. "Segregation in Churches—Why It Still Thrives," 16; "Church on racism? 'Disinterest deafening,'" *National Catholic Reporter*, September 26, 1975: 1, 4; David Gooch, "News Releases Concerning Conference" in *Race: New Directions For A New Day, Addresses from Conferences at Ridgecrest Baptist Conference Center* (Nashville: Christian Life Commission, 1973), 68 (second quotation), 70 (first quotation).

13. Nicholas, "Race Relations: Southern Baptists and Blacks Today," 23–24.

14. *Annual*, SBC, 1974, 81, 209 (first quotation), 210 (second quotation).

15. "Promotion Committee Minutes, CLC Annual Meeting—September 11, 1974," Box 2, Folder 14, SBC Christian Life Commission Minutes, SBHLA; *Annual*, SBC, 1974, 208–210; 1977, 55–56; 1978, 57–58; 1979, 169–70; 1980, 54–55.

16. *Southern Baptist Periodical Index*, 1974–1980 (Nashville: Historical Commission of the Southern Baptist Convention, 1975–1981); Emmanuel L. McCall, "Where Are We?," *Contempo* 5 (June 1975): 5, 33; *Crossing Barriers Through Ministries with National Baptists* (Atlanta: Home Mission Board, 1974); Emmanuel L. McCall, "Home Mission Board Ministry in the Black Community," *Baptist History and Heritage* 16 (July 1981): 36–37 (quotation on p.37).

17. Mark Newman, "Getting Right with God: Southern Baptists and Race Relations, 1945–1980" (Ph.D. diss., University of Mississippi, 1993), 682–83, 724–25, 777–78, 780.

18. Walker L. Knight, "Black Churches Multiply In Southern Baptist Convention," *Baptist Press*, December 1, 1976; Moore, *His Heart is Black*, 91; Sid Smith, "Growth of Black Southern Baptist Churches in the Inner City," *Baptist History and Heritage* 16 (July 1981): 52; *Study of Black Southern Baptists* (Nashville: Baptist Sunday School Board, 1980), 4, 7 (quotation).

19. "Segregation in Churches—Why It Still Thrives," 16; Jere Allen, "Alabama Baptists Respond to the Transitional Community Church Crisis," *Alabama Baptist*, February 17, 1977; "Alabama Baptist Church Removes Racial Barrier," *Baptist Press*, June 5, 1975; Dan Martin, "Exclusion of Selma Church Branded As 'Racist,'" *Baptist Press*, November 19, 1976.

20. James C. Hefley, "A Change of Mind in Plains," *Christianity Today* 21 (December 3, 1976): 50–53; Eileen Keerdoja and Holly Camp, "The Plains Baptists," *Newsweek* 76 (October 17, 1977): 12–13; Mark Newman, "The Georgia Baptist Convention and Desegregation, 1945–1980," *Georgia Historical Quarterly* 83 (Winter 1999): 709–10.

21. *Annual*, Florida, 1975, 51–52, 1976, 50–51; *Minutes*, South Carolina, 1976, 54; William M. Pinson, Jr., "The Future of Race Relations," *Contempo* 5 (June 1975): 7; Wilkinson, "2 + 2 = Who?," 15, 18–19; *Annual*, SBC, 1979, 56–57.

22. Corbin L. Cooper, "A Study of Orthodoxy, Authoritarianism, and Racial Prejudice among Lay Leaders in Southern Baptist Churches in North Carolina" (Ed.D. diss., North Carolina State University at Raleigh, 1977), 27, 67, 68 (quotations); Mark Newman, "The Baptist State Convention of North Carolina and Desegregation, 1945–1980," *North Carolina Historical Review* 75 (January 1998): 27; Donald L. Grant, *The Way It Was in the South: The Black Experience in Georgia* (New York: Birch Lane Press, 1993), 525; John Shelton Reed and Merle Black, "Jim Crow, R.I.P.," in John Shelton Reed, *Surveying the South: Studies in Regional Sociology* (Columbia: University of Missouri Press, 1993), 98.

23. Harper Shannon, "What Doth The Lord Require of Thee?," *Alabama Baptist*, November 15, 1979 (quotation); Newman, "Getting Right with God," 724–25, 777–81.

24. *ESB*, vol. 4, s.v. "Black Southern Baptists," by Sidney Smith; Lynn Clayton, "Race Relations: A Historical Perspective from the Editor of a State Baptist Paper," in *Proceedings of Southern Baptists and Race* (Nashville: Christian Life Commission, 1989), 19; *Annual*, SBC, 1978, 183; "Minutes of the Annual Meeting of the CLC, 16–17 September 1980," Box 2, Folder 20, SBC Christian Life Commission Minutes, SBHLA; David R. Wilkinson, "Confronting the Klan," *Light* (October–November 1980): 2–3; W. David Sapp, "Southern Baptist Responses to the American Economy, 1900–1980," *Baptist History and Heritage* 16 (January 1981): 8.

25. "Montgomery Baptists mold black/white relations into new community outreach," *Home Missions* 51 (May–June 1980): 63; *ESB*, vol. 4, s.v. "Home Mission Board Program of Black Church Relations," by Emmanuel L. McCall; Newman, "Getting Right with God," 633, 682–84, 781; Dan Martin, "Racism Still Problem for SBC, Panel Says," *Baptist Press*, May 2, 1983.

26. E. Glenn Hinson, "SBC Fundamentalists: Stirring Up a Storm," *Christian Century* 96 (July 18–25, 1979): 725–727; Tom Minnery, "Southern Baptist Conservatives Hold the Line against Moderate Challenge," *Christianity Today* 25 (July 17 1981): 80–82; Richard Marius, "The War Between the Baptists," *Esquire* 96 (December 1981): 46, 48–50, 53, 55; Bill J. Leonard, *God's Last and Only Hope: The Fragmentation of the Southern Baptist Convention* (Grand Rapids, Mich.: William B. Eerdman's, 1990), 151–53, 160, 180–82;

Nancy Tatom Ammerman, *Baptist Battles: Social Change and Religious Conflict in the Southern Baptist Convention* (New Brunswick: Rutgers University Press, 1990), 103 (quotation), 76–79.

27. Walker L. Knight interview with the author, August 11, 1997; Leonard, *God's Last and Only Hope*, 133–34; David T. Morgan, *The New Crusades, The New Holy Land: Conflict in the Southern Baptist Convention, 1969–1991* (Tuscaloosa: University of Alabama Press, 1996), 13–14, 162–68; Wayne Flynt, *Alabama Baptists: Southern Baptists in the Heart of Dixie* (Tuscaloosa: University of Alabama Press, 1998), 480, 494, 542, 549, 566; Cecil E. Sherman, "An Overview of the Moderate Movement," and Robert Parham, "The History of the Baptist Center for Ethics" in *The Struggle for the Soul of the SBC: Moderate Responses to the Fundamentalist Movement*, ed. Walter B. Shurden (Macon, Ga.: Mercer University Press, 1993), 36 (first quotation), 210 (second, third and fourth quotations); Ammerman, "Southern Baptists and the New Christian Right," 227–28.

28. Flynt, *Alabama Baptists*, 477, 526, 566–67; Emmanuel L. McCall interview with the author, August 12, 1997; Walker L. Knight, "Race Relations: Changing Patterns and Practices," in *Southern Baptists Observed: Multiple Perspectives on a Changing Denomination*, ed. Nancy Tatom Ammerman (Knoxville: University of Tennessee Press, 1993), 178 (first quotation); Leonard, *God's Last and Only Hope*, 161; *Proceedings of Southern Baptists and Race*; Ammerman, *Baptist Battles*, 103 (second quotation), 287.

29. Knight, "Race Relations," 177, 179–80 (first and third quotations on p. 180); *Annual*, SBC, 1986, 77 (second quotation).

30. Knight, "Race Relations," 179–80; Jesse C. Fletcher, *The Southern Baptist Convention: A Sesquicentennial History* (Nashville: Broadman & Holman, 1994), 318; Flynt, *Alabama Baptists*, 569.

31. Ammerman, *Baptist Battles*, especially 76–80, 99–106, 264, 271–82, 352 n. 34, 361 n. 17; Ammerman, "Southern Baptists and the New Christian Right," 221–24, 226, 230; Morgan, *The New Crusades, The New Holy Land*, 162–63, 167; Flynt, *Alabama Baptists*, 588; Jeff Manza and Clem Brooks, "The Religious Factor in U.S. Presidential Elections, 1960–1992," *American Journal of Sociology* 103 (July 1997): 69–71.

32. Bruce A. Greer, "Active and Inactive Disciples, Presbyterians, and Southern Baptists: A Comparative Socioeconomic, Religious, and Political Profile," in *A Case Study of Mainstream Protestantism: The Disciples' Relation to American Culture, 1880–1989*, ed. D. Newell Williams (St. Louis: Chalice Press and Grand Rapids, Mich.: William B. Eerdmans, 1991), 386–87, 389, 405–406; Wade Clark Roof and William McKinney, *American Mainline Religion: Its Changing Shape and Future* (New Brunswick: Rutgers University Press, 1987), 197–99.

33. "The Sunday School Board Serving Your Church," *Ebonicity* 1 (Summer 1982): 1 (quotation); Joe Maxwell, "Black Southern Baptists," *Christianity Today* (May 15, 1995): 27, 31; *Atlanta Constitution*, March 5, 1990; Knight, "Race Relations," 175–77.

34. Maxwell, "Black Southern Baptists," 31 (first, second, fifth and sixth quotations); *Annual*, SBC, 1995, 79–81 (third quotation on p. 81); Keith Hinson, "SBC messengers apologize, repudiate racism in historic 'Resolution on Racial Reconciliation,'" *Alabama Baptist*, June 29, 1995; *Birmingham [Alabama] News*, June 21, 1995 (fourth quotation); *The News & Observer* [Raleigh, North Carolina], June 21, 1995.

35. Greer, "Active and Inactive Disciples, Presbyterians, and Southern Baptists," 393; Maxwell, "Black Southern Baptists," 29–31 (first quotation on p. 29; second quotation on p. 30; third quotation on p. 31); Roof and McKinney, *American Mainline Religion*, 80–81, 138, 141–44.

Bibliography

I. Primary Sources

A. Annuals, Minutes and Proceedings

Annual of the Alabama Baptist State Convention. Birmingham, 1941–1981.
Annual of the Arkansas Baptist State Convention. Little Rock, 1941–1981.
Annual of the Baptist General Association of Virginia. Richmond, 1939, 1941–1981.
Annual of the Baptist State Convention of North Carolina. Raleigh, 1941–1981.
Annual of the Florida Baptist Convention. Jacksonville, 1941–1981.
Annual of the Louisiana Baptist Convention. Shreveport, 1940–1981.
Annual of the Mississippi Baptist Convention. Jackson, 1941–1981.
Annual of the Pulaski County Baptist Association. Little Rock, Arkansas, 1958.
Annual of the Southern Baptist Convention. Nashville, 1920, 1939–1995.
Minutes of the Baptist State Convention of South Carolina. Greenville, 1941–1981.
Minutes of the Georgia Baptist Convention. Atlanta, 1941–1981.
Minutes of the One-Hundred-Fifth General Assembly of the Presbyterian Church in the United States. Montreat, 1965.
Minutes of the One-Hundred-Sixth General Assembly of the Presbyterian Church in the United States. Montreat, 1966.
Minutes of the One-Hundred-Eighth General Assembly of the Presbyterian Church in the United States. Montreat, 1968.
Proceedings of the Baptist General Convention of Texas. Dallas, 1941–1981.
Proceedings of the Tennessee Baptist Convention. Nashville, 1941–1981.

B. Official Records

Baptist Joint Committee, Washington, D.C.
Office files.

Baptist Sunday School Board Archive, Nashville, Tennessee.
H. Franklin Paschall Papers.

North Carolina Baptist Historical Collection, Wake Forest University, Winston-Salem, North Carolina.

Wendell R. Grigg Papers.

Southern Baptist Historical Library and Archives, Nashville, Tennessee.
Executive Committee Records.
J. D. Grey Papers.
Brooks Hays Papers.
Herschel H. Hobbs Papers.
SBC Christian Life Commission Minutes.
SBC Christian Life Commission Papers.
K. Owen White Collection.

C. Oral Histories and Interviews

Oral Histories

Historical Commission of the Southern Baptist Convention, Nashville, Tennessee.
Lawrence Brooks Hays, by A. Ronald Tonks, 1975–1977. (1985).
The Mississippi Oral History Program of the University of Southern Mississippi, Hatties-
    burg, Mississippi.
Owen Cooper, by Graham Lee Hales, Jr., December 11, 1972. Vol. 17 (1975).
William Penn Davis, by Harold K. Gower, March 24, 1972. Vol. 15 (1973).

Interviews

Walker L. Knight, by author, August 11, 1997.
Emmanuel L. McCall, by author, August 12, 1997.

D. Pamphlets

*An Address by Dr. W. A. Criswell, Pastor, First Baptist Church, Dallas, Texas, to the Joint Assembly,
    State of South Carolina, Wednesday, February 22, 1956, 12.30 P.M.* N.p., n.d.
Bellamy, Guy. *Negro Missions*. Atlanta: Home Mission Board, n.d. [1950].
The Bible Speaks on Race. Dallas: Christian Life Commission, n.d.
The Bible Speaks on Race. Nashville: Christian Life Commission, n.d.
Christian Principles Applied to Race Relations. Nashville: Christian Life Commission, n.d.
    [1965].
Coggins, Ross. *Missions and Race*. Nashville: Christian Life Commission, n.d. [1963].
Cook, Montague. *Racial Segregation Is Christian: Two Sermons on Racial Segregation*. N.p.,
    n.d.
Crossing Barriers Through Ministries with National Baptists. Atlanta: Home Mission Board,
    1974.
Daniel, Carey. *God the Original Segregationist*. N.p., n.d.
Goerner, Cornell. *Race Relations: A Factor in World Missions*. Nashville: Christian Life Com-
    mission, n.d. [1957].
Hudson, R. Lofton. *Is Segregation Christian?* Nashville: Christian Life Commission, n.d.
Jones, John Hall. *The Unity of Humanity*. Nashville: Christian Life Commission, 1956.
Lee, G. Avery. *Some Quiet Thoughts on a Turbulent Issue*. Nashville: Christian Life Commis-
    sion, n.d. [1956].
Maston, T. B. *The Christian and Race Relations*. Memphis: Brotherhood Commission, n.d.
    [1963].

———. *Integration*. Nashville: Christian Life Commission, 1956.

Miller, A. C. *Race Relations—A Factor In World Missions*. Nashville: Christian Life Commission, n.d.

———. *The Racial Problem Is My Problem*. Nashville: Christian Life Commission, n.d.

Race Relations: A Charter of Principles. Louisville, Ky.: Social Service Commission, n.d.

Resolutions adopted by the American Baptist Convention: Portland, Oregon, June 17, 1961. Valley Forge, Pa.: Division of Christian Social Concern, American Baptist Convention, 1961.

Rogers, S. E. *Christian Love and Segregation*. Montgomery: Baptist Laymen of Alabama, n.d.

Statements Adopted by Religious Groups Re Segregation in the Public Schools. New York: Department of Racial and Cultural Relations, National Council of Churches of Christ in the U.S.A., 1954.

Weatherspoon, Jesse B. *Southern Baptists and Race Relations*. Louisville, Ky.: Social Service Commission, 1949.

———. *Race Relations—A Christian View*. Nashville: Christian Life Commission, n.d. [1957].

E. Southern Baptist Newspapers and Periodicals

Alabama Baptist, 1945–1983, 1995.

Arkansas Baptist, 1945–1960.

Arkansas Baptist Newsmagazine, 1960–1971.

Baptist and Reflector, 1945–1971.

Baptist Courier, 1945–1976.

Baptist Men's Journal, 1967.

Baptist Message, 1945–1971.

Baptist Messenger, December 12, 1963.

Baptist Press, 1959–1988.

Baptist Program, 1953–1980.

Baptist Record, 1945–1988.

Baptist Standard, 1945–1980.

Biblical Recorder, 1945–1980.

Christian Frontiers, January 1946–January 1949.

Christian Index, 1945–1977.

Christian Layman, 1958.

Christian Life Bulletin, September 1955–April 1958.

Contempo, 1975.

Ebonicity, 1982–1983.

Florida Baptist Witness, 1945–1971.

Home Missions, 1958–1980.

Light, May 1948–October 1952, March–April 1959 to March–April 1960, 1964 and October 1978–1980. Published sporadically.

Religious Herald, 1945–1971.

Royal Service, 1949–50, 1957, 1964–1980.

Tell, 1964.

The Window of Y.M.A., 1945–1950.

World Comrades, 1948.

F. Miscellaneous

Christianity and Race Relations: Addresses from Conferences at Glorieta and Ridgecrest. Nashville: Christian Life Commission, 1964.

Christianity and Race Relations: Messages from the Sixth Annual Christian Life Workshop. Dallas: Christian Life Commission, 1962.

Proceedings of Southern Baptists and Race. Nashville: Christian Life Commission, 1989.

Race: New Directions For A New Day, Addresses from Conferences at Ridgecrest Baptist Conference Center. Nashville: Christian Life Commission, 1973.

Study of Black Southern Baptists. Nashville: Research Services Department, Sunday School Board, 1980.

G. Magazines, Newsletters, Newspapers

American Baptist News Service, December 23, 1969.

Atlanta Constitution, November 3, 1957, March 5, 1990.

Birmingham [Alabama] News, May 22, 1968, June 21, 1995.

Chicago Defender, July 19, 1952.

Christian Century, 1945–1986.

Christianity and Crisis, March 3, 1958.

Christianity Today, 1957–1995.

Church News [Episcopal Diocese of Mississippi], January 1970.

Columbia [South Carolina] Record, November 13, 1964.

Delta Democrat-Times [Greenville, Mississippi], 1970.

The Episcopal Society for Cultural and Racial Unity Newsletter, August 6, 1963.

Florence [South Carolina] Morning News, April 19, 1956.

Information Service [National Council of Churches], December 1, 1956.

Jackson [Mississippi] Clarion-Ledger, 1945–1984.

Jackson [Mississippi] Daily News, 1949–1967.

Jackson [Mississippi] State Times, June 12, 1958.

Look, April 30, 1957.

National Catholic Reporter, September 27, 1975.

News & Courier [Charleston, South Carolina], April 16, 1957.

News & Observer [Raleigh, North Carolina], June 21, 1995.

Newsweek, October 21, 1963, June 1, 1964, October 17, 1977.

New York Times, 1954–1983.

Religious News Service, 1954–1973.

Star-Tribune [Chatham, Virginia], May 24, 1979.

The State [Columbia, South Carolina], March 4, 1956.

U.S. News and World Report, November 29, 1976.

United Methodist Information, June 27, 1972.

Washington Post, May 21, 1957.

H. Books

Anderson, Margaret. *The Children of the South*. New York: Farrar, Strauss and Giroux, 1966.

Bennett, G. Willis. *Confronting A Crisis: A Depth Study of Southern Baptist Churches in Metropolitan Transitional Areas*. Atlanta: Home Mission Board, 1967.

Brown, Robert R. *Bigger Than Little Rock*. Greenwich, Conn.: Seabury Press, 1958.

Campbell, Ernest Q. and Thomas F. Pettigrew. *Christians in Racial Crisis: A Study of Little Rock's Ministry*. Washington, D.C.: Public Affairs Press, 1959.

Carter, Hodding III. *The South Strikes Back*. Garden City, N.Y.: Doubleday, 1959.

Carter, Jimmy. *Why Not The Best?* Nashville: Broadman Press, 1975.

Cook, James Graham. *The Segregationists*. New York: Appleton-Century-Crofts, 1962.

Egerton, John. *Promise of Progress: Memphis School Desegregation, 1972–1973*. Atlanta: Southern Regional Council, 1973.

Ezell, Humphrey K. *The Christian Problem of Racial Segregation*. New York: Greenwich, 1959.

Gilmore, J. Herbert, Jr. *They Chose To Live: The Racial Agony of an American Church*. Grand Rapids, Mich.: Eerdmans, 1972.

Hays, Brooks. *This World: A Christian's Workshop*. Nashville: Broadman Press, 1958.

———. *A Southern Moderate Speaks*. Chapel Hill: University of North Carolina Press, 1959.

Holmes, Thomas J., with Gainer E. Bryan, Jr. *Ashes for Breakfast*. Valley Forge, Pa.: Judson Press, 1969.

Hunt, Alma. *Reflections from Alma Hunt*. Birmingham: Woman's Missionary Union, 1987.

LaFarge S.J., John. *The Catholic Viewpoint on Race Relations*. Garden City, N.Y.: Hanover House, 1956.

Lee, Dallas. *The Cotton Patch Evidence*. New York: Harper & Row, 1971.

Maston, T. B. *"Of One": A Study of Christian Principles and Race Relations*. Atlanta: Home Mission Board, 1946.

———. *The Bible and Race*. Nashville: Broadman, 1959.

———. *Segregation and Desegregation: A Christian Approach*. New York: Macmillan, 1959.

McClellan, Albert. *The Executive Committee of the Southern Baptist Convention, 1917–1984*. Nashville: Broadman Press, 1985.

McDonald, Erwin L. *Across the Editor's Desk: The Story of the State Baptist Papers*. Nashville: Broadman Press, 1966.

Quint, Howard H. *Profile in Black and White: A Frank Portrait of South Carolina*. Washington, D.C.: Public Affairs Press, 1958.

Record, Wilson, and Jane Cassels Record, eds. *Little Rock, U.S.A.: Materials For Analysis*. San Francisco: Chandler Publishing, 1960.

Sapp, Phyllis Woodruff. *The Long Bridge*. Atlanta: Home Mission Board, 1957.

Sullivan, Clayton. *Called to Preach, Condemned to Survive: The Education of Clayton Sullivan*. Macon, Ga.: Mercer University Press, 1985.

Sullivan, James L. *God Is My Record*. Nashville: Broadman Press, 1974.

U.S. Commission on Civil Rights. *Justice In Jackson: Hearings Held in Jackson, Miss. February 16–20, 1965*. Vol 2. New York: Arno Press, 1971.

I. Articles

Bagby, Grover C. "Race Relations and Our Concern." *Methodist Story* (January 1965): 3–5.

Barnette, Henlee. "Negro Students in Southern Baptist Seminaries." *Review and Expositor* 53 (April 1956): 207–10.

Campbell, Ernest Q., and Thomas F. Pettigrew. "Racial and Moral Crisis: The Role of Little Rock Ministers." *American Journal of Sociology* 64 (March 1959): 509–16.

"The Churches Speak." *New South* (August 1954): 1–6.

Erskine, Hazel. "The Polls: Demonstrations and Race Riots." *Public Opinion Quarterly* 31 (Winter 1967–1968): 655–77.

Jordan, Clarence. "Christian Community in the South." *Journal of Religious Thought* 14 (Autumn-Winter 1956–1957): 27–36.
Marius, Richard. "The War Between the Baptists." *Esquire* 96 (December 1981): 46, 48–50, 53, 55.
"Southern Ministers Speak Their Minds." *Pulpit Digest* 39 (December 1958): 13–17.
Toby, Jackson. "Bombing in Nashville." *Commentary* 25 (May 1958): 385–89.

II. SECONDARY SOURCES

A. Books

Allen, Catherine B. *A Century to Celebrate: History of Woman's Missionary Union*. Birmingham: Woman's Missionary Union, 1987.
Alvis, Joel L., Jr. *Religion & Race: Southern Presbyterians, 1946–1983*. Tuscaloosa: University of Alabama Press, 1994.
Ammerman, Nancy Tatom. *Baptist Battles: Social Change and Religious Conflict in the Southern Baptist Convention*. New Brunswick: Rutgers University Press, 1990.
———, ed. *Southern Baptists Observed: Multiple Perspectives on a Changing Denomination*. Knoxville: University of Tennessee Press, 1993.
Bagwell, William. *School Desegregation in the Carolinas: Two Case Studies*. Columbia, S.C.: University of South Carolina Press, 1972.
Bailey, Kenneth K. *Southern White Protestantism in the Twentieth Century*. New York: Harper & Row, 1964.
Barnette, Henlee H. *Clarence Jordan: Turning Dreams into Deeds*. Greenville, S.C.: Smith & Helwys, 1992.
Bartley, Numan V. *The Rise of Massive Resistance: Race and Politics in the South During the 1950's*. Baton Rouge: Louisiana State University Press, 1969.
———. *The New South, 1945–1980*. Baton Rouge: Louisiana State University Press, 1995.
Bass, Jack, and Walter DeVries. *The Transformation of Southern Politics: Social Change and Political Consequence Since 1945*. New York: Basic Books, 1976.
Belew, Wendell. *A Missions People: The Southern Baptist Pilgrimage*. Nashville: Broadman Press, 1989.
Berger, Peter L. *Invitation To Sociology: A Humanistic Perspective*. Garden City, N.Y.: Doubleday, 1963; repr. Harmondsworth, England: Pelican Books, 1966.
———. *The Sacred Canopy: Elements of a Sociological Theory of Religion*. Garden City, N.Y.: Doubleday, 1967.
Black, Earl. *Southern Governors and Civil Rights: Racial Segregation as a Campaign Issue in the Second Reconstruction*. Cambridge, Mass.: Harvard University Press, 1976.
Black, Earl, and Merle Black. *Politics and Society in the South*. Cambridge, Mass.: Harvard University Press, 1987.
Bourne, Peter G. *Jimmy Carter: A Comprehensive Biography from Plains to Postpresidency*. New York: Scribner, 1997.
Brackenridge, R. Douglas. *Eugene Carson Blake: Prophet with Portfolio*. New York: Seabury Press, 1978.
Bryan, G. McLeod. *Dissenter in the Baptist Southland: Fifty Years in the Career of William Wallace Finlator*. Macon, Ga.: Mercer University Press, 1985.
Campbell, Will D. *The Stem of Jesse: The Costs of Community at a 1960s Southern School*. Macon, Ga.: Mercer University Press, 1995.

Carey, John C. *Carlyle Marney: A Pilgrim's Progress*. Macon, Ga.: Mercer University Press, 1980.

Carter, Dan T. *The Politics of Rage: George Wallace, The Origins of the New Conservatism, and the Transformation of American Politics*. New York: Simon & Schuster, 1995.

Cauthen, Baker James, et al. *Advance: A History of Southern Baptist Foreign Missions*. Nashville: Broadman Press, 1970.

Chafe, William H. *Civilities and Civil Rights: Greensboro, North Carolina, and the Black Struggle for Freedom*. New York: Oxford University Press, 1981 [1980].

Chappell, David L. *Inside Agitators: White Southerners in the Civil Rights Movement*. Baltimore: Johns Hopkins Press, 1994.

Dittmer, John. *Local People: The Struggle for Civil Rights in Mississippi*. Urbana and Chicago: University of Illinois Press, 1995.

Durkheim, Emile. *The Elementary Forms of the Religious Life: A Study in Religious Sociology*. Translated by Joseph Ward Swain. London, England: George Allen & Unwin; reprint Glencoe, Ill.: Free Press, 1947.

Edgar, Walter B. *South Carolina in the Modern Age*. Columbia, S.C.: University of South Carolina Press, 1992.

Eighmy, John Lee. *Churches in Cultural Captivity: A History of the Social Attitudes of Southern Baptists*. With revised introduction, conclusion, and bibliography by Samuel S. Hill. Knoxville: University of Tennessee Press, 1987.

Ely, James W., Jr. *The Crisis of Conservative Virginia: The Byrd Organization and the Politics of Massive Resistance*. Knoxville: University of Tennessee Press, 1976.

Encyclopedia of Southern Baptists. Volumes 1–4. Nashville: Broadman Press, 1958–1982.

Estep, William R. *Whole Gospel Whole World: The Foreign Mission Board of the Southern Baptist Convention, 1845–1995*. Nashville: Broadman & Holman, 1994.

Fairclough, Adam. *Race & Democracy: The Civil Rights Struggle in Louisiana, 1915–1972*. Athens: University of Georgia Press, 1995.

Findlay, James F., Jr. *Church People in the Struggle: The National Council of Churches and the Black Freedom Movement, 1950–1970*. Oxford: Oxford University Press, 1993.

Fletcher, Jesse C. *Baker James Cauthen: A Man for All Nations*. Nashville: Broadman Press, 1977.

———. *The Southern Baptist Convention: A Sesquicentennial History*. Nashville: Broadman & Holman, 1994.

Flynt, Wayne. *Alabama Baptists: Southern Baptists in the Heart of Dixie*. Tuscaloosa: University of Alabama Press, 1998.

Foner, Eric. *Reconstruction: America's Unfinished Revolution, 1863–1877*. New York: Harper & Row, 1988.

Gaillard, Frye. *The Dream Long Deferred*. Chapel Hill: University of North Carolina Press, 1988.

Glock, Charles Y., and Rodney Stark. *Religion and Society in Tension*. Chicago: Rand McNally & Co., 1965.

Goldfield, David R. *Black, White, and Southern: Race Relations and Southern Culture 1940 to the Present*. Baton Rouge: Louisiana State University Press, 1991.

Graham, Hugh Davis. *Crisis in Print: Desegregation and the Press in Tennessee*. Nashville: Vanderbilt University Press, 1967.

Grant, Donald L. *The Way It Was in the South: The Black Experience in Georgia*. New York: Birch Lane Press, 1993.

Greene, Glen Lee. *House Upon a Rock: About Southern Baptists in Louisiana*. Alexandria: Executive Board of the Louisiana Baptist Convention, 1973.

Greene, Lee Seifert. *Lead Me On: Frank Goad Clement and Tennessee Politics*. Knoxville: University of Tennessee Press, 1982.

Greene, Melissa Fay. *The Temple Bombing*. London: Jonathan Cape, 1996.

Hamby, Alonzo L. *Liberalism and Its Challengers: F.D.R. to Reagan*. New York: Oxford University Press, 1985.

Harvey, Paul. *Redeeming the South: Religious Cultures and Racial Identities among Southern Baptists, 1865–1925*. Chapel Hill: University of North Carolina Press, 1997.

Hennesey, James, S.J. *American Catholics: A History of the Roman Catholic Community in the United States*. New York: Oxford University Press, 1981.

Hill, Samuel S., Jr. *Southern Churches in Crisis*. New York: Holt, Rinehart and Winston, 1967.

——, ed. *Encyclopedia of Religion in the South*. Macon, Ga.: Mercer University Press, 1984.

Hughey, Michael W. *Civil Religion and Moral Order: Theoretical and Historical Dimensions*. Westport, Conn.: Greenwood Press, 1983.

Isaac, Rhys. *The Transformation of Virginia, 1740–1790*. Chapel Hill: University of North Carolina Press, 1982.

Keith, Billy. *W. A. Criswell: The Authorized Biography*. Old Tappan, N.J.: Fleming H. Revell, 1973.

Kelsey, George D. *Social Ethics Among Southern Baptists, 1917–1969*. Metuchen, N.J.: Scarecrow Press, 1972.

K'Meyer, Tracy Elaine. *Interracialism and Christian Community in the Postwar South: The Story of Koinonia Farm*. Charlottesville: University Press of Virginia, 1997.

Key, V. O., Jr. with the assistance of Alexander Heard, *Southern Politics in State and Nation*. New York: Vintage Books, 1949.

Leonard, Bill J. *God's Last and Only Hope: The Fragmentation of the Southern Baptist Convention*. Grand Rapids, Mich.: William B. Eerdmans, 1990.

Loescher, Frank S. *The Protestant Church and the Negro: A Pattern of Segregation*. New York: Association Press, 1948.

McClemore, Richard Aubrey, ed. *A History of Mississippi*. Vol. 2. Hattiesburg: University & College Press of Mississippi, 1973.

McGuire, Meredith B. *Religion: The Social Context*. 2d ed. Belmont, Calif.: Wadsworth Publishing Co., 1987.

McMillen, Neil R. *The Citizens' Councils: Organized Resistance to the Second Reconstruction, 1954–64*. Urbana and Chicago: University of Illinois Press, 1971.

Manis, Andrew Michael. *Southern Civil Religions in Conflict: Black and White Baptists and Civil Rights, 1947–1957*. Athens: University of Georgia Press, 1987.

Marable, Manning. *Race, Rebellion and Reform: The Second Reconstruction in Black America, 1945–1990*. 2d ed. Houndmills, England: Macmillan, 1991.

Miller, Robert Moats. *American Protestantism and Social Issues, 1919–1939*. Chapel Hill: University of North Carolina, 1958.

Moore, W. T. *His Heart is Black*. Atlanta: Home Mission Board, 1978.

Morgan, David T. *The New Crusades, The New Holy Land: Conflict in the Southern Baptist Convention, 1969–1991*. Tuscaloosa: University of Alabama Press, 1996.

Muse, Benjamin. *Virginia's Massive Resistance*. Bloomington: Indiana University Press, 1961.

Nevin, David, and Robert E. Bills. *The Schools That Fear Built: Segregationist Academies in the South*. Washington, D.C.: Acropolis Books, 1976.

Norwood, Frederick A. *The Story of American Methodism: A History of the United Methodists and Their Relations*. Nashville and New York: Abingdon Press, 1974.

Osborne, William A. *The Segregated Covenant: Race Relations and American Catholics*. New York: Herder and Herder, 1967.

Peirce, Neal R. *The Deep South States of America: People, Politics, and Power in the Seven Deep South States*. New York: W. W. Norton, 1974.

Pinson, William P., Jr., comp. *An Approach to Christian Ethics: The Life, Contribution, and Thought of T. B. Maston*. Nashville: Broadman Press, 1979.

Pride, Richard A., and J. David Woodard. *The Burden of Busing: The Politics of Desegregation in Nashville, Tennessee*. Knoxville: University of Tennessee Press, 1985.

Prichard, Robert W. *A History of the Episcopal Church*. Harrisburg, Pa.: Morehouse, 1991.

Queen, Edward L. II. *In the South the Baptists are the Center of Gravity: Southern Baptists and Social Change, 1930–1980*. Brooklyn, N.Y.: Carlson Publishing, 1991.

Reed, John Shelton. *The Enduring South: Subcultural Persistence in Mass Society*. Chapel Hill: University of North Carolina Press, 1986 [1972].

———. *Surveying the South: Studies in Regional Sociology*. Columbia: University of Missouri Press, 1993.

Reid, A. Hamilton. *Baptists in Alabama: Their Organization and Witness*. Montgomery: Paragon Press, 1967.

Reimers, David M. *White Protestantism and the Negro*. New York: Oxford University Press, 1965.

Roof, Wade Clark, and William McKinney. *American Mainline Religion: Its Changing Shape and Future*. New Brunswick: Rutgers University Press, 1987.

Rutledge, Arthur B. *Mission to America: A Century and a Quarter of Southern Baptist Home Missions*. Nashville: Broadman Press, 1969.

Sarratt, Reed. *The Ordeal of Desegregation: The First Decade*. New York: Harper & Row, 1966.

Shurden, Walter B., ed. *The Struggle for the Soul of the SBC: Moderate Responses to the Fundamentalist Movement*. Macon, Ga.: Mercer University Press, 1993.

Sitkoff, Harvard. *The Struggle for Black Equality, 1954–1992*. Rev. ed. New York: Hill and Wang, 1993.

Smith, H. Shelton. *In His Image, But . . . Racism in Southern Religion, 1780–1910*. Durham, N.C.: Duke University Press, 1972.

Snider, P. Joel. *The "Cotton Patch" Gospel: The Proclamation of Clarence Jordan*. Lanham, Md.: University Press of America, 1985.

Southern Baptist Periodical Index, 1965–1980. Nashville: Historical Commission of the Southern Baptist Convention, 1966–1981.

Spain, Rufus B. *At Ease In Zion: A Social History of Southern Baptists, 1865–1900*. Nashville: Vanderbilt University Press, 1967.

Storey, John W. *Texas Baptist Leadership and Social Christianity, 1900–1980*. College Station: Texas A & M University Press, 1986.

Storey, John W., and Ronald C. Ellison. *Southern Baptists of Southeast Texas: A Centennial History, 1888–1988*. Beaumont, Tex.: Golden Triangle Baptist Association, 1988.

Sumner, David E. *The Episcopal Church's History: 1945–1985*. Wilton, Conn.: Morehouse-Barlow, 1987.

Thompson, Ernest Trice. *Presbyterians in the South*. Vol. 3: 1890–1972. Richmond, Va.: John Knox Press, 1973.

Thompson, James J., Jr. *Tried as by Fire: Southern Baptists and the Religious Controversies of the 1920s*. Macon, Ga.: Mercer University Press, 1982.

Tindall, George Brown. *The Emergence of the New South, 1913–1945*. Baton Rouge: Louisiana State University Press, 1967.

Troeltsch, Ernst. *The Social Teaching of the Christian Churches*. Vol. 1. With an introduction by H. Richard Neibuhr. Translated by Oliver Wyon. London, England: George Allen & Unwin, 1931; Chicago: University of Chicago Press, 1976.

Wagy, Tom R. *Governor LeRoy Collins of Florida: Spokesman of the New South.* Tuscaloosa: University of Alabama Press, 1985.

Wang, Xi. *The Trial of Democracy: Black Suffrage and Northern Republicans, 1860–1910.* Athens: University of Georgia Press, 1997.

Weatherford, W. D. *American Churches and the Negro: Historical Study From Early Slave Days to the Present.* Boston: Christopher Publishing House, 1956.

Williamson, Joel. *The Crucible of Race: Black-White Relations in the American South Since Emancipation.* New York: Oxford University Press, 1984.

Wilson, Charles Reagan. *Baptized In Blood: The Religion of the Lost Cause, 1865–1920.* Athens: University of Georgia Press, 1980.

Wuthnow, Robert. *The Restructuring of American Religion: Society and Faith since World War II.* Princeton: Princeton University Press, 1988.

B. Articles

Ammerman, Nancy T. "Southern Baptists and the New Christian Right." *Review of Religious Research* 32 (March 1991): 213-36.

Bailey, Kenneth K. "The Post-Civil War Racial Separations in Southern Protestantism: Another Look." *Church History* 46 (December 1977): 453–73.

Baker, N. Larry. "C. W. Scudder: Ethicist and Advocate for Kingdom Causes." *Baptist History and Heritage* 33 (Spring 1998): 19–33.

Barnette, Henlee Hulix. "The Southern Baptist Theological Seminary and the Civil Rights Movement: From 1859–1952. Part One." *Review and Expositor* 90 (Fall 1993): 531–50.

———. "The Southern Baptist Theological Seminary and the Civil Rights Movement: The Visit of Martin Luther King, Jr. Part Two." *Review and Expositor* 93 (Winter 1996): 77–126.

Bass, S. Jonathan. "Not Time Yet: Alabama's Episcopal Bishop and the End of Segregation in the Deep South." *Anglican and Episcopal History* 63 (June 1994): 235–59.

Bodo, John R. "The Pastor and Social Conflict." In *Religion and Social Conflict,* edited by Robert Lee and Martin E. Marty, 159–72. New York: Oxford University Press, 1964.

Bradley, J. C. "Profiles of Home Mission Board Executives." *Baptist History and Heritage* 30 (April 1995): 26–34.

Branch, Harold T. "Implications of Multiple Affiliation for Black Southern Baptists." *Baptist History and Heritage* 16 (July 1981): 41–48.

Bryant, James C. "Georgia Baptists and the Integration Crisis." *Viewpoints: Georgia Baptist History* 13 (1992): 5–17.

Chancey, Andrew S. "'A Demonstration Plot for the Kingdom of God': The Establishment and Early Years of Koinonia Farm."*Georgia Historical Quarterly* 75 (Summer 1991): 321–53.

Cleveland, Mary L. "A Baptist Pastor and Social Justice in Clinton, Tennessee." *Baptist History and Heritage* 14 (April 1979): 20–23.

Colburn, David R. "Florida's Governors Confront the *Brown* Decision: A Case Study of the Constitutional Politics of School Desegregation, 1954–1970." In *An Uncertain Tradition: Constitutionalism and the History of the South,* edited by Kermit L. Hall and James W. Ely, Jr., 326–55. Athens: University of Georgia Press, 1989.

Colburn, David R., and Richard K. Scher. "Race Relations and Florida Gubernatorial Politics Since the *Brown* Decision." *Florida Historical Quarterly* 55 (October 1976): 153–69.

Crowther, Edward R. "Alabama's Fight to Maintain Segregated Schools, 1953–1956." *Alabama Review* 43 (July 1990): 206–25.

Dorgan, Howard. "Response of the Main-Line Southern White Protestant Pulpit to *Brown v Board of Education*, 1954–1965." In *A New Diversity in Contemporary Southern Rhetoric*, edited by Calvin M. Logue and Howard Dorgan, 15–51. Baton Rouge: Louisiana State University Press, 1987.

Eighmy, John Lee. "Recent Changes in the Racial Attitudes of Southern Baptists." *Foundations* 5 (October 1962): 354–60.

Eisenberg, Ralph. "Virginia: The Emergence of Two-Party Politics." In *The Changing Politics of the South*, edited by William C. Havard, 39–91. Baton Rouge: Louisiana State University Press, 1972.

Glaser, James M. "Back to the Black Belt: Racial Environment and White Racial Attitudes in the South." *Journal of Politics* 56 (February 1994): 21–41.

Greeley, Andrew M., and Paul B. Sheatsley. "Attitudes toward Racial Integration." *Scientific American* 225 (December 1971): 13–19.

Greer, Bruce A. "Active and Inactive Disciples, Presbyterians, and Southern Baptists: A Comparative Socioeconomic, Religious, and Political Profile." In *A Case Study of Mainstream Protestantism: The Disciples' Relation to American Culture, 1880–1989*, edited by D. Newell Williams, 386–415. St. Louis: Chalice Press and Grand Rapids, Mich.: William B. Eerdmans, 1991.

Hankins, Barry. "Southern Baptists and Northern Evangelicals: Cultural Factors and the Nature of Religious Alliances." *Religion and American Culture* 7 (1997): 271–98.

Horowitz, David Alan. "White Southerners' Alienation and Civil Rights: The Response to Corporate Liberalism, 1956–1965," *Journal of Southern History* 54 (May 1988): 173–200.

Hyman, Herbert H., and Paul B. Sheatsley. "Attitudes toward Desegregation," *Scientific American* 195 (December 1956): 35–39.

——. "Attitudes toward Desegregation." *Scientific American* 211 (July 1964): 16–23.

Irvin, Michael T. "J. B. Weatherspoon: Christian Statesman." *Quarterly Review* 42 (April-June 1982): 45–53.

Johnson, F. Ernest. "Do Churches Exert Significant Influence on Public Morality?" *Annals of the American Academy of Political and Social Science* 280 (March 1952): 125–32.

Jones, Phillip Baron. "An Examination of the Statistical Growth of the Southern Baptist Convention." In *Understanding Church Growth and Decline: 1950–1978*, edited by Dean R. Hoge and David A. Roozen, 160–78. New York: Pilgrim Press, 1979.

Kelley, Jonathan. "The Politics of School Busing." *Public Opinion Quarterly* 38 (Spring 1974): 23–39.

Knapp, Melvin J., and Jon P. Alston. "White Parental Acceptance of Varying Degrees of School Desegregation: 1965 and 1970." *Public Opinion Quarterly* 36 (Winter 1972–1973): 585–91.

McBeth, Leon. "Origin of the Christian Life Commission." *Baptist History and Heritage* 1 (October 1966): 29–36.

——. "Southern Baptists and Race Since 1947." *Baptist History and Heritage* 7 (July 1972): 155–169.

McCain, R. Ray. "Reactions to the United States Supreme Court Segregation Decision of 1954." *Georgia Historical Quarterly* 52 (December 1968): 371–87.

McCall, Emmanuel L. "Home Mission Board Ministry in the Black Community." *Baptist History and Heritage* 16 (July 1981): 29–40.

McClellan, Albert. "The Southern Baptist Convention, 1965–1985." *Baptist History and Heritage* 20 (October 1985): 7–24, 63.

McGreevey, John T. "Racial Justice and the People of God: The Second Vatican Council, the Civil Rights Movement, and American Catholics." *Religion and American Culture* 4 (Summer 1994): 221–54.

Manis, Andrew M. "Silence or Shockwaves: Southern Baptist Responses to the Assassination of Martin Luther King, Jr." *Baptist History and Heritage* 15 (October 1980): 19–27, 35.

Manza, Jeff, and Clem Brooks. "The Religious Factor in U.S. Presidential Elections, 1960–1992." *American Journal of Sociology* 103 (July 1997): 38–81.

Martensen, Katherine. "Region, Religion, and Social Action: The Catholic Committee of the South, 1939–1956." *Catholic Historical Review* 68 (April 1982): 249–67.

Mertz, Paul E. "'Mind Changing Time All Over Georgia': HOPE, Inc. and School Desegregation, 1958–1961." *Georgia Historical Quarterly* 77 (Spring 1993): 41–61.

Mohl, Raymond A. "The Pattern of Race Relations in Miami since the 1920s." In *The African American Heritage of Florida,* edited by David R. Colburn and Jane L. Landers, 326–65. Gainesville: University Press of Florida, 1995.

Newman, Mark. "The Mississippi Baptist Convention and Desegregation, 1945–1980." *Journal of Mississippi History* 59 (Spring 1997): 1–31.

———. "The Baptist General Association of Virginia and Desegregation, 1931–1980." *Virginia Magazine of History and Biography* 105 (Summer 1997): 257–86.

———. "The Arkansas Baptist State Convention and Desegregation, 1954–1968." *Arkansas Historical Quarterly* 56 (Autumn 1997): 294–313.

———. "The Baptist State Convention of North Carolina and Desegregation, 1945–1980." *North Carolina Historical Review* 75 (January 1998): 1–28.

———. "The Tennessee Baptist Convention and Desegregation, 1954–1980." *Tennessee Historical Quarterly* 57 (Winter 1998): 236–57.

———. "The Baptist State Convention of South Carolina, 1954–1971." *Baptist History and Heritage* 34 (Spring 1999): 56–72.

———. "The Alabama Baptist State Convention and Desegregation, 1954–1980." *Alabama Baptist Historian* 35 (July 1999): 3–40.

———. "The Florida Baptist Convention and Desegregation, 1954–1980." *Florida Historical Quarterly* 78 (Summer 1999): 1–22.

———. "The Georgia Baptist Convention and Desegregation, 1945–1980." *Georgia Historical Quarterly* 83 (Winter 1999): 683–711.

Orser, W. Edward. "Racial Attitudes in Wartime: The Protestant Churches During the Second World War." *Church History* 41 (September 1972): 337–53.

Parham, Robert. "A. C. Miller: The Bible Speaks on Race." *Baptist History and Heritage* 27 (January 1992): 32–43.

Reed, John Shelton. "How Southerners Gave Up Jim Crow." *New Perspectives* 17 (Fall 1985): 15–19.

Ringer, Benjamin B., and Charles Y. Glock. "The Political Role of the Church as Defined by Its Parishioners." *Public Opinion Quarterly* 18 (Winter 1954–1955): 337–47.

Sapp, W. David. "Southern Baptist Responses to the American Economy, 1900–1980." *Baptist History and Heritage* 6 (January 1981): 3–12.

Sitkoff, Harvard. "Harry Truman and the Election of 1948: The Coming of Age of Civil Rights in American Politics." *Journal of Southern History* 37 (November 1971): 597–616.

Smith, Sid. "Growth of Black Southern Baptist Churches in the Inner City." *Baptist History and Heritage* 16 (July 1981): 49–60.

Taylor, D. Garth, Paul B. Sheatsley, and Andrew M. Greeley. "Attitudes toward Racial Integration." *Scientific American* 238 (June 1978): 30–37.

Valentine, Foy. "Baptist Polity and Social Pronouncements." *Baptist History and Heritage* 14 (July 1979): 52–61.

Wheeler, Edward L. "An Overview of Black Southern Baptist Involvements." *Baptist History and Heritage* 16 (July 1981): 3–11, 40.

Willis, Alan Scot. "A Baptist Dilemma: Christianity, Discrimination, and the Desegregation of Mercer University." *Georgia Historical Quarterly* 80 (Fall 1996): 595–615.

Wood, James R. "Authority and Controversial Policy: The Churches and Civil Rights." *American Sociological Review* 35 (December 1970): 1057–69.

C. Theses and Dissertations

Akerman, Robert Howard. "The Triumph of Moderation in Florida Thought and Politics: A Study of the Race Issue from 1954 to 1960." Ph.D. diss., The American University, 1967.

Byrd, Harry Emerson. "An Analysis of Pronouncements on Major Issues by the Social Service Commission of the Southern Baptist Convention From 1914–1946." Th.M. thesis, Southeastern Baptist Theological Seminary, 1959.

Cooper, Corbin L. "A Study of Orthodoxy, Authoritarianism, and Racial Prejudice among Lay Leaders in Southern Baptist Churches in North Carolina." Ed.D. diss., North Carolina State University at Raleigh, 1972.

Cunnigen, Donald. "Men and Women of Goodwill: Mississippi's White Liberals." Ph.D. diss., Harvard University, 1987.

Dunn, James M. "The Ethical Thought Of Joseph Martin Dawson." Th.D. diss., Southwestern Baptist Theological Seminary, 1966.

Fairclough, Adam. "A Study of the Southern Christian Leadership Conference and the Rise and Fall of the Non-Violent Civil Rights Movement." Ph.D. diss., Keele University (United Kingdom), 1978.

Gaddy, Curtis Welton. "The Christian Life Commission of the Southern Baptist Convention: A Critical Evaluation." Th.D. diss., Southern Baptist Theological Seminary, 1970.

Godwin, Roy Edward. "The Role of the Church in Racial Integration in Urban Areas of Transition." Th.M. thesis, Southern Baptist Theological Seminary, 1967.

Hill, Davis C. "Southern Baptist Thought and Action in Race Relations, 1940–1950." Th.D. diss., Southern Baptist Theological Seminary, 1952.

McCain, Raymond R. "A Description and Analysis of Speaking by Atlanta Ministers on Public School Desegregation from February, 1961, to August 30, 1961." Master's thesis, Louisiana State University, 1961.

Newberry, Anthony Lake. "Without Urgency or Ardor: The South's Middle-Of-The-Road Liberals and Civil Rights, 1945–1960." Ph.D. diss., Ohio University, 1982.

Newman, Mark. "Getting Right with God: Southern Baptists and Race Relations, 1945–1980." Ph.D. diss., University of Mississippi, 1993.

Porter, Lee. "Southern Baptists and Race Relations, 1948–1963." Th.D. diss., Southwestern Baptist Theological Seminary, 1965.

Roberts, Anthony Dale. "Jesse Burton Weatherspoon: The Ethics of Advocacy in a Southern Baptist Context." Ph.D. diss., Southern Baptist Theological Seminary, 1983.

Stewart, George R. "Birmingham's Reaction to the 1954 Desegregation Decision." Master's thesis, Samford University, 1967.

Tillman, William M., Jr. "Representative Actions and Statements Among Southern Baptists Concerning Black-White Relations, 1964–1976." Ph.D. diss., Southwestern Baptist Theological Seminary, 1978.

Valentine, Foy Dan. "A Historical Study of Southern Baptists and Race Relations, 1917–1947." Th.D. diss., Southwestern Baptist Theological Seminary, 1949.

D. Miscellaneous

Badger, Tony, "The Southern Manifesto." Paper presented at the annual meeting of the Southern Historical Association, Orlando, Florida, November 11, 1993.

Index

About the Author

Mark Newman is Senior Lecturer in History, University of Derby,
United Kingdom.